EXPLORING THE OLD TESTAMENT

Volume 2

The Historical Books

Philip Satterthwaite studied at Oxford, Cambridge and Manchester. He is Registrar and Lecturer in Old Testament and Hebrew at Biblical Graduate School of Theology, Singapore, where he has taught since 1998. Before that, he was Lecturer in Classical Languages, University of Transkei (South Africa) and Kirby Laing Research Fellow in Hebrew and Aramaic (Tyndale House and Oriental Studies Faculty, Cambridge). He is a member of the Society for Old Testament Studies and the International Organization for Septuagint and Cognate Studies. He has published a number of essays and dictionary articles, mainly on topics relating to Biblical Studies. *Exploring the Old Testament, Volume 2: A Guide to the Historical Books* is his first book.

Philip belongs to a Presbyterian church, where he is active in preaching and teaching. Such spare time as he has he likes to spend making or listening to music, swimming, walking or cooking. He is married to Eileen, who also lectures in Biblical Studies.

Gordon McConville studied Modern Languages at Cambridge and Theology at Edinburgh and Belfast. He is Professor of Old Testament Theology in the University of Gloucestershire, having previously taught the Old Testament in Bristol and Oxford. He has written a number of books on Deuteronomy and the Prophets, and most recently on Old Testament political theology.

Exploring the Old Testament

The Pentateuch by Gordon Wenham

The Historical Books by Philip Satterthwaite and Gordon McConville

The Psalms and Wisdom Literature by Ernest Lucas

The Prophets by Gordon McConville

Exploring the New Testament

The Gospels and Acts by David Wenham and Steve Walton

The Letters and Revelation by Howard Marshall, Stephen Travis and Ian Paul

Exploring the Old Testament

A Guide to the Historical Books

PHILIP SATTERTHWAITE
and GORDON McCONVILLE

Volume Two

InterVarsity Press
Downers Grove, Illinois

InterVarsity Press
P.O. Box 1400, Downers Grove, IL 60515-1426
Internet: www.ivpress.com
E-mail: email@ivpress.com

InterVarsity Press® is the book-publishing division of InterVarsity Christian Fellowship/USA®, a student movement active on campus at hundreds of universities, colleges and schools of nursing in the United States of America, and a member movement of the International Fellowship of Evangelical Students. For information about local and regional activities, write Public Relations Dept., InterVarsity Christian Fellowship/USA, 6400 Schroeder Rd., P.O. Box 7895, Madison, WI 53707-7895, or visit the IVCF website at <www.intervarsity.org>.

The maps on pages 34, 52, 142, 158, 172 and 232 are adapted from maps in the New Bible Atlas, Leicester: Inter-Varsity Press/Tring: Lion Publishing/Wheaton, Ill.: Tyndale House Publishing, copyright © Universities and Colleges Christian Fellowship, Leicester, England, 1985.

Cover design: Kathleen Lay Burrows
Cover image: National Gallery Budapest/SuperStock
ISBN 978-0-8308-2552-3

Printed in Great Britain ∞

Library of Congress Cataloging-in-Publication Data has been requested.

P 25 24 23 22 21 20 19 18 17 16 15 14 13 12 11 10 9 8 7 6 5 4 3 2 1
Y 29 28 27 26 25 24 23 22 21 20 19 18 17 16 15 14 13 12 11 10 09 08 07

Contents

THE HISTORIES

ILLUSTRATIONS

KEY TO PANELS

This key to the panels helps locate the special and suggested exercises that occur throughout the volume. It should be noted that the panels are not exhaustive treatments of topics, and are meant to be read and used in their contexts.

'THINK ABOUT' PANELS

'DIGGING DEEPER' PANELS

OTHER PANELS

PREFACE

Exploring the Old Testament is designed to help the beginning student understand the writings of the Old Testament. It serves the purpose of an introduction, but its unique format is devised to make the volumes accessible to the modern reader. *EOT* engages with the reader, by interspersing interactive panels with the main text. These panels ask for responses, suggest lines of thought, give further information, or indicate ways in which particular topics might be followed up in more depth. This design aims to make the volumes useful either for independent study or as a class text.

EOT aims to show the relevance of Old Testament study both to theology and to modern life. Its four authors, each writing in areas in which they have previously published extensively, believe that the Old Testament has foundational significance for theology and Christian belief and practice.

For that reason *EOT* expressly aims to incorporate modern approaches to interpreting the text. While the traditional historical questions are given their due place, newer approaches such as canonical and rhetorical criticism are represented. It is hoped that this will enable the student to see the potential applications of the books of the Old Testament to modern life.

EOT is a companion series to *Exploring the New Testament*.

Gordon McConville
Series editor

ACKNOWLEDGEMENTS

Thanks are due first to Ruth McCurry of SPCK for her help and encouragement at every stage in the writing, editing and production of this book, and particularly for her patience as the completion date kept receding.

Various scholars have kindly read and commented on draft chapters: Professor Rick Hess of Denver Seminary; Professors Iain Provan and Phil Long of Regent College, Vancouver; Dr Walter McConnell of Singapore Bible College. Their help is gratefully acknowledged.

Three classes of students at the Biblical Graduate School of Theology, Singapore, have read and commented on draft chapters of this book. Many thanks to them as well.

All biblical quotations in this book, as noted above, are taken from the New Revised Standard Version (Anglicized Edition) (Oxford University Press, 1995) unless otherwise stated. Permission to quote from this version is gratefully acknowledged.

Inter-Varsity Press allowed us to reproduce the maps in Chapters 2, 3, 5, 6 and 9.

These maps are taken from pp. 35, 42, 45, 90, 91 and 94 of J.J. Bimson and J.P. Kane (eds), *New Bible Atlas* (Leicester: IVP, 1985). Professor Kenneth Kitchen kindly consented to our reproducing the table representing the chronology of the judges period in Chapter 4. This table is taken from his *On the Reliability of the Old Testament* (Grand Rapids: Eerdmans, 2003), p. 210. We are grateful to Inter-Varsity Press and to Professor Kitchen.

Philip Satterthwaite began work on this book towards the end of his period as Research Fellow in Hebrew and Aramaic at Tyndale House, Cambridge, and the Oriental Studies Faculty, Cambridge, a post which he held from 1993 to 1998. He would like to thank Sir Kirby Laing and his foundation, who provided the funding for the fellowship.

He also records his thanks to the Council and Faculty of the Biblical Graduate School of Theology, Singapore, for granting him two periods of sabbatical leave in 2002 and 2006, without which the book could not have been completed.

INTRODUCTION

The Historical Books of the Old Testament (the Histories) are: Joshua, Judges, 1 and 2 Samuel, 1 and 2 Kings, Ruth, Esther, Ezra, Nehemiah, and 1 and 2 Chronicles. This book is an introduction to the Histories intended for first- or second-year students at theological college or university. Chapter 1 introduces students to the Histories and to recent and contemporary scholarship on them. Chapter 2 briefly surveys the history of the ancient Near East in the period 1550–63 BC. Chapters 3–11 work through the Histories in detail, dealing with critical and interpretative issues.

The series of which this book is a part divides up the Old Testament according to the divisions found in most English Bibles: Volume 1 covers the *Law* (the Pentateuch); Volume 3 covers the *Poetic Books* (Psalms, Song of Songs and the Wisdom Books); and Volume 4 covers the *Prophets*. In this scheme 'Histories' is used as a convenient term of reference. We believe that the books covered in this volume all belong to the category of history writing: they are narratives about past events told with a view to their present relevance. But the use of the term 'Histories' to refer to these books is not meant to imply that other parts of the Old Testament (e.g. the Pentateuchal narratives and the historical sections of some psalms) cannot also be described as history writing.

In this book Chapters 3–11 deal with the Histories in the order in which they occur in Hebrew texts of the Old Testament (the order of the list at the beginning of the first paragraph), not the order found in most English Bibles. The main reason for this is that much scholarship on Joshua, Judges and the books of Samuel and Kings, following the Hebrew order of these books, treats them separately from the other Histories, regarding them, along with Deuteronomy (but not Ruth), as forming a 'Deuteronomistic History'. This is a major issue in scholarship upon these books, and essential for us to address (see Ch. 7). It is most convenient, therefore, to take Joshua–Kings together, postponing treatment of Ruth until later. Having followed the Hebrew order in dealing with Joshua–Kings, we have decided to continue with it for the remaining Histories, and so these are dealt with in the sequence in which they occur in Hebrew Bibles: Ruth, Esther, Ezra, Nehemiah, Chronicles.

HOW TO USE THE BOOK

This book is a guide to the Histories. But we want you to read the Histories for yourself. The frequent biblical references are meant to be looked up. Consulting the biblical text as you read our chapters will make what we say easier to follow. It will also help you decide whether or not you agree with our approach.

Our text contains many panels:

- panels which give background information, or provide a brief, separate treatment of a relevant topic;
- 'Think about . . .' panels, which suggest questions for reflection or discussion which can be answered relatively quickly;
- 'Digging deeper' panels, which will probably require more research and reflection.

Consulting a commentary or an article in a Bible dictionary may help in addressing the issues raised by these panels.

You may find it convenient to ignore these panels at first and return to them when you have read through the main text.

Further reading is suggested at the end of each chapter and in some of the panels. Many of the books and articles listed provide a more detailed treatment of topics introduced in our discussion. We have usually listed only English-language books and articles which we believe will be accessible in most British and North American colleges. We have focused particularly on recent publications. Many of the items listed contain references and bibliographies which will provide further points of access into the copious scholarly literature on the Histories. One recent publication which we particularly recommend, both as a bibliographic resource and as a work of reference on a wide range of topics relating to the Histories, is W.T. Arnold and H.G.M. Williamson (eds), *Dictionary of the Old Testament Historical Books* (Downers Grove/Leicester: IVP, 2005). Rather than refer to it at the end of each chapter, we draw your attention to it here, with the injunction: read it!

DIVINE NAMES; GOD AND MASCULINE PRONOUNS

The Histories refer to the god of Israel mainly by two terms: *elohim* (used about 830 times) and *yhwh* (used about 1,950 times). The New Revised Standard Version (NRSV), the translation of the Bible regularly quoted in this book, translates *elohim* as 'God', the capital 'G' reflecting the fact that the term, which literally translates as 'gods', apparently implies a claim that the god of Israel is the only being worthy of the designation 'god'. NRSV translates *yhwh*, the name particularly associated with the exodus from Egypt (see Exod. 3:13–15; 6:2–3) as 'the LORD'.

In the Outline sections in Chapters 3–11, and sometimes elsewhere, we usually refer to the god of Israel as YHWH, a form which transliterates the Hebrew consonants of this divine name, but without any vowels. (It is not certain what the original Hebrew vowels were.) This includes all biblical quotations where NRSV has 'the LORD'. We have retained all occurrences of 'God' (capital 'G') in biblical quotations. When we use the phrase 'god of Israel' and the like in our own discussion, however, we prefer a small 'g', on the grounds that this phrase normally occurs in passages where we are contrasting Israelite beliefs about their god with competing views. In such passages to speak of the 'the God of Israel' might appear to prejudge the issue, implying that Israel's god is the only one, or that Israel's views of the divine are the only ones worth taking seriously, when the question is whether or not these claims are correct. Further on this issue, see the comments of N.T. Wright, *The New Testament and the People of God* (London: SPCK, 1992), pp. xiv–xv.

The Histories uniformly use masculine grammatical forms in relation to the god of Israel, and when they describe YHWH's purposes and actions using analogies with human beings (as is their regular practice) it is mainly male human figures that they have in mind. The dominant images of YHWH are as King, Judge and Shepherd, female imagery being almost entirely absent. Ruth 2:12, which apparently describes YHWH using the image of a mother hen – not a human mother – is exceptional.

The question whether it is appropriate to use gender-determined language in reference to God is controversial today. Some writers choose to refer to God using 'God/YHWH' in place of 'he' and 'him', and 'God's/YHWH's' in place of 'his', thus avoiding masculine pronouns (though sometimes at the cost of a slight inelegance). Another alternative is to use capitalized forms ('He', 'Him', 'His') to indicate that grammatically masculine forms when used of God do not necessarily have the same connotations that they do when used of human males. On reflection, we have chosen to adopt neither of these courses, but have followed the NRSV in using 'he', 'him' and 'his'. We mostly use these pronouns in the Outline sections of Chapters 3–11, where we are summarizing the contents of the Histories, and so it seemed appropriate simply to reproduce the biblical usage and leave it to readers to decide whether or not they are happy to follow this usage in their own thinking and speaking about God.

We would like to state, however, that we accept the teaching of Genesis 1:26–27, according to which the divine image in humans is most appropriately expressed not by male alone, nor by female alone, but by male and female together (see also Gal. 3:28–29).

WHO WROTE WHAT?

Philip Satterthwaite planned the volume, wrote Chapters 1–7, and edited all the chapters into their present form. Gordon McConville wrote Chapters 8–11. We have each read and commented on the other's contributions and, allowing for some disagreement on points of detail, the book as a whole reflects the thinking of us both.

ABBREVIATIONS

ABD	D.N. Freedman (ed.), *Anchor Bible Dictionary*, 6 vols. New York: Doubleday, 1992.
ANET	J.B. Pritchard (ed.), *Ancient Near Eastern Texts Relating to the Old Testament*, 3rd edition. Princeton: Princeton University Press, 1969.
BAR	*Biblical Archaeology Review*
CBQ	*Catholic Biblical Quarterly*
COS	W.W. Hallo and K.L. Younger (eds), *The Context of Scripture*, 3 vols. Leiden: Brill, 1997, 2000, 2002.
DOTHB	W.T. Arnold and H.G.M. Williamson (eds), *Dictionary of the Old Testament: Historical Books*. Leicester/Downers Grove: IVP, 2005.
DOTP	T.D. Alexander and D.W. Baker (eds), *Dictionary of the Old Testament: Pentateuch*. Leicester/Downers Grove: IVP, 2003.

EOT I	G.J. Wenham, *Exploring the Old Testament, Volume One: A Guide to the Pentateuch*. London/Downers Grove: SPCK/IVP, 2003.	*NEAHL*	E. Stern (ed.), *The New Encyclopedia of Archaeological Excavations in the Holy Land*, 4 vols. Jerusalem: Carta, 1993.
EOT IV	J.G. McConville, *Exploring the Old Testament, Volume Four: A Guide to the Prophets*. London/Downers Grove: SPCK/IVP, 2002.	*NIDOTTE*	W.A. VanGemeren (ed.), *New International Dictionary of Old Testament Theology and Exegesis*, 5 vols. Grand Rapids/Carlisle: Paternoster Press, 1997.
JBL	*Journal of Biblical Literature*	NIV	Holy Bible, New International Version
JSOT	*Journal for the Study of the Old Testament*	NRSV	Holy Bible, New Revised Standard Version
LXX	The Septuagint (an ancient Greek translation of the Old Testament)	*OBC*	J. Barton and J. Muddiman (eds), *The Oxford Bible Commentary*. Oxford: Oxford University Press, 2001.
MT	The Masoretic Text (the standard Hebrew text of the Old Testament)	*SJOT*	*Scandinavian Journal of the Old Testament*
NDBT	T.D. Alexander and B.S. Rosner (eds), *New Dictionary of Biblical Theology*. Leicester/Downers Grove: IVP, 2000.	*TB*	*Tyndale Bulletin*
		VT	*Vetus Testamentum*

Chapter 1

WHAT ARE THE HISTORIES? A SURVEY OF RECENT SCHOLARSHIP

OVERVIEW OF THE HISTORIES

As they now stand in the Bible, the Histories form the continuation of a narrative begun in the Pentateuch. The Pentateuch describes the creation of the world and the beginnings of human history, and then for most of its length focuses on YHWH the creator god's dealings with the people of Israel. YHWH commits himself to Israel by covenant and gives them a calling, to bring blessing to the nations of the world. Deuteronomy, the last book of the Pentateuch, ends with Israel about to enter Canaan, the land which YHWH has promised to give them as their national territory. At this point the Histories begin.

Joshua describes Israel's conquest of Canaan under Joshua's leadership, and the division of Canaan and parts of Transjordan among the 12 tribes of Israel. The later chapters of Joshua imply that by the end of Joshua's life the Israelites have not yet taken complete possession of Canaan.

In *Judges* the generation after Joshua fails to complete the conquest of Canaan. A lengthy period of religious unfaithfulness and political instability follows. Leaders ('judges') arise, but bring only temporary respite. The

book ends with Israel still not in complete possession of the land.

Ruth is set in the period of the judges. Ruth, a Moabite woman, attaches herself to an Israelite family, bringing blessing to herself and others. She is an ancestor of David, future king of Israel.

Samuel is the last of Israel's judges, but the books of *Samuel*, named after him, describe the beginnings of monarchy in Israel. The reign of Saul, Israel's first king, ends in disaster. But David emerges as Saul's successor and completes the conquest of Canaan by capturing Jerusalem. He defeats or forms alliances with surrounding nations and brings stability. During the later years of his reign he has to overcome a rebellion led by his son Absalom.

The books of *Kings* describe the reign of David's son Solomon, who builds a temple for YHWH in Jerusalem. After his death his single kingdom divides into the northern kingdom of Israel and the southern kingdom of Judah. The rest of Kings describes the gradual decline of both kingdoms. The writer attributes this to religious unfaithfulness. The Assyrians destroy the northern kingdom and take its survivors into exile. Some generations later, the Babylonians do the same to the southern kingdom. Jerusalem and the temple are destroyed.

The books of *Chronicles* selectively retell the narrative running through all the books already mentioned. The genealogies in 1 Chronicles 1—9 go back as far as Adam, that is, to the beginning of the Pentateuch, but for the most part Chronicles runs parallel to Samuel and Kings. There are, however, many omissions and additions compared to Samuel and Kings, and many differences of emphasis. The last verses of 2 Chronicles describe how the Persian king Cyrus, who had conquered Babylon, issued a decree permitting the survivors of the southern kingdom and their descendants to return from exile.

The books of *Ezra* and *Nehemiah*, named after two leaders in the post-exilic period, take Cyrus' decree as their starting-point. They describe the return of successive

THE TEXT OF THE HISTORIES

Almost all English translations of the Histories are based on the Hebrew of what is conventionally called the Masoretic Text, or MT. ('Masoretic' comes from a Hebrew word meaning 'tradition': English synonyms for 'Masoretic' might be 'Received' or 'Traditional'.) This text, the work of several generations of the Ben Asher family at Tiberias (in Palestine), reached its final form in the tenth century AD, but it is based on textual traditions going back many centuries before that. The standard modern edition of MT is *Biblia Hebraica Stuttgartensia* (BHS), produced from 1967 onwards by the German Bible Society at Stuttgart.

The Hebrew of MT is sometimes difficult, and it is generally accepted that the traditions on which it is based have at points been affected by textual corruption during earlier stages of transmission. The discipline of Old Testament textual criticism attempts to address this issue. Old Testament textual critics study the many Hebrew manuscripts of MT and also other textual traditions relating to the Old Testament. These other traditions include ancient translations based on earlier forms of the Hebrew text, such as the Septuagint (Greek), the Targums (Aramaic), the Peshitta (Syriac) and the Vulgate (Latin). Since 1947 the biblical manuscripts from Qumran (Hebrew) have entered the discussion. The Qumran manuscripts include some whose text is almost identical to MT, and others which represent divergent textual traditions.

Most English translations, though based on MT, include in their base text non-MT readings suggested by the ancient translations, or attested in the biblical manuscripts from Qumran. The New Revised Standard Version (NRSV), the translation regularly quoted in this book, follows this approach.

We recommend that you use more than one English translation for detailed study of the Histories, for two reasons. First, the translators responsible for the different English translations quite often assess the textual evidence (MT, Qumran, ancient versions) differently. At these points the translations differ because they are based on different views regarding the earliest form of the text. Second, even in passages where the text is not in doubt different translations bring out different nuances of the Hebrew. No one English translation is equally successful at capturing everything in the original. A good version to read alongside NRSV is the New International Version (NIV).

Because of space limitations we have not commented on textual questions relating to the Histories except in the case of Esther. For discussion of textual issues you should consult the commentaries and also the suggestions for further reading at the end of this chapter.

groups from Babylon to the former territory of Judah, the rebuilding of the temple and the walls of Jerusalem, and the regulation of the restored community in Judah on the basis of the law of Moses.

Esther is set in Persia in the post-exilic period. It also describes what happened to descendants of the former citizens of Judah, but focuses on those Jews (the term begins to be used in Nehemiah and Esther) who did not return there. It relates how Esther and Mordecai, two Jews who became involved in the doings of the Persian royal court, managed to avert a threat to Jews throughout the Persian empire.

The above summary follows the order of English Bibles, according to which the Histories are placed after the Pentateuch and arranged chronologically. Hebrew editions of the Old Testament follow a different order. (See p. 17, 'The Histories as part of a larger story'.) In treating Joshua–Judges–Samuel–Kings separately from the other Histories (Ruth included) this textbook follows the lead of the Hebrew Bible.

SOME QUESTIONS

The above summary of the Histories may already have raised in your mind issues which need to be explored. The rest of this chapter will describe different approaches scholars have followed in their attempts to understand and interpret the Histories. These approaches may be formulated as a series of questions.

One set of questions focuses on the historical context in which the Histories originated, that is, on the ancient Near East in the second and first millennia BC. What is known

of the history of this region in general? Are there other texts originating from the ancient Near East with which the Histories may be compared, and which help us to understand the Histories better?

Another set of questions concerns particular literary features of the Histories (e.g. the frequent use of repetition) which can be interpreted in a variety of ways. Can we identify the narrative techniques used by the writers? Do the Histories have a distinctive literary artistry? How should we understand the processes of their composition?

A further set of questions concerns the status of the Histories as historical documents. What kind of history of Israel do they offer? How do they compare to other historical texts from the ancient Near East? How reliable is their account of Israel's history when set in the light of these other texts and when compared with the findings of archaeology?

A final set of questions shifts the focus to more contemporary concerns. What are the implications of the fact that the Histories have at a later stage been incorporated into larger collections designed to function as Scripture within Judaism and Christianity, and which still have this function today? Does it make a difference to read the Histories in the context of a larger Bible, whether this is defined as Law, Prophets and Writings, as in Judaism, or as Old and New Testaments, as in Christianity? And, regardless of how we answer this question, can the Histories, which stem from a culture remote from our own, be used as a resource for theological and ethical thinking today?

These questions will occupy us throughout our study of the Histories. The rest of this chapter sets out the issues in more detail.

THE HISTORIES IN THEIR ANCIENT NEAR EASTERN CONTEXT

Chapter 2, a sketch of the history of the ancient Near East, 1550–63 BC, describes the general context in which the Histories originated. The dates chosen give the outer limits of the period within which, on any understanding, the Histories and those responsible for producing them are to be located.

The Histories are by no means the only surviving ancient Near Eastern texts. Mesopotamia, Anatolia (modern Turkey), Syria and Egypt have all yielded large numbers of texts which provide a literary and historical context for the Histories. These texts include creation accounts and other stories relating to the gods; cultic texts and hymns; treaty documents and law codes; historical accounts and annals; wisdom texts, love poetry and much more. They will almost certainly not be familiar to you, but we will refer to some of them and hope you will follow up these references.

At appropriate points Chapters 3—11 will draw comparisons between the Histories and ancient Near Eastern texts. In some cases the biblical account seems to belong to a recognizable ancient Near Eastern literary type (see the comparison of the account of David's rise in 1 and 2 Samuel with a Hittite apologetic text, Ch. 5). In other cases ancient Near Eastern texts suggest new ways of understanding the literary conventions of the biblical text (see the comparison of Joshua 1—12 with ancient Near Eastern conquest accounts, Ch. 3). In yet other cases ancient Near Eastern texts and the biblical text present different perspectives on the same events (see the panel on Sennacherib and Jerusalem, Ch. 6).

Apart from the Moabite Stone (see Ch. 6) and later texts such as the books of Maccabees and the writings of Josephus, Palestine and Transjordan have yielded few lengthy texts which may be compared with the Histories, though we shall refer to the Tel Dan Stela in connection with David and later kings of Israel and Judah (Chs 5 and 6).

THE HISTORIES AS LITERARY TEXTS

How should the Histories be described from a literary point of view? The following features emerge as one reads through them.

- They include many kinds of writing: memoir-like material (Neh. 1—7), lists (Josh. 13—19), building accounts (1 Kgs 6—7), legal texts (Josh. 20), prayers (Neh. 9) and poetry (Judg. 5). Narrative forms the bulk of the Histories, but there are different kinds of narrative: battle reports (Josh. 6—12), historical surveys (Judg. 1:1—3:6), and accounts which focus on the lives of a few individuals (Ruth); accounts of public speeches (1 Sam. 12) and of apparently private conversations (2 Sam. 13:1—20); accounts of miracles (2 Kgs 4—6) and sections in which the miraculous is absent (2 Sam. 9—20).
- The Histories are written in different styles. Sometimes great literary skill is apparent; at other times we wonder whether what we are reading can properly be called literary at all. There is a clear contrast between well-shaped narratives such as Ruth and Esther and the much more uneven Ezra and Nehemiah; or between the gripping opening chapters of Joshua and the (frankly) monotonous boundary descriptions in the second half of the book.
- Some narratives follow a clear sequence of events (e.g. 1 Sam. 16—31) or have a

clear structure (e.g. Judges 3:7—16:31). Elsewhere episodes are juxtaposed with no obvious link between them: the section of Kings containing the narratives of Elijah and Elisha, 1 Kings 17—2 Kings 13, has a number of examples of this sort.

- The Histories seem to be incoherent at points. There are apparently conflicting views expressed, e.g. regarding whether Joshua completely conquered Canaan, or whether Samuel decisively defeated the Philistines at the battle of Mizpah (compare 1 Sam. 7 and 1 Sam. 13). There are surprising omissions (e.g. Samuel's absence from the account of 1 Samuel 4—6 or Elijah's from 1 Kings 20). Some texts are placed out of chronological sequence (e.g. Judg. 17—21), or seem to go over the same ground as other texts (compare Judges 1:1—2:5 with 2:6—3:6; or Ezra 2 with Nehemiah 7).

- Some narratives seem over-full: words, phrases or ideas are repeated; the same actions are described two or three times (Josh. 3–4; Judg. 20). There are other narratives which seem over-brief, passages where we would welcome explanatory comment or moral evaluation from the narrator but find none (Judg. 19; 2 Sam. 21:1–14).

What are we to make of all this? Much scholarship has been devoted to this topic, employing a variety of methods. In what follows we first consider 'literary-critical' or 'historical-critical' approaches to the Histories. We then turn to the more recent approach known as 'narrative criticism' before briefly considering other approaches which emphasize the role of the reader in interpretation. The question how to explain the distinctive literary features of the Histories is important, and the answer given to some extent determines how we answer most other questions relating to the Histories (e.g. dating, authorship, historical value, theology and ethics). We will, therefore, go into some detail here.

LITERARY-CRITICAL APPROACHES

Literary-critical approaches to the Histories include source criticism, form criticism and redaction criticism, approaches which dominated Old Testament scholarship for much of the twentieth century. The term 'literary-critical' in this context does not mean what it might mean in the study of, say, English Literature. In Old Testament scholarship 'literary-critical' approaches usually focus on the literary *history* of the text: hence an alternative term for them is 'historical-critical'. Scholars who apply such approaches to the Histories often conclude that they are the product of a long and complex compositional process involving many people, writing at different times and influenced by diverse theological perspectives. The different stages in the formation of the Histories can, it is argued, be traced by careful attention to textual details.

Source criticism is the detailed analysis of biblical texts with the aim of identifying their constituent parts, both their sources (earlier, independent texts which have been incorporated into them) and also the editorial changes (additions, omissions, alterations) which have helped to shape them. Source criticism pays particular attention to repetition, gaps, differences of perspective, inconsistencies and contradictions in the text. Such features of the text, though they do not always (it is held) require a source-critical explanation, usually form the raw material of source-critical arguments. This approach has been applied in a particularly thoroughgoing way to the Pentateuch (see *EOT I*, pp. 159–85), but it has also been widely employed in the study of the Histories.

Examples of source-critical arguments applied to the Histories are: the suggestion that repetition in the account of the crossing of the Jordan (Josh. 3—4) shows that more than one hand has worked over it (Ch. 3, 'Outline'); and the view that Judges has two introductions (1:1—2:5; 2:6—3:6), which derive from different stages in the editing of the book (Ch. 4, 'Outline').

Form criticism is also concerned with literary history, but it operates mainly by classifying different types of text according to structure and function. The texts in question may vary in size, but have in common that they form a distinct unit within their context, one whose bounds can be identified. 'Form' is used in two senses in this approach: it can refer to unique features of individual texts, such as their shape and structure; or it can refer to features shared by a number of texts, which may suggest that these texts constitute a distinct category or *genre*. Form criticism has created a number of terms to classify these different genres. Among the genres which have been identified in the Histories are: saga, prophetic legend, aetiology, farewell speech, and battle report.

When a genre has been identified, it may be possible to specify with some precision the kind of situations in which texts belonging to that genre originated or were used. It may also be possible to draw conclusions about the literary history of the narrative(s) in which these texts now stand. See, for example, Soggin's argument that Judges 2:1–5, 6:11–24 and 6:25–32 originated as 'shrine aetiologies', narratives explaining the origins of particular local shrines, and did not originally belong in their present contexts (Ch. 4, 'Outline'). See also the discussion of form criticism in relation to the Elisha narratives (Ch. 6, 'Outline').

Redaction criticism ('redaction' means 'editing') usually works on a large scale, pulling together numerous smaller-scale source- and form-critical observations and fashioning them into an argument regarding the literary history of several chapters of narrative, a whole book or even a group of books. If there is evidence that a biblical text once existed in a different form, since altered by the work of a later editor, redaction criticism focuses on the possible historical context and theological viewpoint of this later editor. How did his perspective differ from that of the base text? What alterations did he make in order to produce a text which reflected his views? (These alterations, if reasonably extensive, are collectively described as an 'editorial layer' or 'redactional layer'.) Has this editor done the same thing in other parts of the Old Testament? Is there evidence that more than one editor has been at work on a particular text?

Along these lines, it has been suggested that those parts of 1 and 2 Samuel which portray David negatively (mainly 2 Sam. 11—20) are a redactional layer inserted into the books in order to counter claims made on behalf of the Davidic dynasty in the post-exilic period (see Ch. 5, 'Literary-critical issues'). A further example of a redaction-critical argument is the widespread view that Deuteronomy–Kings form a 'Deuteronomistic History' in which one or more layers of Deuteronomistic editing can be detected (see Ch. 7).

Source, form and redaction criticism work on somewhat different scales, and focus on different aspects of the text, but they work largely hand in hand. These three approaches, which dominated Old Testament studies until recently, are still widely represented in scholarship on the Histories.

On the basis of the brief summary above you may feel that these approaches offer a generally reasonable way of handling the biblical text. Alternatively, you may find them problematic, perhaps because of views you hold concerning the Bible as God's Word, or because you find some of the examples cited unconvincing considered purely as literary analysis. Whatever your initial response, you should neither embrace nor dismiss these approaches too hastily. It is easy to present them in a parodied form, as 'scissors-and-paste scholarship' and the like, or to parade some of the more extreme examples of this kind of work as though they were representative. But that does not do these approaches justice. They are based on detailed study of the biblical texts and raise fair questions. You may not agree with the answers given, but you cannot simply brush the questions aside. Serious engagement with source-, form- and redaction-critical treatments of the Histories will usually help you to see more in the text than you might otherwise have done. Having said this, we turn to an approach which may be considered a mirror image of the literary-critical approaches just considered.

NARRATIVE CRITICISM

Narrative criticism has emerged in the last 30 or so years. Most scholars who adopt this approach ('narrative critics', or, following Amit's term, 'story scholars') have some or all of the following in common:

• A belief that Old Testament narrative displays great literary artistry: this is reflected in the title of Alter's now-classic work, *The Art of Biblical Narrative*.

• A concern to understand and rightly interpret the literary conventions and techniques of Old Testament narrative: these, it is argued, are partly the same as those of modern Western literature, but also partly different from them.

• A working assumption of literary unity: narrative critics are reluctant to invoke theories of multiple sources, later editing and the like, though such theories are not in principle excluded.

• An awareness of the role of the reader in interpretation.

Narrative critics focus on many of the same features of the biblical text as 'literary-critical' approaches: for example, literary structure, recurring words and phrases, similarities shared by different narratives or sections of narrative, gaps in the narrative, and differences in perspective. But they interpret these features differently. Thus *repetition*, whether small-scale (words, sentences) or large-scale (entire narrative episodes), whether exact or involving some *variation* between the repeated elements, is generally seen as intentional. The same applies to *gaps* in the narrative, the presentation of information out of chronological sequence and the withholding of information or evaluation at points where we might have expected them. (Sternberg, p. 89, sums up this aspect in the phrase 'the interplay of the truth and the whole truth'.) The *play between narration and dialogue* is seen as a prime example of narrative artistry: spoken words, measured against their narrative context, can tell us much about the characters who say them. Old Testament narrators, it is argued, have a fascination with human character and motives.

7

Here are some examples of narrative criticism as applied to the Histories:

- In Joshua 3—4 (the crossing of the Jordan) and Judges 20:29–48 (the defeat of Benjamin) the narrator uses frequent repetition to slow down the narrative and focus on the events described.
- The framework of the accounts in Judges 3:7—16:31 is an example of repetition and variation: the framework suggests a recurring pattern in Israel's history, while variations in the framework (additions, omissions, expansion of particular elements) draw attention to differences between the accounts of the 'major' judges.
- 1 Kings 11—12, the account of Jeroboam's rebellion, is told in a way that suggests ironic parallels with the account of Israel's exodus from Egypt (Exod. 1—14). This is an example of what is termed *narrative analogy*, in which one narrative is deliberately written so as to echo another.
- The Histories contain many dialogues where the participants are characterized by contrast: for instance, the episodes of Micah and the Danites (Judg. 18:22–26), Abner and Paltiel (2 Sam. 3:15–16), David and Michal (2 Sam. 6:20–23), and Obadiah and Elijah (1 Kgs 18:7–16).
- Other texts in the Histories seem to invite the reader to reflect on the difficulties of understanding human character and motives. In Judges 19, what can the Levite be thinking of when he tells his (dead) concubine to 'get up' (v. 28)? In 2 Samuel 12:15–24, why does David respond as he does to his son's death? When Bathsheba enters David's presence in 1 Kings 1, why does the narrator mention that 'Abishag the Shunammite was attending the king' (v. 15)? Is it so that we may speculate on what goes through her mind as she sees her decrepit husband and his beautiful companion?
- Joshua 22 is an example of *gapping*, the withholding of information to create ambiguity. Why have the Transjordanian tribes built their altar (v. 10)? The answer emerges at the climax of the narrative, when it becomes clear that they have acted in good faith, but this fact is only revealed at this point, and not at the beginning (Sternberg, pp. 317–18).
- Judges 1, Judges 17:1–5 and 1 Kings 9—10 may all be seen as examples of *pseudo-objective narration* (Sternberg, p. 480), in which events are narrated without comment, so as to raise questions in the reader's mind, and thus make the reader more receptive to the evaluation which the narrator finally provides.

A central claim of this approach is that Old Testament narrative presupposes readers and hearers who are actively involved in the interpretative process: the writers expected their audience to note key-words, repeated elements, narrative gaps and the like, and then attempt to make sense of them. As we do this we become aware of an *implicit commentary* running through the narrative: the narrator, without actually stating his views, presents words and events in such a way as to suggest a particular interpretation of them. The Histories also, of course, contain passages of *explicit* commentary, where the narrator makes his interpretation of events perfectly plain (e.g. Judg. 2:6—3:6; 1 Kgs 11:1–13; 2 Kgs 17); but this is not the only kind of evaluative comment found in Histories. The Histories, it is claimed, aim to influence readers by both implicit and explicit modes of persuasion; and the implicit modes are the more effective for being more subtle. (For an extended discussion of this topic, see Sternberg, pp. 441–81.)

Narrative critics see the techniques and conventions of Old Testament narrative as vehicles for a distinctive world-view. The frequent presence of gaps in the narrative, which means that the full significance of an event often only becomes clear at a late stage, suggests a contrast between divine omniscience and the limitations of human knowledge. The play between narration and dialogue is tied to a view of humans as fallible and sometimes deceitful. Sometimes human characters tell the truth, and this can be conveyed by a close match between their words and the narrator's. Sometimes human characters have a particular perception of the truth, or misrepresent the facts (deliberately or unintentionally), and in these cases their words may differ quite significantly from those of the narrator or another character. The interest in human character shows a respect for human personality and a belief that human motives, words and actions play an important part in YHWH's unfolding purposes. The literary artistry of Old Testament narrative is thus inseparably bound up with a particular vision of God and humanity.

Narrative critics, then, focus on the same textual phenomena as source, form and redaction critics, but explain them differently. Where these other critics see greater or lesser degrees of literary incoherence, to be explained by theories of multiple authorship, narrative critics tend to see an artistry reflecting a single authorial purpose. Thus: repetition is not a sign of the conflation of separate sources; the presence of discernible sub-units in a text does not mean the text is composite; gaps in the narrative have been deliberately created; unexpected details are

revealed out of sequence to heighten their impact; and so on. In Chapters 3–11 we will note examples where the two approaches read the same textual data differently.

How convincing are the alternative explanations offered by narrative criticism? Responses to this question will vary from case to case and from reader to reader. An interpretative approach which claims that Old Testament narratives contain much implicit commentary may provoke the response that the commentary is not so much implicit as non-existent, and that narrative critics have 'detected' things that are not really in the text. Given the will and sufficient ingenuity, it may be argued, one can usually find *some* way of interpreting even the most unliterary and composite-seeming text as a literary unity. But over against this, we should take seriously the suggestion that the conventions of Old Testament narrative may be different from those with which we are familiar: maybe we need to accustom ourselves to reading the biblical text in ways which at first seem to us over-subtle. (For a helpful discussion of how historical-critical and narrative-critical approaches may interact, see Amit 1999, pp. 22–32.)

It will be obvious from Chapters 3–11 that narrative criticism is the mode of literary analysis we favour. Indeed, one of the chief points of interest in this book may be that it bases its interpretation of the Histories on this approach, in contrast to earlier introductions which favoured historical-critical analyses. We should, however, emphasize that narrative criticism is often open-ended in its implications. If the main lines of narrative criticism are correct, Old Testament narratives contain intentional gaps and frequently refrain from drawing explicit links between events, leaving it to the reader to grasp the significance of what is narrated. This is not a narrative style which sets out everything clearly and unambiguously. The result is that the text can often be taken in more than one way, and many examples can be cited of texts which different narrative critics have interpreted differently. The same point underlies the frequent use of words such as 'seems' and 'apparently' in the 'Outline' sections of Chapters 3–11. In some cases one may feel confident in choosing one reading over another, perhaps because it accounts better for the details of the text or fits the larger literary context better. But sometimes two different readings may seem equally plausible: see, for example, the panel on Ziba and Mephibosheth (2 Sam. 16:1–4; 19:24–30, Ch. 5 'Outline'). If you follow this approach, this is something you are going to have to learn to live with!

Narrative-critical approaches are also open-ended as regards the literary history of the text. It is true that narrative critics tend to interpret biblical texts as literary wholes, and usually do not see gaps, repetitions and so on as evidence that these texts are composite. But conclusions of this sort relate to the biblical text in its present form, and are often accompanied by an agnosticism about possible earlier forms of the text. As regards the Histories, it is very likely, given their nature (the lengthy period they cover, their literary diversity), that they are based on a number of originally separate traditions, and that some of them existed in earlier versions (now lost). Our claim in this book is not that the earlier stages did not exist, but that they are not as easy to recover as source, form and redaction critics argue.

In principle narrative-critical readings might imply early dates for large stretches of the Histories, the literary-critical arguments for distinguishing earlier and later sources (or base text and editorial additions) having been countered by alternative, unitary readings of the same textual data. But this conclusion does not necessarily follow. For example, the narrative analogies that will be noted between Joshua, Judges, Samuel and Kings (Chs 3–6) may suggest the opposite: if these books contain many cross-references to each other, this may imply that, whatever may be said about possible earlier versions of these books, the present form of these books can be dated no earlier than the latest of them, Kings, that is, no earlier than 560 BC. Narrative criticism is not necessarily tied to early dates for texts.

Finally, we have noted how some narrative critics speak of the narrators as attempting by a variety of means to persuade readers towards a particular viewpoint. This raises further questions: should I allow myself to be persuaded? Do I accept the narrator's interpretation of events? Are my values and world-view the same as his? Literary interpretation of any text tends to bring the interpreter's own intellectual and ethical commitments into play, and many modern literary readings of the Histories are quite open about this: reader-response criticism, post-structuralist criticism, feminist criticism and others. (See the essays by Gunn and Fewell; also the chapter 'Readers and Responsibility', in Gunn and Fewell, pp. 189–205; Barr, pp. 102–62.) We will return to such readings later in this chapter, when we consider the use of the Histories as a contemporary theological and ethical resource.

THE HISTORIES AS HISTORICAL DOCUMENTS

Taken at face value, the Histories claim that certain events happened at specific times in particular parts of the ancient Near East. This raises questions relating to the Histories as historical documents. What kind of history writing are they? Is 'history writing' the best classification? When were they written and by whom? How reliable are they?

ARE THE HISTORIES HISTORY WRITING?

In answering this question we can note the following points:

- The Histories present a highly selective account of Israel from the conquest to the exile and beyond, and the coverage varies from period to period. Even where the coverage is most extensive, for example in the account of David in 1 Samuel 16—2 Samuel 20, the Histories are far from giving us all the detail we could desire.
- The writers of the Histories clearly intended what they wrote to influence the thinking and conduct of their contemporaries. This has affected their selection and presentation of events.
- The Histories contain many skilfully composed narratives.
- These Histories describe matters which by their nature one might expect to be widely known, such as tribal history and royal building projects, and also matters which are not normally a matter of public record, such as private conversations between two parties.
- The Histories reflect the writers' theological views. This is seen particularly in the Histories' understanding of causality, which emphasizes the role in events played by Israel's god: YHWH's acts of salvation and judgment to a large extent shape the course of events within and outside Israel.
- The dating and authorship of the Histories have been extensively investigated, but with few generally accepted conclusions. It seems clear that Joshua, Judges, Samuel and Kings in their present form are some kind of literary unity, consequently that the final form of these books cannot be dated earlier than *c.* 560, the date of the latest incident recorded in Kings (see 2 Kgs 25:27–30). But this allows for a wide range of views regarding possible earlier stages in the formation of these books and earlier sources for these books. Chronicles is a post-exilic composition based to a considerable extent on material now found in other biblical books (the Pentateuch and, especially, Samuel and Kings); but questions still remain regarding other sources used by the Chronicler. Ezra, Nehemiah and Esther are clearly post-exilic, but the precise date of composition remains unclear. Finally, different scholars have suggested a wide range of dates for the composition of Ruth, from the early monarchic to the post-exilic periods. All the Histories are basically anonymous.

All these points are perfectly compatible with a view of the Histories as genuine historiography. All history writing must be selective, focusing on particular times, places, people and events, and not even the most detailed account can give comprehensive coverage. The fact that the biblical writers told their accounts with one eye on lessons to be learned by their contemporaries and later generations, which means that the Histories tell us about the writers' own perspectives as well as about the events narrated, also does not make the Histories unusual. Miller (p. 18) argues that this is true of almost all history writing, and speaks of history as 'an ongoing conversation between the past and the present', in which 'as we . . . seek to understand the present, we naturally look to the past for bearings'.

The literary artistry of the Histories, particularly the fact that they contain many passages of apparently private dialogue (e.g. Judg. 6:11–23; 1 Sam. 1:12—18; 2 Sam. 6:20–23), may seem to compromise them as genuinely historical in intent. Do they, as Alter suggests in a discussion of the Ehud account (Judg. 3), include passages of 'fictionalized history', that is, 'history in which the feeling and the meaning of events are concretely realized through the technical resources of prose fiction' (p. 41)? Do they contain a certain amount of imaginative reconstruction of what may have been said on particular occasions?

It is easier to raise these questions than to answer them definitively. Every historical account must be a narrative of some sort, if it is not to be simply incoherent: there must be a certain amount of literary shaping which presents events in a particular order and brings out their significance. The fact that the Histories contain narratives of considerable literary skill cannot by itself disqualify them as history writing. The Histories may contain many passages of reconstructed dialogue, but that is probably true of many other works of ancient historiography. Provided we have no reason to suspect that such passages misrepresent the substance of what was said on a particular occasion, a reconstructed dialogue need not be a worse guide to the course of events than a verbatim report.

As well as providing a clear narrative, every historical account must include analysis of the events narrated, that is, an interpretation which investigates the causes for these events and assesses their significance. The Histories do indeed provide interpretation of the events narrated, though it is debatable whether the kind of theological explanations found in the Histories (e.g. a statement such as 'the Israelites again did what was evil in the sight of YHWH . . . so YHWH sold them into the hands of King Jabin of Canaan', Judg. 4:1–2) counts as 'analysis' according to the canons of modern Western history writing. Most modern histories, whatever period they are describing, do not invoke divine causation to explain events, and many modern histories of Israel tend to replace the references to YHWH's agency in the biblical accounts with historical explanations which seem 'more reasonable' in the sense that they are 'more in keeping with our modern Western perception of reality' (Miller, p. 18).

Why the conventions of modern Western historiography are as they are is too big a topic to explore here. We simply note that the decision to exclude from the category of history writing all works, like the Histories, which do not adopt an effectively secular perspective involves metaphysical commitments which reach beyond the domain of historiography and which cannot be justified by purely historical arguments. Put simply, if you believe in a god somewhat like the god of Israel there is no reason in principle why you should dismiss the theological perspective of the Histories. Certainly the fact that the Histories are theological in character does not make them unique in their ancient Near Eastern context. Many ancient Near Eastern texts which purport to give an account of historical events (e.g. royal annals, campaign reports, descriptions of temple building) speak of gods as guiding the course of events (Averbeck, pp. 107–13). What may make the

Histories unusual among ancient Near Eastern writings is their monotheistic perspective, which gives them what Averbeck (p. 113) terms a 'metanarrative' quality: the Histories, along with the Pentateuch, form an account of human history from creation on, which 'claims to make sense of all other stories and the whole of reality'.

The issue of evidence is another point on which the Histories seem to differ from modern history writing. The histories quite often cite sources (e.g. the reference to the Book of Jashar at Joshua 10:13, and the frequent mention of the 'Book of the Annals of the Kings of Israel/Judah' in Kings). References to phenomena still in existence or places which retain a certain name 'to this day' may similarly be intended as evidence for the historicity of particular events (e.g. Rahab's family, Josh. 6:25; the Valley of Achor, Josh. 7:26; the custom of lamenting Jephthah's daughter, Judg. 11:39–40). But there are few signs of the kind of sifting of evidence, the evaluation of conflicting testimonies and differing viewpoints, which plays a key role in contemporary historical method. Or at least: such a sifting and evaluation may have taken place, but this is not obvious from the biblical text. In fact, one searches the Histories in vain for a statement of historical method. This again is something the Histories have in common with other ancient Near Eastern historical texts. It appears that the first historical writers explicitly to address the question of how to handle different types of testimony were the Greek historians Herodotus and Thucydides (fifth century BC), though that need not mean that they were the first writers to evaluate their sources critically.

Regarding the possible time gap between the Histories and the events described, we must distinguish between the likely date of the final form of each of the Histories and the date of possible earlier sources on which they may be based. Chapters 3–11 will discuss questions of sources and dates in relation to each of the Histories. In general, however, an account composed shortly after the events narrated is not necessarily more reliable than one composed (say) several generations later. One can be too close to events as well as too distant from them. A later account, if founded on reliable traditions, may present a truer picture than one written shortly after the events, not least because it is able to take a longer perspective, setting the events in the light of later developments. (See the discussion of 'Earlier and Later Testimony' in Provan, Long and Longman, pp. 56–62.)

To sum up the argument so far, the Histories have features which are not usual in much modern history writing (most notably, their theological standpoint) and lack other features which are (most notably, extensive documentation and discussion of evidence and sources). They do not read like a modern history book. Yet they have more in common with modern history writing than might at first appear. Literary artistry, a didactic intent, even a theological perspective, are not necessarily incompatible with serious historical concerns. Indeed, they are commonly found in ancient Near Eastern historical accounts. According to many possible definitions the Histories should be classified as 'history writing': accounts of past events told with an eye to contemporary relevance.

ARE THE HISTORIES HISTORICALLY RELIABLE?

But are the Histories reliable accounts? Granted that theological concerns need not undermine sound historical method, have they in fact done so at some points? How far should we rely on the Histories in modern accounts of Israel's history? Many of these issues are hotly disputed at present, and a survey of previous scholarship on this topic may be helpful. (For further details, see the works of Moorey, Fritz and Currid.)

The beginnings of ancient Near Eastern studies (the excavation of sites from the ancient Near East and the decipherment of texts discovered at these sites) can be dated to about 1800. Excavations in Palestine began about 1850. Work in these areas has gone on more or less uninterrupted ever since, with ever more refined methods. For over 100 years, then, historians of Israel in the biblical period have based their accounts both on the biblical texts and on a growing body of data unearthed in the lands of the ancient Near East. These scholars were aware of literary-critical scholarship (e.g. regarding the dating of texts, or the source criticism of particular chapters), and the conclusions of literary critics influenced the use they made of biblical texts in reconstructing Israel's history. The history of Bright, once a standard text, illustrates this point. But there was generally no question that, used with appropriate caution, the biblical texts were a proper source for historians to draw on, along with ancient Near Eastern texts and archaeological data.

Such views, according to which archaeology and the biblical text were mutually illuminating, came to seem increasingly problematic in the later decades of the twentieth century. It was felt that biblical studies had set the agenda of archaeology to an unhealthy extent, with too great a focus on sites mentioned in the Bible and not enough on the archaeology of the region as a whole. The attempt to correlate the findings of archaeology with the biblical text had led to a circularity in some of the arguments used, whereby, for example, a destruction layer might be dated to the thirteenth century, attributed to invading Israelites, and then used as an argument for the historicity of an Israelite conquest, when perhaps there were no other grounds for a thirteenth-century dating, and nothing to prove that Israelites were responsible for the destruction.

Scholars began to argue for a methodological separation between archaeology and biblical studies, so that archaeology could speak with a more independent voice. 'Biblical archaeology' should be replaced by a 'Syro-Palestinian archaeology' in which the archaeological data would be assessed by themselves before the question was raised how they related to the biblical account. The full range of archaeological data should be gathered in order to form as comprehensive a picture as possible of life in Palestine at a given period. Attention should be paid not simply to those data which seemed most relevant to politics and religion (the primary focus of the biblical texts), but also to data which illuminated the culture, social structure and other aspects of the life of the inhabitants of Palestine. (See Dever, pp. 53–95 for a convenient summary of this approach.) These concerns are reflected in studies such as those of King and Stager and Borowski, which consider biblical and archaeological data relating to many aspects of daily life in biblical Israel, and in social-scientific approaches to Israelite society such as those of McNutt.

Another, related development which became noticeable in the 1970s was a growing tendency to question the biblical account of Israel's origins. First the historicity of the patriarchal period and the exodus was questioned, then that of the Israelite conquest of Canaan: all this on the grounds (1) that the biblical texts were maybe centuries later than the events they claimed to report, and seemed to reflect the theological views of these later writers; and (2) that there was scanty extra-biblical evidence, whether archaeological or inscriptional, to support the biblical accounts. Thus Miller and Hayes in their 1986 volume gave a brief summary of Genesis–Joshua and surveyed various theories of Israelite origins, but refused to offer their own reconstruction of these origins, beginning their detailed treatment of Israelite history with the period of the Judges (pp. 54–79).

In the 1990s this questioning was extended to later parts of the biblical account, the period of the Israelite monarchy and beyond. Was the biblical picture of the reigns of David and Solomon plausible? There was little extra-biblical evidence for a Solomonic empire. What about the period of the divided monarchy? Granted that from the ninth century on some names of Israelite and Judean kings begin to appear in Assyrian and Babylonian accounts of campaigns in Syria and Palestine, biblical texts (Kings, Chronicles) were still the major source for Israelite history in that period. And these texts seemed to be no less influenced by their writers' ideology than the biblical texts relating to earlier periods, which had already been found wanting, partly for this very reason. In what was in one sense a logical development, similar arguments began to be employed against the biblical picture of the Babylonian exile. The biblical texts might speak of the kingdom of Judah going into exile (Kings, Chronicles) and of descendants of the exiles returning to the former territory

of Judah in the Persian period (Ezra, Nehemiah), but there was little extra-biblical testimony to all these events. Might not this part of the biblical picture also be largely an invention?

A scholar who argued along these lines was Thompson (1992). In his view the Bible was deeply problematic as a historical source, a late compilation, uneven, contradictory and full of variant traditions (pp. 353–99). Where previous historians of Israel had used literary-critical arguments to distinguish between early sources and later additions, and thus isolate what they considered the more reliable parts of the biblical account, Thompson felt that these arguments were severely flawed. Claims that, for example, some passages in Joshua–Kings could be dated to the time of Josiah's reforms and that other texts reflected a less optimistic, probably exilic perspective (see Ch. 6) themselves depended on a historical framework largely derived from the Bible, and were therefore circular. It might be that there were some earlier traditions embedded within the Bible, but it was uncertain how far these had been altered by the later compilers, so that any literary-critical salvage operation was more or less impossible.

In other sections of his book (e.g. pp. 402–15) Thompson offered an account of Palestine and surrounding regions which made virtually no appeal to the Bible, and was based largely on archaeology (particularly surveys of settlement, farming and trade patterns at different periods) and extra-biblical texts (chiefly Egyptian, Assyrian, Babylonian and Persian), along with studies relating to other long-term trends in the region, such as climate change. He believed that the Assyrian and Babylonian deportations of the eighth to sixth centuries removed virtually all the former inhabitants of these regions and moved new groups into the area, so that there was little continuity between the population of these regions in the sixth century and that of earlier centuries. He argued that what is described in biblical texts as a return of descendants of the former citizens of Judah to their ancestral lands was nothing of the sort. Rather, the Persian province of Yehud (Judah) was a new foundation tendentiously represented as the return of a captive people to their former territories, in line with a Persian imperial ideology which portrayed the Persian rulers as benign restorers of patterns of life disrupted by the previous Babylonian rulers. Persian imperial policy was thus the catalyst for the shaping of diverse (and now largely unrecoverable) traditions into a single account according to which Israel (12 tribes linked by common descent) had entered the land of Canaan together, had been linked by the worship of one god, and had later existed as a united monarchy and then two separate kingdoms, with the heirs of the kingdom of Judah returning to their territories after exile in Babylon (pp. 415–23). Similar views are advocated by Davies and Lemche.

These views may seem extreme, and they have drawn criticism. Kitchen argues at length that scholars such as Thompson ignore or misuse the ancient Near Eastern data: they fail to note good parallels to things described in the Histories, and draw invalid inferences from gaps in the evidence. Further, the Histories look nothing like what we would have expected if they had been mainly composed in the Persian or the Hellenistic periods. They contain a wealth of accurate information about earlier centuries which could hardly have been invented at a later period (Kitchen, pp. 459–64; Dever,

pp. 97–157). In particular, there are serious objections to the view that the Old Testament is basically a Hellenistic book (Albertz). Barr (pp. 97–101) suggests that the approach of Thompson and others suffers from a methodological imbalance. Its advocates are over-suspicious towards the Old Testament, and over-accepting of other data (or interpretations of the data) which support their position. They impose a high burden of proof on those who attempt to relate, say, the biblical accounts of David and Solomon to the realities of tenth-century Palestine, but a much lower burden of proof on those who read these same accounts as Persian- or Hellenistic-period ideology.

However, even scholars who do not accept a very late dating of the Histories may still be highly critical of the Histories as a historical source. An example is the volume by Finkelstein and Silberman (2002), which argues among other things that there was no conquest of Canaan as described in Joshua; that the Israelites were mainly Canaanite in origin; that Judges contains little in the way of reliable historical data; that there never was a united monarchy ruled by David and Solomon with its capital city in Jerusalem; and that what Kings describes as the kingdoms of Israel and Judah had separate origins, the biblical texts which represent them as once both parts of a single kingdom being a fiction invented for propaganda purposes in the reign of Josiah.

Finkelstein and Silberman's volume is not the last word on the topic, nor do we in fact agree with most of their conclusions. Their work, like that of the other scholars mentioned above, has been cited simply to give a sense of recent developments in the field. Some further studies are included in the suggestions for further reading at the end of this chapter. Chapters 3–11 will each pursue particular historical issues in more detail. Underlying much of the detailed discussion in those chapters are some general issues which we have touched on above, which it is worth summarizing here:

- *The relationship of literary reading and historical assessment*: evaluation of the Histories as historical documents cannot be separated from consideration of them as literary texts. A dispute over historical reliability will sometimes centre upon questions which are clearly literary in character (e.g. regarding the dating, coherence or viewpoint of a particular text).
- *The theological character of the Histories*: is this feature of the Histories (which they have in common with most ancient Near Eastern historical accounts) a serious obstacle to accepting them as reliable accounts?
- *External attestation*: is it valid to argue (as many of the scholars cited above in effect do) that one should only believe the biblical account, or is better justified in believing it, when it is supported by extra-biblical data (e.g. ancient Near Eastern texts or archaeological data)? How far can one take this principle? In the absence of external attestation are there other lines of argument one can develop regarding the general plausibility or otherwise of the biblical text?
- *Archaeology and the biblical text*: granted that archaeology must have a certain methodological independence from biblical studies, the attempt must at some point be made to relate biblical text and archaeological data to each other. How is this to be done in a way that is fair to both of them?

THE HISTORIES AS PART OF A LARGER STORY

A first-time reader of the Histories normally encounters them as part of a Bible, either Jewish or Christian, and soon notices that they presuppose and at many points refer to the narrative of Israel's earlier history in the Pentateuch. There are also many links between the Histories and other parts of the Old Testament. The New Testament makes many clear references to the Histories and the events described in them.

Why, it may be asked, have we not considered the relation of the Histories to other biblical books before considering the ancient Near Eastern context? Do these other books not form a more immediate and obvious interpretative context? Answering that question is in fact far from straightforward. It involves examining the links between the Histories and other biblical books. What kind of links are they? How may they have come about? Such questions are explored at various points in Chapters 3–11 (e.g. the '. . . in the canon' sections). Chapter 7, in particular, asks what role Deuteronomy (perhaps an earlier form of Deuteronomy) may have played in the formation of Joshua–Kings. The placing of the Histories within a larger literary entity (a biblical canon) can be seen as a major hermeneutical step, reflecting a particular interpretation of them. A further issue is that there are different biblical canons, which vary in the number of books they include and in the order of the books included (see the panel 'The place of the Histories in three Old Testament canons'). A particularly significant feature of the Hebrew canon, also to be picked up in Chapter 7, is the separation of Joshua–Kings from the other Histories and their designation as 'Former Prophets'.

We do not have space to discuss theories regarding the origins of the different biblical canons, or the significance of the different positions of the Histories in Hebrew and Greek canons. (Some of the '. . . in the canon' sections in Chapters 3–11 will touch on this issue.) A more fundamental issue is whether or not to read the Histories in the light of the New Testament, that is, as part of Christian Scripture, along the lines suggested by advocates of what has come to be called biblical theology. This leads on to the next section.

THE HISTORIES AND BIBLICAL THEOLOGY

Biblical theology has until recently been practised almost exclusively by Christians. The books of the Bible (Old and New

THE PLACE OF THE HISTORIES IN THREE OLD TESTAMENT CANONS

Hebrew Bible	Septuagint	English translations	Hebrew Bible	Septuagint	English translations
Law	*Pentateuch*	*Pentateuch*	*Writings*	Song of Songs	*Prophets*
Genesis	Genesis	Genesis	Psalms	Job	Isaiah
Exodus	Exodus	Exodus	Job	Wisdom of Solomon	Jeremiah
Leviticus	Leviticus	Leviticus	Proverbs	Sirach	Lamentations
Numbers	Numbers	Numbers	RUTH	Psalms of Solomon	Ezekiel
Deuteronomy	Deuteronomy	Deuteronomy	Song of Songs		Daniel
			Ecclesiastes	*Prophets*	Hosea
Former Prophets	*Histories*	*Histories*	Lamentations	Hosea	Joel
JOSHUA	JOSHUA	JOSHUA	ESTHER	Amos	Amos
JUDGES	JUDGES	JUDGES	Daniel	Micah	Obadiah
1 SAMUEL	RUTH	RUTH	EZRA	Joel	Jonah
2 SAMUEL	1 REIGNS	1 SAMUEL	NEHEMIAH	Obadiah	Micah
1 KINGS	2 REIGNS	2 SAMUEL	1 CHRONICLES	Jonah	Nahum
2 KINGS	3 REIGNS	1 KINGS	2 CHRONICLES	Nahum	Habakkuk
	4 REIGNS	2 KINGS		Habakkuk	Zephaniah
Latter Prophets	1 PARALIPOMENON	1 CHRONICLES		Zephaniah	Haggai
Isaiah	2 PARALIPOMENON	2 CHRONICLES		Haggai	Zechariah
Jeremiah	1 ESDRAS	EZRA		Zechariah	Malachi
Ezekiel	2 ESDRAS	NEHEMIAH		Malachi	
Hosea	ESTHER	ESTHER		Isaiah	
Joel	Judith			Jeremiah	
Amos	Tobit	*Poetic Books*		Baruch	
Obadiah	1 Maccabees	Job		Lamentations	
Jonah	2 Maccabees	Psalms		Letter of Jeremiah	
Micah	3 Maccabees	Proverbs		Ezekiel	
Nahum	4 Maccabees	Ecclesiastes		Susanna	
Habakkuk		Song of Songs		Daniel	
Zephaniah	*Poetic Books*			Bel and the Dragon	
Haggai	Psalms (+ Odes)				
Zechariah	Proverbs				
Malachi	Ecclesiastes				

Testament together) are seen as forming a single, diverse but unified account of God's purposes of salvation for humanity from creation (Gen. 1) to new creation (Rev. 22) (Dumbrell, p. 9). Scholars who adopt this approach focus on the developing 'story-line' of the Old Testament. The books of the Bible are taken in historical sequence, usually according to the historical period each book describes or refers to, rather than the date the book was composed or edited. Much attention is paid to recurring themes and patterns which link narratives from different periods. These are then pursued into the New Testament.

The themes 'God', 'people', 'land', for example, form a trio which recurs constantly throughout the Bible: Genesis 1 (God, Adam and Eve, the earth); Genesis 12 and 15 (where Abraham is promised many descendants who will occupy the land of Canaan and enjoy YHWH's blessing); Joshua (where YHWH blesses the obedient Israelites, Abraham's descendants, and enables them to occupy the land of Canaan); Kings (where the people are exiled from the land because of their rebellion against YHWH); the Prophets (who speak of the relationship between YHWH and people being restored and the people returning to their land); and finally Revelation 21–22 (where a redeemed people worships YHWH in a renewed heaven and earth). In a similar way the motifs associated with the exodus from Egypt recur in later texts which describe God's salvation or God's victory over his opponents (Josh. 3–4; 2 Kgs 2; Isa. 40–55; the Gospels; Rev. 15).

Ideas and themes introduced at the beginning of the Old Testament and subsequently are developed, sometimes in unexpected ways. Not all later developments are necessarily clear in the early stages. Thus a sense of historical perspective is important in biblical theology. Linked to this, biblical theologians argue that it is necessary to hear the different voices of the individual books of the Bible. Synthesis (as happens when one traces theological themes from book to book) should not mean assimilation of one viewpoint to another, so that the entire Bible ends up saying the same thing. In this sense, biblical theology accepts literary approaches to the Bible which highlight the different features of the various biblical genres, and the distinctive ideas of each biblical book. It can also welcome at least some historical-critical views about the composition, editing and dating of parts of the Bible (Goldingay, pp. 183, 186–7).

For examples of biblical-theological readings of the Histories, which illustrate how the larger biblical context may affect the interpretation of particular texts, see the discussion of the following texts: 2 Samuel 5–7, where it is suggested that reading these chapters against the background of the promises to Abraham in Genesis may alter our view of the role of Israel's monarchy in YHWH's purposes (Ch. 5, 'Outline'); Ezra and Nehemiah, where the decision to read these books against the background of prophetic texts relating to Israel's restoration may lead to a more negative assessment of what was achieved by those who returned from exile (Ch. 10, 'Key themes'); Esther, where the question arises whether to read the book from a diaspora perspective or a Jerusalem perspective like that found in the Prophets and Ezra and Nehemiah (Ch. 9, 'Esther in the canon').

Questions naturally arise: what is the status of this 'story-line' which unifies both Testaments? Is it simply the creation of later Christian commentators following the lead of the New Testament, which throughout presents Jesus as the fulfilment of Old Testament hopes and promises? That suggestion does not do justice to the many thematic links within the Old Testament noted earlier: biblical theologians are arguably responding to a tendency already present in the Old Testament (so, too, the New Testament writers). Is the presence of a story-line within the Old Testament, then, due to the fact that books composed later were written in dependence on earlier ones? Is it (alternatively or in addition) the result of later, editorial shaping, which has multiplied the links across Old Testament books? Is it true that there is only one story-line running through both Testaments, or is there something to be said for Brueggemann's view according to which the Old Testament contains different, partly conflicting 'testimonies' about the god of Israel? (A testimony is simply a story by another name.) These are questions to keep in mind throughout Chapters 3–11.

As indicated, most practitioners of biblical theology are Christians. The biblical story is seen as spanning both Old and New Testaments, with Jesus as the fulfilment of the Old Testament. Jews, who do not regard Jesus as the focal point of God's purposes, naturally question this aspect of the approach. But in principle there is no reason why those who do not accept the New Testament as the continuation of the Old Testament should not follow similar interpretative steps within the Old Testament (Law, Prophets and Writings in Jewish terminology), reading later parts in the light of earlier, and then finding continuations of the story in other places than the New Testament. Some of the contributors to the volume edited by Bellis and Kaminsky move in this direction.

Consideration of the Histories as part of a larger story shades into the question of their modern interpretation and appropriation. Should we follow the lead of those who produced the various biblical canons and emphasize the links between the Histories and other biblical books? Or should we bracket out the larger story (if only temporarily) and interpret the Histories as far as we can by themselves? What if we refuse to be led by the biblical story-line, either because we find the notion of a single story-line implausible, or because we are as interested in other voices apparently suppressed by those responsible for the Bible (the voices left out of the story or left on its margins), or because our world-view fundamentally contradicts that (those) of the Bible? Exploring this topic to its fullest extent inevitably draws one's personal commitments into the discussion.

THE HISTORIES, THEOLOGY AND ETHICS

As well as making claims about events on the human level, the Histories frequently make statements about God. According to the Histories, many things that happen to Israel and other nations reflect YHWH's purposes. Further, many of the events described are assessed within an ethical framework that clearly reflects a particular view of the divine (e.g. the claims in Judges and Kings that certain actions were 'right' or 'evil' in YHWH's sight).

All this raises the question of theological perspective noted earlier in this chapter: do the Histories have a unified theological and ethical standpoint? But it also raises other questions with more contemporary relevance: do we believe in a god like the god of Israel described in the Histories?

Can we accept the ethical viewpoint of the Histories, or is the gap between the world of the Histories and our own world too large to be bridged? On what basis do we make such judgments?

For those who do accept the theology and ethics of the Histories, whether wholly or in part, the question of contemporary application arises: can we simply transplant the theology and ethics of the Histories into our own historical and social context, or must there be some process of reinterpretation and updating? How might the Histories translate into contemporary living? We survey some of these issues in what follows.

YHWH IN THE HISTORIES

What picture of YHWH the god of Israel do the Histories present? YHWH is personal, and has created men and women to relate to him (note the frequent references to prayer and prophecy in the Histories). YHWH called the nation Israel into being, committing himself to their ancestors by covenant (Josh. 1:6; 2 Kgs 13:23), rescuing Israel from Egypt (2 Sam. 7:23), giving them laws which reflect his own character (Josh. 1:8; 2 Kgs 17:16; 22:8–13), and bringing them to the land he promised them. In the Histories as in the Pentateuch these actions are foundational, revealing key aspects of YHWH's nature. In his dealings with Israel YHWH shows himself just, noting and responding to righteousness and wickedness in his people. He is jealous for his own glory, hating it when his people turn away from him to other gods. Keeping YHWH's law is as important in the Histories as in the Pentateuch. But YHWH also shows an unexpected patience, always responding when people repent (Judg. 3:9; 1 Sam. 7:2–5; 1 Kgs 21:27–29), rescuing Israel

again and again from their enemies, and holding back judgment even when there seems no reason for him to do so (2 Kgs 13:4, 23; 14:26–27).

The Histories often give a sense of what the god of Israel is like by a kind of negative characterization, showing what happens when people turn away from YHWH. Part of the point of Judges, for instance, is that as the people repeatedly turn away from YHWH, they become progressively more corrupt and spiritually apathetic. And in general there are many passages where the underlying logic seems to be: see what happens when you forsake YHWH. See, for example, Judges 17—21, 1 Kings 9—11 and 1 Kings 20—22. In short, the Histories claim that to turn away from YHWH is to reject what is good and right for what is twisted, cruel, wicked, oppressive and dehumanizing.

(These examples have all been taken from Joshua–Kings: Esther and Ruth add to this picture with their depictions of YHWH's providential working; Chronicles, Ezra and Nehemiah say little not already found in Joshua–Kings.)

The portrayal of YHWH in the Histories, then, is broadly consistent with the Pentateuchal presentation, though some Pentateuchal themes (e.g. YHWH as creator) are not frequently mentioned, and function as unstated presuppositions.

The Histories have a strongly monotheistic world-view. (On the question of the appropriateness of the term 'monotheism' to describe the viewpoint of the Old Testament in general, see Bauckham.) YHWH is ruler of the nations, and directs their affairs as he sees fit. Sometimes he defeats them before Israel (Josh. 1—12; Judg. 3:10–11; 2 Sam. 5:17–25; 1 Kgs 20). At other times he uses them as an instrument of judgment (Judg. 3:7–8; 4:1–3; 1 Sam. 4; 2 Kgs 5:1; 18:25–26; 24:20). Foreign nations who underestimate YHWH's power are brought to book, as in the case of the Arameans who imagine that the god of Israel is only a god of the hills (1 Kgs 20:23–25, 28); or as in the account of Sennacherib's siege of Jerusalem (2 Kgs 18—19), perhaps the most explicitly monotheistic text in the Histories.

Other gods are referred to in the Histories. Some texts are even framed as contests between YHWH and other gods: Judges 6 and 1 Kings 18, in which Israelites engaged in the worship of Baal are challenged to transfer their allegiance to YHWH; 1 Samuel 5—6, in which YHWH displays his superior power against the gods of the Philistines. But such texts never describe these other gods as *doing* anything, and the implication seems to be that they have no existence outside the minds of those who worship them.

In contrast, some texts do suggest that it is possible for non-Israelites to acknowledge YHWH's power and even enjoy his blessing: the accounts of Rahab (Josh. 2 and 6) and the Gibeonites (Josh. 9); the accounts of Hiram (1 Kgs 5:7) and the queen of Sheba (1 Kgs 10:6–9); and, perhaps most striking of all, the account of Naaman the Aramean commander (2 Kgs 5:1–20). More commonly, of course, non-Israelite nations and their leaders feature as Israel's enemies. But the texts cited do seem to hold that it is possible for all humans, not Israelites alone, to relate to the god of Israel. This seems to be another presupposition that the Histories share with the Pentateuch, especially with Genesis.

The above paragraphs may suggest that the Histories are somewhat simplistic in their theology, and we should qualify what we have just said by recalling the comments made earlier about the subtlety of biblical narrative. The text does not always make clear whether or not YHWH is involved in particular events, or what YHWH's attitude to these events is. Sometimes it seems that YHWH is portrayed as standing back and letting people who should know what to do 'get on with it' (as in the accounts of Israel's 'testing' in Judges 3, and of the dynastic succession in 1 Kings 1—2). Sometimes YHWH apparently chooses to let events take their course: bad human choices are not prevented from leading to bad consequences (e.g. the people's request for a king in 1 Samuel 8—12). Perhaps this aspect of the narrative reflects a view of men and women as made in the divine image (Gen. 1): because humans have this dignity, what they do cannot simply be overridden whenever it might lead in an unacceptable direction.

Nonetheless, with all these qualifications, here is a most uncompromising picture of divine reality, a strongly monotheistic portrayal clearly at odds both with ancient polytheistic views and with many pluralist strands in contemporary religious thought.

One question that will be taken up later (see Ch. 6) is whether this picture corresponds to historical reality: do the Histories project back into earlier periods religious views which were not held by those who lived then? What about the archaeological evidence from various periods which suggests that many Israelites were not monotheists?

There is also the question of the seemingly narrow religious perspective of the Histories.

22

Is there really as little positive to be said for the religious beliefs and practices of the other peoples of the ancient Near East as the Histories seem to imply? Why does YHWH, the sole creator, select one group, Israel, as his people? Is the religion of the Histories a kind of religious nationalism? And we have not yet addressed the question of seemingly immoral acts attributed by the text to YHWH or his representatives (Josh. 6—11; 1 Sam. 15; 2 Sam. 24). To be sure, passages such as these are not to be taken out of context, as though the killing of Canaanites and others were motiveless actions of an irrational deity (on the contrary, the context usually suggests reasons), or as though the only fact stated about the god of Israel is that he ordered such killings (much else is known, some of which we have summarized above). But these troubling passages and others like them are part of the Histories, and not a minor part at that.

THE HISTORIES AND ETHICS

We have now come to the question of whether, and in what ways, the Histories may be used in contemporary ethics. Some contemporary scholars believe that the Histories are a viable resource for ethics. Much discussion regarding the use of the Old Testament in ethics has focused on the Pentateuchal law and the prophets, but recent scholarship has seen an interest in narrative texts, as in Wenham's monograph, which includes an extensive discussion of Judges, or in some of the work of Barton and Wright.

According to Wenham, care is needed in deducing the narrator's ethical perspective from the text, but there are principles of interpretation which can guide us, and much in Old Testament narrative texts that can

stimulate our own ethical reflection. Wright is similarly optimistic, but he emphasizes that in order to apply Old Testament texts to contemporary ethical questions we need a sense of historical perspective: both in that Israel takes on different forms at different stages of her history (theocracy, monarchy, people in exile), which means that texts from different periods have different viewpoints on the same issue (see, for example, his study, 'The People of God and the State', pp. 213–43); and in that our own world is very different from that of the second and first millennia BC. Other essays in the same volume use Old Testament texts to explore human rights, the theology and ethics of land, unjust political systems, and decision-making. Wright notes that there is often more biblical reflection on such issues in the Old Testament than in the New Testament.

Barton, though he clearly finds parts of the Histories far from morally edifying, nonetheless argues that Old Testament narratives such as the account of David can be read as 'stories with a serious purpose', accounts which handle complex moral issues in a thoughtful and sensitive way (Barton 2003, pp. 5–11). He suggests that narrative is in some ways ideally suited to deal with certain issues (e.g. the interplay of divine and human actions in the outworking of God's purposes) which cannot easily be the subject of legislation or summed up in a proverbial saying. Certainly, narrative functions differently from other types of text, and in a way that makes it particularly difficult to separate 'medium' from 'message'. A text like Judges 19 cannot be reduced to a brief statement of its underlying principles (e.g. 'one must show hospitality to strangers'; 'gang rape is wicked'), true to the text though these in one sense are: a large part of the chapter's impact, and hence its ethical challenge, comes from the way in which the narrative produces in the reader a sense of horror at the events described.

Other scholars are much less convinced that the Old Testament can be used in this way. For Rodd the Old Testament provides merely 'glimpses of a strange land': there is no coherent ethical vision underlying the Old Testament, and the ethical perspectives found there only show us how differently we look at the world nowadays. The Old Testament is a foreign country, and it is problematic to see any of it as ethically authoritative today. Rodd finds parts of the Old Testament (e.g. the texts relating to war) quite irredeemable from an ethical standpoint. In a somewhat similar vein, Penchansky offers studies of six narratives, three taken from the Histories, which he believes show God in a dark and frightening light: as irrational (the account of Uzzah, 2 Sam. 6); as vindictive (David's census, 2 Sam. 24); and as abusive (Elisha and the bears, 2 Kgs 2:23–25). These portrayals of YHWH, he argues, cannot be toned down. Rather, we should admit that these texts do say what they seem to say about God, and then reject these portrayals, seeking out different understandings so as to arrive at a better vision of God and the world. This view of the text as a kind of negative stimulus to theological thought is not unlike Rodd's 'strange land' approach.

Last, we should mention the many feminist readings of the Histories, which in general proceed from the basis that the Histories are suspect as regards their portrayal of the roles of men and women. Some of these readings in effect attempt 'rescue operations', focusing on the minority of texts (in collections generally dominated by patriarchal viewpoints) which seem to portray women in a positive light. Others conclude that rescue is pointless, for even the texts in which women play positive roles are fundamentally patriarchal in perspective (see the discussion of this question with regard to Ruth, Ch. 8).

All the issues we have mentioned during this section will be with us throughout Chapters 3–11.

CONCLUSION

Recent scholarship on the Histories, as on other parts of the Old Testament, shows a great diversity. This chapter has given a sampling of this diversity. To an extent the various approaches applied to the Histories are responding to different aspects of the text, and are based on different types of data, textual and extra-textual. But they are not mutually exclusive: on the contrary, much scholarly writing on the Histories tends to combine insights drawn from a number of them. For instance, analysis of the sources underlying a biblical text may lead to theories regarding the historical context within which that text arose. Or the text may be studied in the light of relevant archaeological findings, with the aim of reconstructing the historical events underlying it. A reconstruction of this sort may in turn form the basis for handling ethical issues relating to the contemporary application of the text.

This is all perfectly legitimate; indeed, any scholar whose work combines study of the biblical text with serious reflection on the text's contemporary relevance must employ a variety of approaches, each with its distinctive method. We believe that each of the approaches represented in our survey deserves serious consideration. But it is also important to understand the assumptions underlying these approaches and to appreciate the possible limitations of each approach.

THE 'OUTLINE' SECTIONS IN CHAPTERS 3—11

Each of the chapters dealing with the Histories themselves (Chs 3–11) contains an extensive 'Outline' section which summarizes and surveys the book(s) in question. There are two reasons for this. First, many students may be unfamiliar with the Histories, and may welcome a 'guided tour' through them. Second, the Outlines set out our interpretations of the Histories, and form the basis for the discussion of other issues in each chapter. A fundamental fact about the Histories, in our view, is that they are artfully constructed texts. The Outlines aim to bring out this aspect and its implications for interpretation. They are not, therefore, simply a neutral (and dispensable) summary of the text, but an essential part of the argument of each chapter.

Our interpretations of the Histories begin with an assumption of literary unity. We are, of course, aware of the large amount of scholarship which treats the Histories as composite at the literary and theological levels, and we interact with a representative selection of it at the appropriate points. We are far from excluding the possibility that many sources and many hands have played a part in the formation of the Histories. But we feel that a judgment cannot be made on these matters before attempting to understand the Histories in their present form, allowing for the possibility that they may operate according to literary conventions to an extent different from those familiar to us. Usually, having investigated contrary viewpoints, we conclude that our

initial, working assumption of literary unity may be allowed to stand. Where others have found literary awkwardness and theological contradiction, we have usually found narrative artistry and a unified (though maybe complex or paradoxical) theology.

On this as on all other positions adopted in this volume, you, student or teacher, must decide whether you agree with us.

FURTHER READING

GENERAL

J. Barr, *History and Ideology in the Old Testament. Biblical Studies at the End of a Millennium*. Oxford: Oxford University Press, 2000.

J. Barton (ed.), *The Cambridge Companion to Biblical Interpretation*. Cambridge: Cambridge University Press, 1998.

V.P. Long, *The Art of Biblical History*. Grand Rapids: Zondervan, 1994.

S.L. McKenzie and S.R. Haynes (eds), *To Each Its Own Meaning. An Introduction to Biblical Criticisms and their Application*. Louisville: Westminster John Knox Press, 1999.

R.D. Nelson, *The Historical Books*. Nashville: Abingdon Press, 1998.

I.W. Provan, 'The Historical Books of the Old Testament', in J. Barton (ed.), *The Cambridge Companion to Biblical Interpretation*, pp. 198–211.

On the text of the Old Testament

J. Trebolle Barrera, *The Jewish Bible and the Christian Bible. An Introduction to the History of the Bible*. Grand Rapids/Leiden: Eerdmans/Brill, 1998.

E. Brotzman, *Old Testament Textual Criticism: A Practical Introduction*. Grand Rapids: Baker, 1994.

E. Tov, *Textual Criticism of the Hebrew Bible*. Minneapolis/Assen: Fortress Press/Van Gorcum, 1992.

THE HISTORIES IN THEIR ANCIENT NEAR EASTERN CONTEXT

Collections of texts

W.T. Arnold and B.E. Beyer (eds), *Readings from the Ancient Near East. Primary Sources for Old Testament Study*. Grand Rapids: Baker, 2002.

W.W. Hallo and K.L. Younger (eds), *The Context of Scripture*, 3 vols. Leiden: Brill, 1997, 2000, 2002.

J.B. Pritchard (ed.), *Ancient Near Eastern Texts Relating to the Old Testament*, 3rd edition. Princeton: Princeton University Press, 1969.

Studies

M.W. Chavalas and K.L. Younger (eds), *Mesopotamia and the Bible. Comparative Explorations*. Grand Rapids: Baker, 2002.

R.S. Hess, 'Ancient Near Eastern Studies' in C.C. Broyles (ed.), *Interpreting the Old Testament*. Grand Rapids: Baker, 2001, pp. 201–20.

H. Tadmor and M. Weinfeld (eds), *History, Historiography, and Interpretation. Studies in Biblical and Cuneiform Literatures*. Jerusalem: Magnes Press, 1983.

LITERARY APPROACHES

R. Alter, *The Art of Biblical Narrative*. New York: Basic Books, 1981.

Y. Amit, *Reading Biblical Narratives. Literary Criticism and the Hebrew Bible*. Minneapolis: Fortress, 2001.

J. Barton, 'Form Criticism (OT)', *ABD* II, pp. 838–41.

D.N. Fewell, 'Reading the Bible Ideologically: Feminist Criticism' in S.L. McKenzie and S.R. Haynes (eds), *To Each its Own Meaning. An Introduction to Biblical Criticisms and their Application*. Louisville: Westminster John Knox Press, 1999, pp. 268–82.

D.M. Gunn, 'Narrative Criticism' in S.L. McKenzie and S.R. Haynes (eds), *To Each Its Own Meaning. An Introduction to Biblical Criticisms and their Application*. Louisville: Westminster John Knox Press, 1999, pp. 201–29.

D.M. Gunn and D.N. Fewell, *Narrative in the Hebrew Bible*. Oxford: Oxford University Press, 1993.

P.E. Satterthwaite, 'Narrative Criticism: The Theological Implications of Narrative Techniques', *NIDOTTE*, I, pp. 125–33.

M. Sternberg, *The Poetics of Biblical Narrative. Ideological Literature and the Drama of Reading*. Bloomington: Indiana University Press, 1985.

C.P.C. Streete, 'Redaction Criticism' in S.L. McKenzie and S.R. Haynes (eds), *To Each Its Own Meaning. An Introduction to Biblical Criticisms and their Application*. Louisville: Westminster John Knox Press, 1999, pp. 105–21.

M.A. Sweeney, 'Form Criticism' in S.L. McKenzie and S.R. Haynes (eds), *To Each Its Own Meaning. An Introduction to Biblical Criticisms and their Application*. Louisville: Westminster John Knox Press, 1999, pp. 58–89.

P.A. Viviano, 'Source Criticism' in S.L. McKenzie and S.R. Haynes (eds), *To Each Its Own Meaning. An Introduction to Biblical Criticisms and their Application*. Louisville: Westminster John Knox Press, 1999, pp. 35–57.

HISTORICAL TEXTS

R. Albertz, 'An End to the Confusion? Why the Old Testament cannot be a Hellenistic Book!' in L.L. Grabbe (ed.), *Did Moses Speak Attic? Jewish Historiography and Scripture in the Hellenistic Period*. Sheffield: Sheffield Academic Press, 2001, pp. 30–46.

Y. Amit, *History and Ideology. An Introduction to Historiography in the Hebrew Bible*. Sheffield: Sheffield Academic Press, 1999.

R.E. Averbeck, 'Sumer, the Bible, and Comparative Method: Historiography and Temple Building' in M.W. Chavalas and K.L. Younger (eds), *Mesopotamia and the Bible. Comparative Explorations*. Grand Rapids: Baker, 2002, pp. 88–125.

O. Borowski, *Daily Life in Biblical Times*. Atlanta: SBL, 2003.

J. Bright, *A History of Israel*, 3rd edition. London: SCM Press, 1980.

J.D. Currid, *Doing Archaeology in the Land of the Bible. A Basic Guide*. Grand Rapids: Baker, 1999.

P.R. Davies, *In Search of 'Ancient Israel'*. Sheffield: Sheffield Academic Press, 1992.

W.G. Dever, *What Did the Biblical Writers Know and When Did They Know It? What Archaeology Can Tell Us about the Reality of Ancient Israel*. Grand Rapids: Eerdmans, 2001.

I. Finkelstein and N.A. Silberman, *The Bible Unearthed. Archaeology's New Vision of Ancient Israel and the Origin of its Sacred Texts*. New York: Touchstone, 2002.

V. Fritz, *An Introduction to Biblical Archaeology*. Sheffield: Sheffield Academic Press, 1994.

L.L. Grabbe (ed.), *Can a 'History of Israel' Be Written?* Sheffield: Sheffield Academic Press, 1997.

L.L. Grabbe (ed.), *Leading Captivity Captive: The 'Exile' as History and Ideology*. Sheffield: Sheffield Academic Press, 1998.

L.L. Grabbe (ed.), *Did Moses Speak Attic? Jewish Historiography and Scripture in the Hellenistic Period*. Sheffield: Sheffield Academic Press, 2001.

P.J. King and L.E. Stager, *Life in Biblical Israel*. Louisville/London: Westminster John Knox Press, 2001.

K.A. Kitchen, *On the Reliability of the Old Testament*. Grand Rapids: Eerdmans, 2003.

J.B. Kofoed, *Text and History. Historiography and the Study of the Biblical Text*. Winona Lake: Eisenbrauns, 2005.

N.P. Lemche, *The Israelites in History and Tradition*. Louisville/London: Westminster John Knox Press/SPCK: 1998.

V.P. Long, D.W. Baker, G.J. Wenham (eds), *Windows into Old Testament History. Evidence, Argument, and the Crisis of 'Biblical Israel'*. Grand Rapids: Eerdmans, 2002.

P. McNutt, *Reconstructing the Society of Ancient Israel*. Louisville/London: Westminster John Knox Press/SPCK, 1999.

J.M. Miller, 'Reading the Bible Historically: the Historian's Approach' in S.L. McKenzie and S.R. Haynes (eds), *To Each Its Own Meaning. An Introduction to Biblical Criticisms and their Application*. Louisville: Westminster John Knox, 1999, pp. 17–34.

J.M. Miller and J.H. Hayes, *A History of Ancient Judah and Israel*. Philadelphia: Westminster Press, 1986.

P.R.S. Moorey, *A Century of Biblical Archaeology*. Cambridge: Lutterworth, 1991.

I.W. Provan, V.P. Long, T. Longman, *A Biblical History of Israel*. Louisville: Westminster John Knox Press, 2003.

T.L. Thompson, *Early History of the Israelite People from the Written and Archaeological Sources*. Leiden: Brill, 1992.

K.W. Whitelam, *The Invention of Ancient Israel. The Silencing of Palestinian History*. London and New York: Routledge, 1996.

K.W. Whitelam, 'The Social World of the Bible' in J. Barton (ed.), *The Cambridge Companion to Biblical Interpretation*. Cambridge: Cambridge University Press, 1998, pp. 35–49.

THE LARGER STORY

R.T. Beckwith, *The Old Testament Canon of the New Testament and its Background in Early Judaism*. London: SPCK, 1985.

A.O. Bellis and J.S. Kaminsky, *Jews, Christians, and the Theology of the Hebrew Scriptures*. Atlanta: SBL, 2000.

W.J. Dumbrell, *The Search for Order. Biblical Eschatology in Focus*. Grand Rapids: Baker, 1994.

J. Goldingay, *Theological Diversity and the Authority of the Old Testament*. Grand Rapids, MI: Eerdmans, 1987.

L.M. McDonald, *The Formation of the Christian Biblical Canon*. Peabody: Hendrickson, 1995.

B.S. Rosner, 'Biblical Theology', *NDBT*, pp. 3–11.

J.A. Sanders, 'Canon: Hebrew Bible', *ABD* I, pp. 837–52.

THEOLOGICAL–ETHICAL RESOURCES

J. Barton, *Understanding Old Testament Ethics. Approaches and Explorations*. Louisville: Westminster John Knox Press, 2003.

R.J. Bauckham, 'Biblical Theology and the Problems of Monotheism' in C.R. Bartholomew *et al.* (eds), *Out of Egypt: Biblical Theology and Biblical Interpretation*. Grand Rapids/Milton Keynes: Zondervan/Paternoster, 2004.

W. Brueggemann, *Theology of the Old Testament. Testimony, Dispute, Advocacy*. Minneapolis: Fortress, 1997.

D. Penchansky, *What Rough Beast? Images of God in the Hebrew Bible*. Louisville: Westminster John Knox Press, 1999.

C.S. Rodd, *Glimpses of a Strange Land. Studies in Old Testament Ethics*. Edinburgh: T. and T. Clark, 2001.

G.J. Wenham, *Story as Torah. Reading the Old Testament Ethically*. Edinburgh: T. and T. Clark, 2000.

C.J.H. Wright, *Walking in the Ways of the Lord. The Ethical Authority of the Old Testament*. Leicester: Apollos, 1995.

Chapter 2

THE ANCIENT NEAR EAST, 1550–63 BC

The term 'Near East' includes the following lands: Egypt; the Arabian peninsula, the Levant (the territory of the modern states of Israel, Lebanon, Jordan and Syria west of the River Euphrates); Turkey; Mesopotamia (Iraq and those parts of Syria east of the Euphrates); Iran.

THE PERIODS OF ANCIENT NEAR EASTERN HISTORY

Period	Subdivisions		Dates
Stone	Upper Paleolithic		43,000–18,000 BC
	Epipaleolithic		18,000–8500 BC
	Neolithic		8500–4500 BC
	Chalcolithic		4500–3300 BC
Bronze	Early Bronze	Early Bronze I	3300–3100 BC
		Early Bronze II	3100–2700 BC
		Early Bronze III	2700–2300 BC
		Early Bronze IV	2300–2000 BC
	Middle Bronze	Middle Bronze I–II	2000–1650 BC
		Middle Bronze III	1650–1550 BC
	Late Bronze		1550–1200 BC
Iron	Iron I		1200–1000 BC
	Iron II	Iron IIA	1000–931 BC
		Iron IIB	931–722 BC
		Iron IIC	722–586 BC
Babylonian			586–539 BC
Persian	Iron III		539–332 BC
Greek			332–63 BC
Roman			63 BC–AD 330

Much of ancient Near Eastern history, following a standard classification, is divided into Stone, Bronze and Iron periods, each of these periods being further subdivided. The major divisions into Stone, Bronze and Iron are named after stages of technological development in the Near East; though this terminology should not be taken to indicate clear-cut divisions, as though no-one used bronze before 3300 BC, or iron before 1200 BC. None of the dates before 1000 BC are exact, in fact. Some, for example, would date the break between Late Bronze and Iron I to 1180, not 1200 BC. Some of the subdivisions have nothing to do with technological developments: the Iron period is subdivided according to different phases of Israelite history. The latest periods are named after four empires which dominated the ancient Near East in succession: Babylonian, Persian (sometimes called Iron III), Greek and Roman.

This mixed naming system produces some anomalies: it gives the appearance that the Babylonians were only dominant from 586 BC on, whereas their major victories against Assyria occurred three decades earlier; also it seems to suggest that the Neo-Assyrian empire (934–610 BC) cannot be compared in importance and scale to those that followed, which is not really true, at least for the period 745–610. In what follows we shall simply divide up ancient Near Eastern history into a series of periods identified by dates (1550–1200 BC and so on).

We focus on the period 1550–63 BC because these two dates set outer limits for the study of the Histories. The first date, 1550 BC, marks the beginning of the Late Bronze Age, and the second,

63 BC, is the date of the capture of Jerusalem by the Roman general Pompey, which began a period of Roman control over Palestine that was to continue well into the Christian era. Scholars are agreed that the events underlying the Histories took place in the ancient Near East within the period 1550–63, though there is a wide range of opinions as to what these events were and what kind of account of

---

CHRONOLOGY OF THE ANCIENT NEAR EAST

The chronological 'backbone' of ancient Near Eastern history is provided by Egyptian and Mesopotamian data. In Egypt, king-lists and observations of datable astronomical phenomena give a fairly precise chronological framework going back to about 3000 BC, though some details can be interpreted in more than one way, with the result that textbooks give alternative dates for some events. In Mesopotamia, astronomical observations, the Assyrian eponym lists ('eponym' = official after whom the year is named), the Assyrian king lists, and correlations with dates for Babylonian rulers give reasonably precise dates as far back as 2400 BC. Before 2400 the dates are less precise. Again, some details are debated, resulting in alternative dates for some events. Events in other parts of the Near East are dated on the basis of correlations with events in Egyptian and Mesopotamian history. The further back one goes, the greater the uncertainty as regards individual dates and the greater the differences between rival chronological schemes. 'High', 'middle' and 'low' chronologies have been proposed for the second millennium.

As regards biblical chronology, while the dates for first millennium are relatively uncontroversial, in the second millennium different dates have been proposed for the exodus and conquest of Canaan, some dating these events to the fifteenth century, others to the thirteenth (see Chs 3 and 4).

them the Histories provide. Similarly, it is generally accepted that by the first century BC the Hebrew text of the Histories had reached a form at least close to that known to us today; though the authorship, editing and dating of the Histories are much debated, and the textual criticism of the Histories also raises some complex questions.

The historical and geographical context of the Histories, then, is the ancient Near East between 1550 and 63 BC. In what follows we survey the main events of this period. We recommend that you have a Bible atlas accessible as you read what follows. For further details, consult the works by Kuhrt and Van der Mieroop, on which the following account is largely based.

Apart from the biblical text, the sources for this survey are ancient Near Eastern texts, inscriptions and other written remains (some of which will be referred to at appropriate points in Chs 3–11); along with archaeological data unearthed by over 150 years of excavations in the lands of the ancient Near East.

1550–1200 BC

Ancient Near Eastern civilization was already thousands of years old by the beginning of the Late Bronze Age (1550–1200 BC).

Egypt, for which a consecutive history can be written from about 3000 BC onwards, had a diverse history before 1550. A number of cities functioned as royal capitals at different times, and in some periods two dynasties exercised control over different parts of the

country at the same time (the so-called First and Second 'Intermediate Periods', dated about 2180–2040 and about 1720–1550 respectively). Between 1648 and 1539 Lower and part of Middle Egypt were ruled by the Hyksos, Canaanite immigrants. ('Hyksos' derives from the Egyptian for 'foreign rulers'.)

Mesopotamia between 3000 and 1550 presents yet more diversity than Egypt. A series of city-states dominated events at different times, exercising power over smaller or greater parts of the region: Sumer, Kish, Akkad, Ur, Asshur (from which the terms 'Assyria' and 'Assyrian' come), Isin, Larsa, Mari and Babylon. Especially noteworthy are the kingdoms of Shamshi-Adad of Asshur (1813–1781), which covered much of northern Mesopotamia and extended west to Mari, and of Hammurabi of Babylon in southern Mesopotamia (1792–1750).

Egypt, Assyria and Babylon all played a significant part in the events of the period 1550–1200, along with two other states: the Hittite kingdom (based in Anatolia = modern Turkey); and the kingdom of Mitanni (northern Syria). These five states divided up much of the Near East between them and, as can be seen from surviving records of their diplomatic exchanges, related to each other more or less on equal terms. Smaller states in the region, for example in Palestine or Syria, usually fell into the sphere of influence of one or other of these five states.

The interactions of these 'great powers' in this period may be summarized as follows. Egypt, which had never previously held territory in the Levant, conducted a series of expeditions from the middle of the sixteenth century on, which brought all of Canaan and also much of Syria under their control. Canaan remained under Egyptian control until the twelfth century, and for much of the Late Bronze Age Egypt disputed possession of the territories north of Damascus – first with the kingdom of Mitanni and later with the Hittites.

The kingdom of Mitanni, whose origins are obscure, was already powerful when Egypt clashed with it the first half of the fifteenth century, and when Egypt and Mitanni entered into friendly relations at the beginning of the fourteenth century, they did so as equals. In the middle of the fourteenth century, however, the Hittites destroyed the capital city of Mitanni, and the kingdom collapsed.

The origins of the Hittites are also obscure, and Hittite chronology is uncertain, but something like a coherent account can be written for the period 1650–1200. This period saw a gradual expansion of Hittite power over most of Anatolia and also parts of north-west Syria, these gains being further consolidated in the second part of the fourteenth century when they took over the western part of the former Mitannian kingdom. The result was that the Hittites came into conflict with Egypt, with whom they fought a notable though inconclusive battle at Qadesh in 1275 (or 1286, following an alternative dating). A peace treaty was concluded between the Egyptians and the Hittites in 1258 (1269).

Mesopotamian history in this period is dominated by two states that had already exercised power in the first part of the second millennium, Babylon and Assyria. Babylon between 1595 and 1155 was ruled by the Kassite dynasty. This was a largely stable period, during which Babylonian power grew, particularly towards the south. At times Babylonian control extended down to the Persian Gulf.

Assyrian history between 1750 and 1350 is largely unknown, but from about 1350 onwards Assyrian control expanded both westwards (taking in parts of the former kingdom of Mitanni) and southwards (at Babylonian expense). For about 30 years at the end of the thirteenth century Babylon was under Assyrian control.

1200–934 BC

Around 1200 (the beginning of Iron I) a change came over the ancient Near East. Hittite power collapsed, and Hattusa, the Hittite capital city, was sacked. Other sites were destroyed around this time: Ugarit on the north Syrian coast and Emar, further inland on the Euphrates river. Egypt, Assyria and Babylon all entered periods of relative weakness in the period after 1200, and their spheres of influence all shrank.

Egyptian control of Syria and Canaan came to an end. After the middle of the twelfth century Egypt rarely ventured into Canaan. In the second half of the twelfth century there was a series of pharaohs most of whom reigned only for brief periods, reflecting internal problems. From 1080 until about 950 control of Egypt was divided between a succession of pharaohs based in Tanis (in the Nile Delta) who ruled Lower Egypt, and a series of priest-kings based in Thebes who controlled Middle and Upper Egypt.

This marked the beginning of the Third Intermediate Period (see p. 35).

The Mesopotamian states were also in decline. For Assyria the twelfth century was a period of internal strife and weakness. Assyrian power briefly revived under Tiglath-Pileser I (1114–1076), who led a series of successful campaigns to the west and against Babylonia to the south. But growing pressure from the Arameans (see p. 34) led to the loss of Assyrian territories in Syria and north Mesopotamia by about 1050. Records become very scanty for over a century from 1050 on, and Assyrian history in this period cannot be reconstructed in detail.

Babylon had troubled relations with Assyria from the beginning of the thirteenth century, and also faced pressure from the Elamites to the east, culminating in an invasion in 1155 which left the Elamites in control of Babylon and brought the Kassite dynasty to an end. A non-Kassite dynasty based on the city of Isin responded to this challenge, and Babylonian control of their territories was restored around 1110. But Aramean raids seem to have posed an increasing problem during the eleventh century. The Isin dynasty was followed by three short-lived dynasties. Little is known about Babylon in the period 1050–900.

How are we to account for all these changes from 1200 onwards? Some have seen the arrival of the 'Sea Peoples' in the Levant in the late thirteenth and early twelfth centuries as a catalyst. These peoples were apparently a mixed group, originating partly in Lycia and Cilicia (southern Anatolia), and perhaps also in the Aegean area. One of the two Egyptian texts which are our chief source of information for these peoples at this period, an inscription of Pharaoh Rameses III, describes how they had wrought havoc in Anatolia, north Syria and Cyprus before he defeated them in a battle dated 1176. Rameses, however, may have exaggerated their previous rampages in order to magnify his own achievement in defeating them, and it is open to question whether they were responsible for the collapse of Hittite power and the destruction of places like Ugarit and Emar. Other factors may have played a part in the changes in the ancient Near East, for instance, drought and famine in the region, or widespread social unrest, as rural populations in a number of states came to resent top-heavy systems in which urban elites held the real power. Relations between the great powers of the previous era may well have been such that the collapse of one power weakened the rest.

Whatever the reason, the transformation of the previous configurations of power in the region is obvious. One aspect of this transformation is the emergence of new peoples. Some of the Sea Peoples settled in south Palestine, to become the Philistines known from Judges and Samuel. According to Joshua and Judges, Israel had by now in some sense established themselves in Canaan, and the earliest extant extra-biblical reference to 'Israel' comes from around this time, the line from an inscription of Pharaoh Merneptah (often referred to as the 'Israel Stela') in which Merneptah claims to have defeated a people named 'Israel' located in Canaan in his fifth year (1209): 'Israel is laid waste, his seed is not.' The Transjordanian states of Ammon, Moab and Edom, whose earlier history in the Late Bronze Age is a matter of some debate, clearly became something like established states in the period after 1200. And finally, a number of Aramean kingdoms emerged in Syria, including the kingdoms of Damascus and Zobah.

The origins of the Arameans are obscure. The first clear references to them are in the annals of the Assyrian king Tiglath-Pileser I, which record campaigns against them in the middle and upper Euphrates area. Aramean groups had probably lived in this region for 300 years previously, but only emerged as a significant force after the general collapse of Bronze Age civilization, after which they exerted growing pressure on Assyria and Babylon, as noted above. Probably they were a group of peoples united by common language. Aramaic became an international language during the Neo-Assyrian period, and continued as such until the end of the Persian period (hence parts of the Persian-period books Ezra and Nehemiah are written in Aramaic).

934–610 BC

The next three centuries were dominated by Assyrian power. This was the era of the Neo-Assyrian empire (934–610), the first of a series of empires that were to shape the history of the ancient Near East in the first millennium BC and beyond (see Map 1). With the beginning of the reign of Ashur-dan (934) Assyrian policy was marked by a determination to regain the territory of the former Middle Assyrian empire and to extend control beyond those former boundaries.

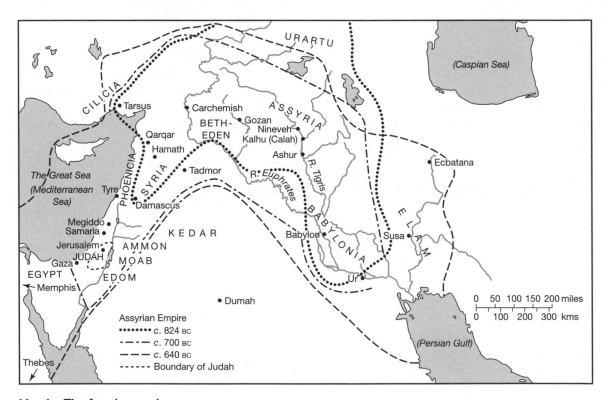

Map I   The Assyrian empire

After a period of consolidation in between 934 and 884, Assyrian power expanded in two main waves. Between 883 and 824 (the reigns of Ashurnasirpal II and Shalmaneser III), Assyrian power expanded first to the north and then to the west, with repeated campaigns into the Lebanon and against the Aramean states of Syria. In 853 Shalmaneser III (858–824) fought a battle at Qarqar (on the Orontes river) against a coalition led by Damascus. An inscription (the 'Kurkh Monolith') numbers this coalition at over 60,000, including '2,000 chariots and 10,000 men of Ahab of Israel' (the first non-biblical reference to the northern kingdom of Israel). A number of campaigns were needed to defeat this coalition, but by 841 Shalmaneser was able to record that King Jehu of Israel gave tribute to him (the 'Black Obelisk'). There were also campaigns in Anatolia, and against Urartu to the north.

There was political instability within Assyria at the end of Shalmaneser's reign, and later within Babylon, where Assyria found it necessary to intervene. From about 785 onwards the kingdom of Urartu (in the region of Lake Van) mounted campaigns west of the Euphrates which threatened Assyrian control of north Syria and Anatolia. These factors combined to check Assyrian expansion in the period 823–745. During the reigns of Tiglath-Pileser III (744–727) and Shalmaneser V (726–722), however, Urartu was driven back from the region of the Euphrates, Babylon came increasingly under Assyrian control (an Assyrian king was installed there in 722), and Assyrian borders in the west were extended to take in the Aramean kingdoms and also the northern kingdom of Israel, whose capital city Samaria fell in 722. Assyria faced some setbacks at the beginning of the reign of

the next king, Sargon II (721–705), and temporarily lost control of Babylon, which was to be a recurring problem in the last century of Assyrian power. But control over Babylon was restored, and campaigns against Urartu and in Anatolia strengthened Assyria's borders in these regions.

The next 70 or so years were mainly a period of consolidation. Sennacherib (705–681) conducted campaigns in the southern Levant (in the course of which he laid siege to Jerusalem) and also in Anatolia. Esarhaddon (680–669) campaigned in Egypt, in response to Egyptian attempts to stir up revolts among Assyria's subjects in Palestine. His son Ashurbanipal (668–627) also mounted campaigns in Egypt, capturing Thebes in 664. No part of Egypt remained long under Assyrian control, however, and as early as the 650s Psammetichus I, first pharaoh of the twenty-sixth dynasty, re-established Egyptian control of Egypt. Relations between Assyria and the twenty-sixth dynasty were more or less friendly. Ashurbanipal led campaigns against Elam, whose support of Babylonian rebellions had been an irritant in recent decades. The Assyrian sacking of Susa, the Elamite capital, in 647 marked the end of Elam as a threat, though a weak Elamite state survived for another 100 years until absorbed by the Persian empire.

In Egyptian history the years 1069–664 are termed the Third Intermediate Period, the third major period in Egyptian history when control of the country was divided. The increasing fragmentation is reflected in the fact that the twenty-second dynasty (945–715), the twenty-third dynasty (818–715) and the brief twenty-fourth dynasty (727–715), each of them of Libyan descent, are given partly overlapping dates in modern histories. Kuhrt (p. 623) describes Egypt in this period as more like a 'complicated network of small states' than a unified nation. The situation is further complicated by another, Nubian, dynasty, the twenty-fifth, whose dates are given as 780–656, and which exercised control over parts of southern Egypt from about 750 on. At some time around 730 (the sources do not permit a precise dating) a ruler from this dynasty named Piye invaded Middle and Lower Egypt, bringing the whole of Egypt under Nubian control by 715. During the years 715 to 656 control of Egypt belongs to the twenty-fifth dynasty alone, this dynasty coming to an end as a result of the Assyrian invasions in the mid-seventh century.

Egypt made only one major excursion into Canaan during these centuries, that of Sheshonq I in 926–925 (cf. 1 Kgs 14:25). Apart from that campaign, Egyptian interventions in Canaan and Syria seem to have been restricted to aiding other states against Assyria: Shalmaneser III lists 1,000 men of Egypt among those who opposed him at Qarqar in 853. Similarly, 2 Kings 17:4 describes how Hoshea the last king of Israel sought help from 'So, king of Egypt' (most likely the pharaoh Osorkon IV), and Sennacherib's inscription describes how he was attacked by Egyptian forces during his campaign in Palestine (cf. 2 Kgs 19:9).

Having reached a peak of power around 650, the Neo-Assyrian empire collapsed with remarkable speed at the end of the seventh century. There were succession struggles in Assyria after Asshurbanipal's death (627), and in 626 Nabopolassar, a Chaldean, mounted a successful claim for the Babylonian throne. In the years following, Babylon threw off Assyrian control, and by 616 Nabopolassar was able to mount attacks on Assyrian territory, in spite of Egyptian support for Assyria. The Medes (see p. 37) also attacked Assyria in 615 and 614, sacking Asshur in 614. In 612 a joint army of Medes and Babylonians captured Nineveh and sacked it after a three-month siege. The last Assyrian king, Asshur-uballit II, hung on to power in Harran with Egyptian help (Josiah of Judah was killed at Megiddo trying to deny Pharaoh Neco passage through Palestine, 2 Kings 23:29–30). Harran was destroyed in 609, and with it Assyrian power came to an end.

610–539 BC

Babylon was one of the two powers that joined in destroying Assyria. We noted above the decline in Babylonian power in the thirteenth and twelfth centuries. Babylon continued to face difficulties during the centuries which followed. They were under pressure from Aramean groups which settled along the Tigris river and from Chaldean groups which settled along the Euphrates and in the south, at the head of the Persian Gulf, establishing themselves in these regions by about 850. (The origins of the Chaldeans are unclear, due to the paucity of texts for the period before 850. They are described in ways which make them seem similar to the Aramean groups, but are always distinguished from the Arameans in Assyrian and Babylonian texts.)

From about 1000 onwards men from a variety of backgrounds held the kingship: Kassites Babylonians, Chaldeans, a man of Elamite descent, and from 722 onwards Assyrians, or men appointed by the king of Assyria. But no dynasty established itself. For much of the eighth century there was conflict between the different people groups in and around Babylonia and even between different Babylonian cities. But towards the end of this century opposition to Assyria seems to have brought Babylonians and Chaldeans into closer alliance, and from about 740 on they were supported against Assyria by a newly resurgent Elam.

The fall of Assyria in 610 marks the beginning of the Neo-Babylonian empire. In the years following, Babylon disputed possession of Syria and Palestine with Egypt, for whom the possibility of re-establishing themselves in these lands beckoned for the first time in centuries. Babylon, led by Nebuchadnezzar, son of Nabopolassar, defeated Egypt at Carchemish in 605. Shortly afterwards his father died, and he had to return to Babylon to secure his succession, but in the years following he conducted a series of campaigns in south Palestine. It proved hard for Babylon to establish control in Palestine, and various states rebelled, hoping for Egyptian help. The southern kingdom of Judah was one of these. Babylonian countermeasures led to deportation of some citizens in 597, and further deportations in 586, at which time Jerusalem was destroyed (2 Kgs 24—25). Babylon also subjugated a number of other states, such as Tyre, which had maintained their independence up to that point. Conflict with Egypt continued intermittently for another 20 years, until the two states concluded a treaty in 567.

Later kings further extended Babylonian power. Neriglissar (559–556) brought Cilicia (south-west Anatolia) within Babylon's borders, and Nabonidus (555–539) took possession of the north Arabian desert as far south as Teima, where he took up residence for about ten years from 552 on, leaving Babylon under the control of his son Belshazzar. Van der Mieroop (p. 262) suggests that this may have been a response to Persian expansion into the Median territories north and west of the Babylonian empire (see p. 38), which posed a threat to Babylonian control of Syria and northern Mesopotamia. As the loss of these possessions would have meant that Babylon no longer had access to the Mediterranean, Nabonidus may have been hoping to establish alternative trade routes to the Mediterranean across the Arabian desert. The Persian king Cyrus was able to make political capital out of Nabonidus' absence from Babylon.

The Medes, a people who originated in the central Zagros region, are known to us chiefly from Assyrian sources. They start to be mentioned in ninth- and eighth-century texts. They appear to have formed something like a centralized state, with Ecbatana as its capital, only in the seventh century, possibly in response to Assyrian campaigns in the Zagros region. By the time of Esarhaddon the Assyrians regarded them as a serious threat. They may well have expanded into formerly Elamite territory after the Assyrian sack of Susa in 647. As noted above, they joined with Babylon in ending Assyrian power in the late seventh century. After this they continued to expand north and west, destroying what remained of the state of Urartu and entering Anatolia, where they concluded a treaty with the Lydian king Alyattes in 585.

Persian origins are obscure. Persia, the Persian homeland (more or less corresponding to the modern Iranian province of Fars) had in the second millennium belonged to Elam, and the city of Anshan was a major centre of Elamite rule in the region. But Anshan declined in importance from the twelfth century on, and almost no sites in the region appear to have been occupied from then until the seventh century when several new sites were settled, this development apparently marking the emergence of Persia as a state. The Persian language belongs to the Iranian family of languages, and one theory holds that the Persians of the seventh and sixth centuries were descendants of groups of Iranian pastoralists who moved into the region during the eleventh and tenth centuries and settled among the local Elamite inhabitants. They appear to have been closely related to the Medes.

It was Cyrus (559–530) who transformed the previously small Persian state into an empire. The Median king Astyages attacked Cyrus in 550, perhaps in response to growing Persian strength. He was defeated and captured, and Cyrus went on to capture the Median capital Ecbatana. The Persians took over all the territory previously occupied by the Medes, from the Zagros region to the Halys river in Anatolia, and extended their gains by conquering Lydia and most of western Anatolia in the early 540s. Persia now occupied all the lands to the north of the Babylonian empire. A major confrontation between the two powers took place in 539, when Cyrus defeated a Babylonian army at Opis, on the Tigris, and laid siege to Babylon, which quickly surrendered, Nabonidus being taken prisoner. In a text known as the Cyrus Cylinder, Cyrus portrays himself as commissioned by the god Marduk to end Nabonidus' unrighteous reign. Nabonidus, he claims, had disrupted the worship of Marduk by his absence. By contrast, Cyrus, who restored the worship of Marduk at

shrines where it had been abandoned, was welcomed by the Babylonians themselves as a deliverer. It is interesting to compare this text with 2 Chronicles 36:23 and Ezra 1:1–4, the account of Cyrus's role in restoring the worship of the god of Israel in Jerusalem.

539–332 BC

By 539, then, Persia had added to her already large possessions the territory formerly occupied by the Babylonians, including Syria and Palestine. Cyrus is also known to have campaigned in eastern Iran and central Asia in the 540s.

Cyrus died in 530. During the previous two or three decades Egypt had built up their naval power and attempted to extend their sphere of influence in the eastern Mediterranean and Aegean. They established themselves in Cyprus and sought alliances with Greek cities in mainland Greece and Anatolia. Persia's response, under Cyrus' son Cambyses (530–522), was to invade Egypt by land and sea in 525. A Persian victory in a battle at the Nile Delta was followed by the siege and capture of Memphis, and Egypt came under Persian control. There were revolts against Persia in 486 and in 460–454, and between 404 and 343 Egypt was ruled by three native Egyptian dynasties, who managed to resist Persian attempts to re-establish control until shortly before Alexander's conquests brought the Persian empire itself to an end. But for the rest of the period from 525 to 332 Egypt was part of the Persian empire, this empire being by some way the largest the ancient Near East had yet seen.

The first half of the fifth century began with the Persians suppressing a rebellion of Greek cities in Anatolia (the Ionian Revolt of 498–494) and then leading campaigns against the cities of mainland Greece (the Persian Wars of 490 and 480–479), both of which ended in Persian defeat. In the 470s and 460s the Greek state of Athens led a largely successful campaign to drive back Persian power in the Aegean, though Persia scored a signal success against them in defeating the Egyptian revolt in the 450s. (The Athenians had sent a substantial fleet to aid the Egyptians, which was lost in the defeat.) In the next century or so, relations between Greece, Persia and Egypt frequently shifted. The Greek states were divided among themselves, most notably in the Peloponnesian War of 431–404, and while Athens and Persia were generally enemies in the fifth century, the Greek state of Sparta and Persia briefly became allies against Athens towards the end of this war. The first half of the fourth century saw Greek contingents at different times aiding Persia against Egypt and Egypt against Persia.

Persia never managed to defeat Greece. Persian control of Egypt was at times broken and revolts in other parts of the empire had periodically to be quashed. There were also internal power struggles: the reign of more than one Persian king ended in murder. Nonetheless the Persian empire lasted for 200 years, reflecting a basically effective internal organization. Alexander of Macedon was able to conquer the Persian empire in the 330s, but he had to fight a long and hard campaign in order to do so.

Certainly Persian control over Syria and the Levant was largely undisturbed in the period 538–332. This is the period in which the distinction between Palestinian and Diaspora Jews becomes significant: the distinction, that is, between Jews who after the Persian capture of Babylon returned to Palestine to rebuild the temple and later the walls of Jerusalem and groups who did not return but remained in various localities throughout the Persian empire. (The books of Ezra and Nehemiah focus on events in Palestine, the book of Esther on a group of diaspora Jews in Susa.)

332–63 BC

This period can be dealt with very briefly. The general outline is clear. After Alexander's death his kingdom divided into a number of smaller kingdoms, including that of the Ptolemies based in Egypt and that of the Seleucids based in Mesopotamia, Syria and Anatolia. Palestine passed from Ptolemaic into Seleucid hands at the end of the third century. It appears that most Jews initially accepted Seleucid rule, but relations were soured in the second century, leading to the Maccabean Wars of the 160s and 150s in which Judas Maccabeus and other members of the Hasmonean family led the resistance to Seleucid rule. Hasmonean leadership continued during the next 100 years, years in which the Jews gained in independence and considerably increased their territory. The last Hasmonean rulers called themselves kings. But Hasmonean rule collapsed in the 60s, when the Romans, whose influence over the eastern Mediterranean area had been growing since the early second century, were asked to arbitrate between the conflicting claims to the throne of two Hasmoneans, Aristobulus II and Hyrcanus II. The result was that the Roman general Pompey invaded their territory, entered Jerusalem, and captured the temple mound.

The events of 332–63, of course, do not fall in the period covered by the Histories, the latest of which only describe events going down to the fifth century. An outline of this period has been included for two reasons: first, for the sake of completeness, because some would argue that large parts of the Old Testament originate from the Greek period; this view may at the moment be a minority position, but as it has its advocates it might seem arbitrary to say nothing at all about this period. Second, whatever view one holds about the date of composition of the Histories, it is clear that the various Hebrew textual traditions on which our modern texts are based were being shaped in this period. This is also the period in which one of the most important ancient translations of the Old Testament, the Septuagint, was produced, much of it probably at Alexandria. This translation plays a significant role in Old Testament textual criticism.

CONCLUSION

We have set out all the above with only the occasional reference to the Histories. We now turn to work through each of the Histories in detail. A question that will occupy us as we do so is: how does their account of Israel's history fit into the picture we have just sketched of the history of the Near East as a whole?

FURTHER READING

ANCIENT NEAR EASTERN HISTORY

M.D. Coogan (ed.), *The Oxford History of the Biblical World*. Oxford University Press, 1998.

A. Kuhrt, *The Ancient Near East, c. 3000–300 BC*, 2 vols. London: Routledge, 1995.

J.M. Sasson (ed.), *Civilizations of the Ancient Near East*, 4 vols. New York: Scribners, 1995 (reprinted in 2 vols, Peabody: Hendrickson, 2000), especially Part 5.

M. Van der Mieroop, *A History of the Ancient Near East, ca. 3000–323 BC*. Oxford: Blackwell, 2004.

CHRONOLOGY

M. Bietak (ed.), *High, Middle or Low? Acts of the Second International Colloquium on Absolute Chronology: The Bronze Age in the Eastern Mediterranean*. Vienna: Akademie Verlag, 1992.

F.H. Cryer, 'Chronology: Issues and Problems' in J.M. Sasson (ed.), *Civilizations of the Ancient Near East*, 4 vols. New York: Scribners, 1995, (reprinted in 2 vols, Peabody: Hendrickson, 2000) pp. 651–64.

J. Finegan, *Handbook of Biblical Chronology*. Peabody: Hendrickson, 1998, pp. 6–138.

ATLASES

Y. Aharoni *et al.* (eds), *The Carta Bible Atlas*. London: Macmillan, 2002.

B. Beitzel, *The Moody Atlas of Bible Lands*. Chicago: Moody, 1985.

J.J. Bimson and J.P. Kane, *New Bible Atlas*. Leicester: IVP, 1985.

Chapter 3

JOSHUA

INTRODUCTION

The book of Joshua describes how the tribes of Israel under the leadership of Joshua entered Canaan, defeated the inhabitants in a series of battles, and divided the land among themselves. Joshua confronts us with most of the literary, historical, theological and ethical issues that will face us throughout the study of the Histories, sometimes in an extremely blunt way.

STRUCTURE OF JOSHUA

1:1—8:35	Crossing into Canaan; initial victories at Jericho and Ai
9:1—12:24	Further victories in the south and north of Canaan, described more briefly (9:1—11:23), ending with a summary (ch. 12)
13:1—21:45	Division of Canaan between the tribes of Israel
22:1—24:33	Conclusion: return of the Transjordanian tribes to their territories (ch. 22); Joshua's farewell to the people (ch. 23); covenant of recommitment at Shechem (ch. 24)

Three main types of material are found within Joshua: narratives, spoken words (speeches and dialogue) and lists (of kings defeated, tribal territories, etc.). Narratives and spoken words dominate in chapters 1—11 and 22—24, lists in chapters 12—21. However, the lists of chapters 12—21 also contain shorter narratives and pieces of dialogue (e.g., 13:1–7; 17:12–18), which make clear the significance of the lists and to an extent prevent them from becoming monotonous.

The book is carefully organized. This can be seen, for example, in chapters 1—4, where a number of narrative strands are woven into a complex and satisfying account. On the larger scale, previews, summaries and explanatory speeches guide the reader through Joshua, and link its different sections together. A particular unifying factor is the law of Moses, often referred to, which provides the justification for many of the events described and also lies behind many of the speeches in Joshua (e.g. 1:6–9; 23:1–16).

OUTLINE

1:1—8:35: CROSSING INTO CANAAN; INITIAL VICTORIES

As noted in Chapter 1, the Histories can be seen as the continuation of a narrative begun in the Pentateuch. Appropriately, then, Joshua begins by taking up themes from the last chapters of Deuteronomy. Deuteronomy ends with Moses dying, having brought Israel to the borders of Canaan. It also introduces Joshua as his appointed successor, who will lead Israel into Canaan (Deut. 31:23; 34:9). Joshua 1 begins where Deuteronomy leaves off, with YHWH speaking to Joshua of the task before him now that Moses has died (1:1).

YHWH's charge to Joshua (1:1–9)

YHWH's words remind Joshua of the events of Moses' life, of Moses' role in the giving of the law, and of the promises given to Moses. At the same time they preview the contents of the entire book: the crossing of the Jordan; the conquest of Canaan and its division among the tribes of Israel; and YHWH's presence with Joshua during his entire lifetime (1:5, 9). Joshua 1:1–9 deliberately links the eras of Moses and Joshua. (Note how 1:4–5 echoes Deuteronomy 7:24 and 11:24–25; and how 1:6 echoes Deuteronomy 31:23.)

It fits with this that Joshua's leadership is modelled on that of Moses: he carries on Moses' work; his success depends on keeping the law of Moses; YHWH will be with him as he was with Moses. He is to be 'strong and courageous'. This is the first of many comparisons, explicit and implicit, which will be drawn between Moses and Joshua.

Joshua's charge to the people (1:10–18)

Joshua 1:10–18 already shows Joshua adopting a Moses-like role. He receives commands from YHWH and issues commands to the people, telling them to prepare to cross the Jordan. In particular, the tribes who have already received territory across

the Jordan must remember their agreement with Moses and fight alongside the tribes who have yet to do so (vv. 12–15; cf. Deut. 3:18–20). The response of the Transjordanian tribes does duty for that of all the tribes: they will obey Joshua as they obeyed Moses, and will not rebel against him (contrast Deut. 1:26–33; 9:23–24).

Joshua 1 is a tightly structured chapter, bringing together ideas that will be central in Joshua and setting the tone for what follows. Under Joshua's leadership the people will (usually) display strength, courage and obedience. Standing where it does, this chapter is programmatic for Joshua–Kings as a whole: YHWH commits himself to Israel, and this is how the people are to respond. Similarly, Joshua is an exemplary leader, bold and faithful to YHWH. He brings the people into their inheritance, and sets a standard by which Israel's later leaders may be judged.

Rahab and the spies (ch. 2)

In 2:1–24 the narrative splits into two: the Israelite army is left preparing to cross the Jordan while spies are sent across to Jericho. The account of the resourceful spies and the brave Rahab is exciting. It ends with the spies encouraging the people: 'Truly YHWH has given all the land into our hands; moreover, all the inhabitants of the land melt in fear before us' (2:24; contrast Num. 13:26–33).

The spies' words echo Rahab's in 2:9–13. These verses are the first of a number of passages describing the reactions of Canaanites to what they have heard about the Israelites (cf. 5:1; 9:1–2; 9:9–11; 10:1–5; 11:1–5). Rahab acknowledges the greatness of Israel's god. The implication is that this was the appropriate response for all the Canaanites, but one that few made.

The crossing of the Jordan (chs 3—5)

The crossing of the Jordan, described in 3:1—4:24, is a key moment in Israel's history. It takes the form of a religious ritual, in which the ark and the priests play a leading role. The account describing it is appropriately slow-moving and solemn, dominated by the pattern 'command–response' (e.g. 3:7–17; 4:1–9; 4:15–18). It is an elaborate, multi-strand narrative, describing several events going on simultaneously, with a number of different groups identified. It uses a repetitive, incremental style.

There are five main strands in Joshua 3—4, relating to: the people (3:1–5, 14, 16, 17; 4:10, 11, 12–13, 19); the priests carrying the ark (3:3–4, 6, 8, 14, 15, 17; 4:10, 11, 15–17, 18); the 12 men representing each of the 12 tribes (3:12; 4:2, 4–5); the waters of the Jordan (3:1, 8, 13, 15, 16; 4:18, 23); the 12 stones taken from the bed of the Jordan (4:2, 6–7, 8–9, 21–24).

The narrative develops different strands in turn. As strands are taken up again they are developed further. Sometimes details are repeated to remind the reader where matters stood previously (e.g. the reference to the priests standing in the middle of the Jordan bed at 4:10a picks up that in 3:17).

The effect of this unusual narrative technique is to create an involved and gripping account which describes the Jordan crossing at length, giving a sense of its significance. Note how some important details are revealed only at the point where they will have the greatest effect: e.g. we are only told that the Jordan was in flood just before the priests step into the water (3:15). The final stage of the crossing, as the priests come out of the Jordan on the west side, is spread over nine verses (4:10–11, 15–18) which also include references to other important themes: the people's obedience to Joshua and to the commands of Moses (vv. 10–12, 14); the obedience of the Transjordanian tribes (v. 12). These verses, along with vv. 19–24 following, form a fitting climax to the narrative.

The crossing of the Jordan parallels the crossing of the Red Sea which began Israel's journey out of Egypt to Canaan, and so there are many allusions to the events of the exodus: e.g. the reference to the first day of the tenth month in 4:19 draws a link with the Passover (cf. Exod. 12:2–3). The parallel is made explicit in 4:23: 'YHWH your God dried up the waters of the Jordan for you . . . *as YHWH your God did to the Red Sea.*' But there are also differences compared to the earlier crossing, most notably in the orderly and disciplined way in which the people cross the Jordan (contrast Exod. 14:10–14). They left Egypt as little more than a rabble; they enter Canaan as an army ready for battle (4:12–13).

Through these events YHWH exalts Joshua before Israel, so that they regard him as they regarded Moses (3:7; 4:14). Joshua in turn exalts YHWH, making it plain before, during and after the crossing that it is YHWH's power which has brought Israel across the Jordan (3:9–13; 4:5–7; 4:21–24). This is also symbolized by the ark going into the Jordan before the people and coming out after them: the crossing takes place under YHWH's protection and through YHWH's power.

Digging deeper:
JOSHUA 3—4: A JUMBLED NARRATIVE?

In the comments above, which draw heavily on Hess 1996 (pp. 97–117), we have treated Joshua 3—4 as a complex but unitary account. But many commentators find these chapters confused and repetitious.

Nelson 1997 (pp. 53–71), for example, finds that there are many 'complications' or seeming contradictions in Joshua 3—4, which produce a muddled effect. He accepts that the narrative makes reasonable sense at most points but he does not believe that it is the work of a single author. 'The convolutions of chapters 3 and 4 result from the concentration of a large number of themes into the narrow nexus of Jordan crossing . . . the thematic threads have tangled and knotted' (p. 55).

Read Nelson's comments and compare his approach with the one offered in the main text. Which do you find more convincing and why? What are the strong and weak points of each position? What are the literary-critical assumptions on which each are based?

(Other multi-strand narratives where similar issues arise are Joshua 8 and Judges 20.)

Chapter 5 reports four incidents which bring out the significance of Israel's entry into Canaan and prepare for the attack on Jericho. First, 5:1 describes how the crossing of the Jordan further demoralizes the kings of Canaan, so that they launch no attack on the Israelites. Second, the male children born during the wilderness wanderings are circumcised (5:2–9). Circumcision symbolizes the promises given to Israel's forefathers, including the promise of land (Gen. 17). It appears that during the wilderness wanderings, when they have been prevented from entering the land of promise, the Israelites have felt it inappropriate to carry out circumcision. That they now do so, at YHWH's command, symbolizes the end of this period of judgment and the fulfilment of a covenant promise. (On 'the disgrace of Egypt', see Exod. 32:11–12 and Num. 14:13–16). Third, on the fourteenth day of the first month the Israelites hold the Passover (5:10–12; cf. Exod. 12). The unleavened bread they eat on the next day is made with grain from the land of Canaan, and the manna, the food YHWH provided for them in the wilderness, ceases to fall. The journey begun with the Passover in Egypt has now come to an end.

The fourth incident in this chapter looks forward to the coming attack on Jericho (5:13–15): an armed man (clearly a manifestation of YHWH; compare Exod. 3:5–6) appears to Joshua and announces himself as 'commander of YHWH's army'. YHWH himself will take the lead in the fighting to come.

Capture of Jericho (ch. 6)

Jericho is 'shut up inside and out' (6:1), but that is no obstacle to YHWH. For six days the Israelites march around the city, accompanied by the ark and by priests blowing trumpets (cf. Num. 10:1–10). The daily procession, like the Jordan crossing, is conducted as a religious ritual. On the seventh day, the people go seven times round the city, shout out when the trumpets sound, and the city wall collapses. The

Israelites then destroy the city, its inhabitants, and everything in it. Rahab and her household are the sole survivors. They are, in effect, treated as Israelites because they have aided Israel, and they become part of Israel from then on (6:17, 25).

Of all the battle accounts in Joshua, none focuses more than Joshua 6 on YHWH's role in Israel's victory. Joshua's fame has spread throughout Canaan, but it is only because YHWH has been with him (6:27). YHWH has been the 'commander', and Israel's part has simply been to follow YHWH's commands, leaving the destruction of Jericho's walls to him. The city, its inhabitants and everything in it are 'devoted to YHWH for destruction', and all metal items considered 'sacred to YHWH' (6:17, 19). YHWH has won the battle, and receives all the spoils as a kind of first-fruits of the conquest.

Capture of Ai (chs 7—8)

The next account, describing the capture of Ai, shows what happens when YHWH ceases to be Israel's commander. Achan, one of those who took part in the assault on Jericho, has kept back for himself some of the items sacred to YHWH. By his action he provokes YHWH's anger against all Israel (7:1). The result is Israel's first military defeat: they attack Ai, a small but strategically important town, and are repulsed with some losses. The defeat is attributed both to Achan's deceit and (implicitly) to Israelite over-confidence after the victory at Jericho (7:3–5). YHWH allows the Israelites to suffer the consequences of Achan's deceit, rather than immediately alerting them to what Achan has done.

> **Think about**
> **ANTHROPOPATHISMS**
>
> 'Anthropopathisms' are expressions which attribute to YHWH emotions and responses like those of humans: love (Deut. 7:8); anger (Josh. 7:1); anguish or frustration (Judg. 10:16); compassion (2 Kgs 13:23). How do you understand such language? What does it attempt to do? If you had to paraphrase these texts while avoiding the language of human emotions, how would you do it?

Now the Israelites are as dismayed as the Canaanites were previously (7:5). Joshua and the elders prostrate themselves before YHWH, and Joshua laments in terms which echo earlier situations of despair or judgment (7:7–9: compare Num. 14:2–4; 20:3–5; and Exod. 32:11–13; Num. 14:13–19). One defeat is enough to bring lurking fears out of Joshua's mind: maybe YHWH does not have good intentions towards Israel after all.

YHWH's response is robust (7:10–15). There is no mystery about what has happened: Israel has fallen into sin, and Joshua must deal with it. Until then the covenant will remain violated, and Israel will continue to be defeated. Joshua assembles the people and Achan is singled out as the guilty party (7:16–18).

Joshua invites Achan to confess in words that are almost kindly ('my son', 7:19). Achan's confession is interesting: it gives a sense of the attractiveness of the forbidden items, how easy it was to desire them. The narrator seems to understand what it means to face temptation, gives a sense almost of sympathy for Achan. But a fierce word of condemnation follows (7:25), and a

Digging deeper:
THE 'DEVOTED THINGS' AND ACHAN'S SIN

Joshua 6—7 are unusual in a number of ways. YHWH does not always demand all the spoils of a conquered enemy city, even when that city is 'devoted to destruction' like Jericho (note the account of the capture of Ai which immediately follows this narrative, Josh. 8:2, 27). While it is a commonplace of the Histories that disobedience to YHWH brings military defeat (Judg. 2:11–15; 1 Sam. 2—4; etc.), it is unusual for one man's disobedience to bring such a judgment upon the entire people, and for the defeat to be traced back to its root cause so quickly and clearly. It is also unusual for children to suffer for their father's sin (cf. Deut. 24:16).

It is as though YHWH makes the Israelites' first battle in Canaan a test of their obedience, giving clear and unusually strict instructions concerning the spoils: when Achan fails the test, the consequences for Israel as a whole and for Achan are severe and obvious. The events ram home a lesson: these are the fruits of disobedience – see how one man's sin can bring disaster upon many in Israel! And if the events themselves were meant as a lesson for the Israelites under Joshua, the well-constructed narrative of Joshua 6—7 aims to apply the same lesson to later generations: it is a 'textbook illustration' of the themes of obedience and disobedience, blessing and curse.

None of this necessarily makes Joshua 7 more acceptable to modern readers. Clements, for example, notes the narrator's didactic intent, but rejects the idea that this chapter has anything worthwhile to communicate: 'It is difficult to find within the story of Achan's sin any residual merit or moral lesson' (p. 125). For Clements perhaps the only lesson of Joshua 7 is that 'faith can promote hatred, intolerance, and a guilt-ridden savagery, as well as love, joy, and peace' (p. 126). Whether or not one agrees with him at all points, it is hard not to feel the force of what Clements says.

Two issues need to be explored here: the act of 'devoting' items or people to YHWH, and the question of corporate responsibility. We shall turn to the larger, related issue of the destruction of the Canaanites later.

'Devoted things'
'Devoted things' translates Hebrew *kherem*, a noun related to a verb which denotes the act of making a person or object entirely over to YHWH. The verb and noun occur in a variety of contexts (Exod. 22:20; Lev. 27; Num. 18). When used in reference to Israel's wars, they denote the destruction of enemy cities, the killing of their inhabitants (Num. 21:3; Deut. 20:16–18), and, in the case of the nations of Canaan, the destruction of their religious images (Deut. 7:25–26). Sometimes the Israelites are allowed to keep some of the spoils of 'devoted' cities, sometimes not. Some texts clearly portray the practice of *kherem* against enemy cities as YHWH's judgment upon them (Deut. 20:16–18; cf. 9:4–5), and that may be implied in other texts as well (Deut. 2:30–35; 3:1–7).

Kherem is a religious concept, linked to other religious concepts such as holiness. Thus in Joshua 6:18–19 the

ferocious act of judgment against Achan and his family. Achan's household suffers exactly what Jericho's inhabitants suffered. YHWH's anger then abates (7:26).

The relationship between YHWH and the Israelites is now restored, and the second attack on Ai goes ahead. Victory comes, not by another Jericho-like miracle, but by means reference to 'devoted things' in v. 18 is followed in v. 19 by the statement that all precious metals are 'sacred to YHWH'. In particular, the devotion of entire cities and their inhabitants to YHWH by fire and sword has connotations of sacrifice (Niditch, pp. 28–55; Kaminsky, pp. 78–81); though it is never implied that the offering of *kherem* to YHWH makes atonement. Niditch (p. 50) suggests that this aspect of the *kherem* can be seen, paradoxically, as underscoring the value of the lives that are thus offered to YHWH: they may be Israel's enemies or great sinners, but their lives must still be returned to YHWH their creator.

The *kherem* is applied to Jericho in a stringent form: everything is to be destroyed or made over to YHWH. This reflects the fact that the capture of Jericho is meant to be exemplary. Though the term *kherem* is not used of Achan's execution, he and his household suffer the fate of the Canaanite inhabitants of Jericho. This is presented partly as an act of retribution (Achan has 'brought trouble' on Israel, and so YHWH 'brings trouble' on him, 7:25), and partly as a sacral act removing pollution from among the people: Achan has stolen what belongs to YHWH (7:1), confusing the realms of the sacred and profane and bringing a kind of contagion upon the people (McConville, pp. 164–5; cf. *EOT I*, pp. 91–5 on the 'holiness' teaching of Leviticus).

Corporate responsibility

Joshua 7 suggests that one person's actions can have consequences for the larger group to which they belong: Achan's sin provokes YHWH's anger against all Israel, rendering them guilty and indeed 'devoted for destruction' in YHWH's sight (7:11–12); Achan's sin brings the destruction of his entire household, including animals and inanimate objects (7:22–26). According to Kaminsky (pp. 85–95) the chapter reflects a view of corporate responsibility, to be linked to the view that misappropriating items designated as *kherem* brings pollution on Israel: the entire Israelite camp becomes unclean because of Achan's act, and the only way to remove the pollution is to destroy the 'infected' part of the camp – Achan and everything belonging to him – thus making the camp clean again.

Joshua 7 presents these ideas within a covenant framework: the ritual pollution is also a transgression of the covenant between YHWH and Israel (7:11), and indeed the punishment Israel suffers, defeat at enemy hands, is one of the covenant curses described at Deuteronomy 28:25. Other factors may also be at work: is it assumed, for example, that Achan's family knew what he had done and did nothing (cf. 7:13), and does this partly explain why they die along with him? But even taking such other factors into account, the concepts of guilt as pollution and of corporate responsibility, so alien-seeming to us, are clearly present in Joshua 7. Kaminsky (pp. 94–5) suggests that these concepts challenge modern, individualistic ways of thinking.

Do you think there is any way of making sense of concepts such as *kherem* and corporate responsibility today?

of an ambush, which succeeds partly because of the defeat of the first attack (8:3–23; esp. vv. 6, 16). YHWH specifically orders an ambush (8:2): perhaps the aim is to reinforce a sense of Israelite solidarity through the use of tactics in which all Israel must act together, thus countering the bad example of Achan's selfishness.

The ambush is related at length. The narrative comes to its climax at the point when the men of Ai realize they have been caught in the open (8:20–22). All the inhabitants of Ai are slaughtered, the plunder and the livestock is divided up, and the king of Ai is executed and symbolically buried at the city gate, the point where his men had previously driven back the Israelites (8:24–29; cf. 7:5).

Verses 30–35 of chapter 8 describe the setting up of an altar and a copy of the law of Moses. This is in accordance with Deuteronomy 27. In the context of Joshua 7—8, which has seen the covenant violated and restored, it also reaffirms Israel's commitment to the covenant.

9:1—12:24: FURTHER VICTORIES AND SUMMARY

Joshua 1—8 have described the initial stages of Joshua's campaign in some detail. The narrator's aim has been to illustrate key theological principles. There is one further extended narrative (ch. 9), but after that the narrator uses a condensed, annalistic style to describe the remainder of the campaign, in which the bulk of the fighting takes place (chs 10—12).

The events of Joshua 9—12 follow on from those in the earlier chapters. The opening verses of chapter 9, which seem to have all the battles of chapters 10—11 in view, represent the hostile attitude of the kings of Canaan and the different response of the Gibeonites as a reaction to the Israelite victories at Ai and Jericho (9:1–5). The narrator continues to note links between events in what follows: Israel's treaty with the Gibeonites leads on to the war against the southern kings (10:1–4), which in turn leads on to the war against the northern kings (11:1–5). These links, along with the change to a more annalistic style, suggest the Israelite conquest gaining momentum, one event leading on to another, and the victories being described more and more rapidly.

The Gibeonites (ch. 9)

The citizens of Gibeon desire a treaty with Israel, and distance themselves from their Canaanite neighbours by pretending that they have come from afar. This episode has parallels with the account of Rahab in chapter 2: like Rahab, the Gibeonites renounce their Canaanite allegiance, confess the power of Israel's god and join themselves to the Israelites. But the treaty is only made because the Gibeonites deceive the Israelites. Seemingly, if YHWH had been consulted the deception would not have worked (9:14). Once made, the treaty is considered binding, but the Gibeonites end up being treated like resident aliens (cf. Deut. 29:11). Unlike Rahab they do not become fully part of Israel.

The account is full of ambiguities. When confronted with their deceit, the Gibeonites admit that they knew of YHWH's command that the inhabitants of Canaan should be destroyed. The deceit was their last, desperate resort, but somehow it worked: YHWH, not consulted by the Israelites, in effect allows his command to be circumvented, and is not angered by what happens (contrast 7:1). One of the questions raised by this narrative is what it implies for YHWH's attitude to the other inhabitants of Canaan. Could other cities similarly have thrown themselves on the Israelites' mercy?

Campaign in the South (ch. 10)

The Israelites have established a foothold in the central hill country, and threaten to isolate Jerusalem and other southern cities (here described as 'Amorite' cities). Reacting to this danger, a major coalition of these cities attacks Gibeon, and the Gibeonites appeal to the Israelites. Joshua honours the treaty, marches by night, launches a surprise attack on the Amorite forces, and wins a great victory. The victory and pursuit are summarized at 10:10 and described in more detail at 10:11–27. If the narrator was reticent about YHWH's attitude to the happenings of chapter 9, in chapter 10 he speaks plainly of YHWH's involvement in events: YHWH assures the Israelites beforehand of victory and plays a major part in the battle, even prolonging the day so that the Israelites can exploit their victory. This event is highlighted by the citation of two lines of poetry from the 'Book of Jashar', and by the comment, 'there has been no day like it before or since, when YHWH heeded a human voice; for YHWH fought for Israel' (10:14).

The victory over the southern coalition is followed by attacks on six southern cities, Makkedah, Libnah, Lachish, Eglon, Hebron and Debir (vv. 28–39), some of whose leaders have already been put to death (vv. 23–26). The army of the king of Gezer is also defeated (v. 33).

The language emphasizes complete destruction, with no survivors remaining (vv. 28, 30, 35). Note especially 10:40–43, which speaks of all the South being captured 'at one time'. This passage, however, needs to be set alongside the accounts of Caleb's later victories in 15:13–16 (cf. Judg. 1:9–15), where it is clear that Hebron and Debir still have some inhabitants. Either the language

here is deliberately exaggerated, or we must suppose that 10:40–43 looks forward to the later exploits of Caleb, sees them as following up Joshua's initial successes, and hence attributes them to Joshua (cf. 11:21–22).

Campaign in the North and summaries of all Israel's victories (chs. 11—12)

The narrative in 11:1–10 is similar to that of 10:1–43, describing Israel's battle against a coalition centring on the northern city of Hazor. This coalition is larger and more formidable than the

---

Think about
YHWH'S ACTIONS IN JOSHUA 1—12

Go through Joshua 1—12 noting the different ways in which YHWH is said to be involved in the events narrated. How would you classify them? Are 'natural' explanations (explanations which do not require YHWH's active involvement in events) possible in some cases? Does YHWH seem to act consistently in these chapters? In general, do you find this aspect of Joshua 1—12 credible?

In particular, how do you understand the language about YHWH 'hardening the hearts' of almost all the Canaanites (11:19–20), which seems intended to evoke similar language used in relation to Pharaoh at the time of the exodus (Exod. 9:12; 10:1, 27; 11:10)? What does this language imply? In what does the 'hardening' consist?

(Regarding the 'long day' of 10:12–14, you can compare the different interpretations surveyed in Hess 1996, pp. 197–9 and Younger 1990, pp. 208–20.)

southern coalition, but it is dealt with extremely briefly and simply (11:4–10): success can now be assumed, provided Joshua and Israel are obedient and trust YHWH. Again YHWH promises victory and again victory follows.

Joshua 11 ends with a survey of land captured – two surveys, in fact: one summarizing the campaign against the northern kings (vv. 12–15); the other more extensive, summarizing all Joshua's victories (vv. 16–23). The Anakites are singled out as an example of intimidating-seeming inhabitants of Canaan whom the Israelites nonetheless defeated (11:21–22; 14:6–15 and 15:13–19 give more details). There is an implicit contrast between the Israelites under Joshua's leadership and those of the previous generation (cf. Num. 13:33; Deut. 9:1–3).

A transition is marked in 11:23, summarizing the events of Joshua 1—11 and leading into the allocations of chapters 13—21. The fighting is over ('the land had rest from war'), and it is time to turn to the question of the tribes' 'inheritance' (a key term in chs 13—21).

Chapter 12 summarizes both Moses' and Joshua's victories, in the form of boundary and territory descriptions (vv. 1–8) and lists of defeated kings (vv. 2, 4, 9–24). The summary ranges even more widely than those of chapter 11, and deliberately links Moses' and Joshua's work.

The list of kings defeated by Joshua roughly follows the order of events in chapters 1—11. However, some of the towns listed have not

---

THE NATIONS OF CANAAN

Joshua 12:8 describes the territory of the people defeated by the Israelites as 'the land of the Hittites, Amorites, Canaanites, Perizzites, Hivites and Jebusites'. As many as eighteen texts listing the nations of Canaan are found in Genesis–Kings (e.g. Exod. 3:8; Deut. 20:17). Some of these texts add 'Girgashites' to the six nations mentioned at Joshua 12:8 (Deut. 7:1; Josh. 3:10; 24:11), others mention only five nations or fewer (Exod. 13:5; 23:28). The order of names also varies. Some of these nations are known from extra-biblical sources, others only from the Bible. Note also that some texts use 'Amorites' and 'Canaanites' as a general designation for some or all of the inhabitants of Canaan ('Amorites': Josh. 7:7; 24:15. 'Canaanites': Exod. 13:11; Josh. 13:4). For further details see Satterthwaite and Baker.

---

been mentioned previously (e.g. Bethel in v. 16; though note the brief reference at 8:17). This suggests that chapters 1—11 are not a complete account (cf. 11:18: 'Joshua made war a long time'). The important site of Shechem is, in contrast, not mentioned here, though the Israelites later treat it as theirs (20:7; 21:21; ch. 24; cf. 8:30–35).

13:1—21:45: DIVISION OF THE LAND
The section 13:1—21:45 describes the division of the land among the Israelite tribes (see Map 2). Like chapters 1—12 this section begins with a divine command to Joshua (13:1–7) and ends with a summary of what has been accomplished (21:43–45).

Time has moved on: Joshua is now old and land still remains to be occupied: 13:1–7 is

JOSHUA 1—12 AND ANCIENT NEAR EASTERN CONQUEST ACCOUNTS

Inscriptions describing military campaigns have been found in many of the lands of the ancient Near East. They date from the second and first millennia BC.

They include:

- Egyptian texts (c. 1550–720): *COS* II, pp. 5–51;
- Hittite texts (c. 1500–1250): *COS* I, pp. 182–204; *COS* II, pp. 82–90;
- Neo-Assyrian texts (c. 850–670): *COS* II, pp. 261–306.

These inscriptions vary in length, detail and style, but share many common features. They are usually royal inscriptions glorifying the king as military leader.

Particular points of contact between these inscriptions and Joshua 1—12 are:

- Reference to divine aid: Rameses II (Egyptian) records how he prayed to Amun at a crucial point during the battle of Qadesh, and was able to rally his men against the Hittites (*COS* II, pp. 34–7); Hattusili III ascribes his many military successes to the aid of 'my lady Ishtar' (*COS* I, pp. 200–4). Compare Joshua 1—12 *passim*.
- Reference to signs of divine power: Thutmose III (Egyptian) records a comet that brought terror upon his enemies (*COS* II, p. 17); Mursili II (Hittite) describes a lightning bolt that preceded one of his victories (*COS* II, p. 85). Compare Joshua 10:1–14.
- Exaggerated language: Thutmose III is described as one who 'immediately overwhelms all foreign lands while at the head of his army', and the same inscription speaks of 'numerous armies of Mitanni . . . overthrown in the space of an hour, annihilated completely like those who had not existed' (*COS* II, pp. 14–15). Shalmaneser III (Assyrian) speaks of 'filling plains' with the corpses of his enemies (*COS* II, pp. 262–3). Compare Joshua 10:28–42; 11:14.
- Descriptions of the fear inspired in the enemy: the enemies of Sethos I (Egyptian) are said to be filled with dread as he advances against them (*COS* II, pp. 30–1); Sennacherib (Assyrian) describes his enemies as traitors and rebels who are thrown into panic as he attacks them (*COS* II, pp. 301–3). Compare Joshua 2:9–11; 5:1.

Younger (1990) has compared Joshua 9—12 and ancient Near Eastern conquest accounts (for his major conclusions, see pp. 197–266). He argues that, to judge by these other accounts, there is nothing in Joshua 9—12 which does not belong in a campaign report (an argument for literary unity). Hoffmeier similarly notes parallels between Joshua 1—11 and the Annals of Thutmose III (*COS* II, pp. 7–13), particularly the combination of detailed narratives and briefer reports. He suggests that the Israelites may have borrowed Egyptian scribal conventions for recording military actions.

Younger also argues that the language of 'total destruction' in Joshua 10—11 and elsewhere is hyperbole typical of ancient Near Eastern conquest accounts, and is not to be taken literally (pp. 226–8). Further, the depiction of the Canaanites in Joshua 9—12 as first seeking to destroy Israel, then filled with terror and finally destroyed in punishment of their sins has many parallels in the ancient Near Eastern accounts (pp. 232–7).

Both Younger and Hoffmeier stress that good parallels to Joshua 1—12 can be found in texts from both the second and first millennium, hence that ancient Near Eastern parallels are not helpful in dating Joshua. Their main value is in helping us to understand the literary conventions of Joshua better. But what follows from the point that other ancient Near Eastern peoples speak of their gods fighting on their behalf and vindicating their cause against a wicked enemy? Does this relativize the claims of Joshua 1—12 on behalf of Israel's god? How do you respond to the suggestion that Joshua 10—12 may contain hyperbole like that found in other ancient Near Eastern battle accounts?

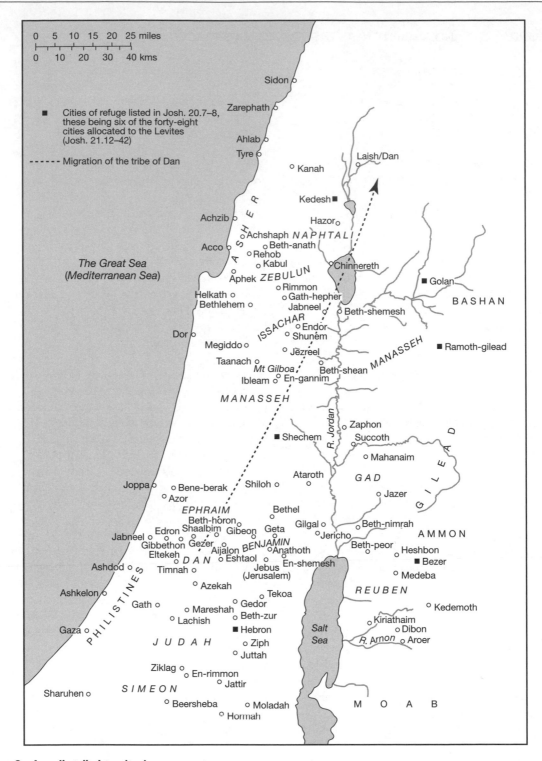

Map 2   Israel's tribal territories

the first explicit statement to this effect. This land lies to the south, west and north (cf. Num. 34:1–12). Other passages in Joshua 13—24 also speak of land remaining to be occupied or nations not yet driven out (18:1–8; 23:4–5, 11–13). The task remains uncompleted by the end of the book.

The tribal allocations take up most of 13:8—19:51. The territory which Moses granted to the Transjordanian tribes (Reuben, Gad and half-Manasseh) is described first (ch. 13). Next come Judah, Ephraim and the other half-tribe of Manasseh (14:6—17:18), separately introduced (14:1–5), whose territories include land already allotted by Moses (14:6–15; 17:3–6). The final section describes the territories which Joshua allocates to the remaining seven tribes at Shiloh (18:1—19:51). This section also has a separate introduction (18:1–10). The last territory to be allocated is Joshua's (19:49–50). This order of presentation follows the order of conquest (Transjordan, south Canaan, north Canaan) and also gives priority to arrangements made by Moses (14:6–15; 17:3–6), suggesting (again) continuity between Moses' and Joshua's work.

In chapters 20—21 the Israelites give back to YHWH some of the territory he has given them, setting apart cities of refuge and cities for the Levites, the tribe dedicated to YHWH's service in worship and sacrifice, who have no allocation of land (ch. 21). This accords with commands given to Moses (cities of refuge: Num. 35:6–15; Deut. 4:41–43; Levitical cities: Num. 35:1–5).

The territories of the Cisjordanian tribes are described with varying amounts of detail. The survey of Judah's territory is the most detailed, a description of the boundaries (15:1–12) followed by a list of the towns in

---

'THE LAND THAT REMAINS'

Joshua 13:1 introduces the theme of the land that 'remains to be possessed'. Verses 2–7 develop this theme in two ways: verses 2–6a describe the extent of this land; and in verses 6b–7 YHWH tells Joshua to divide up this land, much of it as yet unconquered, between the nine and a half tribes who will live west of the Jordan. The two parts of 13:2–7 seem to be linked: YHWH promises to aid the Israelites in taking control of the land (v. 6; cf. 23:4–5), but the tribes have their allotted inheritances, which, it will become clear, they must take active steps to occupy (v. 7; cf. 17:14–18; 18:2–3). Above all, later chapters will emphasize, they must not form alliances with the peoples remaining in the land (23:11–13).

This passage introduces a pair of themes which dominate the second half of Joshua: YHWH will continue to aid the Israelites; but they must remain faithful and obedient to him. These themes are closely linked, and it seems unnecessary to follow scholars who treat parts of 13:1–7 as later interpolations (e.g. Nelson 1997, pp. 163–7).

The boundaries of the land which YHWH here grants to the Israelites (including the land yet unoccupied) correspond fairly closely to those described in other passages (Gen. 15:18; Deut. 1:7; Josh. 1:2–5; 1 Kgs 4:21; 8:65), though the text of 13:1–7 is at points hard to interpret clearly, and the identification of some of the places named is also uncertain (Hess 1996, pp. 229–33; Butler, pp. 145–53). The northern boundaries of this land extend beyond the territories allocated to Asher and Naphtali, the two northernmost tribes (Josh. 18:24–39). According to the biblical texts, the closest Israel came to actually occupying, or at least controlling, this entire territory was during the reigns of David and Solomon. See, further, Kallai, pp. 111–29.

each region (15:20–62). For Ephraim and Manasseh only boundary descriptions are given (16:1–10; 17:7–10), though there are references to towns and villages at 16:9 and 17:9, 11. As regards the seven remaining tribes (18:11—19:48), some have boundary descriptions and town lists of varying length (Benjamin, 18:11–28; Zebulun, 19:10–16; Issachar, 19:17–23; Asher, 19:24–31; Naphtali, 19:32–39) and others have only a town list (Simeon, 19:1–8; Dan, 19:40–46). Chapters 13—19 thus do not present a uniform appearance.

The date of the territory descriptions in Joshua 13—19 has been much discussed, some scholars arguing that they reflect the realities of later periods, for example the reigns of Solomon or Hezekiah or Josiah. For a survey of some of the issues, see Hess 1994 and 1996 (pp. 246–49). Hess argues that the boundary descriptions of Joshua 13—19 are most likely to be pre-monarchic in origin, for the divisions between the tribal inheritances correspond approximately to the boundaries between different city-states of Canaan in the Amarna period. The material in these chapters may, however, have been updated at later periods. This might be expected in an administrative document that remained in use over several centuries. Along these lines one can explain why some of the towns listed in Judah's territory, for example, seem only to have been occupied during the period of the monarchy. In their present context in Joshua the lists are in any case somewhat idealistic, mapping out tribal allocations in a land much of which is yet to be occupied.

The sections of narration and dialogue within Joshua 13—21 bring out key theological ideas. The two narratives about

Caleb (14:6–15; 15:13–19) expand upon the brief summary in 11:21–22. They emphasize his boldness (he attacks the fearsome Anakites, 14:12) and YHWH's blessing on his life (14:13). He captures the land promised to him and shares its blessings among his family (15:13–19), exemplifying the kind of attitude that will see the conquest of Canaan completed.

Two other narratives relating to Ephraim and Manasseh focus on the question of tribal allocations. In the first narrative (17:3–6) Joshua grants the request of Zelophehad's daughters for land, honouring Moses' promise (Num. 36). In the second (17:14–18) Joshua partly agrees to Ephraim's and Manasseh's request for more land, but insists that they must not allow the Canaanites' iron chariots to deter them from occupying their inheritance. Joshua seems more confident than they that the Canaanites can be beaten. The narrative raises the question whether the generations after Joshua will match his boldness and success.

Chapters 13—19 include references to events after Joshua's death: the account of Caleb, Othniel and Acsah (15:13–19; cf. Judg. 1:9–15) and the account of Dan's move north (19:47; cf. Judg. 18). The references to cities which Judah, Ephraim and Manasseh could not capture clearly reflect the perspective of a later period (compare Josh. 15:63 with Judg. 1:21; and Josh. 16:10; 17:11–13 with Judg. 1:21, 27–29). Note how these references occur in a section framed by the accounts of Caleb's conquests (14:6–15) and Joshua's occupation of his inheritance (19:49–50), that is, by accounts of how the two faithful heroes from the previous generation successfully occupied their allotted territories. These chapters thus foreshadow the contrast between Joshua's generation and the next generation in Judges 1—3.

In chapter 20 Joshua sets apart three cities of refuge in Cisjordan, to go with the three already set apart by Moses in Transjordan (Deut. 4:41–43). He does not, however, enact the further provision of Deuteronomy 19:8–9, according to which three further cities can be set apart 'if YHWH your God enlarges your territory . . . and he will give you all the land'. Joshua 20, that is, seems to imply a view according to which the land was not fully occupied under Joshua.

The section 21:41–43 summarizes not only chapters 13—21, but all Joshua so far: YHWH completely fulfilled the promises he made to Israel's forefathers, enabling the Israelites to overcome all their enemies and to settle in the land he had promised them on oath. The details of the tribal allocations may seem tedious to the modern reader, but they are clearly tied to this theme of YHWH keeping his promises. The very weight of detail gives a necessary emphasis, spelling out the fact of fulfilment in concrete terms.

22:1—24:33: CONCLUSION

Joshua 22:1—24:33 describes the departure of the Transjordanian tribes and Joshua's final acts, his farewell exhortation and the covenant-ceremony at Shechem. These events take place after the division of the land. The chapters are united by the theme of religious faithfulness.

The altar of the Transjordanian tribes (ch. 22)

The Transjordanian tribes have played their part in the occupation of Canaan. Joshua blesses them, having warned them to remain obedient to YHWH, and they leave. But before they cross the Jordan they build an 'altar of

great size' on the western side (v. 10). No explanation is given and the other tribes send a delegation to find out what is going on. They assume that the altar is an expression of rebellion against YHWH, and they urge Transjordanian tribes to repent, so as not to bring judgment on all Israel. In reply the Transjordanian tribes explain why they built the altar: not in order to worship other gods or even to offer sacrifices at all, but as a witness to the fact that they are entitled to worship YHWH along with the Cisjordanian tribes. This reply is acceptable to the delegation, and the altar is described as 'a witness between us that YHWH is God' (v. 34). The narrative raises the threats of disunity and apostasy only to dismiss them: the Transjordanian tribes have, after all, remained loyal to YHWH.

Joshua's farewell to the people (ch. 23)

In chapter 23, set 'a long time afterwards' (v. 1), Joshua addresses Israel's leaders in the light of his coming death, exhorting them to remain faithful to YHWH. Only on this basis will YHWH continue to drive out the nations before them (vv. 2–8). This passage is similar to 1:2–9, with a similar focus on the law, but there is a new note of warning (vv. 12–16). In its general shape and in some of its detailed contents, this chapter is like Deuteronomy 28 (blessings for obedience followed by curses for disobedience). Compare also Deuteronomy 11:22–25.

Joshua 23 is clear about what YHWH has already accomplished for Israel: 'rest to Israel from all their enemies' (v. 1); 'YHWH has driven out before you great and strong nations . . . no one has been able to withstand you to this day' (v. 9); 'you know . . . that not one thing has failed of all the good things that YHWH your God promised concerning you; all have come to pass for you, not one of them has failed' (v. 14). But the chapter is equally clear that work remains to be done: note the references to the 'nations that remain' (vv. 4, 7, 12), whom YHWH has still to 'push . . . back before you' (v. 5). The chapter is interesting for containing clear statements both that YHWH has fulfilled his promises to Israel and that Israel does not yet fully possess the land.

The covenant at Shechem (ch. 24)

In chapter 24 Joshua takes matters further, doing all he can to secure Israel's loyalty to YHWH for the future. He summons the whole people to Shechem, addressing his words to them, not simply Israel's leaders (24:2, 16, 19–28), and he leads them in a covenant-ceremony of recommitment to YHWH.

As in the Hittite treaties kings recorded their previous benefactions to those with whom they made the treaty (see, e.g. *COS* II, pp. 93–106), so here Joshua, speaking in YHWH's name, reviews Israel's history from its beginnings down to the present (vv. 2–13). He emphasizes what YHWH has done for Israel, and how dependent on YHWH Israel has been at each stage. The tone of this review is positive: there are no references to the golden calf or other acts of provocation (contrast Deut. 9—10), and the wilderness wanderings to which the previous generation was condemned as a punishment are quickly passed over: 'Afterwards you lived in the wilderness for a long time' (v. 7).

Joshua calls on Israel to respond wholeheartedly to YHWH: other gods are to be 'put away' (vv. 15, 23: this could imply that some Israelites still retained idols, or it could be a metaphor for a mental act of renunciation). The people commit themselves to YHWH alone, even though Joshua makes plain that this is not a light undertaking (vv. 19–20). In context verses 19–20 are clearly an overstatement designed to call forth the people's commitment, as the subsequent dialogue shows (vv. 21–22). But the effect is that a shadow of judgment, of final destruction indeed (v. 20), momentarily hangs over this chapter, as it did over the end of chapter 23. The people will have to be true to their word. The covenant is recorded and a memorial stone set up.

The last verses of Joshua all sound positive notes (vv. 28–33): Joshua finds rest in his inheritance, after he has given the people their inheritances; the people were obedient during Joshua's lifetime; Joseph's bones were finally buried in Canaan (cf. Gen. 50:25); Eleazar the priest (cf. 14:1) was buried in his allotted territory. This conclusion rounds off the account of a generation of Israelites who have in general served YHWH faithfully.

KEY THEMES
Land

Israel occupies and divides the land of Canaan. The territories the tribes receive are their 'inheritances', territory promised to earlier generations by YHWH (cf. Gen. 12:1–13; Exod. 23:23–33). In Joshua YHWH honours this promise. All Israelites are entitled to a share of this land.

Presence of YHWH

Israel defeats the Canaanites because YHWH goes with them and gives them victory. In the earlier chapters YHWH's presence is symbolized particularly by the ark (chs 3—4; 6). Later chapters note YHWH's continuing presence among his people (18:1; 24:1).

Rest

Joshua begins with statements that YHWH will give all the tribes of Israel 'rest' (1:13, 15) and notes that this 'rest' was indeed achieved after the fighting finished (11:23; 14:15; 21:44; 22:4; 23:1). Deuteronomy 12:10 looked forward to a time 'when you cross over the Jordan and live in the land that YHWH your God is allotting to you, and when he gives you rest from your enemies all around', and went on to speak of how Israel should then worship YHWH 'at the place that YHWH will choose' (v. 14). Deuteronomy seemed to envisage a time when Israel was fully in possession of the land, but in Joshua, interestingly, Israel is said to enjoy rest even though much of the land remains to be possessed; and indeed Shiloh, where the tent of meeting is set up, does function in Joshua 18—22 along the lines of the 'place that YHWH will choose' in Deuteronomy. In Judges rest becomes something the Israelites enjoy only fleetingly (Judg. 3:11; 5:31; 8:28), and it is not until the time of David that the possibility of fulfilling Deuteronomy 12 becomes a reality again (2 Sam. 7).

Obedience/disobedience

Because they depend on YHWH, Israel must remain loyal to him, shunning the worship of other gods, otherwise he may turn against them and destroy them. These ideas underlie the warnings of chapter 23 and the covenant ceremonies of 8:30–35 and chapter 24, in which the Israelites bind themselves to keep the law. A key word in chapters 22—24 is 'serve' (sometimes 'worship'), used of Israel's proper response to YHWH.

The law of Moses

Joshua begins and ends with exhortations to keep the law of Moses (1:6–9; 23:6–8; cf. 24:25–26). Many of Joshua's actions as leader are carried out in obedience to the law. Observance of the law does not simply mean right worship: it also has social and ethical implications. In Joshua this can most clearly be seen in the provision of cities of refuge (ch. 20).

Mercy and destruction

Joshua 1—12 is mainly a narrative of destruction: most of the inhabitants of Canaan opposed the invading Israelites and were destroyed by Israel's god. This theme dominates chapters 10—12 particularly. But the accounts of Rahab and the Gibeonites, in which Canaanites are spared and incorporated into Israel, may suggest that destruction did not have to be the order of the day: all Canaanites who cast themselves upon Israel's god found mercy. Our understanding of these issues depends partly on how we understand the passage about the hardening of the Canaanites' hearts at 11:19–20.

Joshua's leadership

At many points Joshua is compared to Moses as a leader. He does not suffer by the comparison. Throughout, he is obedient and responsive to YHWH, no matter what he is commanded to do. At key moments he points to YHWH as the one who has brought about Israel's victories (4:20–24; 10:22–25; 23:1–5), and as he nears death he tries to ensure the people's future commitment to YHWH (chs. 23—24). He unselfishly allocates the tribal inheritances before receiving his own (19:49–50). He is a model for future leaders of Israel.

Israel

Israel is portrayed as generally responsive to Joshua's leadership. There is only one incident of discontent, and that is peacefully resolved (9:16–27; contrast the more serious challenges to Moses' authority in Numbers).

Apart from the Achan incident the people are faithful to YHWH under Joshua. They are also united, a point which emerges particularly in the sections dealing with the Transjordanian tribes and the Levites.

CRITICAL ISSUES

LITERARY-CRITICAL ISSUES

Aspects of Joshua as narrative

Joshua is a carefully structured narrative, with connections between events clearly brought out, giving readers a sense of where the narrative is going. Key ideas are repeated for emphasis: obedience to the law; the idea that the Transjordanian tribes and the Levites are full members of Israel; warnings against apostasy.

There are examples of narrative analogy in Joshua: e.g. echoes of the exodus narrative in Joshua 3—5, which invite the reader to compare the beginning and ending of Israel's journey from Egypt to Canaan. The Caleb narratives in Joshua 14 and 15 can similarly be read in the light of Numbers 13—14: here is a faithful Israelite of the previous generation finally doing what he wanted to do forty years earlier, and as confident of success as he was then.

The narrative of chapters 1—12 is sometimes complex. We have mentioned the 'multi-strand' narratives of chapter 1—4 and chapter 8, narratives which depend on the reader's ability to keep track of the different activities of three or four groups. Chapters 9—10 provide another example: 9:1–2 introduces the theme of Canaanite hostility, but chapter 9 then turns to describe the Gibeonite episode, and Canaanite hostility is not mentioned again until the beginning of chapter 10, now incorporating a reference to Gibeon's treaty with Israel

(10:1–4). The narrative complications are, however, resolved in due course, and the total effect is of an author in control of his material.

Sources, dating, authorship, editing

There are no indications in Joshua as to who the author(s) may have been. As for the date of Joshua, we must distinguish between the traditions on which the book is based and the final form of the book. Verses 12–13 of chapter 10 quote an earlier source, the 'Book of Jashar', but this passage leaves it unclear whether what is quoted is representative (cf. 2 Sam. 1:18), and whether other parts of Joshua are based upon it.

Some passages may reflect the perspective of the early monarchic period or even earlier: the references to Rahab's descendants (6:25), to the Gibeonites' service (9:27, dating from before the Jerusalem temple?), and to Gezer as an unconquered Canaanite enclave (16:10, dating from before Solomon? See 1 Kings 9:15–17). Bear in mind, however, that in these passages the phrase 'to this day' may derive from an earlier source, the author having retained the phrase as a way of indicating that he was using earlier traditions, not because it reflected his own perspective.

We noted that some parts of chapters 15—17 anticipate developments in the period of the judges. The mention of Jair's settlements (13:30) is another example of this (cf. Judg. 10:3–5). The reference to the 'hill-country of Judah' and the 'hill-country of Israel' (11:21) apparently presupposes the division of the monarchy after Solomon (cf. 1 Kgs 12:20–21), but could have arisen through later updating of the text.

Scholars often approach the question of the book's literary history by asking: is Joshua a literary unity? Many argue that it is not (e.g. Curtis, pp. 22–35, Nelson 1997, pp. 5–9). Some of the arguments relate to details of particular texts: for example, Nelson's view (noted above) that Joshua 3—4 contains a number of secondary additions; or Curtis' view that the tribal allocations of chapters 13—19 contain discrepancies (was Kiriath-Jearim in Judah or Benjamin (15:60, 18:28)? Was Eshtaol in Judah or Dan (15:33, 19:41)?) and do not have a consistent format (pp. 26–8), both of which may imply that different parts of these chapters may date from different periods. But it is not simply within narratives that scholars have noted literary tensions: it has been suggested that there are inconsistencies between larger blocks of material, and that the literary structure of Joshua is at points incoherent. Arguments along these lines include the following:

- At 13:1 Joshua is described as 'old and advanced in years'. He is similarly described at 23:1–2, but it is now 'a long time afterwards' (23:1). How much older can he be? Perhaps chapters 13—22 are a secondary insertion, which broke the earlier connection between 13:1 and Joshua's farewell in chapter 23, the words 'a long time afterwards' (23:1) being the editor's attempt to smooth over the hiatus by explaining that Joshua was now even older than at 13:1.
- Chapter 24 has the appearance of a second 'farewell speech' by Joshua, and seems redundant after chapter 23. It may have been added to the book at the same time as 8:30–35 (which may also be secondary to its present context, and is also located near Shechem).
- Most notably, the passages which speak of complete conquest and the utter destruction of the Canaanites (11:16–23; 21:43–45) seem to contradict other passages which speak of land still to be occupied (13:1; 18:2–3) and 'nations that remain' (23:4, 7). Compare also Judges 1,

which make clear that land remained to be occupied after Joshua's death.

On the basis of these and other observations, Curtis envisages the following stages in the formation of Joshua (pp. 30–5):

1 Joshua 2—11 assumed something like their present shape relatively early on, perhaps as early as the tenth century, though it is difficult to date this stage precisely, and also hard to say how much the underlying traditions may have been modified as they were collected together.
2 The conquest account of Joshua 2—11 (or something closely resembling it) was taken up into a Deuteronomistic History (see Ch. 7). At this stage parts of the book clearly reminiscent of the language and theology of Deuteronomy were added: Joshua 1; 12; 21:43—22:6; 23.
3 In fact, there is more than one layer of Deuteronomistic editing. Chapter 24, though it seems to have originated separately from chapter 23, reflects Deuteronomic influence (e.g. vv. 11, 13, 16, 20; cf. Nelson 1997, p. 266, n. 8). Curtis notes the suggestion of Smend, who attributes to a second Deuteronomistic hand passages such as 1:7–9a (the importance of keeping the law), 13:1b–6 (the land the Israelites have yet to occupy) and parts of chapter 23 which dwell on these themes: 'To a version of the history which stressed that the whole land had been conquered a second Deuteronomistic editor has added an element of conditionality, stressing that continued success is dependent on obedience to the law' (p. 35).

Campbell and O'Brien's account of the literary history of Joshua (summarized on pp. 104–6) differs from Curtis's mainly in that they describe the later stages of editing more precisely. They, too, see Joshua 2—11 as the nucleus of the book, which then underwent the following modifications:

1 a first stage of Deuteronomistic editing (seventh century), which added an introduction (1:1–6) and a conclusion (21:43–45); this edition of the book emphasized the idea of total conquest;
2 an exilic (sixth-century) Deuteronomistic revision, which added material emphasizing law-keeping and warning against unfaithfulness (1:7–9; 23:1–16);
3 the insertion of chapters 14—21 (allocations to Cisjordanian tribes; cities of refuge; Levitical cities);
4 the addition of 13:1, 7, followed by 13:2–6 and material relating to the Transjordanian tribes (1:12–18; 22:1–6; 13:8–33; ch. 22). Chapter 24 is also one of the later additions to the book. Campbell and O'Brien stress the uncertainties in reconstructing these stages (pp. 138–9).

Much more has been written on this topic (e.g. concerning the earliest, 'pre-nucleus' stages of the book), and other theories of the formation of Joshua have been proposed. The scholars we have reviewed agree in dating key stages in the formation of Joshua centuries after the purported date of the events narrated. They also agree that Joshua is an obviously composite text, the different stages in the formation of Joshua having left clear traces in the finished book. This entire approach challenges the kind of unitary reading we attempted in the first part of this chapter, and illustrates the point made in Chapter 1 that narrative-critical and source-critical approaches interpret the same textual phenomena differently, because of their different initial assumptions.

A full discussion of this topic would entail setting out these and other scholars' arguments in more detail than is possible here. In response to the source-critical arguments cited above, however, we note the following points.

Campbell and O'Brien argue that Joshua 1 contains material belonging to three different redactional layers (vv. 1–6, 7–9, 12–18). But the themes of these three sections are not contradictory. Joshua 1 hangs together well and, taken by itself, does not obviously require to be divided between three different editorial hands.

What about the view that Joshua 23 and 24 are two mutually exclusive farewell speeches? Chapter 23 does read like a farewell speech, but chapter 24 describes a covenant ceremony, in which Joshua urges the people to recommit themselves to YHWH. Arguably, it forms a logical sequel to chapter 23. Note that in chapter 23 only Israel's leaders, representing all Israel, are addressed: 'all Israel' in verse 2 is immediately glossed as 'their elders and heads . . .' (cf. 2 Sam. 5:1, 3). In chapter 24, by contrast, Joshua addresses all the people ('all the tribes of Israel', v. 1; 'all the people', vv. 2, 27). These are two separate but linked events. It seems unnecessary to assign the two chapters to different hands.

Is there a conflict between 13:1 and 23:1? Perhaps not: a man who dies at 110 may surely be described 'old and advanced in years' for, say, the last twenty years of his life! That would allow enough time for the events of chapters 13—22 (discounting those passages which anticipate developments after Joshua's death).

Last, does Joshua contain contradictory views of the Israelite conquest, with some sections describing a complete conquest under Joshua and other sections describing only a partial conquest? Arguably not (Provan, Long and Longman, pp. 152–6, 166–8; Kitchen 2003, pp. 160–3, 173–4). Phrases such as 'a very great slaughter . . . until they were wiped out' (10:20) or 'a great army, in number like the sand on the seashore' (11:4) look like hyperbole typical of ancient Near Eastern battle accounts. Indeed, in one case the immediate context indicates that this language is not literally intended: 10:20, having spoken of Israel's enemies being 'wiped out', immediately goes on to speak of 'survivors' who were able to flee to fortified towns.

Further, the victories in Joshua 6—12 are not followed by occupation. Rather, the Israelites remain based at Gilgal throughout these chapters (5:10; 9:6; 10:9, 15, 43). Thus at 10:40 it is said that 'Joshua defeated the whole land, the hill country and the Negeb and the lowland and the slopes', a large tract of southern Canaan; but at 10:43 the Israelites return to Gilgal. Nowhere in chapters 10—12 is it said that the Israelites occupied the cities whose populations they annihilated (10:28–39; 11:14 – more hyperbole?). Phrases such as 'defeated the whole land' (10:40) and 'took all that land' apparently imply only the defeat of armies drawn from the regions in question. At 14:6, after the fighting is all over, the Israelites are still based at Gilgal. Thus chapters 13—19 do not allocate land already captured: they map out territory which the Israelites have yet to occupy. This point emerges at 18:1–3, where the land is 'subdued' (v. 1), but the Israelites have still to 'take possession' of it (v. 3).

In line with this, Joshua 21:43–45, which speaks of the fulfilment of *all* YHWH's promises, of Israel defeating *all* their enemies, occupying and settling in *all* the land, must be read in the light of chapter 23. Chapter 23 matches the hyperbole of 21:43–45, speaking of what YHWH 'has done to *all* these nations' (v. 3), such that *'no one* has been able to withstand you' (v. 9), and that *not one* of YHWH's promises has failed (vv. 14–15). But it also refers to 'nations that remain' (vv. 4–5), surviving Canaanites with whom the Israelites must not come to terms (vv. 11–13).

All this suggests that we should understand the 'total conquest' passages as encompassing both reality and potential (cf. Hess 1996, pp. 284–6): they describe what the Israelites can expect to accomplish after Joshua's death as well as what they have actually achieved by the time he dies. A decisive blow has been struck: there really is no reason why the Israelites should not go on to occupy the entire land, with YHWH's help. And so, even though it seems that YHWH is being praised for things he has not as yet done, the hyperbolic language is not empty: YHWH has done enough; the land is as good as occupied. But – the note on which chapter 23 closes – successful occupation depends on the people's continuing faithfulness.

According to Joshua, what territory did the Israelites occupy during Joshua's lifetime? They established themselves in the Gilgal–Jericho–Ai area, this being the base for their campaigns in chapters 9—12. Later (Kitchen 2003, pp. 162–3) they expanded northwards and southwards, perhaps as far north as Shechem (ch. 24), as Ephraim and Manasseh started to take possession of their allocation (17:14–18): hence Shiloh becomes the location of the Israelite camp in chapters 18—22. But, bearing in mind that some passages in chapters 13—21 anticipate developments after Joshua's death (14:6–15; 15:13–19; 15:63; 16:10; 17:11–13) it seems that the area occupied during Joshua's lifetime was relatively small. The argument that Joshua reflects two incompatible views of the Israelite conquest may not be well founded.

In general, then, a good case can be made out for literary unity. When might Joshua have reached its present form? We take up this question in Chapter 7, when we consider the issue of Deuteronomistic editing. To anticipate the conclusion there, Joshua, along with Judges, Samuel and Kings, may have undergone literary reshaping in the seventh and/or sixth centuries; but in the case of Joshua this may have involved only minor changes. We do not have to date major stages in the book's formation to the seventh or sixth centuries.

HISTORICAL ISSUES
Historical context
Canaan was under Egyptian control from the middle of the fifteenth century to around 1160. The Amarna letters, dating from the middle of the fourteenth century and including much correspondence between the rulers of Canaanite city-states and Egypt, may suggest a certain slackening of control around that time. But control was re-established in the thirteenth century and only ended in the middle of the twelfth century, partly (no doubt) due to the Philistines' having established themselves in southern Canaan, but also as one aspect of the collapse of Bronze Age civilization

around this time. Egyptian control was always stronger in the coastal plains of Canaan than in the hill country west of the Jordan. This is the general context in which we must attempt to locate Joshua historically.

The book of Joshua: largely fiction?

The majority of scholars today do not accept the account in Joshua of how Israel established themselves in Canaan (see the surveys in Younger 1999 and Dever, pp. 37–74). It is widely held that this account finds little support in the archaeological data: there is no evidence of destruction at some of the key sites in the account (Jericho, Ai), or of habitation at others (e.g. Gibeon and other Gibeonite cities mentioned at 9:17). An earlier view, according to which the biblical account was held to be partly supported by the presence of destruction layers at sites such as Lachish, Bethel and Megiddo (the 'Conquest Model' associated with W.F. Albright), has come to seem less convincing than it once did: some of the destruction layers previously attributed to the Israelites may have been due to other causes (Egyptians? Philistines?); and in any case the cities seem to have been destroyed at different times, some in the thirteenth century, some in the twelfth.

Facts like these have led many to conclude that the picture in Joshua of invading Israelites winning a series of sweeping victories is largely a fiction. Thus Finkelstein and Silberman (pp. 92–6), basing their approach on the view that Joshua underwent substantial Deuteronomistic editing in the reign of Josiah, link the book to the political realities of the period after the collapse of Assyrian power in the seventh century: it is a thinly veiled programme for Judah's occupation of the territories of the former kingdom of Israel under Josiah, and Joshua himself is simply Josiah in disguise.

How, then, to account for Israel's emergence in Canaan? Finkelstein and Silberman (pp. 72–122) believe that Israel's origins should be sought inside, not outside, Canaan. A key point in their reconstruction is the emergence around 1200 (beginning of Iron I) of about 250 villages, all of them new foundations, in the central highlands of Canaan (an area running from the Judean hills in the south to the hills of Samaria in the north). Many of these sites, whose character only became clear as a result of surveys conducted since 1967, were continuously occupied into the period of the monarchy. On these grounds it is reasonable to call them 'Israelite', though we may question whether the inhabitants of these villages should be viewed as an ethnic group distinct from the Canaanites (Dever, pp. 191–221, surveys the debate on this topic). These foundations were mainly small villages, and their inhabitants appear to have formed an egalitarian society: no large houses or palaces have been discovered, nor, interestingly, any shrines like those found in the Canaanite cities of the plains to the west.

The inhabitants of these new villages, Finkelstein and Silberman argue, had been pastoral nomads living in Canaan, but they now created permanent settlements, likely enough because of the collapse of the Canaanite city-states at the end of the Late Bronze age. Pastoral nomads typically maintain a symbiotic relationship with

THE AMARNA LETTERS

The Amarna letters were discovered at Tel el-Amarna, ancient Akhetaten, a site on the Nile about 180 miles south of Cairo where the Egyptian royal capital was located for a brief period in the mid-fourteenth century (from roughly 1346 to 1330). The letters formed part of a royal archive. They are clay tablets, written in cuneiform script, the majority of them using a form of Akkadian (an international language at the time). Most of the tablets, over 330 in number, were discovered in 1888–9, and fragments of another 40 or so were unearthed at the site in the next 50 years. The most recent edition of the letters (Moran) gives translations of 380 tablets.

All but 32 of the tablets were letters, mainly addressed to the Pharaoh. They date from roughly 1360 to 1330, the earlier letters evidently having been brought to Akhetaten from the previous royal capital, Thebes. The letters consist of 44 letters between Egypt and the major powers of the day (e.g. Babylon, Assyria, Mitanni, the Hittite kingdom) and a much larger corpus of correspondence (over 300 letters) between Egypt and Egypt's vassals (local client-kings) in Canaan and northern Syria. This corpus includes letters from Hazor, Shechem, Gezer, Lachish, Jerusalem and Megiddo. These vassal letters give an interesting picture of relationships between the various Canaanite city-states in the mid-fourteenth century, and of the nature of Egypt's control over Canaan.

One feature of life in Canaan at this period was the presence of various groups referred to as 'apiru. The term is widely attested in the ancient Near East in the second millennium, and usually refers to groups of people displaced in social upheavals, who had to fend for themselves, sometimes in ways that caused them to be viewed as outlaws. In the Amarna letters groups of 'apiru are described as interacting in various ways with the city-states of Canaan and Syria, either acting independently in their own interests, or turning conflicts between local rulers to their own advantage by siding with one or other of them. Individual 'apiru are said to have functioned as mercenaries in the service of Canaanite rulers. The term is often used to describe groups or individuals who (in the writer's opinion) are acting against Egyptian interests. The contrast in the Amarna letters between city-states (mainly in the plain) and nomadic groups who stood in various relations to Canaanite urban society plays a role in some scholars' reconstruction of Israel's emergence in Canaan.

The question has been raised whether some of the references to 'apiru in the Amarna letters might have in view groups of Israelites. Clearly this is not an option for those who date the conquest to the thirteenth century (the view advocated in this book), but those who favour a fifteenth-century dating may find support for their position in some of the references to 'apiru in the Amarna letters. This view does not depend on there being an etymological link between 'apiru and 'Hebrew' ('ibri), the term occasionally used of the Israelites in the Old Testament (e.g. 1 Sam. 14:11). For a cautious statement along these lines, see Provan, Long and Longman, pp. 170–2.

See further: Na'aman, ABD I; Lemche, ABD III.

settled (urban) populations, on whom they depend for products such as grain which are only available to settled populations. When the Canaanite cities collapsed, these Canaanite nomadic groups could no longer obtain these products by trade, and so had to settle down in order to provide them for themselves.

Can we say more about these people? One significant fact is that among the animal remains discovered at these villages (many of which have, however, still to be properly excavated) no pig bones have been discovered, though they have been found at Philistine, Moabite and Ammonite settlements of the same period. This further supports the designation of the inhabitants as 'Israelite' (cf. Lev. 11:2–7).

Israel's origins, then, are to be found in these highland villages. Joshua may preserve some traditions from the early history of these villagers: for example, they may have caused the destruction of Hazor (cf. Josh. 11:10–13; Judg. 4), where archaeology has discovered evidence of a massive fire in the late thirteenth century. But in general, these authors argue, Joshua is not a reliable guide to Israel's emergence in Canaan.

Stager, like Finkelstein and Silberman, sees the Iron I highland villages as the key for reconstructing Israel's origins. These sites suggest a society in which the 'father's house' (an extended family living in a number of linked dwellings) was the main unit (pp. 100–1). Stager, however, notes the sudden rise in the highland population in Iron I compared to the Late Bronze period, from an estimated 12,000 to about 40,000. He thinks it unlikely that this growth can be attributed to sheep- and goat-pastoralists settling down: 'in symbiotic relations the pastoral component rarely exceeds 10 to 15 percent of the total population' (p. 103). That is, if Finkelstein and Silberman were correct, the population in Iron I would have risen to something like 14,000, not 40,000.

Dever agrees with this criticism, and argues that the bulk of the population of the Iron I villages, whom he terms 'proto-Israelite', were peasants from the Canaanite city-states of the plain. He cites the Amarna letters as evidence that already in the fourteenth

---

Digging deeper:
THE MERNEPTAH STELE

An important piece of evidence in identifying the inhabitants of the Iron I villages is the reference to 'Israel' in the Merneptah Stele (*COS* II, p. 41). This inscription mainly describes a campaign by Pharaoh Merneptah against the Libyans, dated 1209. But it ends with a brief description of a campaign in Canaan which mentions the city-states of Ashkelon, Gezer and Yenoam and includes the words, 'Israel is wasted; its seed is not.'

For discussions of this inscription, see Hoffmeier 1997, pp. 27–31, 44–6; Dever, pp. 201–6. Hjelm and Thompson stress the poetic nature of the inscription, and suggest alternative identifications for 'Israel'. Kitchen's response (2004) sets the inscription in the context of other Egyptian New Kingdom campaign reports, and rejects the alternative identifications suggested by Hjelm and Thompson.

'Israel' as described in this inscription is an entity at least on a par with the city-states Ashkelon, Gezer and Yanoam, but the term has the 'people' determinative, indicating that it is a rural or tribal entity, not a state with a city as its centre. (In Egyptian hieroglyphic script, 'determinatives' are signs indicating the category to which a particular entity belongs.) If Merneptah's campaign as described in this inscription is mapped out, the most likely location for the 'Israel' referred to here is in the central hill country. In other words, the 'Israel' described in this inscription is similar in nature and extent to Israel as described at the end of Joshua or in the Song of Deborah (Judg. 5).

Note the boastful rhetoric of the inscription: so far from being without 'seed', Israel was to continue in the land for many centuries! Neither Joshua nor Judges mentions a clash with Egyptians.

century Canaanite society was close to collapse, and argues that these tendencies came to a head in the thirteenth century, causing many to withdraw from a system they saw as oppressive (pp. 170–9). They were probably joined by others: *'apiru* (compare the Amarna letters); local pastoral nomads; maybe even 'an "Exodus group" that had been in Egypt among Asiatic slaves in the Delta' (pp. 181–2). These people came to view themselves as related tribes, owing allegiance to one god. This was a religious expression of a kind of 'social contract', particularly tied up with land ownership rights (pp. 182–9). In effect the move to the Iron I villages was an 'agrarian land reform' (p. 187).

These Iron I villages, Dever argues, are Canaanite in origin. The pottery techniques and styles of Iron I villages show continuity with Late Bronze Canaanite styles (pp. 118–25). Indeed, the villagers must have had some idea what to expect in their new but agriculturally marginal land, and how to adapt their farming techniques to it (as they did, by terracing the hilly land and by building lined cisterns and grain silos). Otherwise it is hard to see how they could have survived and flourished there (pp. 113–17, 176–9).

Why, if Israel's ancestors were Canaanite, are books like Joshua and Judges so negative about the Canaanites? The anti-Canaanite polemic originated as an inner-Canaanite social critique. It really reflects a rejection of Canaanite 'agrarian monarchy and its concomitants . . . it is particularly a protest against a corrupt landed aristocracy that disenfranchised the peasant class. This is evident in early stories of the killing of Canaanite kings . . .' (p. 186).

What does Joshua actually claim?

Part of the impetus for non-biblical models for Israel's emergence such as the above comes from a perception that Joshua gives two contradictory pictures (total conquest vs partial conquest), and from the belief that Joshua was composed centuries after the events it claims to describe. Both of these views we have questioned. But further: what picture of Israel's entry into Canaan does Joshua give? We suggested above that it depicts a series of victories over the peoples of Canaan followed by the occupation of a rather limited area in the highlands west of the Jordan. This (along with the further occupations described in Judges 1) would fit quite well with the emergence of the Iron I villages in this area. Further, the only three sites actually described as being destroyed are Jericho, Ai and Hazor (6:24; 8:28; 11:13, this text explicitly stating that Hazor was the only city destroyed in the north). The 'Conquest model' that sought confirmation of Joshua in destruction levels all over Canaan was to this extent misguided.

Dever and Stager have produced substantial arguments against the view that the inhabitants of the Iron I villages had been Canaanite pastoral nomads. But Dever's suggestion that they were Canaanite peasants who abandoned former overlords is not convincing as a reading of the biblical text. The anti-Canaanite rhetoric of the biblical books simply does not fit with this view. It is not just the kings, but *all* Canaanites who are the enemy in Joshua and elsewhere. If the Israelites really originated in the Canaanite cities of the plain, this fact has left not a trace in the biblical text.

Similarly, Dever's claim that the inhabitants of the Iron I villages cannot have come from

THE CAPTURE OF JERICHO AND AI: HISTORICAL EVENTS?

Assuming a thirteenth-century conquest (see the next panel), the archaeology of Hazor fits with the biblical account. Jericho and Ai are, however, more problematic.

Joshua 2—8 portray Jericho and Ai as towns occupied by men, women and children (also animals), and each ruled by a king (2:2–3; 8:2, 29). Archaeological excavations, however, suggest that both sites were unoccupied between 1500 and 1200. Jericho's substantial mud-brick city walls were destroyed around 1550, but there is only scanty evidence of occupation after that date. Ai has yielded remains of a heavily fortified city from the Early Bronze period, but this city appears to have been destroyed around 2200, and there is no evidence of any substantial occupation until after 1200.

Responses to these facts fall into two main categories.

The events described in Joshua 6–8 never happened (e.g. Dever, pp. 41–50, Finkelstein and Silbermann, pp. 81–2). The biblical account is contradicted by the archaeological data, and cannot be taken at face value.

The archaeological data can be differently interpreted (e.g. Hess 1996, pp. 137–8, 157–9; Howard, pp. 177–80). A number of suggestions have been made along these lines:

- *Jericho*: Wood suggests that the ruins at Jericho usually dated to the Middle Bronze period should be re-dated to the Late Bronze period. This would produce a close fit between archaeological data

and Joshua 6. Wood's suggestion has been disputed (Bienkowski), and requires dating the Israelite conquest to the fifteenth century. An alternative approach (Hess 1996), compatible with a thirteenth-century dating, notes that later levels at Jericho, including those dated to the Late Bronze and Iron I periods, seem to have suffered erosion. Joshua nowhere describes Jericho as a large city (contrast Gibeon, 10:2 and Hazor, 11:10), and the fact that it had a 'king' means nothing, as that could simply denote 'local leader' (cf. Josh. 12:9–24); so perhaps we should not expect extensive remains from a Late Bronze period Jericho.

- *Ai*: Maybe the site of biblical Ai has not been correctly identified. Perhaps the identification is correct but, because of incomplete excavation, the finds which would validate the biblical account have yet to emerge. Such uncertainties make it difficult to draw firm conclusions (Provan, Long and Longman pp. 176–8). Alternatively, Ai may have lain unoccupied for many centuries, but had recently been reoccupied by citizens of Bethel (cf. 8:17) who turned the site into an outpost of their own city, a 'makeshift defence' against the Israelites largely based on the Early Bronze fortifications (Hess 1996, pp. 158–9 and further references there). The name Ai is somewhat unusual: the Hebrew is *ha'ai*, 'The Ruin', which may imply that by the time the Israelites arrived in Canaan the site was still named after these abandoned fortifications, which remained its most notable feature. If this suggestion is correct, the Ai of Joshua 7—8 was more than a fort, for it had a local leader ('king') and contained men, women and livestock (vv. 25–27). But essentially it was a recent (re-) foundation, and substantial Late Bronze remains are not to be expected.

outside Canaan because in that case they would have been totally unprepared to adapt to their new environment seems rather weak. How long does such adaptation take? Terracing and lined cisterns are attested from earlier periods in Canaan, so even people who arrived in the land from

outside would have had examples of the appropriate technology to follow (and every incentive to adapt quickly). The point about the continuity between Late Bronze and Iron I pottery styles is also not decisive: why should a group of outsiders not have adopted the local pottery repertoire when they settled in the land?

In the end, the view that the Israelites came from outside Canaan, defeated many Canaanite kings and during Joshua's lifetime occupied a small amount of territory, which they then expanded in later generations, may give the most convincing reading of the biblical and the archaeological evidence.

Digging deeper:
A FIFTEENTH-CENTURY OR A THIRTEENTH-CENTURY CONQUEST?

Scholars who accept that Israel entered Canaan broadly as described in Joshua are divided into those who date this event 'early' (late fifteenth century) and those who date it 'late' (late thirteenth century).

The early date is supported by 1 Kings 6:1, which places the fourth year of Solomon's reign 480 years after the exodus. This would give a date of about 1446 for the exodus and about 1406 for the conquest. The chronological note at Judges 11:26 also seems to support the early date. It follows from such a dating that the period of the judges extends from the late fourteenth century till about 1040, when Saul became king.

The difficulty with this view is that Canaan was under Egyptian control during the fourteenth and thirteenth centuries, and yet there is no reference to Egyptian power in either Joshua or Judges. Conversely, the earliest Egyptian reference to Israel in Canaan is the Merneptah Stele, dating from the late thirteenth century: this in spite of the fact that the Egyptians campaigned in Syria and Canaan on a number of occasions in the thirteenth century. Further, the Amarna letters, which on this dating would come from the earlier part of the judges period, and which include letters from Hazor, Shechem, Gezer, Lachish, Jerusalem and Megiddo, contain no clear reference to any event described in Judges. The presupposition of all these letters is that Canaan is still under Egyptian control: hence the pharaoh is kept in touch with developments in Canaan, and may be appealed to for help. The Amarna letters cover a period of at most 30 years (c. 1360–1330), and are far from providing a complete record of events in Canaan. Indeed, all the above arguments are arguments from silence: nonetheless, they seem cumulatively quite powerful.

Dating the conquest to the late thirteenth century, when Egyptian control of the hill country seems to have been weaker, removes these difficulties. Further, the only clear archaeological evidence for the presence of Israelites in Canaan, the Iron I villages, dates from the twelfth, not the fourteenth, century. Hazor was also destroyed in the late thirteenth century (*NEAHL* II, pp. 594–606), which would fit with what is described in Joshua 11:13. There are also considerations relating to the date of the exodus (Kitchen, *ABD* II). A thirteenth-century date does mean, however, that the figures at Judges 11:26 and 1 Kings 6 cannot be taken at face value. For the chronology of the Judges period, see Ch. 4, 'Historical issues'.

For further arguments in favour of a thirteenth-century dating, see Hess 1996, pp. 139–43. For arguments in favour of a fifteenth-century dating, see Chavalas and Adamthwaite, pp. 78–90; Howard, pp. 31–5.

WAR AND KILLING

According to Joshua, YHWH showed his faithfulness by helping the Israelites defeat the Canaanites and possess the land he had promised their ancestors; indeed, YHWH fought for Israel against the Canaanites. Many of the inhabitants of Canaan were killed, including non-combatants (the elderly, women and children), and this took place in accordance with YHWH's will. These claims are made quite openly and without embarrassment, and it may be that some readers of this book are able to accept them without difficulty, perhaps out of a conviction such as that if God commands something, then what was commanded must have been right, whether or not we can understand the reasons (cf. Calvin's view, cited in the panel 'Responses to the *kherem*'). Many other readers, however, will find these claims deeply problematic.

Modern wars have involved extensive civilian deaths, but the systematic killing of non-combatants is treated as a war crime. The *kherem* in Joshua 1—12 seems little different from what we now term 'genocide' or 'ethnic cleansing'. The image of a leader telling his people that it is God's will that they kill other peoples and occupy their land also seems alarming, as does the explanation that this killing is God's judgment on these peoples' wickedness (a point made most clearly in Deuteronomy, but apparently presupposed in passages such as Joshua 23:11–13 in which the surviving Canaanites represent a source of religious and moral contamination).

But Joshua merely expresses with particular clarity and bluntness ideas found elsewhere in the Histories and, indeed, throughout the Bible: wars, including wars that involve the killing of civilians or captives, continue to figure in Israel's history, as does the view, found particularly in the Prophets, that war can be an instrument of YHWH's justice. The roots of Joshua 1—12 spread deep and wide throughout the Bible; though we must balance this by noting that in the Bible as a whole war and destruction are not seen as the ultimate truth about God – rather, God is the source of life and order (Jenson, pp. 15–16).

JOSHUA IN THE CANON

Joshua continues the plot-line of the Pentateuch. There are strong links with Deuteronomy, both in theme and language. There are also clear links with Exodus and Numbers.

The events of Joshua are themselves referred to in a number of psalms (Pss 44:1–3; 78:54–55; 80:8–11; 105:43–45; 106:34–38; 114:1–8; 135:10–12; 136:17–22) and in some prophetic texts (Amos 2:9–10; Mic. 6:1–5; Jer. 2:6–7; 32:20–23; Ezek. 20:5–6). They lie behind prophetic texts which speak of Israel's return to the land after exile (Jer. 31:1–6; 33:6–13; Ezek. 47—48).

In the New Testament, finally, the theme of inheritance is reflected in Jesus' saying that 'the meek shall take possession of the land' (as the Greek of Matthew 5:5, which echoes the Septuagint of Joshua 1:15 and 18:3, can be translated) – a non-militaristic vision of the kingdom of God. The theme of warfare (again modified) is picked up in 2 Corinthians 10:3–6, Ephesians 6:10–18 and Revelation 19:11–21.

Certainly contemporary Christian applications of Joshua need to reckon with the radical transformation in the New Testament of key concepts in Joshua (e.g. land, the people of God). Major strands in

Think about
RESPONSES TO THE *KHEREM*

Consider the following views on this topic, ancient and modern:

- 'The wages of sin is death' (Paul, Rom. 6:23): the fate of the Canaanites in Joshua is in one sense no different from the fate of all human beings who resist the Creator's will.
- These narratives are to be understood in a spiritual sense: they tell us that we are to war against sin in our own lives (Origen, cited by Cadoux, pp. 165–6).
- If God commands the killing of Canaanites, then it must be right even if it seems otherwise (Calvin, cited by Wright, pp. 417–18).
- The Canaanites were offered a choice: 'Like Rahab, others could presumably have escaped the threatened destruction. They needed only to believe and to confess the power of Israel's God' (Hess 1996, p. 96).
- It was a 'tragic necessity', but a 'realistic solution to the problem of idolatry' (Jensen, pp. 14–15).
- It never actually happened: 'however, Joshua becomes somewhat more palatable if the reader understands that its relationship to actual history is not direct. Joshua is describing an idealistic and theoretical picture of Israel's origin in Canaan, not factual history' (Nelson 1998, p. 81).
- Other ancient Near Eastern nations practised the *kherem* (Hess 1996, pp. 42–3, citing second- and first-millennium parallels).
- 'Wickedness, however serious, does not constitute a justification for genocide' (Barr, p. 217, partly responding to attempts to justify the killings on the basis of gross Canaanite wickedness).
- 'Perhaps discomfort with the conquest narratives reveals that faith is, for us, no longer a matter of life and death' (Holloway, p. 65).

Which view do you find most sympathetic? Which do you find most plausible as a reading of Joshua? In your view, could God ever command the kind of things he is said to command in Joshua?

the teaching of Christ and his apostles suggest that physical warfare on behalf of God's kingdom belongs to a past era.

FURTHER READING

COMMENTARIES

T.C. Butler, *Joshua*. Waco: Word, 1983.

L.D. Hawk, *Every Promise Fulfilled. Contesting Plots in Joshua*. Louisville: Westminster John Knox, 1991.

R.S. Hess, *Joshua*. Leicester: IVP, 1996.

D.M. Howard, *Joshua*. Nashville: Broadman and Holman, 1998.

J.G. McConville, 'Joshua', *OBC*, pp. 158–76.

R.D. Nelson, *Joshua*. Louisville: Westminster John Knox, 1997.

OTHER BOOKS AND ARTICLES
W.F. Albright, 'The Israelite Conquest of Canaan in the Light of Archaeology', *Bulletin of the American Schools of Oriental Researach* 74 (1939), pp. 11–23.

J. Barr, *Biblical Faith and Natural Theology*. Oxford: Clarendon, 1993.

P. Bienkowski, 'Jericho was destroyed in the Middle Bronze Age, not the Late Bronze Age', *BAR* 16, 5 (1990), pp. 45–69.

E. Bloch-Smith, 'Israelite Ethnicity in Iron I: Archaeology Preserves What is Remembered and What is Forgotten in Israel's History', *JBL* 122 (2003), pp. 401–25.

C.J. Cadoux, *The Early Christian Attitude to War*. New York: Seabury, 1982 (reprint).

A.F. Campbell and M.A. O'Brien, *Unfolding the Deuteronomistic History: Origins, Upgrades, Present Text*. Minneapolis: Augsburg Fortress, 2000, pp. 101–63.

M.W. Chavalas and M.R. Adamthwaite, 'Archaeological Light on the Old Testament' in D.W. Baker and W.T. Arnold (eds), *The Face of Old Testament Studies. A Survey of Contemporary Approaches*. Grand Rapids/ Leicester: Baker/Apollos, 1999, pp. 59–96.

R.E. Clements, 'Achan's Sin: Warfare and Holiness' in D. Penchansky and P.L. Redditt (eds), *Shall Not the Judge of the All the Earth Do What is Right? Studies on the Nature of God in Tribute to James L. Crenshaw*. Winona Lake: Eisenbrauns, 2000, pp. 113–26.

A.H.W. Curtis, *Joshua*. Sheffield: Sheffield Academic Press, 1994.

W.G. Dever, *Who Were the Early Israelites, and Where Did They Come From*? Grand Rapids: Eerdmans, 2003.

I. Finkelstein and N.A. Silberman, *The Bible Unearthed. Archaeology's New Vision of Ancient Israel and the Origin of its Sacred Texts*. New York: Touchstone, 2002.

R.S. Hess, 'Asking Historical Questions of Joshua 13–19: Recent Discussion Concerning the Date of the Boundary Lists' in A.R. Millard, J.K. Hoffmeier, D.W. Baker (eds), *Faith, Tradition and History. Old Testament Historiography in its Ancient Near Eastern Context*. Winona Lake: Eisenbrauns, 1994, pp. 191–205.

I. Hjelm and T.L. Thompson, 'The Victory Song of Merneptah, Israel and the People of Palestine', *JSOT* 27, 2 (2002), pp. 3–18.

J.K. Hoffmeier, *Israel in Egypt. The Evidence for the Authenticity of the Exodus Tradition*. New York/Oxford: Oxford University Press, 1997.

J.K. Hoffmeier, 'Understanding Hebrew and Egyptian Military Texts: A Contextual Approach', *COS* III (2002), pp. xxi–xxvii.

J. Holloway, 'The Ethical Dilemma of Holy War', *Southwestern Journal of Theology* 41 (1998), pp. 44–69.

P.P. Jenson, *The Problem of War in the Old Testament*, Grove Biblical Series 25. Cambridge: Grove Books, 2002.

Z. Kallai, *Biblical Historiography and Historical Geography*. Frankfurt: Lang, 1998.

J.S. Kaminsky, *Corporate Responsibility in the Hebrew Bible*. Sheffield: Sheffield Academic Press, 1995.

K.A. Kitchen, 'Exodus, the', *ABD* II, pp. 700–8.

K.A. Kitchen, *On the Reliability of the Old Testament*. Grand Rapids: Eerdmans, 2003, pp. 159–239.

K.A. Kitchen, 'The Victories of Merenptah, and the Nature of their Record', *JSOT* 28, 3 (2004), pp. 259–72.

N.P. Lemche, 'Habiru, Hapiru', *ABD* III, pp. 6–10.

A. Mazar, *Archaeology of the Land of the Bible, 10,000–586 B.C.E.* New York: Doubleday, 1990.

W.L. Moran, *The Amarna Letters*. Baltimore: Johns Hopkins University Press, 1992.

N. Na'aman, 'Amarna Letters', *ABD* I, pp. 174–81.

R.D. Nelson, *The Historical Books*. Nashville: Abingdon Press, 1998.

S. Niditch, *War in the Hebrew Bible. A Study in the Ethics of Violence*. New York: Oxford University Press, 1993.

I.W. Provan, V.P. Long, T. Longman, *A Biblical History of Israel*. Louisville: Westminster John Knox Press, 2003, pp. 138–92.

P.E. Satterthwaite and D.W. Baker, 'Nations of Canaan', *DOTP*, pp. 596–605.

L.E. Stager, 'Forging an Identity: The Emergence of Ancient Israel' in M.D. Coogan (ed.), *The Oxford History of the Biblical*

World. New York: Oxford University Press, 1998, pp. 90–131.

J. Van Seters, *In Search of History. Historiography in the Ancient World and the Origins of Biblical History*. New Haven: Yale University Press, 1983, pp. 322–37.

B.G. Wood, 'Did the Israelites Conquer Jericho? A New Look at the Archaeological Evidence', *BAR* 16, 2 (1990), pp. 44–58.

D.F. Wright, 'Accommodation and Barbarity in John Calvin's Old Testament Commentaries' in A.G. Auld (ed.),

Understanding Poets and Prophets. Essays in Honour of George Wishart Anderson. Sheffield: JSOT Press, 1993, pp. 413–27.

K.L. Younger, *Ancient Conquest Accounts. A Study in Ancient Near Eastern and Biblical History Writing*. Sheffield: JSOT Press, 1990.

K.L. Younger, 'Early Israel in Recent Biblical Scholarship', in D.W. Baker and W.T. Arnold (eds), *The Face of Old Testament Studies. A Survey of Contemporary Approaches*. Grand Rapids/Leicester: Baker/Apollos, 1999, pp. 176–206.

Chapter 4

JUDGES

INTRODUCTION

The book of Judges describes the history of Israel in the generations after Joshua's death. In general it is a much less positive book than Joshua, focusing on Israel's failures in this period. The largest part of Judges (3:7—16:31) describes the exploits of a series of leaders raised up by YHWH for Israel, termed 'judges', and said to have 'judged' Israel. (The Hebrew terms have a broader meaning than English 'judge', denoting military and political leadership as well as judicial functions.) Judges begins with an introduction relating the period of the judges to that of Joshua (1:1—3:6), and ends with two narratives which, though they come early in the period, are told with one eye on the later rise of the monarchy (17:1—21:25). Women play a greater role in Judges than in Joshua: whereas in Joshua women feature in only two narratives (Rahab, ch. 2; Achsah, 15:13–19), in Judges there are the narratives of Achsah (1:11–15), Deborah and Jael (chs 4—5), Jephthah's daughter (11:29–40), Samson's first wife (ch. 14), Delilah (ch. 16) and the Levite's concubine (ch. 19).

STRUCTURE OF JUDGES

1:1—3:6 Introduction to the judges period:
  Israelite attempts to occupy the land (1:1—2:5)
  Israelite apostasy in the generations after Joshua (2:6—3:6)

3:7—16:31 The judges of Israel:
  Othniel (3:7–11)
  Ehud (3:12–30)
  Shamgar (3:31)
  Deborah and Barak (4:1—5:31)
  Gideon and Abimelech (6:1—9:57)
  Tola (10:1–2)
  Jair (10:3–5)
  Jephthah (10:6—12:7)
  Ibzan (12:8–10)
  Elon (12:11–12)
  Abdon (12:13–15)
  Samson (13:1—16:31)

17:1—21:25 Narratives from early in the judges period:
  Micah and the Danites (17:1—18:31)
  The Levite's concubine; war against Benjamin (19:1—21:25)

Structuring devices in Judges include: the extensive introduction, especially the preview of the judges period in 2:6—3:6; the use of recurring 'frames' in the accounts of 3:7—16:31 (see pp. 79–82); the 'no king' formula in chapters 17—21. The second and third of the three passages in which YHWH confronts the Israelites (6:7–10; 10:10–16; the first being 2:1–5) also mark sub-divisions within 3:7—16:31.

Judges consists almost entirely of narratives, the exception being the Song of Deborah (ch. 5). There are no long programmatic speeches like those in Joshua 1:1–9 or Joshua 23—24. But the three 'confrontation' passages have a similar function, bringing out key ideas in the surrounding narratives. The same is true of the narrator's summary of the period in 2:6—3:6.

OUTLINE

1:1—3:6: INTRODUCTION TO THE JUDGES PERIOD

The transition between Joshua and Judges is as carefully structured as that between Deuteronomy and Joshua. The second part of Joshua and the beginning of Judges are linked by a network of allusions and cross-references. We noted how Joshua 13—24 are dominated by the theme of the land that the tribes have yet to occupy (Josh. 13:1; 18:2–3), and how at certain points these chapters even anticipated events from the period after Joshua's death (e.g. Josh. 15:13–19; cf. Judg. 1:11–15). The introduction to Judges in turn frequently refers back to Joshua 13—24. It falls into two sections, 1:1—2:5 and 2:6—3:6, each of which mentions Joshua's death, focuses our attention on the issue of the tribal inheritances (1:1–2; 2:6–9) and goes on to describe what happened in the years after Joshua's death. We are clearly meant to read this introduction in the light of the

hopes and warnings expressed in Joshua 13—24.

Israelite attempts to occupy the land (1:1—2:5)
Judges 1 takes up ideas from Joshua 13—19. It presupposes the tribal allocations of those chapters: the tribes all seem to know where their 'allotted territory' (1:3) lies. Joshua 13—19 at points anticipated the later failures of the tribes to drive out the Canaanites (compare Josh. 16:10 with Judg. 1:29, Josh. 17:11–13 with Judg. 1:27–28). Judges 1 takes up these earlier references and adds many more to create a picture of disappointed expectations in the generation after Joshua. In a similar way, the incident of Caleb and Achsah (1:11–15) is repeated from Joshua 15:13–19 in order to contrast the successes of an Israelite from an earlier generation with the failures of the generation after Joshua. This contrast was already hinted at in Joshua 13—19 (Ch. 3, Outline).

The first tribes mentioned in Judges 1 are in fact relatively successful: Judah and Simeon work together, making significant gains (1:1–20); the 'house of Joseph' (Ephraim and Manasseh) also enjoys some success (1:22–26). But as chapter 1 develops, the note of failure becomes increasingly clear. For Judah and Benjamin it is merely stated that they could not take territory (vv. 19, 21); for Manasseh, Ephraim and Zebulun the narrator notes that the Canaanites 'lived among them' (vv. 27, 29–30); this phrase is reversed in the case of Asher and Naphtali, who are said to have 'lived among the Canaanites', implying Canaanite dominance (vv. 32, 33); last, the Amorites do not even allow the Danites into their territory (v. 34). And so a narrative whose purpose has been to describe how Israelite tribes took possession of their allotted territories ends with a verse that describes the 'border of the Amorites' (v. 36).

Digging deeper:
JERICHO AND BETHEL

Compare and contrast the account of the capture of Bethel (1:22–26) with the account of the capture of Jericho in Joshua 2 and 6. Pay particular attention to the roles of Rahab in Joshua and the unnamed citizen of Bethel here.

How and why this happens is not explained at first: we read simply that tribe after tribe 'did not drive out' the inhabitants (vv. 19, 21, 27–33); that the reason for Judah's failure was that the inhabitants had iron chariots (v. 19; cf. Josh. 17:16–18); that other groups of Canaanites were 'determined' or 'prepared' (both translations possible) to live in their territories (vv. 27, 34); and that some tribes periodically subjected Canaanites to forced labour (vv. 28, 30, 33, 35). The narrative, though neutral in tone, becomes increasingly ominous in its implications. YHWH's role in the earlier victories is noted (1:2, 4, 7, 19, 22), but there are no references to YHWH after that. What is YHWH's attitude to all this?

This question is answered at 2:1–5, where YHWH denounces the Israelites: far from driving the Canaanites out, they have made covenants with them, and their covenant with YHWH is near breaking point. YHWH declares that he will no longer help them conquer Canaan (cf. Josh. 23:12–13). But perhaps these words are meant to bring the Israelites to repentance, and are not a final statement of intent. They respond by weeping and offering sacrifices, in a

bid to restore their relationship with YHWH. The episode ends inconclusively: will YHWH bring about what he has threatened?

Israelite apostasy in the generations after Joshua (2:6—3:6)

Judges 2:6—3:6, the second part of the introduction, echoes the language and themes of Joshua 23—24 (see panel 'Echoes of Joshua 23—24'). According to 2:6—3:6 the Israelites in the judges period were disobedient and did the very things Joshua had warned them against.

ECHOES OF JOSHUA 23—24		
	Joshua 23—24	**Judges 2:6—3:6**
Serve, worship	23:7, 16; 24:15–16, 18, 20	2:11, 13, 19; 3:6
Forsake or abandon	24:16, 20	2:12–13
Egypt	24:6, 7, 14, 17	2:12
Other gods	23:16; 24:16	2:12, 17, 19
Bow down	23:7, 16	2:12, 17, 19
YHWH's anger	23:16	2:14, 20
Transgress covenant	23:16	2:20

The echoes of Joshua are clearest in Judges 2:6–10, which is a deliberate reworking of Joshua 24:28–31. Whereas Joshua 24:28–31 was structured so as to emphasize Israel's faithfulness to YHWH during Joshua's lifetime, ending the book on a positive note, Judges 2:6–10 presents basically the same material in a different order, so as to lead into an account of how Israel in the generations after Joshua turned away from YHWH, because they 'did not know YHWH or the work that he had done for Israel' (2:10).

Think about
KNOWING YHWH

Look up the following texts from Deuteronomy–Kings, all of which speak of knowing or not knowing YHWH: Deuteronomy 7:9; 8:5; 9:3, 6; Joshua 2:9; 4:24; Judges 2:10; 14:4; 16:20; 17:13; 1 Samuel 3:7; 17:47; 1 Kings 8:60; 18:37; 20:13, 28; 2 Kings 19:19.

Reviewing these texts, what does the phrase 'know YHWH' mean? Are there clear themes which link these texts?

The consequences of Israel's turning away are predictable: YHWH in anger turns against them and they suffer military defeats (2:11–15). Less predictable is what follows: YHWH responds to Israel's distress by raising up 'judges' as deliverers (2:16–19). YHWH is with these 'judges' and uses them to rescue the people. However, the judges make no lasting impression. The people, apparently not truly obedient to YHWH even during each judge's lifetime (v. 17), turn away from YHWH again when the judge dies. YHWH is 'moved to pity' by their sufferings, and shows this by raising up of judges, but the people repeatedly respond with stubborn contempt.

A new stage is reached (2:20–22): Israel has broken the covenant, and so YHWH is no longer obligated to keep his side of the agreement. The question left hanging by 2:1–5 is answered: YHWH again declares that he will not drive out the nations left by Joshua, and this time his words are addressed, not to Israel as a summons to repentance, but to himself as a statement of fixed intent.

The narrative now recapitulates. In 2:22—3:4, a passage clearly related to Joshua 13:1–7, we are for the third time reminded of how things stood by the time of Joshua's death, with some nations remaining to be driven out of the territory allocated to Israel (cf. 1:1–2; 2:6–9). In Joshua 13 YHWH promised to drive out the inhabitants remaining in these territories, but this, it emerged in later chapters, especially Joshua 23, depended on how faithfully the Israelites would pursue the task of claiming their allotted territories.

In 2:22—3:4 we at last learn why YHWH allowed nations to remain: it was to test later generations of Israelites, so that they might have 'experience of war' and, like Joshua's generation, come to know YHWH's power as they obeyed him. Wenham comments: 'The idea that the Canaanites should serve as a sort of punch-bag to give the Israelites practice in fighting is novel, but that they should serve as a test for Israel's loyalty is not' (p. 58). The Israelites in the period after Joshua were to fight for their territory in obedience to YHWH's command, and success in battle would depend on their faithfulness in keeping YHWH's laws. This passage casts a retrospective light over all of Joshua 13—24 and Judges 1—2: *this* is what YHWH has been doing in allowing events to follow the course they have! Judges 2:22—3:4 is a good example of the narrative technique of delayed revelation.

The fact that in the judges period there was no Joshua-like leader (one designated by YHWH, with authority over all the tribes) was apparently part of the testing. At the end of Joshua no one is chosen to succeed Joshua in the way that Joshua was chosen to succeed Moses: Joshua simply exhorts the people, and sends them away to take possession of their allocations (Josh. 24:28; cf. Judg. 2:6). The narrator does not state why Joshua appointed no successor, but he implies an explanation by focusing on the task lying before the tribes after Joshua's death. This was the time for the individual tribes to show faith in YHWH as they occupied the land allocated to them, refusing to come to terms with the Canaanites. Perhaps the narrator sees the absence of a Joshua-like leader as Joshua's (or YHWH's) way of telling the tribes that success or failure now lay in their own hands.

How long the testing might have gone on is an interesting question but beside the point as far as Judges is concerned, for the Israelites fail the test. The whole passage thus contrasts YHWH's intentions for Israel in the period after Joshua with the disappointing reality of their behaviour. The relationship between YHWH and Israel seems shattered: Israel has compromised its calling and YHWH no longer drives out Israel's enemies. On this note the introduction ends. Before we even come to any of the individual accounts of the judges, we know that the period will be one of decline and failure.

3:7—16:31: THE JUDGES OF ISRAEL

The central section of Judges contains the accounts of Israel's judges. The overall shape of 3:7—16:31 is the same as in the summary

---

Digging deeper:
TWO INTRODUCTIONS TO JUDGES?

The two sections of the introduction, 1:1—2:5 and 2:6—3:6, are often seen as separate texts and assigned to different editorial layers. This does not seem necessary. The two sections taken together form a coherent preface, relating the judges period to the era of Joshua and highlighting the major tendencies of the period. It is true that both passages begin at the same point, Joshua's death, and partly cover the same ground. But the passages differ in scope, style, and final outcome:

- *Scope*: 1:1—2:5 deals with events immediately after Joshua's death; 2:6—3:6 summarizes the entire judges period.
- *Style*: 1:1—2:5 is detailed, and offers no evaluation until 2:1–5; 2:6—3:6 uses heavily evaluative language and deals mainly in generalizations (e.g. the statement that the people 'did not listen even to their judges' simplifies the more complicated picture of relations between people and judges in 3:7—16:31).

- *Outcome*: 1:1—2:5 concludes by holding open the possibility that Israel may repent and YHWH relent of his decision not to drive out the nations left by Joshua; 2:6—3:6 shuts the door on this possibility.

Why begin Judges this way, combining two different types of narrative into one introduction? The two narratives reinforce each other. The 'pseudo-objective' style of Judges 1 'shows' us the increasing compromises of the Israelites. By withholding evaluation it leads us to ask what is going on. The explicitly evaluative style of 2:6—3:6, which takes its cue from 2:1–5, the conclusion of the first part, 'tells' us what happened by explaining events in the judges period as the result of Israelite disobedience. The sheer length of the introduction fixes our gaze upon the transition from Joshua's generation to the judges period, a transition which the narrator clearly sees as crucial for the whole period. This focus on the generation after Joshua is also found in Judges 17–21.

---

in 2:6—3:6, but 3:7—16:31 paints a more detailed picture, charting a lengthy process of decline and fragmentation which 2:6—3:6 only hinted at. Similarly, where 2:6—3:6 spoke of all the judges in general terms, the accounts in 3:7—16:31 bring out their individuality much more clearly. See Table 1.

TABLE I THE JUDGES OF ISRAEL

Name	Reference	Judge's tribe	Nature of enemy threat	Area of Israel affected Tribes involved in battle
Othniel (major)	3:7–11	Judah	Cushan-Rishathaim of Aram Naharaim	(Not specified)
Ehud (major)	3:12–30	Benjamin	Eglon of Moab, aided by Ammonites and Amalekites. Jericho occupied	Area around Jericho and Gilgal (territory of Benjamin). Ephraim involved (and Benjamin?)
Shamgar (?)	3:31	Hurrian?	Philistines	(Not specified)
Deborah, Barak (major)	4:1—5:31	Naphtali	Jabin, Canaanite king reigning from Hazor. Iron chariots	Territory of Zebulun and Naphtali (at least) Ephraim, Benjamin, Manasseh, Issachar, Zebulun, Naphtali involved. Reuben, Dan and Asher reproached for non-participation
Gideon (major)	6:1—8:35	Manasseh	Incursions by Midianites, Amalekites and other eastern peoples. Destruction of crops, plunder of livestock 'all the way to Gaza' (6:4)	Territory of Issachar, Manasseh, Gilead. Manasseh, Asher, Zebulun, Naphtali and Ephraim involved
Abimelech (tyrant)	9:1–57	Manasseh	(Civil war)	Shechem and surrounding areas
Tola (minor)	10:1–2	Issachar	(Not specified)	(Not specified)
Jair (minor)	10:3–5	Manasseh (in Transjordan)	(None mentioned)	(—)
Jephthah (major)	10:6—12:7	Manasseh (in Transjordan)	Ammonites occupy Gilead and make incursions into Judah, Benjamin and Israel	Territory of Gilead, Manasseh and Ammon Manasseh
Ibzan (minor)	12:8–10	Zebulun (cf. Josh. 19:15)	(None mentioned)	(—)
Elon (minor)	12:11–12	Zebulun	(None mentioned)	(—)
Abdon (minor)	12:13–15	Ephraim	(None mentioned)	(—)
Samson (major)	13:1—16:31	Dan	Philistines 'rule over Israel' (14:4; 15:11)	Judah particularly affected (? 15:9ff) Samson fights single-handed

As a convenient shorthand, scholars often distinguish 'major' and 'minor' judges, as reflected in Table 1. 'Major' judges are those who are said to have fought battles and whose accounts are longer. The achievements of the 'minor' judges seem less significant, and their accounts are briefer.

The judges are presented in broadly chronological order. They begin with Othniel, a figure from the generation after Joshua, and end with Samson, whose opponents, the Philistines, still dominate the scene in 1 Samuel. There are other chronological links between the accounts: Shamgar 'comes after' Ehud (3:31) and is mentioned as a contemporary of Jael, hence of Deborah and Barak, at 5:6; the order Gideon–Abimelech–Tola–Jair is established by links between the accounts (8:29–32; 10:1, 3), as is the order Jephthah–Ibzan–Elon–Abdon (12:8, 11, 13). These links and the various numbers of years given in Judges are, however, far from establishing a clear chronology for the period (see p. 101, under 'Historical issues').

The 'major' judge accounts in this section are all structured around a similar narrative framework. The 'minor' accounts differ from the 'major' accounts, but themselves share a similar form.

Othniel (3:7–11)
Othniel son of Kenaz is linked to the tribe of Judah: he is a relative of Caleb, and has already shown something of Caleb's bold resourcefulness (1:9–15). He is raised up to defeat 'Cushan-Rishathaim king of Aram Naharim', whom Kitchen (pp. 211–12) well describes as 'the most exotic and distant' of Israel's enemies in this period. 'Cushan-Rishathaim' can be translated 'Cushan of

double wickedness', and is probably a pun on a name with a different meaning. Kitchen suggests that Cushan styled himself *resh 'athaim*, 'ruler of Athaim': he was an Aramean who established himself as a local leader in Aram Naharaim (= north-west Mesopotamia), and briefly exercised control over part of Israel. (For other proposals concerning Cushan-Rishathaim, see Younger, pp. 106–7.) The biblical account states neither which tribes were involved, nor where and how Othniel defeated him.

The account of Othniel has a more positive tone than the preview in 2:6—3:6. It takes up elements of that passage (particularly 2:11–19; see the panel 'Judges 2:11–19 and 3:7–11 compared'), but reshapes them into a crisp story of success. None of the later 'major' accounts are as short and simple as 3:7–11.

JUDGES 2:11–19 AND 3:7–11 COMPARED		
	Introduction (2:11–19)	Othniel (3:7–11)
Apostasy	2:11–13, 17, 19	3:7
Idolatry	2:11–13, 17, 19	3:7
YHWH's anger	2:14	3:8
Judgment (invasion)	2:14	3:8
Oppression	2:15	3:8
Raising up of judge	2:16	3:9
Deliverance	2:16, 18	3:10
Death of judge	2:19	3:11

Othniel becomes a paradigm of success, against whom subsequent judges are measured. This is clear from the way in which much of the wording of 3:7–11 recurs at key points in subsequent 'major' judge accounts, in either an identical or a varied form. The Othniel account has, as it were, been broken down into separate elements which are repeatedly used to form frames for these accounts.

This may explain why Othniel's account is so brief and stylized. We should not assume that the traditions available to the narrator were as skeletal as the present narrative. Just as likely, the narrator could have made the Othniel account more like that of Ehud or Deborah and Barak; but he chose to present it in an abbreviated, schematic form, whose brief phrases could be used as 'frame-elements' in later narratives.

These elements recur in subsequent accounts; see Table 2.

The pattern sin–judgment–crying out–deliverance in 3:7–11 recurs to some extent in all the 'major' accounts. But as we read through the accounts we note variations in the frame, especially in the later accounts (Gideon, Jephthah, Samson): some elements are expanded; others are missing. This is

part of the editorial shaping of Judges: variations in the frame of a particular account generally highlight important features in the account itself. We shall frequently refer to 'the frame' and 'frame-elements' in the following discussion of 3:12—16:31.

Some have seen a difference of viewpoint between the accounts and their frames: the frames appear to refer to Israel as a whole ('the Israelites did evil in the eyes of YHWH', 'the land had rest'); whereas the accounts portray the actions of the judges as more local, normally taking in a few tribes at most. It is often suggested that a Deuteronomistic editor has imposed an 'all-Israel' perspective on his traditions, presenting each of the accounts as though all the tribes had been affected, when this was not the case (e.g. Mayes 1985, pp. 19–20).

This may not be correct, however. The frames usually refer to 'Israelites', not 'all Israel' (a phrase used only at 8:27 and

---

JUDGES 3:7–11 REPRESENTED AS SEPARATE 'ELEMENTS'

A (Apostasy, v. 7)	The Israelites did what was evil in the sight of YHWH, forgetting YHWH their God,	**G** (Judge, v. 9)	YHWH raised up a deliverer for the Israelites, who delivered them, [judge Y].
B (Idolatry, v. 7)	and worshipping the Baals and the Asherahs.	**H** (Spirit, v. 10)	The spirit of YHWH came upon him,
C (YHWH's anger, v. 8)	Therefore the anger of YHWH was kindled against Israel,	**I** (Deliverance, v. 10)	and he judged Israel; he went out to war, and YHWH gave [oppressor X] into his hand;
D (Enemy, v. 8)	and he sold them into the hand of [oppressor X],	**J** (Dominance, v. 10)	and his hand prevailed over [oppressor X].
E (Oppression, v. 8)	and the Israelites served [oppressor X] for [number N1] years.	**K** (Peace, v. 11)	So the land had rest [number N2] years.
F (Cry out, v. 9)	But when the Israelites cried out to YHWH,	**L** (Death of judge, v. 11)	Then [judge Y] died.

TABLE 2   RECURRENCE OF ELEMENTS IN SUBSEQUENT ACCOUNTS

	Othniel	Ehud	Deborah and Barak	Gideon	Jephthah	Samson
A Apostasy	3:7	3:12	4:1	6:1	10:6	13:1
B Idolatry	3:7			[6:7–10]	10:6	
C Anger	3:8				10:7	
D Enemy	3:8	3:12	4:2	6:1	10:7	13:1
E Oppression (duration)	3:8 8 years	3:13–14 18 years	4:3* 20 years	6:2–6 7 years	10:8–9 18 years	13:1 40 years
F Cry out (response)	3:9	3:15	4:3*	6:6–10 rebuke	10:10–16 rebuke	
G Judge (how chosen)	3:9	3:15	4:6–10 prophecy	6:11–12 angel	11:4–6 elders	13:2–5 angel
H Spirit	3:10			6:34	11:29	13:25; 14:6, 19; 15:14
I Deliverance	3:10	3:27–29	4:14–16	7:22–25	11:32–33	16:30?*
J Dominance	3:10	3:30	4:23–24	8:28	11:33	
K Peace (duration)	3:11 40 years	3:30 80 years	5:31 40 years	8:28 40 years	[12:7] 6 years; no peace formula	[15:20; 16:31] 20 years; no peace formula
L Death	3:11	4:1*		8:32	12:7	16:30–31
(Other)			Song of Deborah	Abimelech		

When the same verse reference is used in connection with more than one 'frame-element', each frame-element takes up only part of that verse. An asterisk (*) after a verse reference means that the verse deviates from the standard pattern (3:7–11) in a way that cannot be captured on the table, e.g. by occurring out of sequence, or by introducing elements not found in 3:7–11. The grey shading indicates that Othniel's time of leadership is the one against which the other judges are assessed.

20:34), and need not have Israel as a whole in view. (See especially 8:33, which speaks of 'Israelites', whereas 9:4, describing the same group, indicates that the reference is to those Israelites based around Shechem.) It appears that Judges conceives of Israel as a political or covenantal unity, so that what happens to a part affects the whole. Hence the individual tribes are referred to as Israelites, not with the aim of implying that all Israel was directly involved in the events narrated, but to remind us that these tribes are part of a larger but fragmented whole. This fits with the portrayal of the judges period as one of increasing disunity.

In short, both the accounts and their frames tell the same story of decline. The frames in 3:7—16:31 are a good example of repetition and variation: they do not reflect a stereotyping mentality, but should be taken as inviting the reader to compare and contrast the separate judges accounts.

(For convenience' sake, the rest of the Outline will follow Judges' use of the terms 'Israel' and 'the Israelites', imprecise though this is in some respects.)

We can divide 3:12—16:31 into three main sections (the 'major' judges are shown in bold type):

- 3:12—5:31: **Ehud**, Shamgar, **Deborah and Barak**;
- 6:1—9:57: **Gideon** [Abimelech];
- 10:1—16:31: Tola, Jair, **Jephthah**, Ibzan, Elon, Abdon, **Samson**.

Ehud (3:12–30)

The left-handed Ehud achieves victory in a more devious manner than did Othniel, but his strategy (a single-handed attack with a concealed weapon) is bold and brilliantly successful. There is an element of farce (even toilet humour) about this account which suggests how easily victory is won: Eglon of Moab is a 'fat fool', and his pretensions are punctured as quickly as his belly. Large numbers of Moabites share Eglon's fate. It is not said which tribes responded to Ehud's call: the narrator focuses on Ehud's bold leadership. It appears that at least Benjamin (in whose territory Jericho lay) and Ephraim (where Ehud rallied support, 3:27) were involved.

Eglon is not mentioned outside Judges. The reality of a Moabite kingdom in the early twelfth century has been queried (Hackett, pp. 153–4). Archaeological finds from the Moabite cities of Dibon, Heshbon and Medeba (cf. Num. 21:25–34) are at present relatively scanty for this period, but an Egyptian inscription suggests that Dibon at least was settled as early as 1270. Evidence is lacking for an organized Moabite state in this period, but the leader of a largely pastoral, tribal society might well have designated himself as 'king', or have been so described by others (Kitchen, pp. 195–7).

It has been suggested that the literary artistry of the Ehud narrative, particularly its use of humour to satirize the Moabites, suggests that it has little historical basis. Brettler (pp. 37–8) argues that the account is largely a later fabrication designed to depict the Israelites as superior to their Moabite neighbours. But this does not necessarily follow. The point of depicting Eglon and the Moabites as blundering and obtuse is that this underscores the ease with which Ehud gains his victory (compare the similar depiction of the Arameans in 1 Kings 20; Ch. 6, Outline). The narrative style is appropriate to a section of Judges in which things are going relatively well for the Israelites: at this stage deliverance is, as it were, laughably simple for them.

Shamgar (3:31)

The narrative of Shamgar son of Anath is extremely brief (he is also mentioned at 5:6). It seems likely that he was a non-Israelite, perhaps a Hurrian, serving in an Egyptian military division named after the Canaanite goddess Anath. Block (pp. 172–5) cites an Egyptian inscription from the time of Rameses III (1198–1166), and suggests that Shamgar won his victories when this division fought against the Philistines, shortly after the arrival of the Sea Peoples in the area. In Judges 3 he is a footnote to the Ehud account, another man whom YHWH used to bring deliverance to Israel with an unorthodox weapon – this though he was a non-Israelite who may not even have intended to help Israel.

Deborah and Barak (4:1—5:31)

The exploits of Deborah and Barak are described in narrative (Judg. 4) and in poetry (Judg. 5, often called 'the Song of Deborah'). The narrative of Judges 4 is different in tone from the Ehud account, and Barak's less-than-heroic response to his commissioning ('if you will not go with me, I will not go', 4:8) marks a new development: this is the first time that a judge has imposed a condition before responding. The consequence is that, as chapter 4 traces in detail, Sisera is 'delivered into the hand of a woman' (4:9, 22), not Deborah but (a further twist) Jael. Judges 4 is the first account in which one of the judges is to some extent criticized. Jael plays the role which Ehud played in Judges 3, whereas Barak ends up playing the role of Eglon's courtiers, entering and finding a dead body.

Barak's victory is striking enough, however. He rallies the Israelites to Mt Tabor, from where he attacks Sisera's forces and drives them back to Harosheth Haggoyim, Sisera's base (4:10; 12—16). Harosheth Haggoyim probably means 'cultivated land of the Gentiles', and is apparently identical to the Taanach and Kishon river areas referred to at 5:10–21. The victory seems to have strengthened Israel's hold on northern Canaan, building on the campaigns of Joshua 11 in a way that Zebulun's and Naphtali's earlier efforts (1:30, 33) had failed to do. Note that the 'King Jabin of Canaan who reigned in Hazor' (4:3) seems to be a different figure from the 'King Jabin of Hazor' of Joshua 11:1: names

are often repeated in royal dynasties (Kitchen, p. 213).

Digging deeper:
JUDGES 4 AND 5: TWO ACCOUNTS?

Block (pp. 175–84) discusses the relationship of Judges 4 and 5, setting out the two accounts in synopsis. He concludes that, though the two accounts follow the same basic sequence, they focus on different aspects, each omitting many things touched on by the other. Judges 4, for example, contains no list of tribes who did or did not participate (5:13–18), no mention of a torrent which swept away Sisera's forces (5:19–21), and no reflection on how Sisera's household will react to the news of his death (5:28–30). Judges 5, in turn, does not mention Jabin king of Canaan (4:2, 23–24), Deborah's role in summoning Barak (4:6–9), Barak's pursuit of Sisera and his army (4:16, 22), or Barak finding Sisera dead in Jael's tent. Judges 4 is a coherent and orderly account; Judges 5 is much more impressionistic, with no clear plot-line. 'If the narrative account were not available, it would be difficult to reconstruct the course of the battle from [Judges 5] alone' (p. 182).

Block argues that the two accounts are complementary: Judges 5 praises YHWH for his crucial role in the victory (vv. 1–5, 9, 11), and is a broad-ranging celebration of what was accomplished; Judges 4 focuses much more narrowly on how Deborah's prophecy to Barak found an unexpected fulfilment. It relies on Judges 5 to fill in further details.

Do you find this a convincing explanation of the relationship of Judges 4 and 5? With Block's approach you can compare the different approaches of Halpern, pp. 76–103 and Brettler, pp. 61–79.

The accounts of Ehud and Deborah and Barak are more complex than the Othniel account. But apart from the references to apostasy and judgment in the frames, there are no strongly negative aspects. The Song of Deborah which concludes this section dwells on the themes of Israelite loyalty to YHWH and the defeat of YHWH's enemies. Some tribes are reproached for not having taken part in the victory over the Canaanites (5:16–17, 23), but the dominant note is of willing Israelite response to YHWH's call. This poem could have been omitted without leaving an obvious gap, but its celebratory tone reinforces the mainly favourable impression left by the accounts in chapters 3—4.

Gideon and Abimelech (6:1—9:57)

The next enemy said to have afflicted Israel in this period is a loose alliance of Midianites, Amalekites and 'people of the east', who made periodic raids upon the land (6:2–4: elsewhere in Judges 6—8 this group is referred to simply as 'Midian' or 'the Midianites', e.g. Judg. 6:6, 7, 11, 14). On the link between Midian and the site of Qurayya (north-west Arabia), inhabited in the thirteenth and twelfth centuries BC and thereafter abandoned, see Kitchen (pp. 213–14). As Kitchen notes, the relatively brief time-frame within which Midian seems to have flourished is an argument for the antiquity of the traditions underlying Judges 6—8.

Gideon, of the tribe of Manasseh, was raised up to deliver Israel from this enemy. The account of Gideon and his son Abimelech marks a turning-point in Judges. From Judges 9 on, Israel's fortunes are clearly in decline.

At the beginning of the Gideon account the 'frame' is significantly expanded: the narrative dwells on the enemy oppression, stressing its severity (element E, 6:2–6); and YHWH, instead of immediately giving aid when appealed to, denounces the Israelites (element F, 6:6–10). Relations between Israel and YHWH have worsened: the judgment is more severe, and salvation is no longer automatically granted. This is reflected in Gideon's words at 6:13: ' "Did not YHWH bring us up from Egypt?" But now YHWH has cast us off, and given us into the hand of Midian.' Note how YHWH's condemnation is supported by the picture of religious life in Ophrah later in the chapter (6:25–32).

> **Think about**
> ### FORM CRITICISM AND JUDGES 2 AND 6
>
> Soggin (pp. 30–1, 104–5, 117) argues that three passages in Judges appear to have originated as 'shrine aetiologies', explaining the origins of places of worship in Israel: 2:1–5; 6:11–24; and 6:25–32. He concludes that they are distinct units within their contexts, and did not originally belong there, though later alterations to the text have to some extent obscured this point.
>
> Read Soggin's arguments. What features do these three passages have in common? Is the description of them as 'shrine aetiologies' justified? How strong do you find Soggin's arguments that they did not originally belong in their present contexts?

What follows is more hopeful (6:11–32): in spite of his rebuke, YHWH sends an angel to summon Gideon, and Gideon, once persuaded that the summons has come from YHWH, responds by destroying Baal's altar and summoning the tribes of Manasseh, Asher, Zebulun and Naphtali for battle.

Think about
THE ANGEL OF YHWH

'Angel' translates a Hebrew word whose root meaning is 'messenger' (English 'angel' in fact comes from a Greek word also meaning 'messenger').

Compare 2:1–5, 6:11–24 and 13:2–23, three passages in which the 'angel of YHWH' figures. What features do these passages have in common? How does the 'messenger' relate to YHWH? Do the three passages allow one to form any clear conception of angels? Is there any clear difference between 2:1–5 and 6:11–24, where an angel appears, and 10:10–16, where no angel is mentioned?

But now Gideon wants reassurances that YHWH will 'deliver Israel by my hand, as you have said' (6:36). In the famous incident with the fleeces, he tries to manipulate YHWH into giving a concrete sign of his favour: first he asks for what might happen anyway, a dew-soaked fleece on a dry ground, then he asks that YHWH 'confirm' the first 'sign' by bringing about something more unusual, a dry fleece on dewy ground (if YHWH does not give this sign too he is inconsistent). Both signs are given, but it seems that Gideon is overly concerned for his own glory as Israel's deliverer.

Chapter 7 continues this theme, as YHWH reduces Gideon's army in size specifically because 'Israel would only take the credit away from me, saying, "My own hand has delivered me"' (7:2). It fits with this that the narrator emphasizes YHWH's role in the victory more than in previous accounts: the prophetic dream of the Midianite (7:9–14) suggests an unexpected reversal brought about by YHWH; and in the battle itself it is YHWH who 'set[s] every man's sword against his fellow and against all the army' (7:22).

In chapter 8 YHWH vanishes from the account. Even though Gideon has secured a great victory, he crosses the Jordan with his 300. Questions mount up as the chapter progresses. Why is he pursuing Zebah and Zalmunna, the Midianite kings, with such zeal, even though his men are tired? Why does he treat the men of Succoth and Peniel so viciously for refusing to help him? The reason, it emerges, is that he is obsessed with a personal vendetta (8:18–19): 'What about the men whom you killed at Tabor? . . . They were my brothers.' This fact, delayed until this point, puts much of the earlier narrative in a new light: there *has* been something self-seeking underlying Gideon's behaviour. His concern has not been solely for YHWH's glory, or Israel's deliverance; he has also been wanting to avenge a private grievance.

To all appearances, however, Gideon has won a great victory, and the Israelites offer him kingship. He refuses with fine-sounding words: 'I will not rule over you, and my son will not rule over you: YHWH will rule over you' (8:23). But he then in effect undermines YHWH's kingship by making an ephod which both symbolizes his victory (it is made from Midianite spoils) and emphasizes his personal authority (he sets it up in his home town). This leads the Israelites into apostasy. At his death idolatry is as firmly entrenched in Israel as ever, and afterwards Baal worship springs up again in a syncretistic form: the name 'Baal-Berith' (v. 33, 'Baal of the covenant') apparently attempts to blend the religions of Sinai and Canaan (cf. 2:19). YHWH, Israel's true saviour, has been forgotten, partly because of Gideon's later actions (8:34; cf. 7:2). Gideon's other name, Jerubbaal, thus acquires an ironic sense: by the time Gideon dies Baal *has* contended for himself most effectively (cf. 6:32), and that seems to be why the name

Jerubbaal is particularly used in the last verses of chapter 8. (In ch. 9 Gideon is *only* referred to as 'Jerubbaal'.)

At the end of chapter 8 there is a further expansion in the frame: frame-elements J–L (8:28, 32), far from concluding the account, are used to bracket the account of Abimelech's birth, and create a transition to the subsequent account of Abimelech. This, in a highly effective variation on the frame-pattern, is an 'ending' which does not in fact end the story. By the time he dies Gideon has already sown the seeds of the decline that will follow: he has encouraged an idolatrous cult, and he has acted like a king in all but name. Abimelech accentuates these tendencies: he is an idolater, helped into power by money from the shrine of Baal-Berith (9:4); and his life reflects all the worst aspects of monarchy – murderous family intrigues and the destructive and vindictive abuse of power. It is a relief when he is himself killed and YHWH's control over events is reasserted (9:53–57).

> **Think about**
> **GIDEON: IS HE SO BAD?**
>
> Do you think the interpretation of Gideon's life offered above is over-harsh? Can the details of the narrative, or at least some of them, be taken differently, putting Gideon in a better light? If you wanted to argue that the narrator is basically sympathetic towards Gideon, what features of the narrative would you point to?
>
> You can consult Wenham's discussion of this issue, pp. 119–27.

Jephthah (10:6—12:7)

In the third section, Jephthah and Samson continue the decline. Like the Gideon account, Jephthah's account begins with an extended description of Israelite idolatry and enemy oppression (10:6–9). These verses refer to both Philistine and Ammonite oppression, but the rest of the Jephthah account will describe only the deliverance from the Ammonites and is set mainly in Transjordan, some distance from the Philistines, so it is likely that the reference to the Philistines is intended to prepare for the account of Samson.

YHWH again condemns the Israelites when they cry for help, this time bluntly telling them 'I will deliver you no more' (10:13). In response the Israelites 'put away their foreign gods' and 'worshipped YHWH'. But is this merely a token gesture? The phrase describing YHWH's response is ambiguous (10:16): either 'he could no longer bear to see Israel suffer' (NRSV) or 'he grew weary of their efforts to win his favour' (Block, pp. 348–9). Maybe the Israelites are on their own now.

In this crisis the leaders of Gilead approach Jephthah, also a Gileadite. Rather as they have tried to negotiate with YHWH, the elders negotiate with Jephthah, persuade him to be their leader, and swear an oath to this effect at Mizpah (Judg. 11:1–11). But it is unclear whether or not YHWH supports Jephthah.

There follows yet another set of negotiations, this time between Jephthah and the Ammonite king. (On the question why Jephthah incorrectly identifies the god of the Ammonites as Chemosh rather than Milcom, see Block, pp. 361–2.) Only when it becomes clear that battle cannot be avoided does the spirit of YHWH come upon Jephthah; and just at this point, when YHWH appears to have shown his support, Jephthah attempts to manipulate YHWH with his vow.

The terms of the vow are somewhat ambiguous, but are more likely to refer to a human than an animal: animals could be kept inside Israelite houses, but it would not be natural for Jephthah to speak of an animal coming 'out of the doors of my house to meet me' (Judg. 11:31). Jephthah has mentioned Chemosh, god of Moab, in his negotiations with the Ammonite king, and now treats the god of Israel as though, like Chemosh, he accepted human sacrifice (cf. 2 Kgs 3:27). Like Gideon he wants to be sure of victory, but he goes much further than Gideon in his desire to secure it. His daughter falls victim to his terrible vow, which he knows no better than to carry out.

Think about
JEPHTHAH'S VOW

How are Jephthah and his daughter portrayed in 11:29–40?

Should Jephthah have gone ahead with his vow? (Compare Lev. 5:4–6; Eccl. 5:4–6.)

Why does YHWH not intervene? (Compare Gen. 22:12–14.)

Negotiation, often in the form of manipulative pleading, is a theme that runs through the account of Jephthah: it dominates the exchanges between the Israelites and YHWH (10:6–16), the Gileadites' approach to Jephthah (10:17—11:11), Jephthah's dealings with the Ammonite king (11:12–28) and finally, Jephthah's dealings with YHWH (11:29–31). Jephthah's painful eagerness to have YHWH on his side echoes the Israelites' earlier on, but he shows no better understanding than they of what YHWH really requires. The gap between Israel and YHWH widens in this account, and it is fitting

that the Israelites, whose pursuit of foreign gods now seems entrenched, should have a leader who acts in an 'outrightly pagan' way (Block, p. 367).

A sequel reveals a growing disunity among the tribes (12:1–6). As they did with Gideon, the Ephraimites reproach Jephthah for not having summoned them to battle (cf. 8:1–3). Seemingly they believe that they must share in every Israelite victory; they certainly feel themselves superior to the Transjordanian tribes (12:4). Unlike Gideon, Jephthah fights with the Ephraimites. Perhaps he is enraged that they criticize him after a victory that has cost him so much personally. The result is a civil war, and the only casualties numbered in Jephthah's account are those from Ephraim, not those of Israel's enemies (vv. 5–6; the Ammonite losses were numbered in terms of cities taken or destroyed, 11:33). It is no accident that Jephthah's account does not end with a 'peace formula' (frame-element K): he has brought no real peace to Israel.

Samson (13:1—16:31)

Samson is an even more alarming figure. In his origins he is the exact opposite of Jephthah, and the lengthy prelude to his birth (ch. 13) raises hopes: he will 'begin to deliver Israel from the hands of the Philistines' (13:5). But Samson seems to do everything wrong: he is a Nazirite who defiles himself by eating honey from a lion's carcass (13:4–5; 14:9; cf. Num. 6:6); an Israelite who demands to marry a Philistine wife (14:2–3). YHWH's spirit comes upon him repeatedly, yet his behaviour remains thoroughly wilful. He seems to be motivated, not by a concern for Israel's deliverance, but by sexual lust (16:1–4) and a lethal regard for his own honour (14:9; 15:3, 7–8, 11). He ends his life with an act of personal revenge (16:28: 'Lord YHWH, remember me and strengthen me . . . so that I may pay back the Philistines for my two eyes'). This may have harmed the Philistines more than his other actions (16:30), but it has not removed them as a threat to Israel. Again there is no peace formula at the end of his account.

(Note how, corresponding to the distinction made in 16:30, the summary of 15:20 is repeated at 16:31; 15:20 concludes the account of what Samson did in his lifetime, 16:31 concludes the account of his death. Once more, a variation in the frame reflects a distinctive feature of the narrative.)

The key to the actions of YHWH's spirit in the Samson account is the reference in 14:4 to YHWH 'seeking a pretext to act against the Philistines': whenever YHWH's spirit acts on Samson, something happens which directly or indirectly increases hostility between Israel and the Philistines.

YHWH'S SPIRIT IN JUDGES 13—16

- 13:25 is followed by 14:1, implying that YHWH's spirit led Samson to stray into Philistine territory.
- 14:6: Samson kills the lion; this leads to his riddle at his wedding, which causes the bad relations in chs 14 and 15.
- 14:19: Samson kills 30 youths from Ashkelon.
- 15:14: Samson kills Philistines with an ass's jawbone.

Is Samson conscious of divine leading on these occasions, or are we to regard these acts as springing from his impulses, which YHWH channels into his own purposes? Certainly Samson is only said to call on YHWH twice, both times in desperate need (15:18; 16:28). His life is not marked by any obvious signs of piety.

But Samson has at least struck some blows for Israel's deliverance (cf. 13:5: 'he shall *begin* to deliver Israel'). That he acts like a loose cannon is partly due to the fact that he has no real support in Israel. Indeed, at 15:11 the Judeans come to hand him over to the Philistines with the words 'Do you not know that the Philistines are rulers over us?' (cf. 15:20). Samson seems to be the only Israelite who does not acquiesce in this situation.

On another level, however, Samson is symbolic of Israel in the judges period: he compromises his holy calling, blunders around, finds himself in difficult situations, is rescued by YHWH, then presumes on YHWH (16:20), and is seemingly deserted by him but not in the end abandoned. All these things are, at a different level, true of Israel. It may be that some features of chapters 13—16 are due to the narrator's desire to point to this second, symbolic level of meaning. The narrative highlights the erratic and self-centred aspects of Samson's behaviour. Parts of chapter 16 in particular seem almost unreal: Samson toys with the Philistine leaders, deliberately putting himself at risk to demonstrate his strength. (Or does he believe that Delilah is joking when she says, 'The Philistines are upon you'?) The presence of folk-tale elements such as a barren woman giving birth (ch. 13), riddles (ch. 14) and 'magical' strength (ch. 16) also give the narrative a stylized feel. This is a narrative which by its very oddness seems to hint that it is not simply to be taken at face value, but is a kind of parable of Israel's position before YHWH.

(Two other narratives in the Histories which also begin with the birth of a son to a barren woman and also seem to offer indirect comment on Israel's state before YHWH are 1 Samuel 1—2 and 2 Kings 4:8–37. For the theme of barrenness in Genesis see Genesis 11:30; 25:21; 29:31.)

Think about
MAGIC HAIR?

How would you explain the fact that Samson loses his strength when his hair is cut (16:16–21; cf. 13:5) and regains it as his hair grows back (16:22, 28–31)?

Tola, Jair, Ibzan, Elon, Abdon (10:1–5; 12:8–15)
So far we have ignored the minor judges. Their accounts come between those of Abimelech, Jephthah and Samson; Table 3 shows their own distinctive frame.

There arc slight variations in the 'minor' accounts: the first two begin with 'X arose after him', the next three with 'X judged Israel after him'; the 'Further information' is slightly varied, though mainly focused on evidence of prosperity (children and possessions). But the presentation is repetitive, something accentuated by the brevity of the accounts and the fact that they are clustered into two groups.

Webb (pp. 160–1) notes a number of points of contact between these accounts and the accounts of Abimelech and Jephthah:

- The large families of Jair, Ibzan and Abdon remind us of Gideon (8:30–31).
- The comment that Tola 'arose after Abimelech to save Israel' and 'resided at Shamir' (10:1) suggests that he provided a period of stability in Ephraim after the destructive rule of Abimelech.
- The account of the prosperous Jair (10:3–5) contrasts with that of Jephthah, also from Gilead. The elders of Gilead do not appeal to any of Jair's 30 sons when thc Ammonites invade: owning

TABLE 3 THE MINOR JUDGES

	Tola (10:1–2)	**Jair** (10:3–5)	**Ibzan** (12:8–10)	**Elon** (12:11–12)	**Abdon** (12:13–15)
Succession	Arose after Abimelech to save Israel (10:1)	Arose after him [Tola] (10:3)	Judged Israel after him [Jephthah] (12:8)	Judged Israel after him [Ibzan] (12:11)	Judged Israel after him [Elon] (12:13)
Origins	Shamir in Ephraim (10:1)	Territory of Gilead (10:3)	Bethlehem in Zebulun (?) (12:8)	Territory of Zebulun (12:11)	Pirathon in Ephraim (12:13)
Further information	Resided in Shamir (10:1)	30 sons riding on 30 donkeys; 30 towns (10:4)	30 sons, each with a wife, 30 daughters, all married (12:9)	(—)	40 sons and 30 grandsons, all riding on 70 donkeys (12:14)
Years he judged	23 years (10:2)	22 years (10:3)	7 years (12:9)	10 years (12:11)	8 years (12:14)
Death, burial	Died, buried at Shamir (10:2)	Died, buried at Kamon (10:5)	Died, buried at Bethlehem (12:10)	Died, buried at Aijalon (12:12)	Died, buried at Pirathon (12:15)

a donkey is one thing, leading Israel in battle another!

- The contrast between Jephthah, childless because of his vow, and the many children of Ibzan (12:8–10) is also thought-provoking.

The details given about the minor judges are teasingly ambiguous. Does the fact that Jair, Ibzan and Abdon were each wealthy and had many children indicate that they brought a temporary stability to parts of Israel (as evidenced by the fact that they could raise large families and acquire possessions)? If so, their careers could be seen as instances of YHWH's provision for Israel in a chaotic period. Or are these three judges minor versions of Gideon, people whose concerns focused unduly on building up their own families and founding a local dynasty (Younger, pp. 278–9)? No obvious spiritual decline is evident; indeed, such concerns hardly surface in the accounts. On the other hand, the minor judges seem to accomplish little. The downward trend begun with Gideon continues through the accounts of Jephthah and Samson; and the minor judges, whose careers lie within this period, do not interrupt it at all, Tola excepted (10:1). The impression left by these accounts is that the narrative has been 'treading water'. These figures provide leadership of a sort, but they appear to leave the problem of YHWH's relationship with Israel unresolved.

NARRATIVES FROM EARLY IN THE JUDGES PERIOD (17:1—21:25)
The narratives in this section come from the period following Joshua's death: see 18:1 (cf. Josh. 19:47); 18:30 (reading 'Moses'); 20:27–28 (cf. Josh. 14:1; 19:51). There are no judges in chapters 17—21, and no narrative framework like that in

3:7—16:31. Instead, the chapters are linked by a repeated formula, given in full at 17:6 and 21:25, more briefly at 18:1 and 19:1: 'In those days there was no king in Israel; all the people did what was right in their own eyes.' Clearly these chapters form a distinct section within Judges.

There are two narratives: Micah's idols and the Danite migration (17:1—18:31); the Levite's concubine and the war against Benjamin (19:1—21:25). Each narrative has similar shape and themes, beginning by describing the doings of individual Israelites, then widening the scope to the tribal and, in the case of chapters 20—21, the pan-tribal level. Both narratives describe a corruption that affects Israelite society at all levels: individual Israelites and Israelite tribes all behave in questionable ways. Many parallels are drawn with incidents in earlier Old Testament books. The effect is always to cast a negative light on what is described in Judges 17—21. YHWH is distant in these narratives, hardly ever intervening in events, and then only in judgment. The theme of judgment is particularly clear at the end of both narratives.

Micah and the Danites (17:1—18:31)
Chapter 17 begins by describing Micah's shrine. It is a private shrine, containing idols made from stolen money. Micah, an Ephraimite, installs his own son as priest, but later hires a passing Levite, because he knows that Levites are more suitable as priests (17:7–12). Every aspect of this shrine violates the Mosaic law (e.g. Deut. 27:15), and the 'no king' formula at 17:6 clearly condemns all Micah's actions and his underlying religious attitudes. These are well summed up at 17:13: 'Now I know that YHWH will prosper me, because the Levite

has become my priest.' That is, the more cult objects and qualified cultic functionaries, the more blessing. This is sheer presumption: the narrator at no point confirms Micah's perspective in his own words.

The Danites in chapter 18 are no better. They pass by Micah's shrine in search of land. Rather than destroying it, they make off with the idols and the priest, and use them to found their own shrine. (Judges 1, unlike Joshua 19, had not mentioned Dan's move to the north: this is treated separately in Judges 18. Samson's exploits take place among southern remnants of the tribe of Dan, but the move to the north has already happened by the time of Deborah. See 5:17.)

The account of the Danites' journey contains many allusions to the accounts of Israel's exodus and conquest of Canaan in Exodus, Numbers and Joshua:

- Spies are sent out to explore the land. They report back, urging conquest (18:2, 9–10; cf. Num. 13:1–33).
- The spies are given a promise of success (18:5–6, 9; cf. Josh. 1:10–11; 3:10).
- A stopping-place on the journey north is named (18:12; cf. Exod. 15:22–25; 17:1–7; Num. 11:1–3).
- Cult objects and a priest are acquired en route (18:19–20; cf. Exod. 25ff.); they become part of a shrine when the destination is reached (18:30–31; cf. Josh. 18:1).
- A foreign city is destroyed and renamed (18:27–29; cf. Josh. 6–8; Judg. 1).

But everything about this conquest is wrong: the spies claim that YHWH has put the land of Laish into the Danites' hands (18:10), but the narrator nowhere confirms that this is YHWH's intent. The spies are as presumptuous as Micah at 17:13. The narrator (unusually in the Old Testament) regards the non-Israelite inhabitants of Laish with sympathy, stressing their defencelessness (18:7, 27–28), and implying that they should not have been destroyed. He also hints that the shrine the Danites set up in their new city is as false as Micah's: twice at the end of chapter 18 he reminds us that the idols the Danites set up were only objects made by Micah (18:27, 31). In Old Testament terms this whole account is a parody of a conquest.

At the end there is a clear hint of coming judgment. Micah thought that YHWH was on his side, and was proved wrong when the Danites ransacked his shrine. The concluding verses of chapter 18 suggest that the Danites will fare no better: the references to 'the time the land went into captivity' (v. 30) and the time 'the house of YHWH was at Shiloh' (v. 31) probably refer to the destruction of the shrine by the Philistines after the battle of Aphek (1 Sam. 4; Ps. 78:60; Jer. 7:12–15; 26:6–9).

The Levite's concubine; war against Benjamin (19:1—21:25)

Chapter 19 starts by describing an unhappy relationship between a Levite from Ephraim and his concubine. She runs away to her father's house at Bethlehem. The Levite travels to Bethlehem to bring her back and on the way back to Ephraim they stay in Gibeah. There the concubine is raped and dies. The narrative echoes the account of the angels and Lot in Sodom (Gen. 19), with the difference that in Judges 19 it is Israelites who are guilty of gross wickedness.

Think about
NARRATIVE TECHNIQUE AND THE MESSAGE OF JUDGES 19

Various aspects of Judges 19 are worthy of attention:

- *Time and place*: Examine the use of place-names and expressions for time, and also the play between 'narrated time' (the length of time an incident is said to last) and 'narrative time' (how slowly or quickly the narrator describes the incident). How do these aspects contribute to the narrative?
- *Characterization*: How are the Levite, his concubine, her father and the old Ephraimite portrayed? (You can also consider the Levite's words at 20:4–7.)
- *Significant omissions*: Does the narrator create deliberate ambiguity by omitting details? In particular, is there ambiguity as to when and how the concubine died (19:27–29; cf. 20:5)? See Block, pp. 541–2; Younger, p. 359.
- *Attitude towards women*: 'Had [the concubine] stayed in her place, under her husband's authority where she belonged, she would not have ended up at the wrong place . . . at the wrong time. By insinuating that women, by the way they behave, are responsible for male sexual aggression, the narrator relies on a fundamental patriarchal strategy for exercising social control over women . . . the message in Judges 19 is a cautionary one: if you do anything that even remotely suggests improper sexual behaviour, you invite male aggression' (Exum 1995, p. 85). Do you agree that this is the intended message of Judges 19 for women?

In chapter 20 all the Israelites gather to punish the wrongdoers. The account of their muster is impressive (20:1–17), as is their determination to 'purge the evil from Israel' (20:13; cf. Deut. 13:5; 17:7). The tribe of Benjamin refuses to hand over the citizens of Gibeath, so Israel mobilizes against them. But, though the Israelites go into battle after YHWH has told them to do so (20:18, 23, 28), they are defeated on the first two days of fighting. They only succeed on the third day by means of an ambush, after which the Benjaminites are reduced to 600 male survivors. The account of the ambush is reminiscent of Joshua 8, but here Israelite is fighting Israelite. Chapter 20 is a long, grinding narrative whose turning-point is the terrible moment at which the Benjaminites realize they are facing death (vv. 39–41). At every point the narrator brings out the losses to Israel caused by this war of retribution. 'What is especially horrific about this war is that it is against one of the tribes of Israel and is executed with a determination and a thoroughness surpassing anything evidenced in Israel's wars with the Canaanites elsewhere in Judges' (Younger, p. 375).

Digging deeper:
JUDGES 20:29–48: A SINGLE NARRATIVE?

The account of the third day of the fighting against Benjamin is another example of a multi-strand narrative; cf. Joshua 3—4 (Ch. 3, Outline). In this case the narrator describes the activities of three separate groups: the main Israelite army, the Benjaminites and the Israelite ambush group. Like Joshua 3—4, this account illustrates the differences between narrative-critical and source-critical approaches. Compare the arguments of Block (pp. 563–7) and Younger (pp. 372–5), who believe that 20:29–48 is complex but unitary, and Soggin (pp. 293–6), who postulates two separate sources.

Reading through chapters 20—21, one can sense the Israelites' initial determination and confidence turning to anguish at the near-destruction of Benjamin. This is reflected in the different questions the Israelites ask as the narrative develops:

- 20:3 (to the Levite): 'How did this criminal act come about?'
- 20:12 (to the Benjaminites): 'What crime is this that has been committed among you?'
- 20:18 (to YHWH): 'Which of us shall go up first to battle against the Benjaminites?' (an ironic echo of 1:1).
- 20:23 (to YHWH): 'Shall we again draw near to battle against our kinsfolk the Benjaminites?'
- 20:28 (to YHWH): 'Shall we go out once more to battle against our kinsfolk the Benjaminites, or shall we desist?'
- 21:3 (to YHWH): 'O Lord, the God of Israel, why has it come to pass that today there should be one tribe lacking in Israel?'

Finally the questions change direction again, as the Israelites stop addressing questions to YHWH (because they get no answer?) and instead concern themselves with the survival of the tribe of Benjamin:

- 21:7: 'What shall we do for wives for those who are left, since we have sworn by YHWH that we will not give them any of our daughters as wives?'
- 21:16: 'What shall we do for wives for those who are left, since there are no women left in Benjamin?'

The questions in the text prompt questions in the reader's mind: is the tribe of Benjamin going to be destroyed? Why are the Israelites defeated on the first two days? These turn out to be two aspects of one larger question:

how does Israel survive at all during this episode?

In chapter 20 Israel has distanced itself from Benjamin ('let us purge the evil out of Israel', 20:13). But in chapter 21 the Israelites, in their eagerness to see Benjamin survive, behave increasingly like Benjamin, bending the terms of oaths they have taken (21:5, 18) and finally even encouraging 200 Benjaminites to seize Israelite women as their wives (21:20–25). Chapter 19 began by describing the rape of one woman; now the Israelites sanction the rape of 200.

This suggests why YHWH on the first two days sends the Israelites into battles in which they are defeated: judgment falls on Benjamin, but it also falls on the other tribes as well, because they are really no different from Benjamin. The narrative is clear: if the oaths had been kept, if Benjamin had been fully punished, it would have been destroyed. But if Benjamin is a miniature version of Israel, what does that imply for Israel? How has Israel survived, if she deserves judgment? With that question hanging the book closes.

Within Judges, chapters 17—21 function as a large-scale example of 'delayed revelation'. At the end of a book in which so many things have gone wrong for Israel, they take us back to the beginning of the judges period and show how the very first generation after Joshua went badly astray, as evidenced by the corrupt behaviour of both individual Israelites and whole tribes. In the light of these incidents it is no surprise that later generations also turned away from YHWH as they did.

Chapters 17—21 also point forward to the books of Samuel, which follow Judges directly in the Hebrew canon. By attributing the moral anarchy of the judges period to the lack of a king they anticipate developments that will be described in those books.

KEY THEMES

Covenant violation

Israel were generally faithful to YHWH in Joshua; in Judges they are generally unfaithful, beginning with the generation after Joshua. Their failure to drive out the inhabitants of Canaan is the root of their shortcomings (1:1—2:5). The problem of 'the nations that remain' is still unresolved at the end of the book.

Canaanization

Block (p. 58) has described the main theme of Judges as 'the Canaanization of Israelite society during the period of the settlement'. The Israelites come to terms with the inhabitants of Canaan, intermarry with them, and worship their gods (2:1–3; 3:5–6). Their behaviour mirrors this switch in their commitments: at different points they are found implicated in idolatry (6:25–32; 8:32—9:6; 17—18), superstition (11:30–35), tyrannous violence (8:13–17; 9:34–52), rape (19:22–26; 21:20–23) and murder (9:4–5). On occasions they return to YHWH, but these examples of evil behaviour seem to represent the level to which they are always in danger of falling back (cf. 2:18–19). It is fitting that near the end of the book Shiloh is described as still 'in the land of Canaan' (21:12).

Fragmentation

Israel in Judges is less united than in Joshua, and less responsive to its leaders. There are instances of rivalry (8:1–3), disloyalty (5:15–17), apathy (15:11–12) and civil war (12:1–7; ch. 20). The account of Abimelech in particular presents a picture of complete chaos. The uncomplicated picture in Joshua of the people regularly assembling before the ark to receive YHWH's commands through Joshua vanishes in Judges.

YHWH and Israel

Linked to all the above, Judges traces a decline in the relations between YHWH and Israel. YHWH seems to distance himself from Israel, and Israel, left to itself, resorts to increasingly dubious measures to deal with its continuing crises. When the Israelites do seek YHWH, the suspicion arises that there is no real repentance and that it is only relief from distress that they seek. By the time of Samson they apparently no longer even call on YHWH: at any rate, chapter 13 contains no such reference (frame-element F).

Grace

If enemy invasions are a sign of YHWH's judgment in this period, YHWH shows grace and compassion by sending a succession of deliverers. If the Israelites give up seeking YHWH (ch. 13), YHWH still finds ways of working towards their deliverance (13:5; 14:4). Even by the end of the book the ultimate threats of Joshua 23—24 have not been carried out. Whereas passages like Joshua 23:15–16 and 24:20 (cf. Deut. 28—29) seemed to suggest that exile and destruction would quickly follow disobedience, by the end of Judges Israel is still a viable entity, albeit severely compromised. The very judgments that fall on Israel can be seen as instances of YHWH's grace: repeatedly the people are shown what turning away from YHWH involves; repeatedly YHWH speaks to them through the consequences of their disobedience and so calls them back.

Leadership

The presupposition of Judges is that YHWH is Israel's true ruler (8:23: Gideon's words were true enough, even if his actions undermined them). But the book also focuses on the human leadership raised up by YHWH. Judges presents us with a number of different forms of leadership: vain and vulnerable enemy kings such as Adoni-Bezek and Eglon (1:6–7; 3:12–30); the judges themselves; the disastrous 'proto-kingship' of Gideon and Abimelech (chs 8—9); and the flawed leadership of Israel's elders in the generation after Joshua (chs 1 and 17—21).

The chief disadvantage of the judges, according to 2:16–19, is that they were unable to alter the people's tendency to apostasy: when the judges died the people reverted to their old ways. This is more an indictment of the people than of the judges, and it is interesting to speculate what might have happened had the people remained faithful to YHWH, or been less consistently unfaithful. Nonetheless Judges clearly regards the non-dynastic and usually localized leadership of the judges as inadequate to maintain the people's covenant loyalty.

The two alternatives to non-dynastic individual leadership considered by Judges are collective leadership (government by tribal elders) and monarchy (dynastic individual leadership). Chapters 1 and 17—21 seem to suggest that leadership by elders was inadequate, but what of monarchy? Texts such as 8:23 and 9:7–15 apparently regard monarchy as, respectively, a denial of YHWH's kingship and a fruitless activity which attracts only those most unsuited for it. In sharp contrast to this, the 'no king' formula of chapters 17—21 seems to present monarchy as a blanket solution to moral anarchy. These texts and others in the books of Samuel are sometimes seen as the literary deposit of an ideological struggle in early Israel, representing respectively 'anti-' and 'pro-monarchic' perspectives.

But we must define our terms more carefully. Perhaps Judges 8—9 does not attack all forms of kingship, but only those forms (like Gideon's) which undermine YHWH's rule or which turn into violent tyranny (as with Abimelech). Perhaps Judges 17—21 does not commend all forms of kingship, but only those which will restrain lawlessness and unite the tribes (cf. Wenham, pp. 52–4). This is a debate that continues into Samuel and Kings (Satterthwaite, pp. 87–8; Mayes 2001).

YHWH's spirit

YHWH's spirit comes upon Othniel (3:10), Gideon (6:34), Jephthah (11:29) and Samson (13:25; 14:6, 19; 15:14). Different terms are used in these texts, perhaps to suggest that YHWH's spirit acts in different ways on each of the judges; but the language ('come upon', 'take possession of', 'stir', 'rush upon') does not aim for psychological or phenomenological precision. YHWH's spirit empowers these judges for leadership and war: at least, what follows in the narratives of Othniel, Gideon and Jephthah is that they muster armies and fight battles; and in the Samson narrative, as noted, whenever YHWH's spirit acts on him the effect, direct or indirect, is to stir up Philistine hostility.

Strikingly, the coming of YHWH's spirit does not mean that the judge's behaviour from that point on is marked by moral purity and devotion to YHWH: Gideon is self-seeking and self-serving even after 6:34 (indeed, these aspects of his character only emerge clearly from then on); Jephthah, shockingly, makes his vow immediately after YHWH's spirit comes on him (11:29–30);

Samson's motives are never free from lust and aggression. This is undoubtedly a puzzle for those accustomed to think of YHWH's spirit as 'holy' (Isa. 63:10–11; Rom. 1:4). It is as though the coming of YHWH's spirit serves to accentuate what is in these three men's hearts, whether good or bad (a similar point could be made about Saul and David in 1 Samuel). Clearly there is a complex view of divine–human interactions lying behind these simple-seeming texts, one in which human beings are not simply a slate which YHWH's spirit can 'wipe clean'. See Younger's discussion of this point (pp. 185–7).

CRITICAL ISSUES

LITERARY-CRITICAL ISSUES

Aspects of Judges as narrative

The narratives of Judges vary considerably in style. Some narratives are brief, supplying only a few details (the tribal conquests in ch. 1; the accounts of the 'minor' judges in chapters 10 and 12); others are much more complex and involved (e.g. the Gideon account; the description of the war against Benjamin in chs 20—21). The accounts of the 'major' judges (3:7—16:31) range in tone from the comic to the tragic. This might be explained by supposing that these accounts are based on different traditions, which have not been heavily reworked. But it could equally be the case that the editor has extensively reshaped the underlying traditions, deliberately using different styles at different points as part of his literary strategy: that has been the approach we have followed in the Outline (cf. Guest, pp. 55–7). In any case, none of the sources of Judges have survived independently, so all theories concerning the shaping of Judges must be based on the book as it stands.

Sources, dating, authorship, editing

No author is named for Judges. Regarding the dating of the book, 1:21 notes that 'the Jebusites have lived in Jerusalem among the Benjaminites to this day', a statement which seems to predate David's capture of Jerusalem. But, as with similar phrases in Joshua, the wording of this phrase may have been retained from an earlier source, and cannot be used to date the final form of Judges. Similar statements elsewhere in Judges (1:26; 6:24; 10:4; 15:19; 18:12) could have been true for centuries after they were made, and offer no help as regards dating. The reference at 18:30 to Jonathan's descendants continuing as priests at Dan 'until the time the land went into captivity' has been taken as a reference to the Assyrian deportations (e.g. Brettler, p. 115), which would date the final form of Judges no earlier than the late eighth century. But the parallel phrase in 18:31 ('as long as the house of God was at Shiloh') makes it more likely, as suggested above, that 18:30 refers to the aftermath of the Philistine victory at Ebenezer (1 Sam. 4). None of the passages we have considered helps to tie Judges down to a particular date, early or late; nor, apparently, was this their purpose.

Literary-critical scholarship on Judges has generally addressed the question of dating by investigating the sources and editing of the book. A representative approach is that of Mayes 1985 (pp. 10–36). Mayes' starting-point is that Judges is part of a larger Deuteronomistic History running from Deuteronomy to 2 Kings, and his analysis of Judges is particularly influenced by his view of this History as an originally continuous work. He divides Judges into prologue (1:1—2:5), central section (2:6—16:31) and epilogue (17:1—21:25). In his view, Judges 2:11 originally followed directly upon

Joshua 24:29–30, and the account of Samson (13:1—16:31) led into the accounts of Eli and Samuel in 1 Samuel 1—7. On this basis he concludes that the prologue (along with 2:6–10) and epilogue are later additions which did not originally belong with the central section. In support of this he cites the different literary structure of the three sections, and the fact that the prologue and epilogue both focus on Israelite moral degeneration and the inadequacy of tribal leadership (pp. 13–16).

In Mayes' view the central section has a complicated literary history. The traditions relating to 'major' and 'minor' judges were originally separate, and variations in the framework of the accounts of the 'major' judges indicate that they were not all edited together at the same time (pp. 16–18).

Mayes argues for the following stages in the formation of Judges (pp. 18–34):

- The nucleus of Judges was the narratives of Ehud, Deborah and Barak, and Gideon and Abimelech. These traditions (themselves amalgams of earlier traditions) had coalesced into a collection of 'deliverer stories' at an early stage, possibly among prophetic circles in the kingdom of Israel which were critical of the northern kings.
- A framework bringing out the pattern sin–punishment–deliverance was added to these narratives. Perhaps this took place in Judea after the fall of the northern kingdom: the implicit theme of this collection, particularly the Gideon and Abimelech narratives, was the illegitimacy of the northern kings and hence the legitimacy of David's line.
- The Othniel account, itself little more than a string of formulaic phrases, was added to the collection, probably also by a

Judean hand. This account included all the framework elements present in the other narratives, and added a number of similar elements ('forgetting YHWH their God and worshipping the Baals and the Asherahs', 3:7; 'the anger of YHWH was kindled against Israel', v. 8; 'the spirit of YHWH came upon him, and he judged Israel', v. 10) which stated in a more explicit form ideas already present in the frameworks of the other narratives.

- The next stage, which Mayes sees as decisive in the formation of Judges, and also the major Deuteronomistic redaction of the book, was the addition of the Jephthah and Samson accounts (themselves compilations of diverse material). The lengthy introduction to the Jephthah account includes the Samson narrative within its scope, as shown by the reference at 10:7 to the Philistines. This introduction also uses formulae most closely paralleled by the Othniel account. Taking these facts together, the Jephthah and Samson accounts must have been added to the collection after the Othniel account. The accounts of the minor judges were also added at this time, as indicated by the fact that the two endings to the Samson account (15:20; 16:31) use phrases elsewhere only used of the minor judges. Much of the introductory material in 2:11–20, paralleling that in 10:6–9, was also added at this time.
- A second, much less extensive, Deuteronomistic redaction added further introductory material which portrayed Israelite sin specifically as covenant violation (2:17, 2:20—3:6; 10:10–16).
- The final stage was the addition of the prologue and epilogue to the central section. The epilogue is probably composite: chapters 17—18 originated separately from chapters 19—21, and

chapters 20—21 seem to be a secondary expansion of chapter 19. In his 2001 article Mayes suggests that a Deuteronomistic hand is probably responsible for the epilogue, modifying his earlier view that the prologue and the epilogue 'cannot be assigned very easily to the work of deuteronomistic editors' (1985, p. 33).

Mayes provides a lucid and, if one accepts the premises, coherent theory. It involves a fair amount of speculation, but that is hard to avoid, given that we have so little direct evidence regarding the composition and editing of the Histories. Mayes' approach is broadly similar to that of Campbell and O'Brien (pp. 165–204). As with similar views of the literary history of Joshua, the implication of this approach is that, while many of the traditions underlying Judges may be relatively old, the major stages in the editing of the book took place centuries after the events narrated.

This chapter has followed a different approach. In the Outline we noted points at which we interpreted the text differently (e.g. the relationship of 1:1—2:5 and 2:6—3:6; the relationship of the framework and the 'major' judges accounts in 3:7—16:31). Where Mayes sees the variations in the framework as evidence for three separate editorial layers, we see the variations as highlighting important features of the different accounts, and find no need to posit more than one author or editor for all the accounts; and so on. You may find it instructive to work through Mayes' treatment in detail, noting how at point after point he interprets the same textual phenomena differently from us.

As with Joshua, we are not convinced that the most important stages in the formation of

Judges date to the seventh and sixth centuries, because we question the view of Deuteronomistic historiography on which this dating is based (see Ch. 7).

Judges 17—21 and 1—16 are different in structure, and might have originated separately. Judges 17—21, written from the perspective of the monarchic period (as indicated by the 'no king' formula), could have originated as a prelude to the account of the early monarchy in Samuel rather than as an epilogue to Judges. On the other hand, Judges 17—21 is closer in tone to Judges 1—16 than to the early chapters of 1 Samuel, and it forms a perfectly convincing conclusion to Judges. Given that in any case care has been taken to create thematic links between Judges and 1 Samuel (Ch. 5, Outline), it is not important to decide this issue either way.

Hidden polemic?

Another approach to the question of dating and authorship has been proposed by Amit, who detects examples of hidden polemic in Judges. In her view the narratives about Bochim (2:1–5) and Micah's shrine (chs 17—18) are indirect attacks on the shrine at Bethel, dating from the period before Josiah's reforms (cf. 1 Kgs 12—13; Amit 2000, pp. 99–129). Similarly Judges 19—21, though it is positive about monarchy (19:1; 21:25), subtly attacks Saul by its negative presentation of Gibeah (Saul's home town) and Benjamin (Saul's tribe). The chapters were meant as a prelude to the books of Samuel, in order to predispose readers to accept those books' presentation of David's line as YHWH's chosen dynasty: they are the work of an editor who entertained messianic expectations concerning David's line (Amit 1999, pp. 348–50).

If valid, this argument might help to date parts of Judges, and might also tell us something about some of those responsible for its editing. But Amit does not seem to have explained adequately why hidden polemic of this sort was felt necessary. Thus, to take the second of her examples, she thinks that the account of David in Samuel left it ambiguous how David should be evaluated; consequently, an editor added Judges 19—21 in order subtly to influence readers of Samuel in what the editor felt was the right direction. This seems a fair reading of Samuel, where the presentation of Saul and David is indeed complex, but it is not a plausible argument for the presence of polemic in Judges 19—21. Would any reader pondering how to assess Saul or David as presented in Samuel be decisively influenced by a polemic to the effect 'Can anything good come out of Gibeah/Benjamin?' (a crude oversimplification of the issues, no matter how subtly presented: it was hardly Saul's fault that he came from Gibeah!).

In any case, one can turn the argument around: the king Israel needs, Judges 19—21 implies, is one who will prevent outrages like the rape in Gibeah and prevent civil wars like the war against Benjamin. But in 2 Samuel David permits a rape in his own family to go unpunished (2 Samuel 13) and later sees his kingdom divided by civil war (2 Samuel 15—18). So maybe Judges 19—21 is a hidden polemic, not against Saul, but against the line of David! Of the two 'polemical' readings, this seems more plausible, because it involves shared themes, not a (possibly chance) association of place and name. But it is just as likely that these chapters contain no hidden polemic at all, but are simply a narrative which mentions some places and names and introduces some themes which also occur in later biblical narratives; and so, probably, for other cases of 'hidden polemic' in Judges.

HISTORICAL ISSUES

The historical context is broadly the same as that sketched for the book of Joshua. Egyptian control of Canaan came to an end during the first half of the twelfth century. As with the period of the Israelite conquest, the Iron I villages in the central highlands of Israel are central to reconstructions of Israel's history in the judges period.

We noted in the previous chapter (Ch. 3, 'Historical issues') how the beginning of Iron I (1200) saw the rise of some 250 new settlements in the central highlands. These were apparently egalitarian communities: the houses in these settlements were all roughly the same size, with no 'great houses' that might indicate the presence of a ruling class. Archaeological surveys seem to indicate that in the eleventh century the inhabitants started to expand into the Jezreel Plain (the area near Megiddo). Based on the size and number of these settlements, a rise in population size may be detected as we move from the twelfth to the eleventh century, from about 55,000 to 75,000 (Dever, p. 110; cf. Mazar, pp. 285–7). The archaeological evidence suggests a population with no centralized leadership settling down in the land. This population originally settled in the hill country but appears gradually to have expanded its territory.

In general terms this all fits with the picture in Judges, which seems to imply an expansion and consolidation of Israelite power in Canaan. (See especially Judges 1 and 4—5. Judges 1 is critical of Israel's achievements, but does suggest that some territorial gains were made.) Similarly, excavations at Tel Dan seem to support the account in Judges 18 of the Danite destruction of the city of Laish (Stager, p. 125).

Philistine power expanded considerably during the twelfth and eleventh centuries. Stager (pp. 113–28) traces the stages in this expansion: (1) a Philistine heartland based around the five cities of Gaza, Gath, Ashkelon, Ekron and Ashdod (*c.* 1180–1150); (2) territorial gains in the coastal plain and lowlands after the end of Egyptian control in Canaan (*c.* 1150–1050); (3) expansion into the central highlands, seriously threatening Israel's control of its territory until the rise of David, who pushed the Philistines back to their heartland (*c.* 1050–975). Again, this picture, derived largely from archaeology, fits with that in Judges: the Philistines are first mentioned in connection with Shamgar (3:31), but do not seem to pose a serious threat until the time of Samson (*c.* 1070).

Judges: oversimplified propaganda?

But can the details of the accounts in Judges be taken seriously as history? Guest, for example, is happy to accept that Judges is a literary unity, arguing that all the features of the book which have been taken as indicating that it is composite can be differently explained. But having reached this conclusion (which builds on other recent literary studies of Judges) Guest goes on to argue that everything in Judges is to be dated late, and that the whole is more or less theological invention: well structured, skilfully composed, but of little value historically.

Others, while less radical in their conclusions, are similarly suspicious of the clear theology and literary patterning of Judges. Miller and Hayes (pp. 87–91) find

that the schematic presentation of the accounts of the judges renders them almost valueless as a historical source: the individual traditions may preserve accurate memories of particular events and of the sociological and religious character of early Israel, but Judges as a whole cannot form the basis for a consecutive account of the period.

Finkelstein and Silberman (pp. 120–2), arguing (somewhat like Amit) that Judges contains hidden polemic, view Judges as essentially a seventh-century tract. Judges 1 opens by contrasting Judah's success in occupying their allotted territory with the failures and compromises of the northern tribes; Judges 3—16 contains accounts (almost none involving Judah) which chart increasing Israelite idolatry and fragmentation; and the book concludes by pointing to the need for a king (chs 17—21), reminding the reader of how David arose after the period of the judges. Judges is in reality covert propaganda for Judean expansion under Josiah into the territories of the former northern kingdom. It is not a reliable source for Israel's early history.

Miller and Hayes partly base their arguments on the view that the narrative framework of Judges 3—16 ('pan-Israelite', theologically loaded) is contradicted by the details of the narratives themselves. We have questioned this view: the point of the frames is not to turn the judges from local leaders into leaders of all Israel, but to remind us that the tribes referred to belonged to Israel, thus underscoring the growing disunity of Israel in the period. Further, it is one-sided to portray Judges as pro-Judean polemic: the book contains passages which describe Judean failure to occupy part of their territory (1:19), Judean acquiescence in Philistine domination (15:9–11) and, most strikingly in a section allegedly anticipating the rise of David's line, Judean defeat at Benjaminite hands on the first day of the battle against Gibeah (20:18–21).

In general these scholars seem to underestimate the complexity of the portrayal in Judges. Certainly, the narrator has a clear theological perspective, but we should not conclude that this has led him to oversimplify his presentation. On the contrary, we should take seriously the implications of his narrative, that Israel's history in this period was one of fragmentation and largely local leadership. This helps us address a problematic aspect of this period, the chronology.

The chronology of the judges period

If all the figures given in Judges for years of oppression, years the judges led Israel, and years of peace achieved by the judges are taken as consecutive, then the total duration of the events described in Judges is 410 years. Assuming the widely accepted date of 1000 for the beginning of David's reign over all Israel, which puts the beginning of Eli's leadership of Israel at about 1100, the beginning of the judges period would date no later than 1510, impossible even for those who date the exodus and conquest to the fifteenth century. But if the judges are seen as a series of local leaders, whose periods of leadership to a considerable extent overlapped, then it is possible to telescope the figures in Judges.

Kitchen (pp. 204–10) suggests a helpful analogy: the period of the judges is an 'intermediate period', like those in Egyptian history, in which different judges exercised leadership over different parts of Israel at the same time. Basing his approach on the indications in Judges as to which judge came

after which and also on the statements as to where each judge was active, Kitchen (p. 210) arrives at a regionally based chronology of the judges period (Table 4).

In this way Kitchen is able to fit all the events of the judges period (and some of those described in 1 Samuel) into about 160 years, from 1200 to 1042, a chronology compatible with a thirteenth-century exodus and conquest. This approach, while it does not require figures such as 40 years' peace after Othniel and 80 years' peace after Ehud to be more than roughly accurate, can accommodate almost all the figures given in Judges. It does, however, entail interpreting the figures of 300 years at Judges 11:26 and 480 years at 1 Kings 6:1 non-literally. For further discussions of chronology, see Block, pp. 59–63 and Provan, Long and Longman, pp. 162–6.

Two accounts of Israel's settlement?

It will be clear from our earlier comments on Judges 1:1—3:6 that we do not accept the common view that Judges 1 and Joshua 1—12 give two variant accounts of how Israel entered Canaan, a view linked to the equally common argument that Joshua 1—12 and 13—21 present two different pictures of the Israelite conquest (Ch. 3, 'Literary-critical issues'). In our view, Joshua and Judges paint a consistent picture: in Joshua Israel wins many victories in Canaan, but much land remains to be occupied by Joshua's death. The early chapters of Judges describe how the Israelites in the generation after Joshua failed fully to occupy this land. Judges 1:1—3:6 is a carefully constructed and logical sequel to the book of Joshua, not a variant account of the same events.

All the points we have discussed in this section illustrate how different literary

TABLE 4   KITCHEN'S CHRONOLOGY OF THE JUDGES PERIOD

South		Centre		North		East
South-west and west Phils, Dan	South Judah and Negev	East centre Benjamin	Centre Ephraim	North centre Manasseh	Galilee, northern areas	East, across Jordan
Dan N 1180? *Philistines* x SHAMGAR x *c.* 1170	*Kushan-R* 8 OTHNIEL 40 *c.* 1195	*Eglon* 18 EHUD x *c.* 1180 80 years' peace				
			Jabin 20 DEBORAH x *c.* 1160 40 years' peace	◄------------►	+ BARAK x *c.* 1160	
----------------	----------------	----------------	----------------	----------------	----------------	----------------
				Midian 7 GIDEON 40 *c.* 1170–50 (Abimelech 3)		
			TOLA 23 *c.* 1125			JAIR 22 *c.* 1100
						---------------- *Ammon* 18 JEPHTHAH 6 *c.* 1070
	IBZAN 7 *c.* 1070			ELON 10 *c.* 1060		
Philistines 40 SAMSON 20 *c.* 1070 *Philistines*	Sons of SAMUEL x *c.* 1045	SAMUEL 20 1062–42	ABDON 8 // *c.* 1050 // ELI 40 *c.* 1100–1060 (SAMUEL)			

Names in italics = Israel's oppressors
--------------- = events above and below this line cannot be placed in exact chronological order
x = indeterminate number of years
// = overlaps with

readings of the biblical text lead to radically different assessments of its historical worth.

JUDGES IN THE CANON

Judges is most clearly linked to Joshua and Samuel. We have also noted allusions to episodes from the Pentateuch. Themes introduced in earlier books are continued in Judges: Israel's calling; the covenant with YHWH; the promises in relation to the land of Canaan. Leadership has been a theme of (particularly) Numbers, Deuteronomy and Joshua, but in Judges the theme is taken further as the possibility of Israel becoming a monarchy draws closer to becoming reality.

Later books also contain references to events in Judges (Neh. 9:27–28; Pss 83:9–12; 106:34–36; Isa. 9:4; 10:26; Hos. 9:9; 10:9). In general, these texts refer to events in the judges period as exemplifying Israel's unfaithfulness and YHWH's mercy in delivering Israel. It is interesting that the deliverance from the Midianites is particularly remembered, as well as the outrage at Gibeah.

The clearest reference to the judges period in the New Testament is Hebrews 11:32–34, where Gideon, Barak, Samson and Jephthah are cited as examples of faith, men who trusted God and whom God used as agents of deliverance. This is not an untrue summary, but it clearly simplifies the much more complex and ambiguous descriptions of these men in Judges.

FURTHER READING

COMMENTARIES
D.I. Block, *Judges, Ruth*. Nashville: Broadman and Holman, 1999.

R.G. Boling, *Judges*. Garden City: Anchor, 1975.

T.J. Schneider, *Judges*. Collegeville: Liturgical Press, 2000.

J.A. Soggin, *Judges*. London: SCM Press, 1981.

K.L. Younger, *Judges and Ruth*. Grand Rapids: Zondervan, 2002.

OTHER BOOKS AND ARTICLES
Y. Amit, *The Book of Judges: The Art of Editing*. Leiden, Brill, 1999.

Y. Amit, *Hidden Polemics in Biblical Narrative*. Leiden, Brill, 2000.

M.Z. Brettler, *The Book of Judges*. London: Routledge, 2002.

A.F. Campbell and M.A. O'Brien, *Unfolding the Deuteronomistic History: Origins, Upgrades, Present Text*. Minneapolis: Augsburg Fortress, 2000, pp. 165–204.

K.M. Craig, 'Judges in Recent Research', *Currents in Biblical Research* 1 (2003), pp. 159–85.

W.G. Dever, *What Did the Biblical Writers Know and When Did They Know It?* Grand Rapids: Eerdmans, 2001, pp. 108–24.

J.C. Exum, 'Feminist Criticism: Whose Interests are Being Served?' in G.A. Yee (ed.), *Judges and Method. New Approaches in Biblical Studies*. Minneapolis: Augsburg Fortress, 1995, pp. 65–90.

I. Finkelstein and N.A. Silberman, *The Bible Unearthed. Archaeology's New Vision of Ancient Israel and the Origins of its Sacred Texts*. New York: Touchstone, 2002.

P.D. Guest, 'Can Judges Survive without Sources? Challenging the Consensus', *JSOT* 78 (1998), pp. 43–61.

J.A. Hackett, ' "There Was No King in Israel": The Era of the Judges' in M.D. Coogan (ed.), *The Oxford History of the Biblical World*. New York: Oxford University Press, 1998, pp. 132–64.

B. Halpern, *The First Historians. The Hebrew Bible and History*. Pennsylvania: Pennsylvania State University Press, 1988.

Z. Kallai, 'Joshua and Judges 1 in Biblical Historiography' in *Biblical Historiography and Historical Geography*. Frankfurt: Lang, 1998, pp. 243–60.

K.A. Kitchen, *On the Reliability of the Old Testament*. Grand Rapids: Eerdmans, 2003, pp. 199–222.

A.D.H. Mayes, *Judges*. Sheffield: JSOT Press, 1985.

A.D.H. Mayes, 'Deuteronomistic Royal Ideology in Judges 17–21', *Biblical Interpretation* 9 (2001), pp. 241–58.

A. Mazar, 'The Iron Age I' in A. Ben-Tor (ed.), *The Archaeology of Ancient Israel*. New Haven: Yale University Press, 1992, pp. 258–301.

J.M. Miller and J.H. Hayes, *A History of Ancient Judah and Israel*. Philadelphia: Westminster Press, 1986, pp. 80–119.

I.W. Provan, V.P. Long, T. Longman, *A Biblical History of Israel*. Louisville: Westminster John Knox Press, 2003, pp. 138–92.

P.E. Satterthwaite, ' "No King in Israel": Narrative Criticism and Judges 17–21', *TB* 44 (1993), pp. 75–88.

L.E. Stager, 'Forging an Identity. The Emergence of Ancient Israel' in M.D.

Coogan (ed.), *The Oxford History of the Biblical World*. New York: Oxford University Press, 1998, pp. 90–131.

B.G. Webb, *The Book of the Judges. An Integrated Reading*. Sheffield: JSOT Press, 1987.

G.J. Wenham, *Story as Torah. Reading the Old Testament Ethically*. Edinburgh: T. and T. Clark, 2000.

G.A. Yee (ed.), *Judges and Method. New Approaches in Biblical Studies*. Minneapolis: Augsburg Fortress, 1995.

Chapter 5

1 AND 2 SAMUEL

INTRODUCTION

The books of Samuel describe the rise of the prophet Samuel and the reigns of Israel's first two kings, Saul and David. In Hebrew Bibles these books follow directly upon Judges, Ruth being placed in the Writings, the third division of the Hebrew Bible.

The books of Samuel are printed as separate books in English translations: 1 and 2 Samuel. The Masoretic (Hebrew) text follows the same book, chapter and verse divisions as in English versions, but has no break between 1 Samuel and 2 Samuel.

STRUCTURE OF 1 AND 2 SAMUEL

1 Sam. 1—7	Samuel's rise and Eli's demise; the journeys of the ark (I)
1 Sam. 8—15	Saul becomes king; Saul's reign
1 Sam. 16—31	David's rise and Saul's demise
2 Sam. 1—7	David becomes king; the journeys of the ark (II)
2 Sam. 8—20	David as king
2 Sam. 21—24	Conclusion

Prophetic speeches play an important part in the plot structure of 1 and 2 Samuel: the prophecy against Eli's house (1 Sam. 2:27–36); Samuel's farewell speech (1 Sam. 12); Samuel's rejection of Saul (1 Sam. 15:17–31; cf. 28:15–19); YHWH's promise to David through Nathan (2 Sam. 7:4–16); Nathan's condemnation of David (2 Sam. 12:7–14). Note the similar themes and vocabulary of the condemnation/rejection speeches.

The poetic passages near the beginning, middle and end of 1 and 2 Samuel, Hannah's prayer (1 Sam. 2:1–10), David's lament (2 Sam. 1:19–27), David's song (2 Sam. 22) and David's 'Last Words' (2 Sam. 23:1–7), have a similar function. They act as structural markers, which underscore major themes such as human and divine kingship.

OUTLINE

1 SAMUEL 1—7: SAMUEL'S RISE AND ELI'S DEMISE; THE JOURNEYS OF THE ARK (I)

The first seven chapters of 1 Samuel have a number of links with Judges. Chronologically these chapters take up where the account of Samson, the last of the judges, ended: the Philistines continue to be a threat to Israel, as they were in Judges 13—16. The plot is also somewhat similar to that of the 'major' judge accounts: Israel falls into sin (represented by the arrogant behaviour of Eli's sons, 2:12–17) and comes under judgment (Israel's defeat at Aphek, ch. 4); Israel repents and seeks YHWH (7:2–6); a leader emerges who 'judges' Israel and leads them to victory over the Philistines (7:7–17). There are even some phrases reminiscent of the frames of the Judges accounts (4:18; 7:13, 15), though 1 Samuel 1—7 as a whole is not structured around such a frame. Last, the narrative has the same shape as the two accounts in Judges 17—21. Like those accounts, 1 Samuel 1—7 begins by focusing on the family of a single man, Elkanah (cf. Judg. 17:1 and 19:1) and broadens out into a portrayal of the situation in Israel as a whole.

It seems, then, that 1 Samuel 1—7 has been written to follow on from Judges. But this section does not simply continue the trends described in Judges. Unlike Micah's and the Levite's families in Judges 17—21, Elkanah's family shows genuine affection and piety (particularly Hannah). While the narrative that follows paints a picture of corruption in Israel (particularly in the priesthood of Eli's sons), that corruption is not allowed to continue unchecked. Samuel emerges as Israel's leader and halts the downward spiral of unfaithfulness and military defeat: the people repent, return to YHWH, and win a significant victory over the Philistines (1 Sam. 7).

Hannah, Eli and Samuel: the capture of the ark (1:1—4:22)
Elkanah's piety sounds a different note compared to Judges 17—21, but Hannah's prayer for a son seems to symbolize something much deeper: the yearning of the

---

Digging deeper:
1 SAMUEL 1—15 AND JUDGES

Here are some further possible connections between 1 Samuel 1—15 and Judges (similar plot elements or thematic links):

- 1:11: another barren woman is enabled to conceive, another Nazirite vow is taken (cf. Judges 13).
- 2:12: Eli's sons 'did not know YHWH' (cf. Judg. 2:10). Samuel, by contrast, comes to 'know YHWH' through the revelation of YHWH's word to him (3:7, 21; cf. 3:1; 4:1), and that word in turn comes to all Israel.
- 4:1–4: another unexpected defeat is followed by questions (4:3; 6:2; 6:20; cf. Judg. 20—21). Like Judges 20—21, 1 Samuel 4—6 depicts YHWH as distant from Israel.
- 7:2–6: the Israelites repent (cf. Judg. 10:10–16).
- 9:21: Saul's response to his call echoes that of Gideon in Judges 6.

- 11:6–7: YHWH's spirit 'comes upon' Saul as it did on Samson (the same Hebrew phrase is used, Judg. 14:6, 19; 15:14); he summons the Israelites to war with a gesture like the Levite's at Judges 19:29–30.
- 12:6–11: Samuel's review of Israel's history (cf. Judges 2:6—3:6).
- Chapters 13—14 echo the account of Gideon at a number of points.
- Most important of all, the issue of kingship, raised in Judges 8—9 and 17—21, becomes the central issue in 1 Samuel 8—15 (and beyond).

Are these links all of the same kind? Are they really deliberate? What view of the composition of Judges and Samuel might this imply?

righteous within Israel for YHWH to bring about deliverance. YHWH grants Hannah's prayer, and her words after dedicating Samuel celebrate YHWH's power to change hopeless situations (1 Sam. 2:1–10): YHWH is sovereign, strengthening the feeble, bringing down the mighty, executing judgment against the wicked, establishing justice throughout the earth, and upholding his chosen king. (Note this anticipation of a theme from later chapters.)

The section 1 Samuel 2:1–10 (often referred to as Hannah's Song) is written in poetry and, like other poetic passages in the Pentateuch and Histories, acts as a focus for the themes of the surrounding narrative. It is a kind of prophecy, which sees in Samuel's birth a sign that YHWH is about to reverse Israel's fortunes. But more than that, the Song sets out a view of YHWH which is programmatic for the books of Samuel. The themes of the Song are already illustrated in the chapters which form its immediate context, 1 Samuel 1—4, where the account of Samuel's birth and growth to maturity is interwoven with the account of judgment falling on Eli's family. The contrast between the fortunes of Samuel and of Eli's house in chapters 1—4 can be summed up in the words of 2:9: 'He will guard the feet of his faithful ones, but the wicked shall be cut off in darkness.'

In a similar way, chapters 4—7 emphasize YHWH's sovereignty: YHWH will not be manipulated or presumed upon. That point comes across in the panicky words of Israel's elders after the first defeat at Aphek (4:3): 'Why has YHWH put us to rout today before the Philistines?' YHWH has not done what they thought he would. The account of the second defeat brings out the idea of unexpected reversal yet more clearly

(4:4–11). The Israelites summon the ark into battle to ensure victory. The Philistines acknowledge that the ark symbolizes a potent divine power and are afraid, like the Canaanites in Joshua (Josh. 2:10; 5:1), yet they go into battle and defeat the Israelites again, even capturing the ark. The Israelites were wrong to believe that the presence of the ark would guarantee victory: it cannot be used to compel YHWH's support.

The ark returns to Israel; victory at Ebenezer (5:1—7:17)

Eli's daughter-in-law assumes that the capture of the ark marks the end of YHWH's involvement with Israel: 'The glory has departed from Israel, for the ark of God has been captured' (4:22). But she is wrong. In chapters 5—6 YHWH's power turns against the Philistines. They bring the ark to the temple of their god Dagon, as a sign of Dagon's triumph, but Dagon is symbolically executed in his own temple, and plagues fall on the Philistines wherever the ark is sent (5:1–12). They realize that Israel's god is not so easily mastered, and that they are in danger of suffering Pharaoh's fate (6:5–6). So they allow the ark to return to Israelite territory. The list of offerings presented by the Philistines reads like another list of defeated cities and rulers (6:17–18; cf. Joshua 12). This is a victory YHWH has won without human aid.

Yet the return of the ark does not mean that YHWH is now unequivocally back on Israel's side. YHWH's presence can be as dangerous for Israelites as for Philistines (6:19–20). The ark is moved to Kiriath-jearim, but this is only a temporary resting place. The fact that the ark remains near the borders of Israelite territory suggests that relations between YHWH and Israel, ruptured by the sins of Eli's household, are not yet fully restored. It fits with this that the people 'lament after YHWH' for 'some twenty years' (7:2), and that the narrative describes an act of repentance, in which Samuel takes the lead (7:3–6).

This repentance seems to be genuine, a change of heart such as the Israelites only mimicked in the days of Jephthah: compare Judges 10:16 ('they worshipped YHWH') and 1 Samuel 7:4 ('they served YHWH *only*). The Israelites find that in spite of their fears YHWH fights for them again, and routs the Philistines (7:7–11). The presumptuousness of chapter 4 has been replaced by a more realistic sense of dependence on YHWH, also reflected in Samuel's words as he sets up a commemorative stone: '*thus far* YHWH has helped us' (v. 12). True: but that does not guarantee YHWH's help in future, unless Israel remains faithful.

The summary of Samuel's achievements in 7:14–17 closes this section. Samuel's leadership has reversed some of the negative trends of Judges. As we read the account of the beginnings of Israel's monarchy in 1 Samuel 8—15, we must remember that it follows a narrative which has shown, in the person of Samuel, what a truly faithful judge can achieve.

This section has also introduced a major theme of 1 and 2 Samuel: the contrast between faithful and unfaithful leaders, and the different outcomes of their lives for themselves and for Israel as a whole. These issues were already raised in Judges, but they are explored more systematically in Samuel. The opening section sets the terms of reference: the different fates of Eli's sons and Samuel, and the different fortunes of Israel under their leadership, establish a pattern that will recur in the lives of Saul and David.

SAMUEL'S VICTORY: A FICTION?

In the light of later texts which speak of Philistines continuing to trouble Israel and invade Israelite territory while Samuel was still alive (1 Sam. 9:16; 10:5; 13:3), how are we to understand the claim in 1 Samuel 7:13 that 'the Philistines were subdued and did not again enter the territory of Israel: the hand of YHWH was against the Philistines all the days of Samuel'? Is the account of Samuel's victory largely a fiction designed to enhance the presentation of him as a faithful leader (so Klein, pp. 69–70)? More likely, 'all the days of Samuel' refers only to the period in which Samuel actively led Israel, before he appointed his sons to succeed him (8:1). Samuel's victory at Ebenezer is not depicted as ending Philistine domination, but as a significant temporary check to it.

---

1 SAMUEL 8—15: SAUL BECOMES KING; SAUL'S REIGN
The choice of Saul (8:1—12:25)

The section 1 Samuel 8—15 describes the beginnings of monarchy in Israel (chs 8—12) and YHWH's rejection of Israel's first king, Saul (chs 13—15). Chapters 8—12 contain a number of interpretative problems. We begin with an outline of events, then discuss issues arising.

Samuel is now old, and his sons are disqualified as leaders because of their dishonesty (8:1–3). The problem noted by Judges 2:19, that a good judge has no lasting influence, surfaces again. Israel's elders approach Samuel and tell him: 'You are old and your sons do not follow in your ways; appoint for us, then, a king to govern us, like other nations' (8:5).

This seems reasonable: something must be done. Furthermore, Deuteronomy 17:14–20, a passage which lies behind this chapter (compare Deut. 17:14 and 1 Sam. 8:5,

19–20), envisages Israel making such a request at some point after entering the land. However, both Samuel and YHWH respond negatively: YHWH speaks of the request as an act of rebellion (vv. 7–8), and Samuel warns Israel that the king will oppress them cruelly (v. 18). Despite an opportunity to reconsider, they insist on a king, and Samuel repeats the request to YHWH. YHWH, surprisingly, tells him to 'listen to their voice' (v. 22). Samuel then sends the Israelites back home: the implication is that he will take the necessary steps to find them a king.

Chapter 9 introduces Saul. We suspect that this is the man who will become king, but the narrative is in no hurry to reach this conclusion. Only at 9:15 are we told that the 'seer' Saul is journeying to meet is Samuel, and that they meet through YHWH's agency. Samuel tells Saul that 'all Israel's desire' is 'fixed' on him (9:20, referring to the events of ch. 8). The next morning he gives him a 'message from God' (9:27). The message comes in several parts: Saul is anointed and told that YHWH has made him 'ruler over his heritage (10:1); various events will take place as he returns home, to confirm his choice as king (10:2–4); last, when he reaches Gibeath-elohim, he will meet a band of prophets, YHWH's spirit will come upon him, and he must 'do whatever you see fit to do, for God is with you'; he is then to go to Gilgal and wait seven days 'until I come to you and show you what you shall do' (vv. 5–8).

These last verses seem enigmatic, but are not so really (see Long 1989, 1994, whose general approach is followed below). At 9:16 YHWH spoke of Saul as the one who would 'save my people from the hand of the Philistines', and the instruction 'do whatever you see fit to do' (10:7) comes after a reference to a Philistine outpost near Gibeah (10:5). Samuel seems to hint that Saul is to attack this outpost and, having provoked a Philistine response, muster the Israelites at Gilgal for a full-scale battle. He is then to await Samuel's arrival. This, at least, is the course that events follow, with certain crucial differences, in chapter 13, and had chapter 10 gone on to describe such a series of events, the meaning of verses 5–8 would have been plain. But in what follows, though all the signs duly occur (vv. 9–12), Saul does nothing regarding the Philistines. YHWH's spirit comes upon him, but, in contrast to what regularly happens in Judges, no act of deliverance follows. Instead, Saul goes up to a high place (it is not said why) and, when questioned by his uncle, hides the fact that Samuel has spoken to him about kingship (vv. 13–16).

On the surface 1 Samuel 9:1—10:16 is more positive about kingship than chapter 8. Saul seems a good choice as king. Both YHWH and Samuel speak with apparent approval of his future role (9:16, 20; 10:1). But this section of narrative closes with a sense of expectations unfulfilled. Saul has not taken Samuel's hint about the Philistines. The fact that he does not mention his anointing as king strikes a dissonant note. Should Israel's king be so unresponsive and reluctant?

By a somewhat indirect route the narrative has described how Samuel found a king for the people. It is logical, then, that Samuel goes on to assemble the people before YHWH at Mizpah (10:17). But his tone changes. He accuses them of rejecting YHWH (vv. 18–19), and we might think that an announcement of judgment is to follow. But instead he publicly selects a king from among them (vv. 20–21). The selection process picks out

Saul's tribe, clan and family, and finally Saul himself. Apparently it is intended as a public demonstration that Saul is the one YHWH has chosen. Saul shrinks from being selected, and YHWH has to tell the people where he is hiding (v. 22), another dissonant note. But Samuel declares Saul to be YHWH's chosen, and the people agree (vv. 23–24). The assembly ends with a covenant ceremony, the writing and deposition of a scroll setting out the 'rights and duties of the kingship' (v. 25). The narrator notes that those who were responsive to YHWH and of good character supported Saul, while those who queried his choice were 'worthless fellows' (vv. 26–27). This section leaves a bitter-sweet impression in the reader's mind: is Saul's selection as king a blessing or judgment upon the people?

Nahash the Ammonite attacks Jabesh-gilead in Transjordan, and the Gileadites send for help (11:1–3). Saul hears of it, YHWH's spirit comes upon him, and he musters the people for war with a symbolic act which suggests that he is responding positively to YHWH's call and turning away from his former way of life (vv. 4–7).

Saul wins a great victory, and the people express their approval to Samuel (11:12). This, after all, was what they wanted a king for (cf. 8:19–20). Samuel leads the people back across the Jordan to Gilgal, where the kingship is 'renewed'. Saul, confirmed in public as YHWH's choice (10:17–27), has acted with a decisiveness appropriate to a king (11:4–11). He is careful to give glory to YHWH, and is appropriately merciful to those who questioned his choice as king (11:13). Saul and Israel rejoice together.

This is the context for Samuel's farewell speech (12:1–25), which marks the transition from his leadership to Saul's kingship. Samuel's words have in view not simply Saul, but to an extent the monarchy as a whole. It is a key point within Joshua–Kings.

Again the tone changes: Samuel confronts the people with the implications of their choice. He reviews events leading up to Saul's kingship (vv. 1–11). He has 'listened to' the people (cf. 8:22) and given them a king. This king is YHWH's 'anointed', the one chosen by YHWH (vv. 3, 5). Nonetheless, Samuel himself has led Israel justly. He invites anyone who will to accuse him of wrongdoing, but no-one does.

YHWH, Samuel continues, has also dealt righteously with Israel (vv. 6–11), bringing them from Egypt into Canaan, forgiving their unfaithfulness, and giving them a succession of leaders. Israel has responded with mistrust. One reason why they requested a king was their fear of the Ammonites (v. 12). They had no confidence in YHWH, their true King.

And so the king they have chosen stands before them, but the terms of the covenant are unchanged: they must still obey YHWH or face the consequences (vv. 13–15). YHWH can bring thunder and rain at any time, and he can bring down judgment as he will (vv. 16–18). The choice of Saul as king need not lead to disaster, provided people and king remain faithful and serve YHWH wholeheartedly. Samuel will continue to pray for them. But if they do evil, they and their king will be swept away (vv. 19–25).

One cannot read these chapters without noting the different attitudes expressed towards the people's request for a king. More than once the people are sharply criticized for their request. It is a wicked act

110

of rejection (10:19; 12:17). Moreover, it is foolish: the king will subject them to hard service and oppress them (8:18; cf. Exod. 2:23; Judg. 3:9; 4:3). Passages like these present kingship as a punishment for the people's folly. By contrast, other sections seem enthusiastic about Saul, the man chosen in response to the people's request: he has been appointed by YHWH to deliver Israel from the Philistines (9:16); he is 'the one whom YHWH has chosen', outstanding among the people (10:24); the reaffirmation of his kingship after his victory is an occasion of rejoicing (11:14–15).

This raises again the question we noted in connection with Judges 8—9 and 17—21: do the Histories reflect conflicting attitudes towards the Israelite monarchy? Some scholars say 'Yes' and point to 1 Samuel 8—12 as a parade example. According to a standard view these chapters are not a literary unity, but a composite account in which pro-monarchic and anti-monarchic sources have simply been interleaved, with no real attempt to harmonize the conflicting viewpoints:

- 8:1–22: anti-monarchic
- 9:1–10:16: pro-monarchic
- 10:17–27: anti-monarchic
- 11:1–15: pro-monarchic
- 12:1–25: anti-monarchic

Thus Noth argued that while the editor of 1 and 2 Samuel 'in general simply reproduced the literary sources available to him and merely provided a connecting narrative for the isolated passages', here, because he strongly disapproved of the Israelite monarchy, he departed from his regular practice, taking his source (a favourable account of Saul's rise) and interspersing it with material, mostly composed by himself, in which he expressed his own negative views (pp. 26, 77–84, 133).

The source-critical approach to these chapters is also held to explain other odd features: e.g. that Saul is apparently made king more than once (10:24; 11:14–15); and that, having been made king in chapter 10, he is next reported as ploughing a field (11:5), not an obviously kingly activity.

It is true that chapters 8—12 can be divided quite neatly into these sections, and that if the 'anti-monarchic' sections were removed, the remaining sections would form a reasonably coherent account of Saul's rise. But there are problems with this approach. First, the editorial policy envisaged by Noth's approach seems strange: why should an anti-monarchic editor have wanted to use a source favourable to the monarchy at all? Why not abandon this source and compose a fresh account which more consistently reflected his views?

Second and more important, to use the terms 'pro-monarchic' and 'anti-monarchic' runs the danger of over-simplifying the issues (Long 1989, pp. 181–2). What is it, precisely, that is being supported or opposed? All forms of monarchy or only some? Is the support or opposition qualified in some way? Clearly these chapters contain passages which express different attitudes towards the institution of monarchy, but we need to inquire more deeply into the reasons for these differing attitudes.

On the basis of these and other considerations, recent scholarship has questioned whether these chapters are as incoherent as was previously accepted. Long's 1989 monograph drew together many arguments along these lines. Following this approach, we argue that 1 Samuel 8—12 form a unified but nuanced account of Saul's rise, whose thesis may be summed up as follows: the people were wrong to ask for a king, not because monarchy was intrinsically unsuitable for Israel, but because they asked with wrong motives; the result was that a wrong sort of king was chosen. The account of Saul's reign and rejection in chapters 13—15 validates this thesis.

As noted, 1 Samuel 8—12 alludes to the discussion of kingship at Deuteronomy 17:14–20. That passage begins:

> When you have come into the land that YHWH your God is giving you, and have taken possession of it and settled in it, and you say, 'I will set a king over me, like all the nations that are around me', you may indeed set over you a king whom YHWH your God will choose.

There follows a list of restrictions: the one chosen must be an Israelite; he must not amass wealth; he must study the law; he must be humble (vv. 15b–20). Nonetheless, Deuteronomy 17 clearly holds that some form of monarchy is acceptable for Israel. But the restrictions imposed mean that Israel's king will be unlike other kings: he is to avoid royal splendour and arrogance; he remains subject to YHWH's law, in many respects a typical obedient Israelite such as Deuteronomy wishes all the people to be (v. 20).

The section 8:1–22, then, quotes a passage which permits Israel to have a form of kingship: surely this suggests that it cannot simply be described as 'anti-monarchic'? If we accept that 10:25 also alludes to Deuteronomy 17 (the reference to 'the rights and duties of the kingship'), the same

argument applies to 10:17–27, the second 'anti-monarchic' passage. These two passages are more complex than first appears.

What, then, is criticized in these two passages and in chapter 12? Two passages, 8:19–20 and 12:12, suggest an answer. At 8:19–20 the people repeat their request: '. . . we are determined to have a king over us, so that we also may be like other nations, and that our king may govern us and go out before us and fight our battles'.

These words reveal their motives more clearly than vv. 4–5: they see a king primarily as someone who will win battles for them (cf. the people's request to Gideon at Judges 8:22). Apparently they feel insecure, uncertain that YHWH will deliver them; they would be happier if they had a human king.

Samuel's words at 12:12 develop this idea: 'But when you saw that King Nahash of the Ammonites came against you, you said to me, "No, but a king shall reign over us", though YHWH your God was your king.' That is, the request expresses lack of faith in YHWH, who, as Samuel states at length (12:6–11), is the one who has delivered them from their enemies until now.

The focus of the critique in 1 Samuel 8—12, then, is a king sought for the wrong reasons. The people use the phrase 'a king . . . like all the nations that are around' (Deut. 17:14) as a slogan, and are not interested in the conditions that follow (vv. 15–20). YHWH may acquiesce in the people's choice, even using language that speaks of his having chosen Saul (9:16; cf. 10:24); but the fundamental choice is the people's. The question raised by these chapters is: will such a king be obedient to YHWH, and lead the people by example? For faithfulness and obedience are what YHWH still requires (12:14–15):

If you fear YHWH . . . and if both you and the king who reigns over you follow YHWH your God – good! But if you do not obey . . . his hand will be against you, as it was against your fathers.

Saul's reign (13:1—15:35)

Saul's reign begins, and he carries out the first part of Samuel's earlier instructions: his son Jonathan provokes the Philistines and Saul summons the Israelites to Gilgal (13:1–4; cf. 10:5–8). The Philistines respond in force, and many of Saul's men desert him, while the rest are fearful (13:5–7). Saul waits seven days for Samuel, but when Samuel does not appear he offers the sacrifices that Samuel was supposed to offer. Samuel, tantalizingly, arrives just as he has finished (vv. 8–10), and tells Saul that he has failed to keep YHWH's commandment. YHWH will not establish his kingdom; instead he will seek out 'a man after his own heart' (vv. 13–14).

In the light of what follows in chapter 15, Samuel's words at 13:13–14 can be interpreted as a sharp warning to Saul rather than a final rejection of him as king. Nonetheless Samuel seems to treat Saul very harshly: Saul was in a desperate situation, seeing his men slipping away (v. 11), and yet he is condemned on a seeming technicality. Is Samuel, the rejected leader, making life difficult for his successor out of spite?

Perhaps not. This chapter echoes earlier battle accounts in which Israel faces numerically superior enemies, in particular the account of Gideon (Judg. 6–7): the Israelites are summoned by a trumpet; the enemies are 'like the sand on the seashore' (13:3–5; cf. Josh. 11:4; Judg. 6:33–34; 7:12);

the Israelites 'tremble' (13:7; cf. Judg. 7:3), and their numbers are reduced, in Judges 7 at YHWH's command, here through simple desertion (13:6).

In other words, the situation Saul faced was not unprecedented. The command to wait for seven days (10:8) was apparently intended to test him. Would he follow YHWH's word given through his prophet? Would he trust that YHWH was with him (cf. 10:7), even if many of his men (predictably) deserted? Samuel's aim, seemingly, was that the Israelites should defeat the Philistines in a way that made it clear that the real victor was YHWH (cf. Judg. 7:2). But Saul's actions have obscured this point. The grounds for Samuel's rebuke are not trivial. The underlying issue is the one highlighted by Samuel in chapter 12: will Saul as king uphold or undermine YHWH's rule?

Having failed his test, Saul still has the Philistines to deal with. He lapses into inertia, withdrawing to Gibeah with his 600 men (13:15) apparently for some days (13:17—14:3), doing nothing about the raiding parties the Philistines send out. Jonathan and his armour-bearer, in contrast, take on a Philistine garrison single-handed, trusting in YHWH's guidance (14:6–10). The Philistines view their attack with contempt, but it unexpectedly succeeds and spreads panic among them (vv. 11–15). The panic develops into a rout as Saul, seeing what is developing, leads his men into battle and Israelites rally from other quarters (vv. 16–23).

Unlike Saul, Jonathan clearly sees that YHWH does not need large numbers to deliver Israel (14:6; contrast 13:11). This is, indeed, the main point at issue in chapters 13—14 (again, compare Judges 7). Jonathan's words and actions implicitly condemn Saul's earlier approach as timid and faithless.

When Saul does take an active hand in the battle, his leadership is not impressive: he lays an oath on his men, wanting to impose his authority on events, and to show his commitment to YHWH (v. 24), but it has the result of limiting the Israelite victory, and leading some into ritual impurity (vv. 30–32). He finds that YHWH will not answer his enquiry as to whether he should continue the pursuit, deduces that his oath has been violated, and identifies Jonathan as the guilty party (vv. 36–42). The narrative at this point echoes the Achan narrative (Josh. 7), and Saul seems to cast himself as a second Joshua, willing to execute even his own son to expiate guilt (vv. 43–44). But this display of zeal is undercut by the people's protest (v. 45): how can the one through whom YHWH has brought victory be executed? The people's 'commonsense' approach, which echoes Saul's own words after the victory over the Ammonites (11:13), makes him seem ludicrous and inconsistent. Saul calls the pursuit off (v. 46). Throughout he has been like an actor missing his cues.

The passage 14:47–52 describes other events from Saul's reign which portray him more favourably: his victories over neighbouring nations; his creation of a standing army; the beginnings of royal administration. Instead of developing any of this material into a longer account (unless we see ch. 15 as an expansion of 14:48), the narrator presents it so briefly that it is overshadowed by the negative account of Saul's first campaign against the Philistines; and by what follows.

Samuel approaches Saul: 'YHWH sent me to anoint you king over his people Israel; now therefore listen to the words of YHWH' (15:1).

This is Saul's last chance: YHWH raised him up as king, so he must listen to YHWH's prophet. The command, given in unambiguous terms, is that he should destroy the Amalekites and their livestock (v. 3). Like the Israelites in Joshua 6, Saul is set a test whose terms are clearly spelled out. Saul wins a victory, but does not fully carry out the command: he had no mandate to spare Agag or keep the choicest animals to make sacrifices of his own (vv. 8–9).

In chapter 13 Saul was told that his kingship stood under judgment, but subsequent events suggest that this was a warning rather than a final rejection, and the warning came only from Samuel's lips. Now, however, YHWH tells Samuel: 'I regret that I made Saul king, for he has turned back from following me, and has not carried out my commands' (15:11; cf. v. 1). Saul has again failed a test, and this time his kingship is forfeit. Samuel goes in search of Saul.

On his journey he learns that Saul has set up a monument and gone on to Gilgal. Saul seems to be playing up his achievements: he wants to sacrifice the spoils of his victory to YHWH; he has set up a monument, 'for himself' (v. 12). Perhaps he has gone to Gilgal because Gilgal featured in Samuel's earlier instructions (cf. 10:5–8). Certainly when he meets Samuel he claims that he has obeyed YHWH's command (v. 13).

Samuel disagrees: if Saul has obeyed YHWH, what are all these sheep and cattle doing? The argument between them (vv. 14–26) once more concerns an apparent technicality (the distinction between 'utter destruction' and sacrifice), but the point is again that Saul has not done as he was commanded. Saul is more argumentative than in chapter

13, and does not immediately concede Samuel's point. He tries to suggest that the people are responsible for sparing the animals (vv. 15, 21); and as for King Agag, it is not as though he has escaped (v. 20). What more must Saul do to please 'YHWH your God' (vv. 15, 21)?

Samuel will not have this: Saul has rebelled, he has rejected YHWH's word, and he has himself been rejected as king (vv. 22–23). This is now irrevocable: 'YHWH has torn the kingdom of Israel from you this very day, and has given it to a neighbour of yours, who is better than you' (v. 28: cf. 13:13–14).

Samuel accompanies Saul as he worships YHWH (vv. 27–31), but this is more a face-saving exercise than a celebration of victory. Samuel kills Agag (pointing up Saul's disobedience) and leaves Saul, never again to see him. He grieves for him and YHWH regrets having made him king (v. 35; cf. v. 11). Saul's reign is effectively over.

Think about
THE *KHEREM* IN I SAMUEL 15

The issue of the *kherem* has already been discussed in connection with Joshua 6—7. Does I Samuel 15, in which YHWH commands the Amalekites and their possessions to be 'utterly destroyed' (v. 13) in a similar manner, throw any light on the issue? Alternatively, does it seem to make the issue even more difficult? How do you respond to YHWH's reason for ordering the Amalekites' destruction (vv. 2–3) and to Samuel's justification for killing Agag (vv. 32–33)? Do the events of I Samuel 30 offer a retrospective justification for what is commanded here?

I SAMUEL 16—31: DAVID'S RISE AND SAUL'S DEMISE

Chapters 8—15 have been treated at length because they are some of the more obviously difficult chapters in 1 Samuel, and because much of what follows flows from them. Chapter 16 introduces David, the man who will replace Saul as king: chapters 16—31 interweave the accounts of David's and Saul's different fates just as chapters 1—4 interwove the accounts of Eli's house and Samuel. It is a long narrative, but one whose main lines are clear.

David is singled out in the same manner as Saul: a feast (sacrifice), followed by anointing and the coming of YHWH's spirit on him, but with no public acclamation for the moment. David's long rise to kingship begins. YHWH's spirit leaves Saul and an 'evil spirit from God' begins to trouble him. This leads to David being taken into his service (16:14–23).

David's suitability to lead Israel emerges in the very first incident where he plays an active role, the account of his duel with Goliath the Philistine champion. His first words characterize him as zealous for YHWH (17:26): 'What shall be done for the man who kills this Philistine, and takes away the reproach from Israel? For who is this uncircumcised Philistine that he should defy the armies of the living God?' His words before he kills Goliath are equally striking (17:45–47):

You come to me with sword and spear and javelin; but I come to you in the name of YHWH of hosts, the God of the armies of Israel, whom you have defied. This very day YHWH will deliver you into my hand . . . so that all the earth may know that there is a God in Israel, and that all this assembly

Digging deeper:
THE EVIL SPIRIT FROM YHWH

'Now the spirit of YHWH departed from Saul, and an evil spirit from YHWH tormented him' (16:14). What does this mean? Does the narrator conceive of YHWH having in his service evil spirits, spiritual beings perhaps somewhat like the 'demons' in the Gospels? How does the 'evil spirit from YHWH' relate to the 'spirit of YHWH' referred to earlier in the verse? In using the phrase 'from YHWH' rather than 'of YHWH' does the narrator imply that YHWH is not personally implicated in evil even though he sends the evil spirit?

The closest parallel to this verse is Judges 9:23: 'God sent an evil spirit between Abimelech and the lords of Shechem'. In that passage 'evil spirit' could simply mean 'bad attitude' or 'poisoned relationships'. 'Spirit' (*ruakh*) in some Old Testament texts can mean something like 'mood' (Gen. 26:35, where NRSV 'made life bitter' is literally 'were a bitterness of spirit'; 1 Kgs 21:5, literally, 'why is your spirit resentful?'). In this passage and other references to the 'spirit of YHWH' in Judges and Samuel, does 'spirit' denote a being which may in some sense be called personal? Or does it describe an emanation of divine power which, though it may be an expression of the divine will, is no more intrinsically personal than the 'fire of YHWH' in 1 Kings 18:38?

Certainly, the narrative of Saul's decline would be psychologically intelligible even if there were no mention of the 'evil spirit of YHWH'. Indeed, the depiction of Saul in 1 Samuel 16—31 at many points suggests some kind of mental illness, and does so with striking realism. It seems (bearing in mind the difficulties of psychoanalysing characters in a text) that one aspect of what is going on in Saul's mind as the 'evil spirit' afflicts him is suppressed guilt at continuing as king even though YHWH's prophet has rejected him (16:2 has already hinted at his determination to continue as king) and, later, intense jealousy of David's successes against the Philistines (18:8–10; 19:8–10). But if 'evil spirit' is understood as something like 'fit of depression' or 'psychosis', how are we to understand the phrase 'from YHWH'?

Another approach to this issue is to ask (rather as we asked in connection with the Samson narratives of Judges 14—16): what are the consequences of Saul's affliction by the evil spirit? Note that the references to the evil spirit are limited to the section of narrative which describes David entering Saul's service and the breakdown of relationship between them, chs 16—19.

may know that YHWH does not save by sword and spear . . .

Like Jonathan in chapter 14, David is confident that he can defeat any enemy if YHWH is with him. Saul has never said anything like this. Here, the narrator suggests, is someone who understands YHWH's power and his purposes for Israel; in short, here is someone acting like a king.

Saul now looks at him with new eyes, and for the first time expresses interest in the question of David's lineage (17:55–58). Perhaps he begins to suspect that David is the threatened 'neighbour of yours, who is better than you' (15:28). Certainly it is obvious from here on that David is destined for power. YHWH is with him and nothing can stop him. Chapters 18—31 trace the stages in his rise.

From chapter 18 on Saul sees David as a possible rival for the throne. Soon he is expressing open hostility against him, and David has to flee him. The narrative then focuses on 'David's rise and Saul's demise' (Gordon 1980). Simply put, everything Saul does in chapters 18—31 (much of it with the aim of killing David) ends in failure, whereas David puts hardly a foot wrong. This can be set out in point form.

Saul:

- Saul twice attacks David with his spear (18:10–11; 19:9–10; cf. 20:33) and twice misses. He is never able to harm him.
- He sends David on military expeditions, hoping he will be killed, but only adds to David's glory. He is forced to let his daughter Michal marry David (18:17–30).
- He tries to turn his children against David, but finds that Jonathan and Michal take David's side (19:1–7, 11; 20:30–34).
- On one occasion when he might have captured David, YHWH's spirit comes upon him and delays him while David escapes (19:18–24).

- He kills the priests and other inhabitants of Nob, believing them to sympathize with David (22:11–19). But this violence rebounds on him: Abiathar escapes and comes to David with the ephod (an item of priestly clothing to which were attached the Urim and Thummim, used for divination; see Meyers, *ABD* II) and David uses it to escape Saul (23:6–13).
- On another occasion when David is in danger of being captured, Saul is diverted by a Philistine attack (23:24–29).
- He drives away from Israel his most skilful commander and the resourceful warriors who have gathered around him (27:1–4).
- He is killed in battle, along with three of his sons and many other Israelites (31:1–7). Many Israelites abandon their towns, and the Philistines proclaim a great victory (vv. 8–10). Saul's kingship has ended in disaster for Israel.

David:

- David wins the love of Michal and Jonathan (18:1–4, 20). They both secretly aid David against Saul (19:11–17; 20:35–42; 23:15–18).
- He is always successful in battle against the Philistines. His reputation grows within Israel (18:5–6, 12–16, 30; 23:5; cf. 2 Sam. 3:17–18; 5:1–2).
- Jonathan even predicts David's future kingship and binds himself to David by covenant (20:13–17, 42; 23:17–18).
- David is helped by Ahimelech, priest at Nob (21:1–9).
- He unwisely seeks refuge with the king of Gath, but manages to escape (21:10–14).
- At Adullam in Judah he attracts followers to himself, mainly social outcasts (22:1–2).
- He takes care of his family (vv. 3–4).
- He receives YHWH's guidance through Gad the prophet (22:5), through the ephod

(23:2, 4, 10, 12; 30:6–8) and even through an Egyptian captive (30:11–15).

- Though on the run, David remains concerned for Israel's welfare: he delivers Keilah from the Philistines (23:1–6). He flees Keilah to prevent Saul from destroying the town on his account (vv. 10, 13).
- Twice he refuses to kill Saul even though circumstances have placed Saul in his hands (24:1–7; 26:7–12). On these occasions even Saul acknowledges that David is in the right, and will be king (24:17–20; 26:21, 25). David gives Saul an oath that he will not harm his descendants (24:21–22).
- Though sorely tempted to avenge himself on Nabal, he is kept from blood-guilt and gives thanks to YHWH (25:32–35).
- When he again flees into Philistine territory, he and his men are able to live an extraordinary double life, attacking Israel's enemies, but convincing Achish that they are attacking Israelites (27:1–12).
- When it appears that David will have to join the Philistines in fighting Saul (28:1), the other Philistine commanders refuse to let him come along, and he has a plausible excuse for leaving the field of battle (29:1–11).
- The Amalekites have meanwhile attacked his city, but David pursues and defeats them, rescuing his and his men's women and children (30:1–20). He is in 'great danger', but is rescued through YHWH's guidance (30:6–8).
- In the aftermath of that battle he shows himself to be a fair leader (30:21–25). He gives some of the spoil to his supporters in Judah (30:26–31).

Of course, to dissect chapters 18—31 in this way completely fails to convey their skill and drama. But it underscores how the narrative

brings out David's fitness to be king and Saul's unfitness. David in these chapters shows what a 'man after [YHWH's] own heart' (13:14) looks like, and Saul shows what it means to have forfeited YHWH's favour. See, for example, Samuel's words at 28:16–19:

> . . . YHWH has turned from you and become your enemy. YHWH has done to you just as he spoke by me; for YHWH has torn the kingdom out of your hand, and given it to your neighbour, David. Because you did not obey the voice of YHWH . . . therefore YHWH has done this thing to you today. Moreover, YHWH will give Israel along with you into the hands of the Philistines; and tomorrow you and your sons shall be with me . . .

These words restate Samuel's earlier prophecy (15:26–28), and confirm that what has happened since then has simply been the outworking of that prophecy. All Saul's attempts to hang on to the kingship have been futile; worse, they have brought disaster on himself, his family and Israel.

David, by contrast, is favoured by YHWH, commits his way to YHWH (22:3), looks to YHWH to vindicate him rather than taking matters into his own hand (26:9–11), always seeks Israel's welfare, and is recognized as Israel's future ruler even before he comes to power (23:17; 24:20; 25:30). We sense YHWH preserving David and his men in the midst of dangerous circumstances, as David weaves a path between hostile Philistines and an equally hostile Saul.

On one level, then, the narrative can be read as apologetic (justification) for David. It prepares for 2 Samuel 1—4, which describe the last stages of David's rise to power. In these chapters, as we shall see, the narrator had to explain some incidents which were potentially damaging to David's reputation.

But the narrative goes beyond mere justification of David's rise to power. The narrator is fascinated with the character of Saul, and portrays him with a complexity which goes beyond the needs of a simplistic apologetic. These chapters must be one of the earliest attempts in human literature to depict mental instability, and they do so with great skill. We see Saul becoming increasingly paranoid (22:6–10; 23:21–23), almost monomaniac in his pursuit of David (note the telling description of him as sitting 'with his spear in hand' at 22:6). But he is still capable of remorse (as in his exchanges with David in chs 24 and 26). Certainly chapter 28 confirms that YHWH has rejected Saul as king, but it also captures the desperation of a man rejected by YHWH: YHWH no longer speaks to him, but he so longs for a word of reassurance that he is prepared to consult a medium and raise the spirit of Samuel, a man from whom he can hardly hope for encouragement (vv. 5–7, 15).

Think about
SAUL'S SEANCE

What is going on in 28:3–19? Was it really possible (though forbidden to Israel) to communicate with the dead through a medium? Is a naturalist (psychological) explanation of the whole episode viable (e.g. that the 'communication' from Samuel is a projection of Saul's guilt feelings)? How do you explain the medium's reaction in v. 12?

You may find Goldingay's treatment of this episode (pp. 168–82) helpful.

We feel something like pity for him as he hears Samuel's prophecy of his death and

falls prostrate (28:20). Indeed, the last verses of this episode are unexpectedly moving. None of those involved is a model Israelite – Saul the rebel king, the woman who engages in prohibited religious practices, and the servants who have brought the two together – and yet the woman's concern to feed Saul before he leaves adds a brief touch of human warmth to this eerie chapter (vv. 21–25). Saul leaves knowing that he will die, yet having experienced kindness of a sort before he goes. And he does not in the end shrink from his death (Goldingay, pp. 180–2).

Saul in decline is one of the most haunting and problematic characters in the Old Testament. Nabal in chapter 25 is, perhaps, little more than a cartoon villain, but that is not true of Saul in his last years.

Nor is Saul's legacy entirely bad. The inhabitants of Jabesh-gilead, in a touching gesture, rescue his and his sons' bodies and dispose of them decently (31:11–12). They at least have reason to honour Saul (ch. 11). The narrator thus reminds us of the event which began Saul's reign, and of a time when YHWH was still with him. It is a thought-provoking note on which to end his account.

Anyone who takes seriously the possibility that there is a god who (at least sometimes) deals with people as he deals with Saul in 1 Samuel must find this account troubling. Some interpreters of 1 Samuel place the issue of YHWH's justice centre-stage, and argue that the narrator portrays YHWH and his servant Samuel negatively (Gunn 1980; Exum, pp. 16–42): they are both vain, sensitive and vindictive when their authority is challenged. In effect YHWH, through Samuel's agency, punishes Israel for daring to voice criticism of him, and Saul is little more than the innocent victim of YHWH's malevolence.

We have interpreted 1 Samuel differently. Israel and Saul bear some responsibility for the disasters of Saul's kingship. In different ways they are both guilty of disobedience and unbelief. And when Samuel prophesies Saul's rejection as king, Saul's response is to cling on to the kingship for himself and Jonathan (16:2; 18:8–9; 20:31), and to persecute the one he sees as his likely successor. More than once Saul is challenged with the irrationality of his behaviour (19:4–5; 24:9–15); indeed, he himself sometimes sees that YHWH is with David (18:28) and that David will succeed him (24:20–21; 26:25). But he does not finally change his ways. Thus he makes a bad situation worse and leads Israel to disaster.

Chapters 24—26 fit in here. They are an example of 'narrative analogy', the use of a repeated plot structure to bring out the links between thematically related episodes (Gordon 1980). (See Table 5.)

The parallels between chapters 24 and 26 are clear: similar events unfold in more or less the same order. The parallels between these two chapters and chapter 25 are less exact, but chapter 25 handles the same themes: the possibility of David avenging himself against an enemy who treats him unjustly; the intervention of YHWH to vindicate David. The narrator spells out the parallel between Nabal and Saul by describing Nabal as holding a feast 'like the feast of a king' (25:36).

Why tell essentially the same account in three varied forms? Clearly all three chapters portray David favourably, as one

who abstains from bloodshed and vengeance (or in chapter 25, one whom YHWH restrains from bloodshed). But perhaps the chapters also function as an implicit theodicy. The narrator in chapter 24 seems to suggest that Saul is given a chance to repent, and abandon his pursuit of David. He is confronted with evidence of David's good intentions, and also with the possibility of his own death. Has YHWH brought about the meeting for this purpose (and not, as David's men suppose, as an opportunity for vengeance, v. 4)? Saul responds with remorse. Seemingly he accepts that David will be king, even to the extent of making him swear an oath of protection (vv. 21–22). David and Saul go their separate ways, but the chapter leaves open the possibility that Saul will now relinquish the kingship in favour of David.

But by the beginning of chapter 26 this possibility has vanished: by giving Michal to another man and resuming his pursuit of David, Saul has shown that he will not stand aside in favour of David. Events follow a similar course in this chapter, but different points are made: that reconciliation between David and Saul is now impossible, for David can no longer trust Saul (vv. 21–22; cf. 27:1); that YHWH will vindicate David by bringing about Saul's death (vv. 10, 23–24; David has, after all, seen what happened to Nabal). Saul, for his part, can no longer bear to admit that David will be king (v. 25; cf. 24:20). Is there a sense that Saul has passed the point of no return, that he must now face the consequences of having raised his hand against 'YHWH's anointed' (26:9, 11: the words apply to Saul as much as to David; cf. 16:13)?

Chapters 18—31, then, suggest that Saul, though rejected as king, did not have to end

TABLE 5   THEMATICALLY RELATED EPISODES IN I SAMUEL 24—26

Plot element	I Samuel 24	I Samuel 25	I Samuel 26
Opportunity for David to avenge himself on his enemy	Saul is alone and at David's mercy (3)	David has 400 men to lead against Nabal's household (12–13) and wants to destroy it (21–22)	Saul is asleep and at David's mercy (7). YHWH has sent sleep on Saul's camp (12)
Reasons for David to avenge himself	Saul is pursuing David (1–2). David's men suggest that YHWH means David to kill Saul (4)	David's men have helped Nabal's shepherds, but Nabal will not give a favour in return (2–11, 14–17)	Saul has given Michal, David's wife, to another man (25:44), and continues to pursue David (1–4). Abishai suggests YHWH intends David to kill Saul (8)
David does not avenge himself	Cuts off a piece of Saul's cloak, prevents his men from attacking Saul (4–7)	Abigail, Nabal's wife, persuades him not to (26–31)	Prevents Abishai from killing Saul, takes Saul's spear and water-jar (7, 12)
Reasons for David's action	Will not treat 'YHWH's anointed' with violence (5–6)	Abigail's intervention (26–31)	Will not treat 'YHWH's anointed' with violence. Saul will die as YHWH wills (9–11)
David accuses his enemy, expresses his grievances	Saul is pursuing him even though he means no harm (9–10)	Nabal has returned him evil for good (21–22)	Mocks Abner (13–16). Saul is pursuing him without cause and driving him from YHWH's presence (17–18)
David confronts his enemy with evidence that he has spared his life	The piece of cloak (10)	[No parallel]	Spear, water-jar (16, 22)
David calls on YHWH to vindicate him	'May YHWH judge between me and you!' (12,15)	David praises YHWH for keeping him from avenging himself (32–35)	'May my life be precious in the sight of YHWH' (24)
David's enemy responds	'You are more righteous than I. You did not kill me when you could have. You will be king' (16–21)	[No parallel]	'Blessed be you, my son David! You will do many things and succeed in them' (25)
The final outcome	Saul and David go separate ways (22)	YHWH strikes Nabal. Nabal dies. David praises YHWH for vindicating him. David marries Abigail (36–42)	Saul and David go separate ways (25). David goes into Philistine territory (27:1–2)

as he did: it was his continuing resistance to YHWH's will that made his last years as king so disastrous for himself and for Israel. He was not simply a puppet in the hands of a vindictive YHWH, but a complex human being who for a long time had it in his power to make real choices about the way he would go.

Yet how culpable was Saul? Here is a man, we might say, who was thrust against his will into a position which exposed his weaknesses and who was then condemned for his failures. Was that fair? Is it realistic to suggest that, once informed of his rejection as king, he should have given up kingship and lent his support to David? Perhaps. Maybe the narrative of Eli, which provides the theological categories for so much of 1 and 2 Samuel, suggests the appropriate response for a rejected leader: 'It is YHWH; let him do what seems good to him' (1 Sam. 3:18). This, however, was not Saul's response.

But here we come to the question of the 'evil spirit from YHWH': was Saul actually driven into irrationality by YHWH? The text could certainly be taken that way, though there are other possibilities (see above). The question is impossible to resolve because, like all such language in the Histories, the phrase is imprecise: what is involved when a spirit from YHWH comes upon a person? Does the coming of an evil spirit (depression?) leave a man responsible for his actions? It is hard to answer such questions.

Similarly, if Israel is taught a lesson (that there are right and wrong ways to choose leaders), the lesson comes at great cost. Admittedly it is not the first nor the last time in the Histories that Israel is left to face the consequences of particular choices. But the narrator in these chapters does not gloss over the difficult aspects of YHWH's acts of judgment. This is a narrative that was apparently *meant* to be troubling.

2 SAMUEL 1—7: DAVID BECOMES KING; THE JOURNEYS OF THE ARK (II)

David learns of Israel's defeat from an Amalekite (1:4–10). He mourns Israel's loss, and laments Saul's and Jonathan's deaths as a tragedy for Israel (1:17–27).

War with the house of Saul (2 Sam. 2—4)

Following YHWH's guidance, David and his men leave Philistine territory and move to Hebron. There David is anointed king by his own tribe, Judah (2:1–4), and attempts to widen his power base (vv. 5–7). However, Abner, the commander of Saul's army, has made Ishbosheth (NRSV 'Ishbaal') king over the other tribes (v. 9). This leads to a 'long war between the house of Saul and the house of David' (3:1), between 'all Israel' (2:9–10; 3:12, 17; 4:1) and 'the house of Judah' (2:10–11; 3:10). The war apparently lasts several years (2:11), but is represented in the narrative only by the account of the battle of Gibeon (2:12–32), which the narrator presents as a futile waste of life: Abner does not want to kill Asahel (vv. 21–22); and the exchange between him and Joab in vv. 26–27 suggests the folly of Israelite killing Israelite. The war drags on, and David's side starts to gain the upper hand (3:1–5); but it is a war that should never have happened, a further negative legacy of Saul's reign.

Abner has been strengthening his own position, and transfers his loyalty to David (3:6–11), who he now accepts is YHWH's chosen king. He negotiates with David and works to win Israel over to him (vv. 12–18). He then reports to David and departs with the stated intention of summoning Israel to make David king. Joab, however, publicly condemns Abner's motives, pursues him and kills him (vv. 19–27). David is quick to distance himself from Joab's action (vv. 28–39): he curses Joab's house, publicly mourns Abner's death, fasts for a day, and continues to express regret privately before his servants. 'All the people took notice of it, and it pleased them . . . So all the people and all Israel understood that day that the king had no part in the killing of Abner son of Ner' (vv. 36–37).

Think about
ABNER'S DEATH

The narrator spends most of chapters 2—3 describing Abner's death and events leading up to it. It was clearly important to him to persuade later readers of David's innocence, just as it was important for David to persuade Israel at the time (3:36–37).

Consider the following in relation to 2 Samuel 2—3:

- What are Abner's motives? Why does he switch sides? Is Joab's account of his motives (3:24–25) plausible?
- In what ways does the narrator try to convince the reader that David had nothing to with Abner's death?
- How might Abner's death have benefited David, and how might it have harmed him?
- Why does David not punish Joab beyond cursing him? Are his words at 3:39 convincing?
- Look at other references to the violence of the sons of Zeruiah: I Samuel 26:8–11; 2 Samuel 16:9–12; 19:21–23; cf. also I Samuel 22:2 and 24:4–7. How has it come about that David has such people among his supporters?

Things are now falling apart in Ishbosheth's camp. Rechab and Baanah, two of his officers, take matters into their own hands, killing Ishbosheth and carrying his head to David (4:2–7). They assume that David will welcome their action, even see it as YHWH's vindication of him. But David condemns them as having murdered a 'righteous man', and has them killed (vv. 8–12). Their hands and feet are displayed by the pool of Hebron, whereas Ishbosheth's head is honourably buried. The message is clear: David does not want revenge over his former enemies in Israel.

Israel's elders come to commit themselves to David: 'We are your bone and flesh' (5:1). Perhaps David's treatment of Ishbosheth's killers has assured them of his good intentions, but they speak as though they needed little persuading: they recognized his leadership even under Saul, and they now believe that YHWH has chosen him to rule them (v. 2; cf. 3:17–18). It is also true that with Ishbosheth's death they have few options left. David makes a covenant with them before YHWH (cf. 1 Sam. 10:25) and they anoint him as king. The narrator marks the event with an accession formula: David ruled for 40 years, seven years over Judah alone and 33 over all Israel (5:4–5). He implies that David has been king since his anointing at Hebron, though not recognized as king by all Israel until now.

David becomes king (2 Sam. 5—7)
The rest of chapter 5 describes how David consolidates his kingship: his capture of Jerusalem (vv. 6–10); his alliance with Hiram of Tyre (vv. 11–12); and his victories over the Philistines (vv. 17–25). (Up to this point the Philistines seem to have regarded David as their ally – he was, after all, fighting the remnants of Saul's house.) These are significant achievements. The conquest of Jerusalem, one of the last remaining Canaanite cities in the land, is important for Israel and for David as king. By defeating the Philistines David regains territory lost after Saul's defeat and strengthens Israel

politically. The narrator sees behind these events the hand of YHWH, who has 'exalted [David's] kingdom for the sake of his people Israel' (vv. 10, 12). But he describes the events quickly. The account of Jerusalem's capture is so brief that it remains unclear how the stronghold was breached. The battles against the Philistines are covered at greater length, but mainly so as to highlight YHWH's role (vv. 19–20, 23–25): the account has nothing like the length or narrative skill of, for example, 1 Samuel 17. The narrator's main interest is in what follows: he plays down the events of chapter 5 so that chapters 6—7 may stand out in their context.

Chapter 6 is devoted to one topic: David brings the ark from Kiriath-jearim into Jerusalem. There is a terrible accident on the way (vv. 6–8), which causes him to doubt whether the ark is meant to come to Jerusalem, but it becomes clear that YHWH intends blessing, and the ark finally arrives in the city, to general rejoicing (vv. 9–15). David offers sacrifices and blesses the people (vv. 17–19)

This is a highly significant event, for at least three reasons:

- It implies YHWH's blessing for Israel. If the Philistine capture of the ark was an act of judgment on Israel's disobedience (1 Sam. 4), and the sojourn of the ark at Kiriath-jearim suggested an uneasy truce between YHWH and Israel (1 Samuel 6:10—7:2), the fact that David, Israel's king, is able to bring the ark into Jerusalem, a stronghold where it can rest undisturbed, suggests a restored relationship: YHWH now dwells among his people, at the newly established centre of the kingdom of Israel.

- It also declares YHWH's kingship. The ark enters a recently captured Canaanite stronghold, symbolizing YHWH's rule over the land. It fits with this that David brings the ark to Jerusalem after a narrative describing victories over the Philistines.

- It has implications for David as king. In the ancient Near East, if a deity permitted a king (through oracles) to build a temple, that was taken as a sign that the deity favoured the king and would bless his dynasty (Hurowitz, pp. 131–67). In a similar way, the fact that David can bring the ark into the city he has captured (the 'city of David', vv. 12, 16) validates him as YHWH's chosen king. David is not himself permitted to build a temple, but his son is. This legitimates David's line (ch. 7).

However, the ark is not simply a religious symbol which David co-opts for his own purposes. It represents the potentially dangerous presence of the god of Israel, who must be treated with respect, as the Uzzah incident shows (vv. 6–8). YHWH enters Jerusalem on his own terms, not at David's compulsion. The ark, moreover, contains the tablets of the law (cf. Deut. 10:1–5; 1 Kgs 8:9) and is a reminder of the covenant requirements of Sinai. This whole narrative in which YHWH, as it were, takes up official residence among his people seems to emphasize that this is not an inevitable or necessarily permanent arrangement: if YHWH is to remain in Zion and bless his people, then (by implication) the people must fear him and keep his commandments.

The same applies to David's kingship. As the ark makes its way to Jerusalem, David dances before it, showing gratitude and humility before YHWH (vv. 14, 16). Michal, his wife (and Saul's daughter), deeply disapproves: such behaviour is unworthy of the 'king of Israel' (vv. 16, 20). David, equally angry, reminds her that YHWH chose him as king in place of her father Saul. Which is better, to abase oneself before YHWH or to resist YHWH and be removed as Saul was (vv. 21–22)? Michal and David represent two opposed views of kingship: Michal emphasizes royal dignity, David humility before YHWH. The future lies with David's line (v. 23). But the point is that David does not believe that because the ark is in his city he is free to behave as he wishes: rather, YHWH has chosen him and he must obey YHWH. We should bear this point in mind as we read chapter 7.

> **Think about**
> **THE ACCOUNT OF MICHAL**
>
> Look up the following references to Michal: 1 Samuel 14:49; 18:20–28; 19:11–17; 25:44; 2 Samuel 3:13–14; 6:16–23. This is 'the story of Michal'. What strikes you about it? How is Michal portrayed? How do you respond to this portrait?

Deuteronomy 12 anticipated a time when Israel would enter Canaan and YHWH would give them 'rest from your enemies all around so that you live in safety' (v. 10). At that time the Israelites would bring their offerings 'to the place that YHWH your God will choose as a dwelling for his name' (v. 11). Deuteronomy 12 clearly underlies 2 Samuel 7.

In this chapter David sees that YHWH has given him 'rest from all his enemies around him', and tells the prophet Nathan of his intention to build a permanent dwelling for the ark (vv. 1–3). These verses explicitly relate the two themes of Deuteronomy 12 (rest in the land, worship at a central sanctuary) to David's kingship: Israel has found rest in the land through him; and now David, by building a temple, wants to establish his city definitively as the promised 'place' where the Israelites will gather to worship. David, like any ancient Near Eastern ruler, is seeking legitimization for his kingship: if he is allowed to build a temple for the god of Israel, that will put beyond doubt that YHWH has chosen him and his descendants as Israel's royal dynasty. But the references to Deuteronomy 12 remind us that David's request raises larger issues relating to YHWH's purposes for Israel. Both sets of issues are addressed in chapter 7.

At first Nathan sees no objection. But then YHWH gives Nathan a long message for David (vv. 5–16). This falls into three sections, each of them introduced by a 'speech formula' (vv. 5a, 8a and 11b), and makes three main points:

- vv. 5–7: The building of a temple will be a major turning-point in Israel's history: never before has Israel's god had such a dwelling among the Israelites. (Apparently the building in which the ark was housed at Shiloh, 1 Samuel 1—3, does not count.)
- vv. 8–11a: David is YHWH's 'servant' (the term puts him on a par with Moses and Joshua: Joshua 1:1–2; 24:29). YHWH has chosen him to lead Israel (cf. 5:12), has defeated his enemies, and will give him a great 'name' (reputation). Israel will enjoy security as never before; David will have rest from his enemies (v. 11). This acknowledges that the time is ripe for YHWH to choose a place 'as a dwelling for his name': the conditions in Deuteronomy 12:10–11 have been fulfilled.
- vv. 11b–16: YHWH will 'make' a 'house' (= dynasty) for David: David's son will become king after him. This son will 'build

a house for my name', and his rule will be established 'for ever' (v. 13). YHWH will adopt him as his own 'son': though he may be punished for disobedience, YHWH will continue to love him. His dynasty will be unlike Saul's, for YHWH will not abandon him (vv. 14–15). David's 'house' and rule will last 'for ever' (v. 16).

So David is not allowed to build the temple, but he is promised everything that temple-builders in the ancient Near East hoped for: security for himself and a lasting dynasty for his descendants.

Why can David not build the temple? Apparently it is more appropriate for his son to build it because this will more clearly highlight YHWH's grace towards David and Israel. That is why these verses dwell on what YHWH has done and will do for David and Israel (vv. 8–11). The word-plays involving 'build', 'house' and 'name' make the same point: the 'house' YHWH makes for David comes before that which David's son will build for him (vv. 5, 7, 11, 13, 16); YHWH gives David a 'great name' before David's son builds a house for YHWH's name (vv. 9, 13). David receives these promises before a stone of the temple has been laid, and this is more fitting: whatever the future glories of David's line, they are ultimately due to YHWH's prior initiative.

Digging deeper:
DAVID AND THE TEMPLE

Compare with 2 Samuel 7:5–16 the following passages, which also give reasons why David was not allowed to build the temple: 1 Kings 5:3–5; 8:17–20; 1 Chronicles 22:7–10. How do you explain the difference in perspective between these passages and 2 Samuel 7?

David responds at length: he acknowledges YHWH's goodness to him and to Israel (vv. 18–24). He prays that YHWH will do what he has promised, implying that these promises are so great that he need ask for nothing else. The result will be that YHWH's own name will be upheld in Israel (vv. 25–29).

Even more than chapter 6, chapter 7 stands out in its context. YHWH's and David's words survey past and future in a way reminiscent of 1 Samuel 12: 2 Samuel 7 is another turning-point within Joshua–Kings. The promises to David are presented as a natural continuation of YHWH's previous dealings with Israel. Both YHWH and David speak about Israel's past history (vv. 6–7, 23–24), implying that what YHWH is doing through David fits with what he has done for Israel previously. In particular, YHWH's promise of blessing for David and his descendants uses terms clearly reminiscent of the promises to Abraham: 'I will make for you a great name' (v. 9; cf. Gen. 12:2); 'I will raise up your offspring . . . who shall come forth from your body' (v. 12; cf. Gen. 12:7, 15:4). The implication is that through David the promises to Abraham come closer to completion.

The same point emerges when we note that in 2 Samuel 5—7 David's kingdom in many respects expresses in reality what Moses in Deuteronomy could only present as a vision: David rules over an obedient and united Israel which is established in the land and will now worship YHWH in the place he has chosen (cf. Deut. 12); Israel enjoys the blessings of the land, as symbolized by David's gifts of food to the people at 6:19 (cf. Deut. 8:7–10; 28:3–5); David himself fits Deuteronomy's description of the kind of king Israel is permitted to have (cf. Deut. 17:14–20).

According to 2 Samuel 5—7, then, kingship, at least the kind of kingship represented by David, fulfils YHWH's purposes for Israel. It does not undermine what YHWH has done in Israel up to this point. Any attempt to sum up 1 and 2 Samuel's view of the Israelite monarchy must take these chapters into account along with more negative-seeming chapters such as 1 Samuel 8—12.

How should we understand the promise that David's descendants will form a dynasty which will last 'for ever', which, unlike Saul's dynasty, will never come to an end, even if is necessary to discipline some members for disobedience (2 Sam. 7:14–16)? Is this literally meant, or is it 'royal rhetoric' (cf. 1 Kgs 1:31; Neh. 2:3)? Does YHWH commit himself to David's line without reserve? Passages in Kings will restate this promise in an apparently more conditional sense (e.g. 1 Kgs 9:4–5), and the issue will return to us there. Here it is enough to note that, on the one hand, David's response to YHWH does treat this promise as very great; but that, on the other, chapter 6 tends, as argued above, to suggest conditionality. The issues of obedience and covenant faithfulness are not explicitly raised in 2 Samuel 7, but they are clearly present in the narrative immediately preceding. We must also read chapter 7 in the light of the chapters following.

2 SAMUEL 8—20: DAVID AS KING
Obedience and blessing (2 Sam. 8—10)
Chapter 7 of 2 Samuel, the conclusion of the account of David's rise, sets out a vision of how YHWH can bless Israel through his chosen king. How do the later years of David's kingship match up to the vision?

That is the subject of 2 Samuel 8—20. (We thus agree with Gordon 1984, pp. 81–94, that 'History of David as King' is a better rubric than 'Succession Narrative' for these chapters.)

Chapter 8 describes further victories of David over surrounding nations. It notes that 'YHWH gave David victory wherever he went' (vv. 6, 14). Obedient Israel wins military victories (cf. Deut. 28:7). The nations are coming to know the power of Israel's god (cf. 1 Sam. 17:46). Israel in this period is internally healthy too: David's administrative structures ensure just rule (vv. 15–18). Chapter 9, in which David treats Mephibosheth kindly because of his oath to Jonathan, ties up a loose end from earlier in the account (2 Sam. 4:4) in a way that is similarly to David's credit (though note that the way in which David 'shows kindness' means that he is able to keep an eye on a survivor of Saul's line who might be a threat to his rule.)

In 2 Samuel 10 and 11 a decline sets in, barely perceptible in chapter 10, very clear in chapter 11. Israel fights again, this time against a coalition of Ammonites and Arameans (ch. 10). In contrast to chapter 8, David is absent from the first battle. The narrative instead dwells on the bold leadership of Joab and Abishai (10:9–14). But in the second battle David wins a striking victory, putting a wedge between Ammon and Aram (vv. 15–19). At the beginning of chapter 11, 'Joab with his officers and all Israel' continue the war against the Ammonites, again without David, even though, as the narrator notes, this is 'the time when kings go out to battle' (v. 1). This time David's absence has serious consequences: while in Jerusalem, he seduces Bathsheba, the wife of one of his soldiers.

To cover up the fact of her pregnancy he has her husband Uriah killed in battle. After mourning, she becomes his wife and bears him a son.

Sin and death (2 Sam. 11—20)

This is a terrible abuse of royal power. The narrator comments: 'the thing that David had done displeased YHWH' (11:27), and in chapter 12 Nathan is sent to denounce David. In chapter 7 Nathan announced YHWH's intention to establish a 'house' for David's son, and to bring peace for Israel. In chapter 12, using language which reminds us of the earlier promise, Nathan pronounces a judgment on David: 'the sword shall never depart from your house' (v. 10); 'I will raise up trouble [literally, 'evil'] against you from within your own house' (v. 11); 'the child ['son'] that is born to you shall die' (v. 14).

Nathan's rebuke echoes Samuel's rejection of Saul ('your neighbour', 2 Sam. 12:11; cf. 1 Sam. 15:28). David, who proclaimed to Michal his humility before YHWH (2 Sam. 6:20–23), is now accused of contempt for YHWH's word (vv. 9–10; cf. 1 Sam. 15:1, 24–26). The only differences between Saul and David are that David's line is not explicitly rejected (2 Sam. 12:11; cf. 1 Sam. 15:28); and that David immediately admits his sin and is forgiven (2 Sam. 12:13). The promise of chapter 7 is not set aside, then, but the judgments pronounced by Nathan work themselves out in the death of his son by Bathsheba (12:15–19), in the death of Amnon (ch. 13) and, most devastatingly, in the rebellion and death of Absalom (chs 15—18).

The narrator suggests how these catastrophes follow from David's crime and YHWH's judgment of it. In 2 Samuel 13:1 Absalom and Amnon are introduced, each described as 'son of David'. Amnon's rape of Tamar, sister of Absalom, is a more brutal and emotive version of David's adultery with Bathsheba (vv. 2–20). David himself apparently sees the similarities, for, though 'very angry' (v. 21) at Amnon, he does nothing. (So a king permits things which in Judges 19—21 were attributed to the absence of a king.) Absalom now hates Amnon. He has Amnon killed at a feast where 'all the king's sons' are present (vv. 27–29), and flees into exile. A false report reaches David that all his sons are dead, and David briefly believes it (vv. 29–31). The narrator thus momentarily toys with the possibility that YHWH's promise to David will fail. He also characterizes David as out of touch with events in his own family: Jonadab, his nephew, knows what is going on (vv. 32–33) but David does not, or he would not have let Amnon go to Absalom's feast.

Chapter 14 describes Absalom's restoration to David's court. The lengthy parable of the Tekoan woman (similar to Nathan's in ch. 12) part persuades, part deceives David into agreeing to Absalom's return (vv. 1–21). But David does not permit Absalom to see him (vv. 23–24). Seemingly he cannot bring himself either to condemn or to acquit Absalom: perhaps the ambiguity of his own survival in spite of his sin with Bathsheba continues to haunt him. Two years elapse, bracketed by the narrator's comments that Absalom 'did not come into the king's presence' (vv. 24, 28). In between those comments the narrator places material which portrays Absalom as a growing threat to David: he is handsome and proud (vv. 25–26); he still bears a grudge, for he names his daughter after the sister Amnon violated (v. 27). The passage suggests his resentment, symbolized by his fire-raising in v. 30. When Absalom finally is restored (v. 33), he has become a dangerous man.

The narrator immediately describes Absalom's conspiracy against David (15:1–12). Absalom wins support by claiming that David no longer administers justice. These claims are clearly plausible to the hearers, though the narrator does not comment either way. Certainly Absalom is driven by a sense that David has not acted justly in regard to Tamar.

Again, David is unaware of these developments. When he does hear of them, his response (15:14) echoes Nathan's prophecy: 'Hurry, or he will soon overtake us, and bring disaster ['evil'] down upon us, and attack the city with the edge of the sword' (cf. 12:10–11). Again the possibility is raised of Nathan's words being fulfilled in an act of destruction (this time involving the city of David) which will undo the promise of chapter 7. This does not happen (David flees to prevent it happening, v. 14), but the consequences for Israel will be severe: note the general weeping as David leaves (v. 23).

As he once fled Saul, David now flees Absalom. There are parallels between this part of 2 Samuel and 1 Samuel 19—31. As he earlier moved his family to Moab until it should become plain 'what God will do for me' (1 Sam. 22:3), so now David again entrusts his fate to YHWH (2 Sam. 15:25–26). However, in the earlier narrative it was clear that David would in the end become king. This time the possibility that YHWH has rejected David is real. David's refusal to have the ark with him (2 Sam. 15:24–26) reflects this: the ephod in 1 Samuel was a symbol of YHWH's presence (see especially 23:6), but now David will not presume that YHWH is

with him. As he departs, David leaves supporters in Jerusalem to undermine Absalom's position: Ahimaaz, Jonathan and Hushai (15:27–29, 32–37). But the immediate news is not good: Mephibosheth appears to have abandoned David (16:1–4). Shimei, one of Saul's relatives and a representative of those in Israel who remain hostile to David, comes to curse David, and David will not stop him (16:5–14). Perhaps Shimei is right: perhaps YHWH has removed David in favour of his son (v. 8), an unexpected fulfilment of Nathan's prophecy, and all David can do is acquiesce, in the hope that YHWH will relent.

The role of Ahithophel, David's counsellor who has gone over to Absalom (15:12), also creates uncertainty. David has prayed that YHWH will 'turn the counsel of Ahithophel to foolishness' (15:31), and has sent Hushai to counter him (vv. 32–36). But Ahithophel's first advice to Absalom, to sleep with David's concubines publicly, though terribly abusive of these women, seems tactically sound; indeed, it fulfils Nathan's prophecy (16:16–22; cf. 12:11–12). Perhaps YHWH has not answered David's prayer, but is using Ahithophel to fulfil his own purposes. It is only when Hushai's advice is preferred to Ahithophel's that it becomes plain which way events will go, a turning-point marked by the narrator's comment that 'YHWH had ordained to defeat the good counsel of Ahithophel, so that YHWH might bring ruin ['evil'] on Absalom' (17:14). The message that Hushai has succeeded reaches David, not without difficulty (17:15–21); Ahithophel hangs himself; and provisions reach David's men before the battle with Absalom (17:27–29). The balance has shifted in David's favour.

The narrator's comment in 17:14 anticipates David's eventual victory, but it does so in a double-edged way: another of David's sons will die. Israel, too, bears the cost of Absalom's rebellion, and many lives are lost in the decisive battle (18:6–8). Rather than describing the battle between David's men and Absalom's in detail, however, the account in chapter 18 focuses on Absalom's death and David's response.

Absalom's aim has apparently been to kill David – a sound policy, as David's own men recognize (18:1–4). David, less realistically, has asked his three commanders to 'deal gently' with Absalom (18:5), advice which Joab ignores, though he would rather not have had to kill Absalom himself (vv. 9–15). There follows another scene involving messengers, which focuses on David as he awaits the outcome (18:19–32; cf. 13:30–33 and, more distantly, 1 Sam. 4:12–18). David's hopes are cruelly raised and then dashed, and his grief is, in Old Testament terms, shockingly unrestrained: 'O my son Absalom, my son, my son Absalom! Would I had died instead of you, O Absalom, my son, my son!' (18:33; cf. 19:4). These words form the climax of the narrative since chapter 12, and as David laments, we realize that Nathan's prophecy has indeed worked itself out in terrible ways: David has lost three sons; his house has been torn apart by violence; and Israel as a whole, described as enjoying peace and security at the beginning of chapter 7, has fallen into civil war.

David learns that the tribe of Judah at least is willing for him to return as king. They come down to the Jordan to escort him and his men across (19:11–15). There follow three dialogues, as David speaks in turn with Shimei, Mephibosheth and Barzillai (19:16–40). The first exchange is ambiguous. Shimei has come to meet David with a

thousand Benjaminites, and, as he begs David's mercy, takes care to present himself as the 'first of all the house of Joseph' to greet him (19:20). David forgives him, but we do not know whether he does so out of magnanimity or because it would send the wrong message to the other tribes if he did not. In the second dialogue, David, faced with the competing claims of Mephibosheth and Ziba, cannot decide who is in the right, and divides Mephibosheth's property between them. Mephibosheth's words notwithstanding, he is far from being 'like the angel of God' (19:27): he is an ordinary man, limited in his knowledge, who can provide no more than an approximate solution. Both these exchanges leave a sour taste. As for Barzillai, who has helped David, he gives his son into David's service, but does not himself desire the king's luxuries, preferring his home town in Transjordan (19:33–38). We are perhaps reminded of the trees in Jotham's parable (Judg. 9:7–15): there are better things to do than live out one's days in the royal court.

> **Think about**
> **ZIBA AND MEPHIBOSHETH**
>
> Which of them is lying? Compare 2 Samuel 16:1–4 and 19:24–30. Can you see any way of adjudicating between the conflicting claims? Does the narrator give us any hint to help us?

In general the account of David's return to Jerusalem reminds one of the earlier account of his rise to power (chs 1—5), but suggests that things have changed for the worse since then. Whereas chapters 2 and 5 told how David was accepted as king first by Judah and then by the other tribes of Israel, this account is marked by rivalry between Israel and Judah as to who should have welcomed him back. The result is that David is almost rejected by Israel again (19:41—20:2).

Another changed factor is that Joab is now the dominant figure. It is he who tells David to stop lamenting Absalom's death and welcome his men back (19:1–8). He later kills Amasa, whom David has appointed as commander in his place (20:8–11). No protest on David's part is recorded, even though Joab had not even the shadow of a pretext: Amasa simply stood in the way of his ambitions. Joab also deals with the troublemaker Sheba son of Bicri in a characteristically cynical and brutal way, by a 'wise plan' which involves Sheba's execution (20:14–22). The picture of Sheba's head being thrown over the city wall is not a happy image with which to end the narrative of David as king. The account ends by listing David's officials at this stage of his reign (20:23–26; cf. 8:15–18): Joab is once again army commander (v. 23).

Much of the blessing promised in chapter 7 has vanished by the end of chapter 20. David is still king: he has not been rejected like Saul; he still has sons to succeed him, and a kingdom to rule over. But his reign has fallen under a shadow, and the account of his later years fills one with a sense of what has been lost. In contrast to chapters 5—7, there is no reference to YHWH's involvement in the events of chapters 19—20. This seems fitting.

2 SAMUEL 21—24: CONCLUSION

The books of Samuel conclude with one of the most motley-seeming collections of texts in the Old Testament. Chapters 21—24 consist of two poetic passages enclosed by two sections summarizing military exploits of David and his men, and further enclosed by two narratives of divine judgment and mercy. This is a chiastic structure.

STRUCTURE OF 2 SAMUEL 21—24

A   Famine narrative (21:1–14)
B   David and his heroes: battles with the Philistines (21:15–22)
C   David's Thanksgiving (22:1–51)
C′   David's Last Words (23:1–7)
B′   David and his heroes: battles with the Philistines; the list of the Three and the Thirty (23:8–39)
A′   Plague narrative (24:1–25)

The structure is not entirely symmetrical, for the paired elements vary considerably in size (especially C and C′), but it seems deliberate. Note especially the similar wording of 21:14 and 24:25, and how each of the B elements contains a narrative expressing the concern David's men feel for him (21:15–17; 23:13–17).

Why has the narrator/editor brought such disparate material together? Some of the incidents in these chapters seem to belong in the period described by 2 Samuel 5—8. And why is this material placed where it seems to separate the account of David as king (2 Sam. 8—20) from the account of his last days and death in 1 Kings 1—2? Noth (p. 86, n. 3) argued that these chapters are a later insertion into an earlier narrative in which the present 1 Kings 1—2 followed upon 2 Samuel 20. However, it is not clear that 1 Kings 1—2 was ever the direct continuation of 2 Samuel 20. Many years seem to separate these chapters, and 1 Kings 1—2 is better seen as the introduction to the account of Solomon. 2 Samuel 21—24, in turn, is a fitting conclusion to the account of David as king: it brings together material which reflects both positive and negative aspects of his reign (see Gordon 1984, pp. 95–7).

The positive aspects dominate the poetic texts which form the centrepiece of these chapters. 'David's Thanksgiving' (22:1–51) is a long psalm (largely identical to Ps. 18) which presents David as trusting in YHWH and vindicated by him; and 'David's Last Words' (23:1–7) are an 'oracle' describing the blessings of righteous rule and celebrating YHWH's covenant with David. The two sections describing the exploits of David's warriors (21:15–22; 23:8–39) also portray David in a good light, as a commander who leads a band of remarkable men; his men care for him (21:15–17), and he in turn values their lives (23:13–17). These sections share with David's Thanksgiving the theme of YHWH preserving his faithful and bringing victory even in desperate situations (e.g. 23:8–12; cf. 22:18–20). The poetic texts, however, paint a somewhat idealized picture, which stands in some tension with the account of decline in 2 Samuel 11—20. Much that these texts say of David can be documented from the narratives of 1 and 2 Samuel; but they do not tell the whole story.

The negative aspects of David's reign surface in the mention of Uriah the Hittite at the end of the list of the 'Thirty' (23:39), a brief reminder of a wicked act; and in the highly problematic narrative of David's census (ch. 24), which must be interpreted along with the narrative of the Gibeonites and Saul's sons (21:1–14).

The section 21:1–14 concerns a negative legacy of Saul's reign: Saul's zeal against the Gibeonites has brought blood-guilt on his family and famine on the land (vv. 1–2). David asks the Gibeonites what they want, and they propose retribution: as Saul planned to destroy them, let them execute seven of his sons (vv. 3–6). David permits this, and after the bones of these sons have been properly buried, along with those of Saul and Jonathan, YHWH again hears prayer for the land (vv. 7–14). This, to put it mildly, is a puzzling narrative. Why are Saul's descendants held guilty for his sins? Why are the Gibeonites allowed to determine how they are to be avenged, and to execute judgment on YHWH's behalf ('before YHWH', vv. 6, 9)? Why do the last verses focus on the burial of the bones, not only of Saul's seven sons, but of Saul and Jonathan? What is it to which YHWH finally responds, the death of these sons, or their death *and* proper burial?

But in all this David seems to act properly: he seeks YHWH, follows YHWH's guidance, observes his own oath concerning Mephibosheth (v. 7; cf. 1 Sam. 20:15), treats the bones of the dead respectfully (v. 13; cf. 2 Sam. 4:12), and puts an end to the famine. This assumes, of course, that we accept the narrator's view that the seven sons were killed in accordance with YHWH's will (see the panel 'Two views of 2 Samuel 21:1–14').

By contrast, 2 Samuel 24 describes David himself bringing harm upon Israel. David orders a census of all Israel, and afterwards realizes he has 'sinned greatly' (v. 10). He prays for forgiveness. Like the Gibeonites he is offered a choice, and the judgment he has chosen is then carried out: plague sweeps Israel until it comes to a halt at the threshing-floor of Araunah. At that place David builds an altar and makes offerings: YHWH hears his prayer and the plague comes to an end.

Everyone in the narrative assumes that holding a census is sinful or at least questionable: Joab (v. 3), David (after the event, v. 10), and YHWH, for whom the only question is what form the punishment will

Digging deeper:
TWO VIEWS OF 2 SAMUEL 21:1–14

A sham

David wants to eliminate possible rivals, arranges for a suitable 'divine oracle' and has the Gibeonites do the eliminating for him (see Brueggemann).

But does this take the narrator's words seriously? When the narrator says that YHWH attributed guilt to Saul, and responded to prayer after the death of Saul's sons (vv. 2, 14) are we to understand him to be saying, 'That was the official explanation, and I'm not going to comment further'? What would that imply for our attempts to interpret YHWH's role in Old Testament narrative generally?

Corporate responsibility

Saul as Israel's king has brought blood-guilt upon Israel as a whole, and Saul's descendants carry the guilt for his crimes even after his death. David, Saul's successor as king, takes the necessary steps to remove the blood-guilt (see Kaminsky, pp. 96–113).

This view involves a more straightforward reading of the narrative, and indeed seems to represent the narrator's viewpoint, but the concept of corporate responsibility may well seem alien to us today (cf. the panel 'The "devoted things" and Achan's sin', Ch. 3).

Can this episode be seen as a special case? That is, YHWH does not normally allow sons to suffer for their father's sins (cf. Deut. 24:16), but in this case the injustice was so glaring and the possibility of creating a malign precedent was so great (for it was Israel's *king* who was persecuting those whom he should have protected), that the wrong done to the Gibeonites had to be publicly avenged, even if only against Saul's sons and not Saul himself. The king, in other words, is not an average Israelite, and if he does wrong he and his family are subject to graver sanctions than apply to other Israelites. Or must we conclude that the text cannot mean what It seems to mean, so terrible is the view of divine justice it implies, and so obvious the clash with other Old Testament texts?

take (vv. 12–13). What the sin consists in is not stated, however. We may compare Exodus 30:11–16, where Moses is instructed that when he holds a census of Israel's fighting men each of them is to pay half a shekel as 'a ransom for their lives to YHWH, so that no plague may come upon them for being registered' (v. 12). This passage, interestingly, assumes that taking a census may bring a plague upon the people, but does not explain why.

Does judgment fall because the necessary half-shekel per man has not been paid? The narrator nowhere says so. Is the point, rather, that military censuses encourage a false confidence in human strength rather than YHWH's power, and that YHWH cuts such human pretensions down to size swiftly? Certainly 2 Samuel 24 suggests a contrast between the apparently impressive forces available to David (they took over nine months to be properly counted) and their vulnerability should YHWH desert them (famine, enemy invasion and plague can all cut them down). The end of the narrative, in which David humbles himself before YHWH, would fit with this.

133

So does the account suggest the damage that royal arrogance can cause? The language in which David confesses his wrongdoing reminds us of other occasions on which both Saul and David fell into disobedience: 'I have sinned' (vv. 10, 17; cf. 1 Sam. 15:24, 30; 26:21; 2 Sam. 12:13); 'I have done very foolishly' (v. 10; cf. 1 Sam. 13:13; 26:21). The placing of 21:1–14 and ch. 24 at either end of this section reminds us that both Saul and David were capable of acting in ways that brought YHWH's judgment on Israel, but that David, unlike Saul, knew how to listen to YHWH's prophet and humble himself before YHWH when judgment fell (vv. 18–25). It may also be that the narrator assumes knowledge of the tradition which 1 Chronicles 22:1 makes explicit, that Araunah's threshing-floor became the site of Solomon's temple. Is he then making the further point that the temple must be a place for humbly seeking YHWH's favour, not a symbol of royal glory (cf. 1 Kgs 8:27–51)?

The most alarming feature of this chapter, however, is verse 1: 'Again the anger of YHWH was kindled against Israel, and he incited David against them, saying, "Go, count the people of Israel and Judah."' This seems to portray YHWH as vindictive, leading David to sin so that he may have a reason to punish him and Israel. Hamilton (p. 366) attempts to explain this verse by finding a cause for YHWH's anger against Israel in the preceding chapters of 2 Samuel. Penchansky (pp. 35–51) argues that the narrator genuinely means to portray YHWH as arbitrary and malevolent, and so also takes v. 1 at face value.

A different approach may be suggested. In speaking of YHWH 'inciting' David, does the narrator mean to make us reflect on the implications of YHWH giving Israel a king?

In what did the 'inciting' consist? Perhaps simply in YHWH's appointing David king over Israel: to give such power to one man, even a 'man after God's own heart' (1 Sam. 13:14), would always lay that man open to the temptation to abuse that power. On this understanding, 2 Samuel 24:1 is a striking and sharp statement of a more general truth, and stands for a number of such statements that could have been made throughout the account of David. The beginning of 2 Samuel 12, for example, could have read: 'And God's anger was kindled against Israel, and he incited David, saying, "Go, seduce Bathsheba the wife of Uriah the Hittite"', with the same implication: the tragic consequences of David's adultery ultimately go back to YHWH's choice to appoint David as king. On this view, YHWH remains ultimately responsible for David's sin in 2 Samuel 24, as indeed for everything in David's kingship. The point can be made more strongly: God is actively involved in *all* the events of David's reign: the narrator will not have it otherwise. But YHWH's responsibility or involvement is not to be understood in a way that ignores the human decisions (Israel's, Saul's, David's) which have led to David's kingship taking the form it has.

Taken together, 2 Samuel 21—24 is a contradictory-seeming section, which presents David from two opposed perspectives: at his best, he represents an ideal, but he has not always lived up to this ideal. The question arises: if even David, the founder of Israel's royal dynasty, has fallen short of the ideal, what will happen in the generations when his descendants rule?

KEY THEMES
Rise of the monarchy: theological implications
The section 1 Samuel 8—12 has a complex attitude towards monarchy: not all forms of

kingship are intrinsically wrong for Israel, but it is possible to demand a king for the wrong motives, which may amount to asking for the wrong sort of king. For YHWH to give Israel such a king may be an act of judgment, as 1 Samuel 10:18–19 seemed to imply. Even David, for all the good that he accomplishes in the earlier part of his reign, is not free from the temptation to abuse power, with all the consequences. By the end of 2 Samuel 20 we have read of death, war, misery and even exile (as David and his men flee Jerusalem), this in spite of the promises to David in chapter 7. The prophet who denounces Eli's house in 1 Samuel 2 insists that YHWH blesses only faithful leadership: 'those who honour me I will honour' (v. 30). That point applies to both Saul and David. The books of Samuel clearly raise the question: is kingship truly a blessing? The answer given is: yes, but only if the king obeys YHWH.

Prophecy

More clearly than any book preceding (except possibly Deuteronomy) the books of Samuel develop the idea of prophets as proclaimers of YHWH's will. In 1 and 2 Samuel YHWH uses prophets to warn his servants of impending danger (1 Sam. 22:5), to promise blessing (2 Sam. 7) and, above all, to insist upon obedience from, and denounce disobedience in, Israel's leaders (1 Sam. 2:27–36; 15:1–3, 17–29; 2 Sam. 12:1–15). The idea that Israel's kings are subject to YHWH's word through his prophets is further developed in Kings.

Monarchy: politics, pragmatism and image?

Does the narrator view the institution of kingship as intrinsically corrupting? Certainly the accounts of Saul's and, later, David's reign convey a sense of kingship as a kind of magnet for violent and sordid deeds:

Saul persecutes David in his attempt to hold on to power (1 Sam. 22:6–19); others plunder bodies or even kill to ingratiate themselves with David (2 Sam. 1:1–16; 4:5–12); Joab's hands are red by the end of 2 Samuel. Perhaps Israel has not progressed very far beyond the violence of Abimelech (Judg. 9).

Provan (pp. 162–73) draws attention to the theme of wisdom in 2 Samuel 11—20: David's wisdom is compared to an angel's (14:20; 19:27), but his behaviour and that of others in these chapters often smacks more of cynical pragmatism than anything reflecting the 'fear of YHWH' (Prov. 9:10). Admittedly, David sometimes rises above this level of behaviour, but others, more ruthless than he, step in where he seems to be paralysed by conflicting motives, and manipulate events in their favour: Jonadab in chapter 13; Absalom in chapters 14—15; Joab in chapters 18—20. Part of the point of these chapters is that love or moral scruple may be politically inexpedient. Is this all an inevitable consequence of the coming of monarchy to Israel? The opening chapters of 1 Kings will take up this question afresh.

Monarchy, like any form of leadership, throws a spotlight on the motives of those who exercise it or aspire to it. Alter (1981, pp. 115–19) has commented on the difficulty of determining David's motives in 1 Samuel 18. Everything he says is entirely appropriate for a gifted young man at the start of a promising career. But, because the narrator never tells us what David was thinking (in contrast to Saul, whose motives are painfully obvious, 1 Sam. 18:8–9, 17, 25) we are left to ask: is David sincere, or is he simply a natural politician? Similar questions arise about David's execution of the Amalekite messenger (2 Sam. 1:13–16), his public mourning of Abner's death (2 Sam. 3:31–34), and his kind treatment of Mephibosheth (2 Sam. 9): sincerely meant, probably; good publicity, definitely! Perhaps there is no way of resolving such issues.

Divine–human interaction

The books of Samuel have a subtle view of YHWH's involvement in Israel's history. This is clear in the narrative of the people's request for a king (1 Sam. 8—12). The request displeases YHWH, for it is a rejection of his own kingship, but he grants it nonetheless, and the consequences are worked out to the bitter end, till Saul's death and even beyond that. Presumably YHWH could have brought Saul's reign to an end sooner, striking him down like Nabal or Uzzah (1 Sam. 25; 2 Sam. 6). But he does not do so. And 2 Samuel 24 suggests that what is true of Saul is also true of David: even he is not fit to be king of Israel in every respect, and when he falls into sin, the people, who have chosen him, suffer. The books of Samuel highlight the importance of human choices: people get what they ask for, even if the result is that judgment falls on them, or that YHWH's purposes are temporarily thwarted. As a result, Israel's history does not proceed in a predictable or linear fashion.

Barton (pp. 7–11) makes a similar point when he notes that events in 2 Samuel 11—20 are presented from two different perspectives: on the one hand, the violence that befalls David's house is the outworking of the judgment threatened through Nathan; but on the other hand it takes place as the result of a series of seemingly free human actions and choices, not all of them made with bad motives. The section 2 Samuel 11—20, Barton suggests, may be called a 'philosophical narrative' (p. 9), a story designed to explore moral themes, specifically the interaction of human choice

and divine will. The same point could be made of other parts of the book.

CRITICAL ISSUES

LITERARY-CRITICAL ISSUES

Aspects of 1 and 2 Samuel as narrative

The books of Samuel form a narrative of extraordinary skill, which maintains control of its various themes for over 50 chapters. It is a subtle and complex narrative, reflecting the narrator's awareness that the Israelite monarchy and the character and acts of David were topics about which no simple evaluation was possible. This observation provides a starting-point for evaluating the frequently made suggestion that 1 and 2 Samuel are apologetic for David and the Davidic dynasty.

Apologetic?

The account of David clearly aims to present his rise to power in a favourable light. We should not be surprised at this: David was not Saul's son, and he was vulnerable to the charge of having usurped Saul's throne. Under these circumstances we would expect the account to explain why he was justified in assuming power. We may compare the 'Apology of Hattushili', a thirteenth-century Hittite text, in which Hattushili gives an account of how he became king of the Hittites, deposing his nephew Urhiteshub. This text carefully brings out the rightness of Hattushili's actions, noting incidents of divine blessing and guidance in his life (*COS* I, pp. 199–204). The parallels with the biblical account are quite close.

Other parts of the account of David, however, cannot easily be explained along these lines. Saul is not a caricature such as we might expect in a purely apologetic text, but a complex character for whom the narrator seems to have some sympathy. Above all, the second part of 2 Samuel contains much negative characterization of David himself. It is hard to believe that the narrator of 2 Samuel 11—24 could not have produced a more flattering picture of this period of David's reign, if his sole aim was to act as David's 'spin-doctor'. The books of Samuel are better described as a theological reflection upon the implications of the coming of the monarchy to Israel, which acknowledges both gains (e.g. political stability) and drawbacks (e.g. scope for abuse of power). The ambivalent portrayal of David fits with this.

Sources, authorship, editing

The point about the theological complexity of 1 and 2 Samuel also provides a framework for addressing questions relating to authorship, sources, editing and dating. As will by now be familiar, scholarship approaches these questions using primarily literary-critical tools, there being few convincing alternatives available. No author is named for the books of Samuel, and though there are references to things said to be the case 'to this day' (1 Sam. 5:5; 6:18; 27:6; 2 Sam. 4:3; 6:8; 18:18), these, as with Joshua and Judges, are either too imprecise to date the account or vulnerable to the counter-argument that they may only give the date of the sources used by the author, not the date of the books at later stages of their formation. We shall note below arguments based on the character of the narrative that tend to put large sections, at least, of 1 and 2 Samuel early. But how convincing these arguments seem depends partly on how one evaluates source-critical approaches to the books of Samuel. To these we turn.

At many points in 1 Samuel scholars have argued that the narrative is inconsistent. We have considered a number of these passages already: Samuel's victory at Ebenezer, described in terms (1 Sam. 7:13) which seem to conflict with the references to the Philistines as a continuing threat in 1 Samuel 8—15; seemingly contradictory attitudes towards monarchy expressed in 1 Samuel 8—12; the apparently incoherent narratives of 1 Samuel 10—13 (Saul, having been told to go to Gilgal in 1 Samuel 10, only does so in 1 Samuel 13) and 16—17; the fact that each of 1 Samuel 24, 25 and 26 has the same basic narrative structure, suggesting that they are variants of the same tradition. In most of these cases (apart from 1 Samuel 16—17, which was left for you to reflect upon!) we have interpreted the text as it stands, and found it coherent, complex rather than inconsistent.

One further example is the fact that Samuel is absent from 1 Samuel 4—6, even though 3:19—4:1 seems to imply that he is by now a major figure in Israel. On the basis of this apparent inconsistency, Campbell and O'Brien (pp. 226–7) argue that 1 Samuel 4—6 and (probably) 2 Samuel 6:1–19 originally formed a separate 'Ark Narrative' whose purpose was to explain how the ark's location shifted from Shiloh to Jerusalem. They point to the fact that these chapters are the only extended narratives involving the ark in the Old Testament.

Again, the conclusion does not necessarily follow. Samuel's absence in 1 Samuel 4—6 can be explained by supposing that 3:19—4:1 deliberately anticipates developments after the events of chapters 4—6, so as to continue the theme of Samuel's rise versus the decline of Eli's house (Provan, Long and Longman, p. 206). While 1 Samuel 4—6 and 2 Samuel 6 may be the only chapters in which the ark features, the idea underlying the representation of the ark in these chapters (YHWH's absolute sovereignty) is common to all of 1 and 2 Samuel. And the main narrative developments in 1 Samuel 4—6 (YHWH's departure from and return to Israel, with the implication that his blessing may not be assumed) and 2 Samuel 6 (YHWH's entry into David's citadel, with the implication that he has chosen to bless David and Israel) are both entirely appropriate to their contexts. There is no need to suppose that these chapters ever formed a separate narrative.

Other suggestions concerning the sources of 1 and 2 Samuel are based not so much on perceived contradictions within the narrative as on the fact that they form sub-units in the account, with identifiable themes. On these grounds it has been suggested that 1 Samuel 16:14—2 Samuel 5:25 is based on an earlier 'History of David's Rise'; and that 2 Samuel 9—20 and 1 Kings 1—2 originally formed a 'Succession Narrative' whose main theme was the question of who would succeed David.

But again, there is little evidence that these two blocks of narrative as they now stand ever had an independent existence. As we move from 1 Samuel into 2 Samuel, and as David becomes king and his reign over Israel passes through different phases, the situations described to some extent change. But there is no clear discontinuity at any point: in fact, it is hard to draw the division between the account of David's rise and the account of his kingship. This point may be illustrated by asking the question: does 2 Samuel 2—5 belong with what precedes or what follows? The answer seems to be: both. David's rise, the theme of 1 Samuel 16—31, continues into these chapters, as does the theme of Saul's hostility, represented by the

hostility of 'the house of Saul' (2 Sam. 3:1). But these chapters also hint at themes that will dominate later parts of the account, especially chapters 19—20: violence, deceit, the corrupting effect of power. Part of the point of 2 Samuel 19—20 is that they present a 'tarnished' version of the events of 2 Samuel 2—5.

Regarding the suggestion that 2 Samuel 9—20 were originally part of a 'Succession Narrative', there is the further question: is the succession really the theme of these chapters? The main focus of chapters 13—20, at least, seems to be the outworking of Nathan's prophecy against David. The term 'Succession Narrative' is perhaps best reserved for 1 Kings 1—2 alone, where Solomon's succession genuinely is the focus.

A different approach to 2 Samuel 9—20 suggests that this section, in contrast to earlier chapters, portrays David negatively, and is on this basis to be identified (along with parts of 2 Samuel 1—4) as a separate source, inserted into the books of Samuel at a later stage of editing (Van Seters, pp. 277–91; McCarter 1984, pp. 7–16). But is it necessary to polarize the account of David into positive and negative sections? The links between the different stages of the account of David seem stronger than this suggestion allows; and above all, the narrator's picture of David is more complex.

Last, we may mention Campbell and O'Brien's suggestion (pp. 24–32, 214–15) that one of the sources of 1 and 2 Samuel (and much of Kings) was a 'Prophetic Record' covering the period from Samuel's rise to Jehu's coup (2 Kings 9—10). This record, they argue, was a reworking of traditions relating to David's rise and Elijah's ministry which focused on the roles of successive prophets in the rise and fall of kings: Samuel's role in relation to Saul and David; Ahijah's role in relation to Jeroboam (1 Kings 11 and 14); Elijah's and Elisha's interactions with the house of Ahab and with Jehu (1 Kings 17—2 Kings 10). In the books of Samuel they attribute the following passages to the Prophetic Record: much of 1 Samuel 1—3; much of 1 Samuel 9:1—10:16 and chapter 11; 1 Samuel 15—16; much of 1 Samuel 17—23; 1 Samuel 25—31; 2 Samuel 1—2; much of 2 Samuel 3—5; parts of 2 Samuel 7; 2 Samuel 8:15.

This suggestion helpfully draws attention to a theme which links the books of Samuel and Kings. But the fact that a series of passages in Samuel and Kings each share a theme need not imply that these passages originally formed an independent narrative. We see no reason to separate the passages listed above from sections of narrative such as 1 Samuel 12—14 and (most notably) 2 Samuel 9—20. As we have argued, 1 Samuel 8—15 forms a whole cloth. And the events of 2 Samuel 12—20 flow out of Nathan's prophecy in 2 Samuel 12:7–12, which, as Campbell and O'Brien (p. 298) rightly note, echoes texts (1 Sam. 9:16; 10:1; 15:1, 17) which they assign to their Prophetic Record. (Their arguments for 2 Sam. 11—20 not having belonged to the Prophetic Record are on pp. 295–6, and their argument against the view that the echoes of earlier texts in 2 Sam. 12:7–12 indicate common authorship is on p. 298. We remain unconvinced.)

It is likely that many different traditions, quite possibly originating in different circles, underlie the long and varied account of 1 and 2 Samuel; but that is not the same as saying that constituent sources can now be easily identified in the present text of Samuel. Whatever form the traditions may have taken, they have in our view been skilfully reworked to produce a subtle narrative from which virtually nothing can be removed without loss. In their present form, 1 and 2 Samuel are more or less a seamless robe.

(For further discussion of these issues, see: Gunn 1978, pp. 65–84; Gordon 1984, 1994; Long 1994; Campbell and O'Brien, pp. 215–31. We return to the question of dating in the next section.)

HISTORICAL ISSUES
The historical context
The period covered in the books of Samuel extends from the time of Eli's activity as Israel's judge down to the latter years of David's reign, from roughly 1100 to the first decades of the tenth century. During this period Egypt, Assyria and Babylon, great powers in the Late Bronze Age, remained relatively weak, and other people groups, relative newcomers to the region, played a significant role: the Aramean kingdoms to the north of Israel; the Philistines, whose power expanded north, south and east for much of the eleventh century. The Transjordanian kingdoms of Ammon, Moab and Edom also feature (2 Sam. 8 and 10).

CHRONOLOGY OF SAUL'S, DAVID'S AND SOLOMON'S REIGNS

(based on Provan, Long and Longman, pp. 200–2)

Dates	King	Years	Biblical text
c. 1032–1010	Saul	22	1 Sam. 13:1
(c. 1006–1004)	Ishbosheth	(2)	2 Sam. 2:10
c. 1010–970	David	40	2 Sam. 5:5
c. 970–930	Solomon	40	1 Kgs 11:42

The chronological 'peg' for these dates is the reference in 1 Kings 14:25 to the invasion of Israel by Pharaoh Sheshonq (Shishak) in the fifth year of Rehoboam, for which see Kitchen, pp. 32–4.

Israel's first two kings

The books of Samuel are a theological account of David and Saul, which focuses mainly on a few central characters. Many matters on which we might have welcomed more information are not included, or are only briefly described: for example, many of Saul's achievements are summarized in a few verses (1 Sam. 14:47–52), and the account of Absalom's revolt in 2 Samuel 15 gives few details about who supported him and why.

Some modern historians of Saul's and David's reigns have reservations about those parts of 1 and 2 Samuel in which theological concerns are prominent or where the narrator may have engaged in imaginative reconstruction (e.g. scenes involving dialogue). Where these scholars base their accounts upon the biblical text, it is primarily the 'factual', apparently non-theological sections of narrative on which they draw (e.g. 1 Sam. 13:1; 14:47–52; 2 Sam. 3:2–5; 5:1–5; 8:1–18; 20:23–26).

A good example of this is the essay by Meyers. Her account of the early monarchy is based on the annalistic material in the accounts of Saul and David (less than 10 per cent of each account), on selected details from elsewhere in the accounts, and on archaeological data. She also draws on insights from the social sciences.

She explores factors such as: Israelite population growth in the eleventh and tenth centuries; the need for greater political stability; the role of the monarchy in making trade possible (particularly in meeting the demand for iron implements); the nature of the Philistine threat; the relationship between local, kinship-based authority structures and centralized control; the different conditions imposed by urban and rural life; the continuing role of Israel's elders in the government of Israel; and much else. Among the archaeological data she cites in connection with David's reign are evidence of greater settlement in the Negev (southern Judea), likely carried out with the aim of fortifying Israel's southern borders, and indications of expansion into the coastal areas of the plain of Sharon (pp. 183–5, 190; cf. Mazar, pp. 374, 390–6; Kitchen, pp. 98, 100).

The result is an interesting survey which complements the biblical account but is essentially non-theological in character. One question raised by Meyer's chapter is: if YHWH's will really is a determining factor in history, as the Histories uniformly assume, may not other parts of the biblical account (for instance the many narratives and dialogues concerned with theological issues such as the standing of individuals before YHWH and YHWH's responses to human actions) count as properly historical data? Even if we do not share the biblical writers' aim of producing a theological history of the period, it may still be appropriate to draw on parts of the biblical text other than those used in an account such as Meyers'. Modern historians of the ancient world (not least the ancient Near East) regularly draw on texts that are at least as explicitly theological as the biblical texts, and do not see the fact that the gods feature in these texts as an obstacle to this procedure.

The account of David: a 'cover-up'?

Another approach to the books of Samuel focuses on those sections which Meyers downplays, but does so under the rubric of 'royal propaganda'. A number of deaths occurred in the course of David's rise and reign, many of them convenient for him, in that the people who died either opposed him or could have become a threat to him: Nabal; Saul and Jonathan; seven other sons of Saul; Abner; Ish-bosheth; Uriah; Amnon; Absalom; Amasa. The biblical account emphasizes that David bore no responsibility for any of these deaths except Uriah's. But does it protest too much? Was David in reality a multiple murderer? Two recent accounts, those of Halpern (pp. 73–93) and McKenzie (pp. 89–127) suggest he probably was.

Such arguments are hard to refute: some of the deaths do look suspicious, and were apparently regarded as at least potentially incriminating during David's lifetime (2 Sam. 3:36–37; 16:7–8). But some points may be made in response:

- As noted above, the account of David is not simply apologetic for him. The narrator admits that David was responsible for Uriah's death. Perhaps for that reason we should also believe the narrator's claims that he was not guilty of the other deaths.
- Halpern and McKenzie come close to regarding any attempt to defend David as automatically suspect (see especially McKenzie, pp. 44–5). But this seems self-defeating, particularly given that the circumstances of David's rise would have made a defence of his actions desirable. Is David to be held guilty simply because the defence was attempted?
- When someone emerges as the likely victor in a power struggle, others sometimes do try to seek favour by killing that person's remaining opponents, without that person having wanted it (cf. 2 Sam. 4).
- Abner's death, at least, occurred at the worst possible time from David's point of view, just when it might have deterred the tribes which had previously supported Saul

from transferring their allegiance to him. Joab was the main beneficiary of Abner's and Amasa's deaths.

David's kingdom: a later retrojection?
Finkelstein and Silberman suggest that the biblical account of David's kingdom is more radically misleading than in the 'propaganda' approach discussed above. In their view there never was a united monarchy: the kingdoms of Israel and Judah had separate origins, and the biblical accounts of David and Solomon are essentially inventions of the seventh century, propaganda for Josiah's expansionist ambitions (pp. 142–5, 153–9).

In Chapter 7 we will question the tendency to see the seventh and sixth centuries as significant periods in the formation of the books of Samuel. Other features of 1 and 2 Samuel make an early dating of the books (tenth or ninth century) likely. McKenzie (pp. 35–6) argues that the presence of apologetic elements in 1 and 2 Samuel suggests that the books contain genuine historical information about David. He concludes: 'Who would invent such allegations against David just to try to explain them away?' Along similar lines Barr (p. 87) argues,

I just cannot see that anyone in the [post-exilic] period, inspired by ideology, would just *invent* all the material about Abner and Asahel and Ittai the Gittite and Paltiel the son of Laish. Elements of invention, yes, one can see in any story, but the invention of material on such a scale seems entirely unconvincing.

In addition, three inscriptions which refer, or may refer, to David make the suggestion that David is not a historical figure unlikely:

the Tel Dan Stela, the Moabite Stone, and Sheshonq's topographical list.

INSCRIPTIONAL REFERENCES TO DAVID?

Tel Dan Stela

This is a fragmentary inscription in Aramaic from Tel Dan, discovered and published in the 1990s (see Kitchen, pp. 36–7). In lines 8 and 9 an Aramean king describes his victory over a '[xxx]ram son of [xxxx] king of Israel' and '[xxx]iah son of [xxxx.xx]? the house of David' (x = missing letter; ? = uncertain letter).

On the basis of 2 Kings 8—9 the names of the kings can plausibly be reconstructed as 'Jehoram (= Joram) son of Ahab' and 'Ahaziah son of Jehoram (= Joram)', kings of Israel and Judah, whom Hazael of Aram is said to have defeated. This would make the author of the inscription Hazael, and the date 841 or shortly afterwards. The key point is the reference to 'the house of David', which suggests that a foreign king knew that David was the founder of Judah's royal dynasty.

Moabite Stone or Mesha Stela

This inscription was discovered in 1868, and dates from the mid-ninth century. Line 31 of this inscription (somewhat damaged) has been restored to read 'and the house of [Da]vid dwelt in Horonem' (Lemaire, pp. 30–7). If the restoration is correct, this text apparently also refers to the kingdom of Judah as 'the house of David'.

Sheshonq's topographical list

An inscription of Pharaoh Sheshonq I commemorating an invasion of Israel in 926/5 lists the places his army passed through. The section of the list covering south Judah and the Negev includes a reference to 'the heights of *Dwt*'. Kitchen (p. 93) suggests that *Dwt* may be the Egyptian equivalent of 'David'. David is said to have been active in the Negev in the period before he became king (1 Sam. 24:1; 27; 30); this inscription, dating from fewer than 50 years after David's death, may echo that historical connection.

These inscriptions, however, even on the most optimistic reading, only confirm that a 'David' existed and that he founded a dynasty that could in the ninth century be paired with that of the kings of Israel. There are no extra-biblical texts which attribute to David an 'empire' like that described in 2 Samuel 8 and 10. There is also very little archaeological evidence from Jerusalem which might support the biblical picture of it as David's royal capital, and no inscriptions have been found in Israel which refer to David.

Map 3   David's kingdom

Some aspects of this question will be addressed when we discuss Solomon's kingdom in Chapter 6. But again, some points may be made regarding these facts:

- David's 'empire' (see Map 3) is said to have consisted of a heartland (Israel), conquered states under Israel's control (Edom, Moab, Aram-Damascus and perhaps Zobah) and subject allies (Hamath, Ammon and perhaps Geshur), a substantial territory, but not impossibly huge, particularly given that powers such as Egypt, Assyria and Babylonia were in decline in this period. See further Kitchen (pp. 98–104), who notes evidence for other empires of a similar size and structure in the Levant in the twelfth to ninth centuries.
- It is not surprising that inscriptions of David, Solomon and later kings of Judah should have failed to survive the invasions and occupations of later centuries, particularly in Jerusalem, the site where they are most likely to have stood at one time. Other comparable first-millennium kingdoms have left similarly scanty inscriptional remains: Aram-Damascus; Aleppo; Moab; Ammon; Edom; Tyre and Sidon (Kitchen, pp. 90–1).
- The archaeology of Jerusalem is much debated at present (see the essays edited by Vaughn and Killebrew). However, the absence of extensive tenth-century remains at Jerusalem may not be a good argument against the site having functioned as David's capital. Many parts of the ancient city have been built over by modern dwellings or are otherwise inaccessible (e.g. the Temple Mount). In any case Jerusalem has suffered much destruction and rebuilding during its long history: how much of tenth-century Jerusalem should we expect to have survived down

to the present? Few remains of Bronze Age Jerusalem have been discovered, and yet the Amarna letters from Jerusalem indicate that it was a regional centre for Egyptian rule in the fourteenth century. This being so, the lack of tenth-century remains should not exclude the possibility of Jerusalem's having acted as the centre of David's administration (Kitchen, pp. 150–4).

The books of Samuel, to sum up, remain our major source for Israel's early monarchy. The general picture painted in these books is plausible, and the grounds urged for rejecting it are not compelling.

SAMUEL IN THE CANON

We have noted links between 1 Samuel and Judges, and also how the patriarchal promises of descendants, land and blessing are substantially fulfilled in David's reign, this point being particularly clear in 2 Samuel 7. Only the promise about blessing to other nations seems to remain unfulfilled: Israel has dealings with the nations around, but they are mainly warlike (2 Sam. 5; 8; 10, etc.)

The events and themes of 1 and 2 Samuel resurface in later biblical books, most obviously in the books of Kings and Chronicles, which each continue the history of Israel's monarchy; but also in other books.

The Psalms which highlight the role of Israel's king in YHWH's purposes (e.g. Pss 2, 72, 89, 110, 132) and YHWH's rule over the nations (e.g. Pss 2, 46–48, 65, 99) also have their roots in the books of Samuel, particularly 2 Samuel 6—7. The same could be said of those prophetic texts which speak of the nations coming to Zion to worship YHWH (Isa. 2:1–4; 60:1–3; Zech. 8:20–23) and which predict the restoration of David's line after judgment (Isa. 11:1–9; Jer. 23:5–6; Ezek. 37:24–28).

These prophetic texts are explicitly messianic: they speak of a future anointed king from David's line, a messiah ('messiah' is simply the English transliteration of *mashiakh*, 'anointed one') whose glorious reign will rescue the line from the disgrace into which it has fallen. The books of Samuel are not messianic in that sense, but they do draw a contrast between David at his best, David as God's ideal for kingship, and the failures of the later part of David's reign. Already in 1 and 2 Samuel there is a gap between ideal and reality which partly anticipates the thinking of the later prophetic texts. We can speak of a 'proto-messianism' in the books of Samuel. (See further the essay by Satterthwaite.)

The New Testament also develops ideas introduced in Samuel. The New Testament titles for Jesus, 'Christ' ('anointed one') and 'Son of God', have roots in the books of Samuel (1 Sam. 16:13; 2 Sam. 7:14). Many New Testament texts base their presentation of Jesus on the claim that he is God's chosen king, but handle this theme in radically new ways. Thus, Jesus enters Jerusalem as the promised king of David's line (Mark 11:1–10), but announces judgment on Jerusalem and the temple (Mark 11:12–17). The kingdom of God is present in Jesus' ministry, but takes an unexpected form (Mark 1:5; Luke 17:20–21). Most unexpectedly of all, Jesus is declared to be king by death on a cross and resurrection from the dead (Mark 15:18–26; Rom. 1:3–4). In Revelation, similarly, the figure announced as the 'Lion of the tribe of Judah' and 'Root of David' proves to be 'a Lamb standing as if it had been slaughtered' (Rev. 5:5–6). Later in Revelation, however, the visions of a king riding out to war against God's enemies (19:11–21), and of a new Jerusalem in which a temple is no longer needed (ch. 21), recall David and his royal city in a more straightforward way, though with a splendour which transcends the Old Testament archetypes.

FURTHER READING

COMMENTARIES

R. Alter, *The David Story*. New York: Norton, 1999.

A.A. Anderson, *2 Samuel*. Dallas: Word, 1989.

R.P. Bergen, *1, 2 Samuel*. Nashville: Broadman & Holman, 1996.

R.P. Gordon, *I and II Samuel*. Carlisle: Paternoster, 1986.

H.W. Hertzberg, *I and II Samuel*. London: SCM Press, 1964.

R.W. Klein, *1 Samuel*. Waco: Word, 1983.

P.K McCarter, *I, II Samuel*. New York: Doubleday, [1980] 1984.

OTHER BOOKS AND ARTICLES

R. Alter, *The Art of Biblical Narrative*. New York: Basic Books, 1981.

J. Barr, *History and Ideology in the Old Testament. Biblical Studies at the End of a Millennium*. Oxford: Oxford University Press, 2000.

J. Barton, *Understanding Old Testament Ethics. Approaches and Explorations*. Louisville: Westminster John Knox, 2003.

A. Brenner (ed.), *A Feminist Companion to Samuel and Kings*. Sheffield: Sheffield Academic Press, 1994.

W. Brueggemann, '2 Samuel 21–24: An Appendix of Deconstruction?', *CBQ* 50 (1988), pp. 383–97.

A.F. Campbell and M.A. O'Brien, *Unfolding the Deuteronomistic History: Origins, Upgrades,*

Present Text. Minneapolis: Augsburg Fortress, 2000, pp. 215–321.

J.C. Exum, *Tragedy and Biblical Narrative*. Cambridge: Cambridge University Press, 1992.

I. Finkelstein and N.A. Silberman, *The Bible Unearthed. Archaeology's New Vision of Ancient Israel and the Origin of its Sacred Texts*. New York: Touchstone, 2001.

J. Goldingay, *Men Behaving Badly*. Carlisle: Paternoster, 2000.

R.P. Gordon, 'David's Rise and Saul's Demise: Narrative Analogy in 1 Sam. 24–26', *TB* 31 (1980), pp. 37–64.

R.P. Gordon, *1 and 2 Samuel*. Sheffield: JSOT Press, 1984.

R.P. Gordon, 'In Search of David: The David Tradition in Recent Study', in A.R. Millard, J.K. Hoffmeier, D.W. Baker (eds), *Faith, Tradition and History. Old Testament Historiography in its Ancient Near Eastern Context*. Winona Lake: Eisenbrauns, 1994, pp. 285–98.

D.M. Gunn, *The Story of King David. Genre and Interpretation*. Sheffield: JSOT Press, 1978.

D.M. Gunn, *The Fate of King Saul. An Interpretation of a Biblical Story*. Sheffield: JSOT Press, 1980.

B. Halpern, *David's Secret Demons. Messiah, Murderer, Traitor, King*. Grand Rapids: Eerdmans, 2001.

V.P. Hamilton, *Handbook on the Historical Books*. Grand Rapids: Baker Book House, 2001.

V. Hurowitz, *I Have Built You an Exalted House. Temple Building in the Bible in Light of Mesopotamian and Northwest Semitic Writings*. Sheffield: Sheffield Academic Press, 1992.

J.S. Kaminsky, *Corporate Responsibility in the Hebrew Bible*. Sheffield: Sheffield Academic Press, 1995.

K.A. Kitchen, *On the Reliability of the Old Testament*. Grand Rapids: Eerdmans, 2003, pp. 81–158.

A. Lemaire, ' "House of David" Restored in Moabite Inscription', *BAR* 20, 3 (1994), pp. 30–7.

V.P. Long, *The Reign and Rejection of King Saul. A Case for Literary and Theological Coherence*. Atlanta: Scholars Press, 1989.

V.P. Long, 'How did Saul become King? Literary Reading and Historical Reconstruction', in A.R. Millard, J.K. Hoffmeier, D.W. Baker (eds), *Faith, Tradition and History. Old Testament Historiography in its Ancient Near Eastern Context*. Winona Lake: Eisenbrauns, 1994, pp. 271–84.

P.K. McCarter, 'The Apology of David', *JBL* 99 (1980), pp. 489–504.

S.L. McKenzie, *King David. A Biography*. New York: Oxford University Press, 2000.

A. Mazar, *Archaeology of the Land of the Bible, 10,000–586 B.C.E.* New York: Doubleday, 1992.

C. Meyers, 'Ephod', *ABD* II, p. 150.

C. Meyers, 'Kinship and Kingship. The Early Monarchy' in M.D. Coogan (ed.), *The Oxford History of the Biblical World*. New York: Oxford University Press, 1998, pp. 165–205.

M. Noth, *The Deuteronomistic History*, 2nd edition. Sheffield: Sheffield Academic Press, 1991.

D. Penchansky, *What Rough Beast? Images of God in the Hebrew Bible*. Louisville: Westminster John Knox, 1999.

R. Polzin, *Samuel and the Deuteronomist. A Literary Study of the Deuteronomistic History, Part 2: 1 Samuel*. Bloomington: Indiana University Press, 1989.

R. Polzin, *David and the Deuteronomist. A Literary Study of the Deuteronomistic History, Part 3: 2 Samuel*. Bloomington: Indiana University Press, 1993.

I.W. Provan, 'On "Seeing" the Trees while Missing the Forest: The Wisdom of Characters and Readers in 2 Samuel and 1 Kings' in E. Ball (ed.), *In Search of True Wisdom: Essays in Old Testament Interpretation in Honour of Ronald E. Clements*. Sheffield: Sheffield Academic Press, 1999, pp. 153–73.

I.W. Provan, V.P. Long, T. Longman, *A Biblical History of Israel*. Louisville: Westminster John Knox Press, 2003; pp. 193–238.

P.E. Satterthwaite, 'David in the Books of Samuel: A Messianic Hope?' in P.E. Satterthwaite, R.S. Hess, G.J. Wenham (eds), *The Lord's Anointed. Interpretation of Old Testament Messianic Texts*. Grand Rapids/Carlisle: Baker/Paternoster, 1995, pp. 41–65.

E. Tov, *Textual Criticism of the Hebrew Bible*. Minneapolis: Augsburg Fortress, 1992.

J. Van Seters, *In Search of History. Historiography in the Ancient World and the Origins of Biblical History*. New Haven: Yale University Press, 1983.

A.G. Vaughn and A.E. Killebrew (eds), *Jerusalem in Bible and Archaeology: The First Temple Period*. Atlanta: Society of Biblical Literature, 2003.

Chapter 6

1 AND 2 KINGS

INTRODUCTION

The books of Kings describe Solomon's reign, the division of Solomon's kingdom into the (northern) kingdom of Israel and the (southern) kingdom of Judah during the reign of his son Rehoboam, the gradual decline of both kingdoms, and their eventual destruction by Assyria and Babylon respectively.

They are printed as two separate books (1 and 2 Kings) in English translations.

The Hebrew text follows the same book, chapter and verse numbering as in English Bibles, with minor deviations (e.g. 1 Kgs 4:21—5:18 in English Bibles = 1 Kgs 5:1–32 in MT). However, it has no division between 1 Kings and 2 Kings. For this reason 1 and 2 Kings together are often referred to simply as 'Kings'.

In spite of its length Kings is a highly selective narrative. Generally the kings about whom most is said are those who stand at turning-points in the narrative: Solomon;

STRUCTURE OF KINGS

1 Kings 1—11	Solomon's reign
1 Kings 12—16	The division of the kingdoms; early history of Israel and Judah
1 Kings 17—2 Kings 10	The two kingdoms; Elijah and Elisha
2 Kings 11—17	The last years of Israel
2 Kings 18—25	The last years of Judah

The above structure is a simplification. In Kings the narrative often weaves together a number of separate strands. This is particularly true of 1 Kings 17—2 Kings 10, the long central section which contains the accounts of the prophets Elijah and Elisha.

Particular features of Kings unify the narrative and clarify its structure and meaning:

- 'regnal formulae' (see the panel 'Regnal formulae in Kings');
- a recurrent pattern of prophecy and fulfilment (e.g. 1 Kgs 13:1–2 and 2 Kgs 23:15–16);
- 'narrative analogy', in which later narratives are patterned upon earlier narratives;
- speeches at key points and comments by the narrator (e.g. Solomon's address and prayer at 1 Kings 8; the narrator's explanation of Israel's exile at 2 Kings 17).

Ahab and Jehu of Israel; Hezekiah, Manasseh and Josiah of Judah.

OUTLINE

I KINGS 1—11: SOLOMON'S REIGN

Solomon becomes king (1 Kgs 1—2)

This opening section forms a bridge between the accounts of David and Solomon. It presupposes knowledge of the characters and incidents in 2 Samuel 8—20, but it marks a new phase. David is now an old man, and the question arises: who will succeed him as king?

David seems weak and indecisive. He has not nominated his successor publicly, though he has apparently given a private oath that Solomon will succeed him (1:17, 29–30; cf. 2 Sam. 12:24–25). Adonijah, another of David's sons, sees an opportunity to become king, and enlists powerful individuals to his cause (1:7–10). He represents a threat to Solomon's succession: indeed, his feast constitutes a public claim to the kingship (cf. 2 Sam. 15:11–12) and is so described by Nathan and Bathsheba when they report the matter to David (vv. 18, 24–25). But once these two have persuaded David to declare Solomon king, Adonijah's claim collapses. Even in his weakness David knows how to undermine his pretensions. Adonijah's feast is interrupted by people acclaiming King Solomon, and his supporters quickly scatter (vv. 41–49). Seemingly he never had much popular support. He has to beg Solomon for mercy.

David approaches the day of his death. He gives Solomon farewell advice (2:1–9). Solomon must be faithful to YHWH. He must show favour to the sons of Barzillai, the Gileadite (non-Judahite) who helped David;

but he must ensure that Joab and Shimei meet their deaths. Joab and Shimei in different ways represent tribal rather than national interests: Joab the Judahite who sometimes acted in a way that threatened David's acceptance by the other tribes; and Shimei, the Benjaminite who cursed him. David advises Solomon to favour those who foster tribal unity and get rid of those who might cause division (Provan 1995, pp. 33–4).

This is in one sense reasonable advice: Israel needs a king who will unite the tribes. But the question arises: if Solomon is the right king, is this the right way to be king? David's exhortation to Solomon to walk in YHWH's ways (2:2–4; cf. Josh. 1:1–8) sits uneasily with his advice to kill Joab and Shimei (2:6, 8–9). These are terrible last words. They reflect 'wisdom' of a kind (vv. 6, 9): experienced, disaffected men like Joab and Shimei could be a threat to the young Solomon. But is this all really wisdom from YHWH?

The accounts of Adonijah's, Joab's and Shimei's deaths increase our unease. True, Adonijah still has designs on the kingship, and to that extent can be represented as harbouring wicked schemes (cf. 1:52). But the narrative emphasizes his self-delusion (2:15) and folly: can he really believe that Solomon will not see what the request to marry Abishag implies? Is this political incompetent such a threat? And where is Solomon's evidence for a conspiracy involving Abiathar and Joab (v. 22)?

It seems that Solomon is simply looking for reasons to remove potential trouble-makers. He attempts to justify his actions, and invokes YHWH's blessing on his own house (vv. 23–24, 33, 44–45), but his words seem increasingly shrill and unconvincing. In Chapter 5 we suggested that the account of David's rise could partly be seen as pro-Davidic apologetic, designed to exonerate him of possible guilt in the deaths of his rivals. But 1 Kings 2 cannot ever have been meant as propaganda for Solomon (against Jones, pp. 48–57). The narrator simply presents Solomon's questionable deeds alongside his hollow statements and lets us draw the conclusions.

The theme of political shrewdness runs through 1 Kings 1—2. Since the rise of the monarchy people have learned skills that will enable them to survive in this new system: how to extend one's influence; how to manipulate those in authority. It is because he lacks such skills that Adonijah fails. These chapters describe the first genuine dynastic succession in Israel. But is this how YHWH's chosen dynasty is to be established? David may urge faithfulness and righteousness on Solomon (2:1–4) and Solomon at Gibeon may claim that David showed these qualities (3:6); but we know that this is only part of the story. If David's line survives, it is not because of the consistent righteousness of its members, but also because of divine forbearance. This is true of the first two members of the line, and it will continue to be true in later generations.

Solomon seeks YHWH (1 Kgs 3—5)

Chapters 3—5 of 1 Kings develop three themes: (1) Solomon's wisdom; (2) the blessings of Solomon's rule for Israel; (3) the preparations to build the temple.

Solomon is now king. The first three verses of chapter 3 introduce leading themes of chapters 3—11: Solomon's marriages with foreign women (v. 1); Solomon's building works (v. 1); the question of the people's loyalty to YHWH (v. 2: when the temple is built, will they abandon their previous practices as Deuteronomy 12 implied they must?); the question of Solomon's own loyalty (v. 3: he loves YHWH, but he also worships at the high places). How these themes are worked out in the following chapters determines the character of Solomon's reign.

The account of Solomon's dream (3:4–15) explicitly addresses the question: what kind of rule is Solomon to exercise? YHWH says to him, 'Ask what I should give you' (v. 5), an open-ended request which invites Solomon to reveal what is in his heart. Strikingly, Solomon confesses his inexperience and asks for wisdom to govern YHWH's people justly (3:7–9), tacitly admitting that the 'wisdom' he has followed so far has been of a different sort. This is the response YHWH was looking for: 'It pleased the Lord that Solomon had asked this.' YHWH gives Solomon what he asks, and riches and honour as well (vv. 12–13; note also v. 11: 'you . . . have not asked . . . for the life of your enemies' – an implicit criticism of Solomon's earlier actions?).

This encounter is a turning-point. The next episode (3:16–28) shows Solomon's new wisdom in action, and ends, 'all Israel . . . perceived that the wisdom of God was in him, to execute justice' (v. 28). This represents an advance upon the events of chapters 1—2.

Chapter 4 describes Solomon's kingdom: his officials, Israel's strength and security, Solomon's horses, the royal provisions and Solomon's wisdom. There are echoes of Israel's earlier history. The list of Solomon's administrative districts reminds us of the division of the land under Joshua (though these districts do not follow the earlier division at all points, and to that extent 'represent a new order': Provan 1995, pp. 54–5). The phrase 'as numerous as the sand by the sea' (v. 20) alludes to the patriarchal promises (Gen. 15:5; 22:17), as does the description of the bounds of Solomon's kingdom (vv. 21, 24; cf. Gen. 15:18). The reference to people coming 'from all the nations to hear the wisdom of Solomon' (v. 34) echoes Deuteronomy 4:5–8, and Moses' hope that Israel's national life would attract the attention of the surrounding nations by its manifest wisdom. This chapter suggests how far Israel has progressed since its beginnings. Under Solomon Israel comes as close as it ever does to fulfilling the Pentateuchal vision.

Chapter 5 continues the positive tone of chapter 4. Solomon builds the temple in token of the fact that he has inherited a kingdom at peace with its neighbours (vv. 2–6; compare Deut. 12; 2 Sam. 7). Hiram's response to his request for aid praises his wisdom (v. 7; cf. v. 12). The materials for the building are assembled (vv. 13–18).

Solomon's temple (1 Kgs 6:1—9:9)

The lengthy and intricate account of the building and dedication of the temple forms the capstone of the Solomon narrative. With some variations it follows a six-fold structure attested in Mesopotamian temple-building accounts: (1) divine approval for building (5:3–5); (2) preparations for building (5:6–18); (3) description of the work and the complete building (6:1—7:51); (4) dedication celebrations (8:1–11, 62–66); (5) dedication prayers (8:12–61); (6) divine

promises, curses and blessings (9:1–9). (See Hurowitz, especially pp. 311–21).

The narrator links the beginning of the temple-building with Israel's exodus from Egypt (6:1), suggesting that all Israel's history so far has been leading up to this point (cf. Exod. 15:13–17). From now on Israel is to be known as the nation which worships YHWH in this temple. If David's bringing up of the ark to Zion set the seal on his rise to kingship, then Solomon's building of the temple confirms YHWH's choice of David's line. As Meyers notes (pp. 360–2), the temple is a visual symbol of the legitimacy of David's dynasty. It represents a stable social order in which the king enjoys divine favour and upholds justice. In Kings, as in ancient Near Eastern thought generally, the political and the religious are indivisible.

(For illustrations of possible reconstructions of Solomon's temple, see Meyers, pp. 356–7).

After the account of the temple (6:1–38) comes an account of the building of Solomon's palace complex (7:1–12). This complex is considerably larger than the temple, and takes longer to build. The relative smallness of the temple does not mean that it is less important than the palace: its smaller size implies, rather, its greater importance (access to it is more restricted). But the suspicion arises that royal splendour is going to Solomon's head. For the moment, though, the narrator does not develop this point.

When the temple is complete, the ark is installed in it (8:1–13). All the Israelites assemble for this final stage in its journey. The narrative again recalls the past, referring to the tablets of the law and to the exodus (v. 9). Finally a cloud representing YHWH's glory fills the temple (vv. 10–11), reminiscent of the pillar of smoke which led the Israelites (see also Lev. 9:22–24). Solomon proclaims the fulfilment of YHWH's promise (vv. 12–22), in words which echo 2 Samuel 7. Indeed, 1 Kings 8 is like 2 Samuel 7: it surveys past and future and focuses on key theological themes.

Most of chapter 8 consists of Solomon's prayer of dedication (8:22–53). The temple is now a visible symbol of YHWH's presence in Israel, and so Solomon envisages Israelites praying in or towards the temple when they seek YHWH's blessing (vv. 30, 31, 33, etc.). He praises YHWH's faithfulness (vv. 23–24): the completed temple testifies to that faithfulness. But it cannot 'contain' YHWH (v. 27): it does not place him under obligation to bless his people. And so Solomon asks (v. 30): 'Hear the plea of your servant and of your people Israel when they pray towards this place; O hear in heaven your dwelling place; heed and forgive.'

Israel will often need to seek YHWH's forgiveness: this becomes the central theme of the prayer. Solomon envisages seven situations in which people will pray in or towards the temple. In the first of them the prayer is an oath of innocence (vv. 31–32), in the fifth the one who prays is a foreigner (vv. 41–43), and in the sixth the prayer is for victory in battle (vv. 44–45). But in the remaining four cases those who pray are Israelites who have sinned and fallen under various judgments: military defeat (vv. 33–34); drought (vv. 35–36); famine and plague (vv. 37–40); and, most seriously, exile (vv. 46–53). These four judgments echo the covenant curses of Deuteronomy 28, and so the prayer is essentially that YHWH

will forgive covenant violations if the people repent. Solomon does not once refer to the temple as a place of sacrifice, though this idea is clearly implied elsewhere in the chapter (vv. 5, 62–64). His sole focus is Israel's need for forgiveness. He almost assumes that Israel will sin (v. 46).

Solomon's prayer frequently echoes Deuteronomy 28—30 and follows the pattern of those chapters, in which sin leads finally to exile, but the people are restored when they repent. The verses dealing with exile (vv. 46–53) do not explicitly mention return to the land, speaking merely of YHWH granting Israel in exile 'compassion in the sight of their captors' (v. 50), and so might seem to differ at this point from Deuteronomy 30:1–10. But v. 34 has already spoken of YHWH bringing people back to the land, and the two references to the exodus from Egypt (vv. 51, 53) also seem to imply this idea. If there is a difference between Deuteronomy 28—30 and 1 Kings 8:22–53, it is that one passage is a prophecy and the other a prayer. The prayer form brings out more clearly the people's utter dependence on YHWH. It fits with this that Solomon only hints at a possible return from exile, as though even to mention it openly would be presumptuous.

Finally Solomon addresses the people (vv. 56–61), praying that YHWH will remember his words, so that the lives of king and people may be a witness to the surrounding nations, and calling the people to recommit themselves to YHWH. The chapter ends with a description of the sacrifices offered and the celebrations of the people (vv. 62–66).

In 9:1–9 YHWH answers Solomon in a vision which balances the earlier vision at Gibeon (v. 2). If that vision focused on what YHWH would give Solomon, the focus here is on what YHWH requires: integrity, obedience and loyalty. Only on this basis will Solomon's line continue to rule Israel, Israel remain in the land, and the temple continue as a place of worship. Failing that, the covenant curses will fall (vv. 4–9; cf. Deut. 28:37; 29:22–28). It is not that Solomon's prayer has been rejected: on the contrary, YHWH has 'consecrated' the newly built temple and put his name there 'for ever' (v. 3). Not only his eyes (cf. 8:29) but his heart will be there 'for all time' (v. 3). This is the language of firm commitment. But none of this means that the temple cannot be destroyed: on the contrary, verses 8–9 envisage precisely this possibility. 'For ever' and 'for all time' are not an unconditional pledge of non-destruction. The same is true of Israel's nationhood and the rule of Solomon's descendants over Israel: these things can come to an end if king and people are disobedient. No sooner is the temple built, no sooner has Solomon prayed for YHWH's continuing blessing, than YHWH speaks to him of possible destruction and exile. This is a sobering note on which to end.

YHWH has now fulfilled much of what was promised to David in 2 Samuel 7: Solomon is on the throne, and the temple is built. Both David and Solomon have at points fallen short; and yet YHWH has kept his word. But what will follow? Throughout 8:1—9:9 there is an unresolved tension: the people must keep YHWH's laws, but will need to seek YHWH's mercy; YHWH is gracious, yet also judges his people's disobedience; YHWH promises Solomon much, but he and his descendants must walk in YHWH's ways. This tension between judgment and grace runs through the rest of Kings. The narrator is also interested in what happens to the temple; but Solomon's prayer makes clear

that YHWH's purposes, like YHWH, are bigger than the temple.

Solomon's folly (I Kgs 9:10—11:43)

Some details in earlier chapters have raised questions (e.g. Solomon's marriage, 3:1; his extravagant palace, 7:1–12), but the narrator has made no comment. During 9:10—10:29 similar details mount up more noticeably: the narrator continues to withhold comment.

Chapter 5 contained sections describing economic relations with Hiram (5:7–12) and the organization of the labour for the construction of the temple (5:13–18: 30,000 conscripted labourers and 150,000 other workers). These two themes recur in chapter 9 with a more clearly negative cast: Hiram continues to co-operate with Solomon, but now, far from praising YHWH, complains at Solomon's hard bargain (9:10–14; contrast 5:7). A further description of Solomon's forced labour (9:15–22; cf. 5:13) notes that the first, conscripted group of labourers (identified as such by the use of the same Hebrew term, *mas*: compare 5:13 [MT 5:27] and 9:21) were drawn from the original inhabitants of the land, whom the Israelites had not driven out. We are reminded of Judges 1—3, and how failure to drive out the Canaanites led Israel into idolatry (cf. Deut. 7:1–6).

Chapter 10 describes the Queen of Sheba's visit (10:1–13; Sheba = south-west Arabia), and continues with a long description of Solomon's wealth. This chapter parallels chapter 4. There are the same references to wealth and splendour, to Solomon's wisdom, and to foreign rulers coming to learn from him (vv. 8, 23–24). But the balance of chapter 10 is different. In chapter 4, Solomon's wealth was described in terms of food and, importantly, the contentment and security of all Israel (4:20, 25); in chapter 10 gold and luxury items dominate the description (9:26–28; 10:2, 10–25), and Israel as a whole seems to recede from view. YHWH has promised Solomon wealth (3:13), but did he mean Solomon to acquire so much? Compare Deuteronomy 17:17: '. . . silver and gold he must not acquire in great quantity for himself'. In a similar way, Solomon's horses and chariots (10:26–29) clearly violate the terms of Deuteronomy 17:16.

So far the narrator has simply reported facts. But in chapter 11 he abandons his 'pseudo-objective' stance, and passes a negative judgment on Solomon's old age, using heavily loaded language and drawing a sharp contrast between what YHWH had commanded and what Solomon did (vv. 2–3, 9–10). Our misgivings in chapters 9—10 are confirmed: Solomon's heart has strayed from YHWH. Solomon has loved his wives rather than YHWH, and they have led him to worship other gods, exactly as Deuteronomy 17:17 warned. In the end he has not followed the example of his father David (vv. 4, 6), though he did so, at least in a qualified sense, earlier in his life (3:1).

The narrator's evaluation is followed by a word of divine judgment (11:11–13): the kingdom is to be 'torn' from Solomon. But this judgment is lightened in two ways (vv. 12–13): it will happen not in Solomon's own lifetime but in that of his son; and Solomon's son will still have one tribe to rule over.

The narrative then describes the rise of various adversaries: Hadad and Rezon, who begin to weaken Solomon's empire while he is still alive, and Jeroboam, who will dismantle the kingdom after his death (11:14–40). There are exodus echoes, but these are no longer positive: instead, Solomon's kingdom has become a kind of Egypt from which the oppressed flee.

Ahijah approaches Jeroboam with a word from YHWH (11:29–39). He tears his cloak (cf. Samuel and Saul in 1 Sam. 15:27–28), ripping it into 12 pieces, of which he invites Jeroboam to take ten, in token of the fact that Jeroboam will rule over ten tribes. One tribe is for Solomon and his descendants (cf. v. 13). This tribe, chapter 12 will make clear, is the tribe of Benjamin, a point already implied in the mathematics here, in which Jeroboam has ten tribes, Solomon one, and one tribe is unaccounted for (vv. 31–32, 35–36) – most likely Judah, whose loyalty to David's line is throughout assumed (for alternative views, see Jones, p. 244; Provan 1995, pp. 95, 98). Ahijah cites YHWH's commitment to David and to Jerusalem as the reason why the kingdom is divided only after Solomon's death and why Solomon's descendants will still rule over a part of this kingdom (vv. 32–36; cf. vv. 12–13). He repeatedly mentions David. The point is clear: Jeroboam can be king over ten tribes, but he must acknowledge the continuing legitimacy of David's line and Jerusalem. He must also, verse 33 implies, deal with the people's growing unfaithfulness. This is a difficult calling. But he is promised that YHWH will bless him as he blessed David (v. 38).

Ahijah's prophecy contains two apparently contradictory themes. YHWH's promise to Jeroboam (vv. 31–39) involves the break-up of Solomon's kingdom. Solomon has not walked before YHWH with 'integrity of heart and uprightness', and so the promise to David that 'there shall not fail you a successor on the throne of Israel' is broken (cf. 1 Kgs 9:4–5): Chapter 12 will make clear that Jeroboam, and not Solomon's son Rehoboam, has the better claim to rule over the 'throne of Israel'. YHWH promised David that his house would be 'made sure for ever' and his throne 'established for ever' (2 Sam. 7:16); but already in Solomon's lifetime YHWH announces the intention of tearing the kingdom from David's line.

But the prophecy also dwells on YHWH's commitment to David and Jerusalem: David will always have 'a lamp before me in Jerusalem' (v. 36), which implies that the promise to David is somehow still in force. The giving of the ten tribes to Jeroboam does not completely destroy David's kingdom; indeed, this new state of affairs is not necessarily permanent (v. 39).

The division of the kingdom is a severe blow, but still falls into the category of 'blows inflicted by human beings' (2 Sam. 7:14). In spite of the earlier parallels between Solomon's punishment and Saul's, Solomon has not ended by sharing Saul's fate, and his son succeeds him as king, though with a reduced kingdom.

The account of Solomon ends with his death and Rehoboam's succession (11:41–43). Verse 41 refers to a 'Book of the Acts of Solomon' as giving a full account of 'all that he did and his wisdom'. Coming as it does after three chapters describing Solomon's mounting folly and its consequences, the reference to wisdom seems ironic.

The Solomon narrative is not a simple account of a good king failing at the end of his life. Some of Solomon's early actions are questionable. He then seems to change his ways and for a time leads Israel righteously and wisely, bringing them blessing. But in his later years he declines, falling into apostasy which brings down judgment. If David fell short of being an ideal king, Solomon falls far shorter, in spite of what he inherited from David.

(The above account of Solomon's reign often follows Provan 1995, which you can consult for more details.)

1 KINGS 12—16: DIVISION OF THE KINGDOM; EARLY HISTORY OF ISRAEL AND JUDAH

Chapter 12 describes the fulfilment of Ahijah's prophecy. 'All Israel' comes to Shechem to make Rehoboam king (12:1): this phrase apparently means representatives of all the tribes, for when Rehoboam later musters Judah and Benjamin for war, he has to return to Judah to do so (12:21).

**EARLY KINGS OF ISRAEL AND JUDAH
(1 Kgs 12—16)**
(dates based on Kitchen, pp. 26–32, simplified for
easy reference)

Israel	**Judah**
Jeroboam (930–910)	Rehoboam (930–914)
	Abijam (914–911)
Nadab (910–909)	Asa (911–870)
Baasha (909–886)*	
Elah (886–885)	
Zimri (885)*	
Omri (885–874)*	
Ahab (874–853)	

* = beginning of new dynasty/denotes usurper

The representatives wish to know what kind of a king Rehoboam intends to be (12:2–4). They have invited Jeroboam to join their assembly, an indication that they are prepared to consider alternatives. They ask for the burdens imposed by Solomon to be lightened. However contented the people once were (4:20), they are no longer so. Having taken advice from court elders and from his younger companions, Rehoboam answers the people harshly (12:5–14). The people reject him with equal bluntness (cf. 2 Sam. 20:1).

Rehoboam's response is foolish, but not unbelievably so: a prince who had grown up during the later, more unbalanced years of Solomon's reign might well have found the advice that he become his people's 'servant' offensive (12:7), particularly if his friends egged him on. The narrator, as elsewhere in the Histories, notes YHWH's hand in events (12:15) but also suggests other levels of explanation for the course of events.

The tribal representatives are still near Shechem ('to their tents' in 12:16 is probably literal). Perhaps they are debating their next step. Rehoboam compounds his folly by sending Adoram, apparently to impose forced labour upon them. But they kill him, and Rehoboam has to flee. Israel's 'rebellion' is now irreversible, and they make Jeroboam their king. Judah, however, follows Rehoboam, turning its back on the decision of the other tribes (12:18–20).

Rehoboam's first reaction is to try to regain his kingdom by force (12:21–24). He musters Judah, and also Benjamin. (Did the Benjaminites change sides when they saw Judah mustering? A further detail of Ahijah's prophecy is fulfilled.) But now there comes a prophecy: 'You shall not go up or fight against your kindred the people of Israel. Let everyone go home, for this thing is from me' (v. 24). Rehoboam and his men take the prophecy seriously, abandoning their intention of going to war against their 'kindred'. Jeroboam's next action, by contrast, deliberately widens the gap between the southern and northern tribes. Afraid of what may happen if his people continue to worship in Jerusalem, he makes two golden calves, tells the people that these are 'your gods . . . who brought you up out of the land of Egypt' (v. 28; cf. Exod. 32:4), and places them in shrines at Bethel and Dan. He appoints non-Levitical priests, and institutes a festival which is 'like the festival that was in Judah' except that, unlike the festival of Tabernacles, it is held on the fifteenth day of the eighth, not the seventh, month (cf. Lev. 23:33–36).

The text emphasizes Jeroboam's role: he has created a new form of worship to suit his purposes, and this is a 'sin' that leads his people astray (v. 30). Behind Jeroboam's actions lies unbelief: YHWH promised him ten tribes (11:29–39), but he is unable to trust the promise (12:26–27). In effect he decides that it is more important for the ten tribes to remain loyal to him than loyal to YHWH. Jeroboam's shrines are the first instance of a recurrent theme in Kings: the tendency of kings to adopt forms of worship that suit their own interests.

The narrator's perspective on Jeroboam's actions could not be more clear. It is less clear what Jeroboam ought to have done instead: Ahijah's prophecy noted the people's apostasy (11:33), implying Jeroboam's duty to bring his subjects back to YHWH, and emphasized YHWH's continuing commitment to Jerusalem (11:32, 36). But he gave no instructions regarding the people's worship. Should Jeroboam have allowed the people to go to Jerusalem (if Rehoboam would permit this), trusting that they would remain loyal to him? Should he have set up within his own territory imageless shrines, designed not to rival the Jerusalem temple but to testify that his people were entitled to worship in Jerusalem (cf. Josh. 22:10–34)? Why does he not seek YHWH? One can imagine a different narrative in which Jeroboam in perplexity prays to YHWH and receives guidance: but events take another course. From this point on Jeroboam's shrines are the standing reproach of the North (1 Kgs 15:26, etc.).

Jeroboam is about to inaugurate his new shrine, when a prophet from Judah appears and denounces it (13:1–3). His words imply that the North is doomed: Bethel, the royal shrine, and the high places will be destroyed by Josiah, a descendant of David. (This implies that the South will outlive the

---

Think about
JEROBOAM: WAS HE SO BAD?

Is Kings unfair to Jeroboam? It has been suggested that Jeroboam did not intend to lead his people away from YHWH: his aim in setting up his shrines was, rather, to provide his people with centres of worship which (unlike Jerusalem) had no historic associations with David. The calves were not meant as idols, but simply as symbols of YHWH's presence or as a kind of throne on which YHWH was thought to sit, like the cherubim in the Jerusalem temple. Indirect support for this position is found at 1 Kings 19:14, in the words of Elijah, who, over 60 years later, seems to believe that the altars of the North were in some sense altars for the worship of YHWH (Miller and Hayes, pp. 242–4; Gnuse, pp. 186–7).

Elijah's brief words, however, spoken at a time when the people have (as he believes) rejected YHWH in favour of Baal, cannot be taken as an endorsement of Jeroboam's shrines: it is likely that he would have viewed even (what he felt to be) a corrupt form of YHWH worship as better than outright abandonment of YHWH. And Jeroboam's reforms have been viewed as a deliberate attempt to recreate a form of Canaanite worship (Wyatt), a suggestion which fits with the apparently polytheistic theology attributed to Jeroboam at 1 Kings 12:28 and also with the reference to 'sacred poles' at 14:15.

What in your view does the narrator principally find fault with: the religious aspects of the reforms, or Jeroboam's personal motives in carrying out the reforms?

North.) Jeroboam is unable to silence or bribe the prophet (13:4–10), and the lengthy sequel makes clear that the Judean prophet spoke truly: he rightly predicted his own death for disobedience, and so he may be trusted in what he said about the North (13:32). His fate, indeed, parallels what he prophesied for the North: he is punished for transgressing a divine command (13:21–22), having been lured into sin by a plausible counterfeit claiming YHWH's authority (13:14–19).

In spite of the warning, Jeroboam does not change his ways (13:33–34). Even after the prophecy he apparently could have repented, but did not. Judgment begins to fall: Jeroboam's son Abijam falls ill. Jeroboam sends his wife to Ahijah in disguise, apparently believing that a favourable prophecy, even one obtained by deceit, brings blessing. Ahijah sees through the deception and pronounces judgment: Abijam will die, Jeroboam's line will come to an end, and Israel will be an unstable kingdom, eventually going into exile in Assyria ('beyond the Euphrates', v. 16). Already YHWH's promise to Jeroboam and the ten tribes has run into the sand, though the end still lies nearly 200 years in the future.

The account of Jeroboam raises difficult questions (cf. Campbell and O'Brien, pp. 325–6). On the one hand the rebellion of the ten tribes is justified because of Rehoboam's foolish behaviour. Indeed, that rebellion was YHWH's will (12:15). But the result is that Jeroboam leads the ten tribes away from YHWH. It is as though their separation from Judah and Jerusalem brings out what is really in their hearts. And the ten tribes ('Israel' as they are called from now on) share in Jeroboam's guilt: it was they who summoned Jeroboam and made him king; and they later chose to accept the idolatrous worship which he devised. Like Jeroboam, the kingdom of Israel is guilty of unfaithfulness to YHWH (14:15).

Judah under Rehoboam is little better. The brief account of Rehoboam's reign (14:21–31) tells how Judah also fell into idolatry, and then describes the invasion of Shishak, who plundered the Jerusalem temple. The implication is that YHWH's hand lay behind the invasion. The removal of Solomon's golden shields and their replacement by bronze shields symbolizes the vanished glory of Solomon's kingdom.

And yet the two kingdoms, equally corrupt and worthy of judgment, are not on a par. Abijam, Rehoboam's son, is no more faithful than his father, and yet 'for David's sake YHWH his God gave him a lamp in Jerusalem, setting up his son after him, and establishing Jerusalem' (15:4). Asa, Abijam's son, pulls Judah back from the brink, ridding the land of idolatry, and warding off Israel's attacks in the reign of Baasha (15:9–24). His son Jehoshaphat succeeds him: David's line still survives.

By contrast, Nadab, Jeroboam's son, is assassinated by Baasha, and all of Jeroboam's descendants are killed (15:25–32). Baasha in turn follows Jeroboam's sin and like Jeroboam receives a prophecy that his line will come to an end (15:34—16:4). This theme dominates the account of Baasha: not only are the prophet's words cited in 16:2–4, but the narrator refers to the prophecy in verse 7, explaining God's anger as due to Baasha's having followed Jeroboam's sins and also (paradoxically) to his having eradicated Jeroboam's line. Baasha is characterized as the founder of a dynasty which he doomed by his own disobedience.

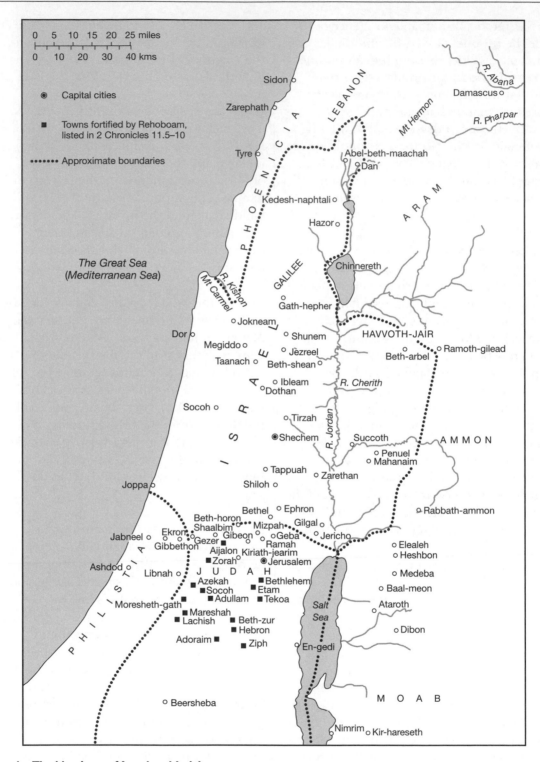

Map 4   The kingdoms of Israel and Judah

There follows a period of civil war in Israel (16:8–23): Omri, the army commander, overcomes a further rival, Tibni, and stability is restored. Omri founds a new dynasty and builds a new royal city, Samaria.

Omri brings stability, but not righteousness: the reverse, for 'he did more evil than all who were before him' (16:25), continuing to follow the false worship of Jeroboam. His apparently considerable military victories (see the panel 'The Moabite Stone') are dismissed in a brief reference to 'the power that he showed' (16:27), and the main impression that his narrative leaves is of wicked apostasy.

Omri's son Ahab outdoes even his father in wickedness, not only following the 'sins of Jeroboam' (16:31) but marrying Jezebel, a Phoenician princess, and introducing the worship of Baal, one of the Phoenician gods, into Samaria.

Everything that follows in the books of Kings is a logical consequence of the events of 1 Kings 12—16: the differing assessments of Israelite and Judean kings in the 'regnal formulae' (see the panel 'Regnal formulae in Kings'); the different characters of the two kingdoms (Israel has a number of dynasties, each of which ends violently; Judah has one); the different fates of the two kingdoms (2 Kings closes holding out some hope for Judah, but with no hint of hope for Israel, at least not as a separate kingdom).

1 KINGS 17—2 KINGS 10: THE TWO KINGDOMS; ELIJAH AND ELISHA

The long central section of Kings (1 Kgs 17—2 Kgs 10) contains most of the narratives of the prophets Elijah and Elisha. The different episodes in this section are diverse in character, and the connection between them is not always apparent. Some have explained these facts by arguing that a number of sources have been combined,

---

THE MOABITE STONE

The Moabite Stone, also known as the Mesha Stela (*COS* II, pp. 137–8), an inscribed stone which came to light at Dhiban in the former territory of Moab in 1868, was produced around 835 BC to commemorate the achievements of Mesha king of Moab (cf. 2 Kgs 3:4).

The stela is written in a language closely related to biblical Hebrew. It tells us (lines 5–8) that Omri 'oppressed Moab for many days', occupying the region of Medeba, and that Omri's 'son' (quite probably Joram rather than Ahab, 'son' here denoting 'grandson') attempted but failed to reimpose Israelite control on Moab (a possible reference to the events described in 2 Kings 3). It also describes Israel as having 'gone to ruin for ever' (line 7), possibly an (exaggerated) reference to the aftermath of Jehu's

coup. It describes Mesha's defeat of Israelites living in Transjordan (lines 9–21, and his subjecting of the inhabitants of Nebo to 'the ban' (the root is *khrm*, the same root as in Joshua 6). The stela attributes setbacks to the anger of Chemosh, god of Moab, in the same way that the Histories see Israel's national fortunes as dependent upon YHWH's anger or favour. Last, Mesha speaks of having taken the 'vessels of YHWH' and brought them 'before the face of Chemosh' (lines 17–18): this is the earliest reference to the name of Israel's god in an inscription. (For a possible reference to 'the house of David' in line 31, see Ch. 5.)

For further discussion of the Moabite Stone, see Hobbs, pp. 39–41.

REGNAL FORMULAE IN KINGS

'Regnal formulae' are the phrases which introduce and conclude the accounts of all the kings of Israel and Judah. Such phrases have occurred already in connection with David (2:10–11), Solomon (2:12; 11:41–43), Jeroboam (14:20) and Rehoboam (14:21, 29–30). But from 15:1 on, reflecting the fact that the two kingdoms are now separate entities, the opening formulae follow a new pattern, in which each king of Judah is dated in relation to the king of Israel reigning at the time he came to power and vice versa. Nelson summarizes the general pattern of the formulae as follows (1981, p. 32):

Introductory:

- synchronism (only up to Hoshea of Israel);
- age at accession;
- length of reign;
- capital city;
- name of queen mother (Judah only);
- verdict.

Concluding:

- source citation;
- death and burial;
- notice of the succession.

These formulae, as the term implies, use stereotyped language, but with some flexibility: e.g. the concluding formula for Solomon contains an appropriate reference to his 'wisdom' (1 Kgs 11:41), and that for Omri a reference to the 'power that he showed' (1 Kgs 16:27). Formulae tend to be disrupted or replaced with other types of material in narratives of major crises, as for example in the case of Jehu (because of how he came to power). There are no concluding formulae for Jehoiachin or Zedekiah of Judah, because of the unusual ways their reigns ended (2 Kgs 24:12; 25:6–7).

Patterns can be seen in the formulae. Thus the first eight kings, Jeroboam to Joram, all 'walk in the way of Jeroboam' and cause Israel to 'provoke YHWH to anger' (e.g. Omri, 1 Kgs 16:26). For the next eight, from Jehu to Pekah, the characteristic expression is that the king 'did not depart from all the sins of Jeroboam' (e.g. Jeroboam II, 2 Kgs 14:24). The last king, Hoshea, 'did what was evil . . . yet not like the kings of Israel before him (2 Kgs 17:2). (For all this, see McKenzie, pp. 302–3.) In McKenzie's view the 'entire list is well balanced and seems to convey a clear message': the first eight kings are the 'true apostates'; after Jehu the reformer Israel's kings 'are not so bad, but they perpetuate the sin of Jeroboam'; Hoshea 'is not to blame for Israel's demise; he is only the last in a long line of evil rulers'. (For tables setting out the data, see Campbell and O'Brien, pp. 478–85.)

The synchronisms in the formulae also highlight one of the narrator's main interests, the intertwining of the fates of Israel and Judah: the two kingdoms, though separate, continue to interact with each other, fighting (1 Kgs 15) or forming alliances (generally seen as unwise for Judah: 1 Kgs 22; 2 Kgs 3). Sometimes the kings of Judah sin by imitating the kings of Israel (2 Kgs 8:18, 26–27), and share the fate of the northern kings (2 Kgs 9:27–29). At times the narrative, building on the 'cross-referencing' tendency of the formulae, seems to suggest analogies between what happened at the same period in the two kingdoms, noting both similarities and divergences (see the comments on 1 Kgs 15—16 and 2 Kgs 10—12).

The formulae, finally, highlight an unhappy truth: the way in which each king's accession is described continually reminds us that there were two kingdoms where there should only have been one.

producing an account in which both continuity and chronological accuracy have suffered (See, for example: Jones, pp. 64–73; Dietrich, pp. 247, 251). Clearly, these chapters develop a number of narrative strands which could be disentangled and function as largely independent accounts. But these strands are more closely linked than at first appears, and it seems legitimate to treat 1 Kings 17—2 Kings 10 as a complex but single literary entity (Provan 1995; Satterthwaite).

KINGS IN THE PERIOD OF ELIJAH AND ELISHA (1 Kgs 17—2 Kgs 10)

(based on Kitchen, pp. 26–32)

Israel	Judah
Ahab (874–853)	Jehoshaphat (870–848)†
Ahaziah (853–852)	
Joram (852–841)	Joram (848–842)
Jehu (841–813)*	Ahaziah (842–841)

* = beginning of new dynasty/denotes usurper
† = possible co-regency with predecessor

Elijah, Elisha, Ahab and Baal

Elijah is said to have been active in the reigns of Ahab and Ahaziah, kings of Israel; Elisha, his successor, in the reigns of Ahaziah, Joram, Jehoahaz and Joash. Elisha, in particular, played a role in major political events of the time (wars waged against Aram and Moab; Jehu's coup). Both prophets were engaged in the struggle against Baal worship. The narrative presents this as their main achievement. No sooner has Ahab introduced Baal worship into Israel than Elijah makes his striking entry into the narrative (1 Kgs 17:1). The famine which follows is YHWH's challenge to the claims of Baal, god of storm and fertility. The entire central section of Kings develops this theme

announced at its beginning, tracing the stages in the eradication of Baal worship from Israel and (a linked theme) the destruction of Ahab's line.

THE BATTLE AGAINST BAAL AND AHAB'S LINE

The main stages are:

- 1 Kings 17—18: famine in Israel; Elijah's contest at Mt Carmel;
- 1 Kings 19: Elijah's discouragement at Jezebel's impenitence; his meeting with YHWH at Horeb;
- prophecies of judgment against Ahab and his family (1 Kgs 20:42; 21:17–24);
- 1 Kings 22: death of Ahab;
- 2 Kings 1: death of Ahaziah, son of Ahab;
- 2 Kings 9: deaths of Joram, son of Ahab, and Jezebel;
- 2 Kings 10:1–11: destruction of all members of Ahab's line;
- 2 Kings 10:18–28: slaughter of the priests of Baal and destruction of the Baal temple in Samaria. Note especially v. 28: 'Thus Jehu wiped out Baal from Israel.'

In 1 Kings 16—19 the narrator sets out important elements in his portrayal of Ahab's reign: Ahab's promotion of Baal worship as a 'state religion' (16:31–32); the persecution of YHWH's prophets, who are seen as 'trouble-makers' (18:3, 10, 17). This is a picture of oppression and state-sponsored apostasy. Unexpectedly, judgment against Ahab's line is postponed, more than once (19:15–17; 21:27–29). Yet Ahab never returns to YHWH, and the extra years he is granted, described in 1 Kings 20—22, only provide more evidence of the corrupt character of his reign.

In 1 Kings 20 he defeats Aram twice, having received prophecies of victory (vv. 13, 28), yet he does not acknowledge YHWH's power, preferring to make a treaty with Ben-Hadad, who has challenged YHWH (v. 23). Chapter 20 thus ends unexpectedly with a prophecy of judgment on Ahab, and he leaves the battlefield 'resentful and sullen' (vv. 42–43). The same phrase recurs in 1 Kings 21 when Naboth refuses to sell Ahab his vineyard (v. 4). It highlights a common theme in these two narratives: Ahab wishes to exercise kingship as he sees fit, and when he runs up against YHWH's word, whether in the form of a prophecy or in the form of an Israelite who will not violate the law (21:3; cf. Lev. 25:8–17), he responds by sulking.

Think about
WHICH KING AND WHICH PROPHET?

It has been argued that 1 Kings 20 and 22 did not originally belong in the account of Ahab (De Vries, p. 247; Jones, pp. 336–9). Elijah, active in chapters 19 and 21, is absent from these chapters, his place being taken by other prophets. Ahab is only occasionally referred to by name (20:2, 14; 22:20), and more frequently as 'king of Israel' (20:7, 21, 22, 34; 22:2–3, 9–10, 26, 33). But are these convincing arguments? Might there be a reason for Elijah to be absent from these chapters? Might a narrator writing about Ahab have had reasons for referring to him as 'king of Israel'?

For three years there is no war between Aram and Israel (22:1). Ahab then provokes war (vv. 2–4). This seems inconsistent, as he previously sought a treaty with Aram. But apparently Ahab intends to reverse the prophecy of 20:42, which implied that Aram would survive at Israel's expense, and that Ahab would die for having spared Ben-Hadad. How better to invalidate the prophecy than by a further victory over Aram? This final act of defiance leads to his death.

A similar pattern can be seen in the account of the reign of Joram, Ahab's son: a postponement of judgment, followed by the king's decisive rejection of the prophetic word and his death (see p. 164).

ARAM IN 1 AND 2 KINGS

- 1 Kings 15: first reference to Aram: Asa seeks Aramean help against Baasha;
- 1 Kings 20: victories against Arameans; 1 Kings 22: Aramean victory at Ramoth Gilead; death of Ahab;
- 2 Kings 5:1—6:23: healing of Naaman; Elisha's 'capture' of Arameans brings peace;
- 2 Kings 6:24—7:20: Elisha brings deliverance to besieged Samaria;
- 2 Kings 8:7–15: Elisha foretells Hazael's destructive power;
- 2 Kings 8:28–29: wounding of Joram in battle with Hazael;
- 2 Kings 10:32–33: Hazael starts to conquer Israelite territory;
- 2 Kings 13:3–7: destructive power of Aram;
- 2 Kings 13:10–25: Elisha dies: Joash will have only three victories after his death.

Note particularly 2 Kings 10:28–31, which explains why the end of Baal worship was not the end of Israel's troubles with Aram.

The miracles

In this context, what is the significance of Elijah's and Elisha's miracles? Some of them, particularly those of Elisha, seem oddly trivial. Is the fact that Kings contains narratives such as 2 Kings 4:38–41 (the vegetable stew) or 6:1–7 (the floating axe-head) simply due to the fact that these traditions survived, whereas others did not? Perhaps there is more to the miracles than that. Two themes seem to unite the miracle accounts: (1) life and death; (2) relations between prophet and king. These are in fact two aspects of a single theme.

Sometimes the theme of life and death is obvious, as in the narratives in which Elisha provides food during famine (1 Kgs 17:8–16; 2 Kgs 4:38–44), or carries out healings (1 Kgs 17:17–24; 2 Kgs 4:18–37). YHWH is regularly linked with life in these chapters. This is true in a literal sense: YHWH sends rain (1 Kgs 18), provides food, and enables a barren woman to conceive (2 Kgs 4:11–17). But it is true on another level. The Elijah and Elisha narratives for a time hold out the hope that Israel will heed their call, return to YHWH and (in this sense as well) find life. This is why the question of relations between prophet and king is important: if the king listens to the prophet, then all Israel may find life.

Elijah is a second Moses: he meets with YHWH at Horeb (1 Kgs 19); he ends his earthly life outside the land and in such a way that 'no one knows his burial place to this day' (2 Kings 2:9–12; cf. Deut. 34:6). Elisha, Elijah's successor, reminds us of Moses' successor, Joshua: the point becomes clear when Elisha parts the waters of the Jordan to cross back into the land (Hobbs, p. 19; cf. Josh. 3—4). The narrative seems to suggest that, just as Joshua completed Moses' work by conquering Canaan, Elisha and his companions, the 'sons of the prophets', will complete Elijah's work by purging Israel of the quasi-Canaanite Baal worship. The two narratives that follow Elisha's crossing of the Jordan clarify the issues at stake: those who seek the prophet's aid and follow his word will find life, like the citizens of Jericho (2:19–22); those who scorn his word will die, like the 'small boys' of Bethel (2:23–24).

The hope that Israel will find life is particularly strong in 2 Kings 4—6. In chapter 4 Elisha promises a son to the

---

Digging deeper:
THE BOYS AND THE BEARS

The narrative of 2 Kings 2:23–24 seems one of the harshest in the entire Old Testament, particularly if one believes that in general 'small boys' are not entirely accountable for their actions.

Penchansky, in a chapter entitled 'The Mad Prophet and the Abusive God', argues that the narrative is an attempt to come to terms with experiences in which God seems to have acted arbitrarily and vindictively (pp. 81–9). Brichto (pp. 196–8) interprets the Hebrew as saying, not that a group of 'small boys' were 'mauled', but that a gang of 'mean-spirited rascals' (young men) was 'broken up' (scattered) by the two bears.

Read these two alternative approaches to the passage. Is either of them workable?

---

woman of Shunem, and later raises this son back to life (4:8–37). This narrative seems to function partly on a symbolic level, echoing narratives in Genesis in which a barren woman conceives and bears a son: the boy represents Israel, and the incident hints that sick Israel may be restored to life like this boy. In chapter 5 Elisha heals Naaman, the Aramean commander who has previously defeated Israel in battle (5:1–2), an action which leads Naaman to acknowledge YHWH, and which tends in the direction of bringing peace between Aram and Israel (though it does not do so immediately). In chapter 6 Elisha takes increasingly effective steps to counter the military might of Aram, finally leading many Aramean soldiers captive to Samaria (6:17–23), temporarily ending Aramean raids. Relations between Joram and Elisha seem to improve in chapters 5–6, Elisha warning the king of Aramean plans (6:8–10) and the king listening to his word.

But the hope fades: the Arameans return (6:24). They are again defeated, but relations between prophet and king deteriorate (6:30–32). Joram turns his back on YHWH (6:33), and the death of his captain as punishment for mocking Elisha (7:1–2, 17–20) seems to foreshadow his own death. In the next episode (8:1–6) Elisha and Joram are apparently no longer on speaking terms: Joram can only learn of Elisha's mighty deeds at second hand, with no expectation that he may himself see them. In chapter 9 Elisha instigates Jehu to assassinate Joram. In chapter 13, by the end of Elisha's lifetime, there is a clear sense that Israel is dying. The hope of Israel's return to YHWH has come to nothing.

Jehu's coup (2 Kgs 9—10)

No sooner has Elisha sent a young prophet to anoint Jehu than he vanishes from the narrative. The young prophet also flees once he has carried out his task (9:10). But the narrative emphasizes that Jehu's actions fulfil YHWH's will as declared by his prophets (9:6–10). He kills Joram and Ahaziah of Judah (9:16–28), denouncing Joram before he does so (v. 22). He leaves Joram's body in Naboth's plot as a second fulfilment of the prophecy against Ahab (1 Kgs 21:19). Jezebel, too, dies a gruesome death, and again the narrator draws the link with Elijah's prophecy (9:30–37; cf. 1 Kgs 21:23). Next, Jehu wins over the chief officials of Samaria with persuasive threats and has Ahab's sons, his remaining rivals for the throne, executed (10:1–6). The heaping up of their heads outside the gate of Jezreel is a further grisly detail. Jehu points to it as

---

Digging deeper:
FORM CRITICISM AND THE ELISHA NARRATIVES

B.O. Long's commentaries on 1 and 2 Kings are part of a series which is form-critical in its orientation: much of what Long says (regarding structure, genre and possible origins of individual literary units) reflects this perspective. Read his treatment of some of the Elisha narratives in 2 Kings 2—8 to get a sense of how form criticism works out in practice.

Long's approach in these chapters is somewhat unusual in that he often seems to be more comfortable describing how individual narratives function in their present context than discussing the original life-setting and meaning of these narratives. A recurring comment (e.g. pp. 30, 35, 46) is that the *present* literary setting of individual texts is what is crucial for interpretation. In this his commentary seems to resist a tendency to fragmentation which can be detected in form-critical scholarship. Perhaps it also offers indirect support for the unitary reading of 1 Kings 17—2 Kings 10 proposed in this chapter.

---

evidence that YHWH truly is with him (10:9–10).

Ahaziah of Judah has already been killed, and now Jehu captures 42 of his relatives on the way to visit Ahab's family. That fact is enough to damn them, and he has them killed too (10:12–14). Jehonadab son of Rechab, in contrast, a faithful servant of YHWH (see Jer. 35), becomes his ally and witness of his continuing zeal for YHWH (10:15–16). Jehu destroys the remnant of Ahab's family in Samaria, and all of Ahab's associates (10:17, a further reference to

Elijah's prophecy). Finally he ends Baal worship in a kind of parody sacrifice in which Baal's priests are themselves the victims. Baal's house is destroyed and defiled (10:18–27).

The account of Jehu focuses on his role as instrument of YHWH's vengeance: only 10:28–36 deals with other aspects of his reign. The narrative stresses Jehu's obedience to YHWH's command. We might, therefore, expect a 'rave review' for Jehu, and the narrator does have praise for him, but only qualified praise. Jehu destroyed Baal worship, but he did not remove Jeroboam's shrines (vv. 28–29); he dealt with Ahab's line 'in accordance with all that was in [YHWH's] heart' but, because he did not follow YHWH's law scrupulously, was promised descendants only to the fourth generation (10:30–31). This disappointing ending fits with 2 Kings 2—8, which has made clear that the removal of Baal worship will not be the end of Israel's problems. (Perhaps this is why Elisha appeared to distance himself from Jehu at the beginning of ch. 9.) The fact that in Jehu's day YHWH uses Hazael of Aram to 'trim off parts of Israel' is a further fulfilment of prophecy (10:32–33; cf. 8:12–13 and 1 Kgs 19:15–17), and one which suggests that Elijah and Elisha have not fundamentally transformed Israel's situation.

Verses 28–36 of chapter 10 are the key to understanding Israel's fortunes in 2 Kings 11—14. Israel survives in these chapters, and there are references to YHWH's forbearance. Jehu's line has been granted four generations, and it gets them. Indeed, Jeroboam II, Jehu's great-grandson, seems very successful. But underlying the account is a sense that time is running out for Israel.

2 KINGS 11—17: THE LAST YEARS OF ISRAEL

LATER KINGS OF ISRAEL AND JUDAH (2 Kgs 11—17)

(based on Kitchen, pp. 26–32)

Israel	Judah
Jehu (841–813)*	[Athaliah (841–835)]*
Jehoahaz (813–805)†	Joash (835–795)
Joash (805–790)	Amaziah (795–775)†
Jeroboam II (790–749)†	Azariah/Uzziah (775–735)†
Zechariah (749)	
Shallum (749)*	
Menahem (748–738)*	
Pekahiah (738–736)	
Pekah (736–731)*	Jotham (750–730)†
Hoshea (731–722)*	Ahaz (730–715)

* = beginning of new dynasty/denotes usurper
† = possible co-regency with predecessor

Israel and Judah in the period after Jehu's coup (2 Kgs 11—14)

Chapter 11, like chapter 10, describes a conspiracy which comes to its head in a temple. But this time the temple is YHWH's, in Jerusalem, and the conspirators are YHWH's faithful servants, whose aim is to remove a usurper and restore the legitimate dynasty.

It is not clear why Athaliah, queen mother in Judah, tries to destroy the Judean royal family (11:1). Perhaps she sees her opportunity in the fact that Jehu has killed so many rivals to the throne along with her son (10:12–14). But the line of David, to which YHWH is committed (see most recently 8:19), survives in the person of the infant Joash (11:2–3). Athaliah, equally clearly, does not have the support of all her 'subjects'. Those opposed to her bide their time and then act decisively (11:4–12). Many elements in this account suggest the different character of Judah and Israel at this period:

the references to Sabbath, priests and regular temple worship; the mention of shields and spears belonging to David; the presentation to Joash of the 'covenant' (11:12: literally, 'testimony', a copy of the covenant law; cf. Deut. 17:18–20; 1 Kgs 2:3) at his crowning; even the concern to avoid polluting YHWH's house with bloodshed (11:15). In spite of the wicked behaviour of its most recent king (8:25–27), Judah clearly contains significant numbers of faithful people for whom YHWH's promises and law are not a dead letter. Baal has had a foothold in Judah, but king and people now recommit themselves to YHWH and destroy Baal's temple (11:17–20). The people rejoice at the turn of events.

Like a number of kings of Judah before him (Rehoboam, Asa, Jehoshaphat), Joash is assessed as a good king, but one who allowed worship to continue 'on the high places' (12:1–3). The narrative continues to focus on the temple, describing the repairs which Joash ordered to be carried out (12:4–16). But the account ends unexpectedly: Hazael threatens Jerusalem, and the king who was kept safe in the temple in his early years and was concerned for its fabric during his reign ends up plundering its treasuries to buy him off (12:17–18).

The narrator gives no direct comment. It is ironic that YHWH delivers 'apostate' Israel from Aram when the 'evil-doing' Jehoahaz supplicates him (13:4–5), whereas at the same period 'good' Joash of 'faithful' Judah does not seem to turn to YHWH at all when similarly threatened. Joash's assassination by his servants may be linked to this failure of nerve (12:19–20).

The account of Jehoahaz (13:1–9) is the first narrative of a king of Israel since chapter 10.

It picks up the reference in 10:32–33 to YHWH's reducing Israel's territory. Jehoahaz continues in the sins of Jeroboam, and Israel is repeatedly defeated by Aram, their army being reduced almost to nothing. But when Jehoahaz prays for mercy, YHWH relents, and a 'saviour' brings about their deliverance (v. 5). Yet in spite of this, and in a manner reminiscent of the period of the judges, Israel continues in its sins.

Verses 10–13 of chapter 13 are a brief summary of the reign of Joash, Jehoahaz's son, which notes only his continuing in the sins of Jeroboam and his victory over Amaziah of Judah.

It is a surprise to learn in 13:14 that Elisha is still alive, as he has not been mentioned since chapter 9. But now it is time for him to die, a man who like Elijah was worth armies to Israel (cf. 2:12). Joash goes to him, perhaps to seek his blessing. Elisha promises him victories over Aram, but only three (v. 19). The narrative notes YHWH's graciousness to Israel in his father Jehoahaz's day, and how Joash, building on that legacy, duly won the three victories promised, recapturing territory previously lost to Aram (vv. 22–25). But now Elisha's word has been fulfilled, the question arises: what will happen next? The account of Elisha's burial makes the same point symbolically (13:20–21). Elijah held out the hope of life to Israel: even his corpse could revive another corpse! But Elisha has now died, leaving no successor, and it appears that Israel's hope has vanished with him.

Amaziah becomes king of Judah (14:1–6). Like Joash he is a good king, except that he permits worship at the high places to continue. He executes his father's killers once he is established as king, but he observes the law of Moses, and kills no other members of their families, even though that might have been safer for him.

Amaziah attacks Edom and is successful, to some extent reversing the loss of Edom in Joram's day, and reminding us of David's victories (14:7; cf. 8:17–22; 2 Sam. 8:13). But when he attacks Israel, over-confident after his success in Edom, he is defeated, and Judah is humiliated (14:8–14). Israel takes hostages to prevent any further attacks by Judah. YHWH has not given the word for Israel's demise (14:27), and so attempts by Judah to challenge Israel's power are misconceived. (Note how 14:8 traces Jehoash's parentage back to Jehu, reminding us of YHWH's promise to Jehu.)

At this point the closing formula for Jehoash's reign is repeated (14:15–16), dividing the account of Amaziah of Judah, and suggesting that the narrative of Amaziah so far has been as much about Israel as about Judah. The only further information the narrator gives regarding Amaziah concerns his assassination and burial, over 15 years later (14:17–22). The conspiracy arose in Jerusalem, and 'all the people of Judah' played a part in making Amaziah's son Azariah king. Unlike Amaziah, Azariah is not said to have punished his father's killers (cf. 14:5–6), which may imply that he at least went along with the conspiracy. But beyond hinting at a widespread discontent at Amaziah's rule, perhaps with roots in his disastrous attack upon Israel, the narrator does not explain Amaziah's death.

Jeroboam son of Joash (sometimes termed Jeroboam II to distinguish him from the first northern king) continues the paradoxical tendencies of his immediate predecessors (14:23–29). He does not abandon the sins of Jeroboam (I), but enjoys what appear to be considerable blessings: a long reign and, after a period of distress, great military success. He restores Israel's territories 'from Lebo-Hamath to the Sea of the Arabah [Dead Sea]', all this following a prophetic word through Jonah son of Amittai (cf. Jon. 1:1).

The reigns of the three kings who follow Jehu each see a restoration of Israel's fortunes: in Jehoahaz's day a saviour delivers them from Aram (13:4–5); Joash recaptures cities previously captured by Aram (13:24–25); most strikingly of all, Jeroboam II extends Israel's northern border to Lebo-Hamath, which marked the northern boundary of Solomon's kingdom (1 Kgs 8:65). Jeroboam's closing formula, accordingly, plays up his role as military victor (14:28). But these achievements are hollow, due solely to YHWH's grace (13:4, 23; 14:26–27). YHWH has not yet given the word for Israel's destruction (14:27), but that is all that seems to keep destruction away.

Azariah of Judah (also named Uzziah, 15:13) was as righteous (in a qualified sense) as his predecessors, but YHWH afflicted him with leprosy, so that Jotham governed Judah for part of his reign (15:1–7).

The period of Israel's last kings (2 Kgs 15:8—17:41)

Jehu was promised that the fourth generation of his descendants would rule Israel (10:30; 15:12). Once this point is reached, the end of Jehu's dynasty comes quickly. Zechariah becomes king, fails to abandon the sin of Jeroboam, and is assassinated after only six months. Shallum, his successor, lasts only a month. Menachem kills him and takes his place (15:13–16).

The account of Menachem's reign (15:17–22) contains the first reference to Assyrian power

Joash, Amaziah and Azariah of Judah are all basically righteous, and yet all experience unexpected setbacks: Joash and Amaziah are humiliated by enemy armies, and Azariah suffers leprosy; Joash and Amaziah are both assassinated. All these developments are left largely unexplained in Kings. But the accounts of these three kings in 2 Chronicles 24—26 seem to fill in the gaps in Kings, pointing to apostasy or acts of disobedience as the reason for the changes of fortune they suffered.

This aspect of the relationship between Kings and Chronicles is usually only discussed as it relates to the interpretation of Chronicles, Kings being seen as the earlier account, and any significant changes in Chronicles *vis-à-vis* Kings being regarded as theologically motivated and historically suspect. But consider the possibility of inverting the relationship of Kings and Chronicles: is it possible that the writer of Kings had available traditions relating to these three kings substantially like those found in Chronicles, but omitted the material which is now found in the Chronicles accounts? Can you think of plausible reasons why he might have done so?

Further on the relationship of Kings and Chronicles see Auld.

('Pul', v. 19, being another name for Tiglath-Pileser, v. 29). The Assyrian king is bought off with a large amount of silver. Menachem's son Pekahiah succeeds him, but is assassinated after only two years (15:23–26). His assassin, Pekah, rules for 20 years (15:27–31), during which Assyria captures much of Israel's northern and eastern territories, deporting the inhabitants. Pekah is assassinated by Hoshea.

The theme of war with Aram and Israel dominates the account of Ahaz (16:1–20), a wicked and relatively successful king who comes after four good but unfortunate kings. The narrator emphasizes his unfaithfulness (vv. 2–4): 'he did not do right in the eyes of YHWH his God'; he 'walked in ways of the kings of Israel', 'made his son pass through fire, according to the abominable practices of the nations whom YHWH drove out . . .' and sacrificed 'on the high places, on the hills, and under every green tree'. The language recalls the state of affairs under Rehoboam (1 Kgs 14:23–24) and under Jehoram (2 Kgs 8:18).

Aram and Israel attack Judah, and at the same time Edom recaptures Elath. Ahaz escapes the crisis by becoming an Assyrian vassal ('I am your servant and your son', 16:7), and sending him much treasure (16:8, continuing the theme of the spoliation of the temple by Judah's kings). Tiglath-Pileser captures Damascus and invades Israel (16:5–9; cf. 15:29).

The rest of the account of Ahaz describes his religious innovations: the new altar he had built along the lines of one in Damascus and the changes made in the Jerusalem temple (16:10–18). The narrator, having made his view clear at the outset, offers no direct comment on these changes, except to note that some were made 'because of the king of Assyria' (16:18), suggesting that Ahaz's aim was to show himself a loyal vassal. Possibly he had the new altar built for similar reasons. What is clear is that Ahaz has abandoned faith in YHWH's power to save his people, and feels himself at liberty to make religious innovations as he sees fit.

These are not the actions of a king who fears YHWH.

The kingdom of Israel has been reduced to an Assyrian vassal, and the final stage in its dissolution comes quickly (17:1–6). Israel's last king, Hoshea, surprisingly, is said to have done evil, 'yet not like the kings of Israel who were before him', and there is no mention of his having followed the sins of Jeroboam. Whatever this may indicate about the character of his reign, it is not enough to preserve him when he revolts against Assyria. He himself is imprisoned, Israel is invaded, Samaria besieged and captured, and the people taken into exile into regions beyond the Euphrates. The end threatened as early as 1 Kings 14:15 has become reality.

There follows a lengthy statement of the reasons this happened (17:7–23). The narrator's tone becomes strongly condemnatory as he catalogues the people's covenant violations. Almost every phrase in this passage is loaded. But the interesting thing is that mostly it seems to speak about Israel and Judah together. It views the exile of the North as a disaster for all the 12 tribes of Israel, with roots which can be traced to before the division of the monarchy (vv. 8, 15). While many of the terms used here have previously been applied to Israel's sins ('high places', v. 9; cf. 1 Kgs 12:31; 13:2; 'provoking YHWH to anger', v. 11; cf. 1 Kgs 14:15; 16:2), some of them have only been used in connection with Judah's sins: 'pillars and sacred poles on every high hill and under every green tree' (vv. 9–10; cf. 1 Kgs 14:23; 2 Kgs 16:4); 'made . . . to pass through fire' (v. 17; cf. 2 Kgs 16:3). Verses 16–17 use terms that will later recur in the description of Manasseh's reign (2 Kgs 21:1–9). Further, at two points the narrator

specifically includes Judah in his condemnation (vv. 13, 19) leading to the conclusion that 'YHWH rejected *all the descendants* of Israel' (v. 20), which seems to include both kingdoms. Only after this does the narrator specifically mention Jeroboam and Israel, and the exile in Assyria (vv. 21–23). So this passage is not simply a 'funeral oration for the North', as it is sometimes described: it seems also to anticipate the downfall of the South.

The narrator adopts a 'pseudo-objective' style to describe events after Israel's deportation (17:24–41). New peoples are brought into the land from Syria and Babylon. They do not worship YHWH, so YHWH sends lions among them, and the Assyrian king is told that this is happening 'because they do not know the law of the god of the land'. One of the former priests of Samaria is sent to teach them how they should worship YHWH (v. 28). The result is not impressive: the various peoples continue their former worship (including acts which are clearly detestable, v. 31), but now offer worship to YHWH as well. The way in which priests and worship styles are chosen is reminiscent of the worship founded by Jeroboam I (v. 32; cf. 1 Kgs 12:31; 13:33). The conclusion in v. 33 is not so much pseudo-objective as ironic: 'So they worshipped YHWH, but they also served their own gods.' The entire narrative of Kings up to this point has made it quite clear that YHWH cannot be worshipped on this basis. The narrator says as much in v. 34, reverting to an explicitly evaluative style: 'They do *not* worship YHWH.'

The passage ends by quoting at length words originally addressed to Israel, setting out Israel's covenant obligation to YHWH (vv. 35–39), but leading up to a condemnation of the nations brought into

Israel's former territories (v. 40): 'They would not listen, however, but they continued to practise their former custom.' The passage seems both to condemn the Israelites who have gone into exile (for the earlier part of ch. 17 has made clear that they did not heed YHWH's call), and (yet more so) the peoples brought into their territory. It is clear that these peoples and their descendants have no claim to be Israelite, and no claim to be true worshippers of YHWH.

What period is this passage speaking about, the eighth and seventh centuries or the sixth century? If the former, the peoples described here may have included those whose descendants Josiah encountered during his forays northwards (23:15–20). If the latter, perhaps they are in some way related to the groups living in the land who later caused trouble for the people who returned from the Babylonian exile (Ezra 4; Neh. 2 and 4). This question is impossible to answer. It is an example of the difficulties that surround the interpretation of the phrase 'to this day' in the Histories (see vv. 34, 41).

2 KINGS 18—25: THE LAST YEARS OF JUDAH
Hezekiah and Assyria (2 Kgs 18—20)

Hezekiah is the first king of Judah to receive unqualified praise (18:1–8): he is entirely like David (contrast Amaziah, 14:3, and Azariah, 15:3); he removes from the land questionable religious practices which have been tolerated for a long time, centralizing worship in Jerusalem (18:4, 22); he trusts YHWH and holds fast to him, keeping the law of Moses. YHWH is with him, giving him success everywhere. He rebels against the king of Assyria (overturning Ahaz's policy) and wins victories against the Philistines (a further link with David).

Verses 9–12 of chapter 18 summarize briefly what chapter 17 has described at length, the end of Israel and its causes – but now from the perspective of an account focusing on Hezekiah. These verses imply a question: Assyria has destroyed Israel because of its sins, but what will happen when Assyria confronts the righteous Hezekiah?

What follows is disappointing (18:13–16): Assyria overruns Judah, and Hezekiah capitulates, as though he has abandoned trust in YHWH. He acts just like Joash and Ahaz before him, stripping YHWH's temple to buy off a foreign invader. Yet this is not enough; Sennacherib, having accepted Hezekiah's wealth, sends his chief officials to demand complete surrender (18:17–25). Perhaps he sees Jerusalem as a threat to be dealt with once and for all. The Rabshakeh's words mix contempt with an alarmingly plausible reading of recent events: 'YHWH said to me, Go up against this land, and destroy it' (v. 25). This is what has just happened to Israel.

When Hezekiah's representatives ask him to speak in Aramaic, not wanting the people to hear these words, the Rabshakeh instead addresses these people and changes his tone, replacing an apparent pluralism ('your god is on my side') with naked imperialism

---

THE LAST KINGS OF JUDAH

Hezekiah (715–686)†
Manasseh (686–642)†
Amon (642–640)
Josiah (640–609)
Jehoahaz (609)
Eliakim = Jehoiakim (609–598)
Jehoiachin (598)
Mattaniah = Zedekiah (597–586)

† = possible co-regency with predecessor

('your god cannot deliver you from the might of Assyria'). His words become openly blasphemous and crudely scatological, defying the power of Israel's god (18:32–35). Hezekiah's officials tear their robes and report the Rabshakeh's words to Hezekiah.

Hezekiah, too, tears his clothes. The encounter with the Rabshakeh has been bruising, and neither Hezekiah nor his officials have been impressive so far. All Hezekiah can do is send to Isaiah the prophet acknowledging the disgrace that has fallen upon the people, (19:3: the image of a pregnant woman unable to give birth is an interesting point of contact with Isa. 26:17–18). Only YHWH can bring deliverance now, and rescue the 'remnant that is left' (19:4), if he chooses to respond to the Rabshakeh's mockery. Isaiah brings back a word from YHWH urging trust and promising salvation (19:5–7).

In 19:8–34 the pattern is repeated. Rabshakeh delivers another insolent message, claiming that YHWH is no more able to deliver them than the gods of the other peoples Sennacherib has conquered (vv. 10–13: this time he does not even bother to claim that YHWH is on Sennacherib's side). Hezekiah again appeals to YHWH, acknowledging the partial truth of the Rabshakeh's words but also pointing out his crucial error – the assumption that YHWH is like the gods of the nations; and Isaiah gives a prophecy in YHWH's name. This prophecy is much longer (19:20–34): a taunt against Assyria to match the insults of the Rabshakeh, followed by a promise that the remnant will survive and again flourish. Judgment falls and the Assyrian army is destroyed; Sennacherib withdraws to Nineveh, where he is later killed by his sons in the temple of 'his god Nisroc' (who, ironically, was unable to save him).

So now we have the full story: Hezekiah trusted YHWH (cf. 18:5) when he saw there was no other option, apart from abject capitulation. Faced with a crisis like those faced by Jehoash and Ahaz earlier, Hezekiah began unpromisingly, but, when his attempt at a compromise solution had failed, showed the right response for a king of David's line.

Within Kings the account of Hezekiah and Sennacherib is a massive set-piece, showing YHWH's ability to defend his people. If YHWH can defeat the Assyrians, he can defeat any nation. Assyria in 2 Kings 17—19 does exactly what YHWH had always determined, no more, no less: destroying Israel, but being cast back from the gates of Jerusalem.

Digging deeper:
SENNACHERIB AND JERUSALEM

You can compare the account found in 2 Kings 18—19 with Sennacherib's own account (COS II, pp. 302–3). What differences do you note between them? Is it possible to harmonize the two accounts, or are certain parts of them simply contradictory?

Hess's essay provides a helpful discussion of the issues. Particularly interesting is his suggestion that 2 Kings 18:13–16 and 18:17—19:37 follow a standard Old Testament literary technique: an account is given first in summary form and then in more detail.

Further on Sennacherib's invasion, and particularly on the question of the modern historian and the 'miraculous', see Davies, pp. 32–4 and Provan 1997, pp. 57–64.

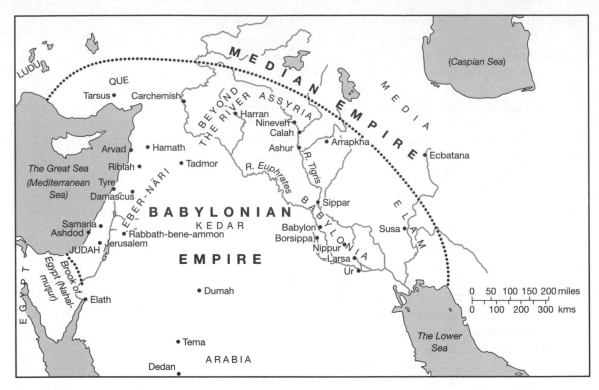

Map 5   The Babylonian empire

Two other incidents from Hezekiah's reign are described in 2 Kings 20. Hezekiah's recovery from illness (20:1–11) follows the same pattern as Jerusalem's deliverance. The parallel between Hezekiah's healing and Jerusalem's deliverance is made explicit in 20:5–6, v. 6 repeating 19:34. But this very parallel raises the question: what will happen to Jerusalem after Hezekiah's death?

Envoys are sent from Babylon. This is a friendly visit, and the men are given a tour of the royal treasure house. But the incident portends a time when Babylon will plunder these treasures, and Hezekiah's own descendants will be taken captive. Babylon will succeed where Assyria failed (20:16–18). Just as Hezekiah will die, therefore, so Jerusalem will be captured in the future: the parallel is exact.

Chapters 18—19 of 2 Kings describe a great act of salvation. Hezekiah was himself an outstanding king (though less flawless than the initial assessment of 18:1–8 suggested). But the account of Hezekiah ends with the first clear prophecy of Judah's destruction by Babylon.

Manasseh, Amon and Josiah (2 Kgs 21:1—23:30)
After a good king who reigned for 29 years comes an evil king who reigned for one and a half times that. Manasseh's evil consists primarily in his religious innovations. The description of these reads like a compendium of the sins of the kings of Israel and Judah up to this point (21:1–9). The narrator's comments bring out the significance of what Manasseh did with increasing clarity: he overturned Hezekiah's reforms; he followed the practices of Ahab of Israel; he defiled

YHWH's dwelling place, with which Israel's security in the land was inescapably linked; he made his people behave worse than the nations of Canaan before them.

After these ominous verses, it comes as no surprise to read of YHWH's word through 'his servants the prophets' (21:10–15): YHWH will cast off his people in an act of judgment like that carried out against Samaria and against Ahab. Judah will suffer exactly the same fate as Israel.

Amon has a brief reign, in which he follows his father's evil practices (2 Kgs 21:19–26). He is assassinated in a palace intrigue. The people, however, make sure that someone from David's line succeeds him – Josiah.

Josiah is presented without qualification as a good king, on a par with David. From the beginning of his account the narrator stresses Josiah's obedience to the law of Moses: he 'did not turn aside to the right or to the left' (22:2: cf. Deut. 17:20; Josh. 1:7). These words also link him with Joshua, the Israelite leader famous for his obedience to the law. (See also 22:13, 'to do according to all that is written', and cf. Jos. 1:8; 8:34; 23:6.) Josiah is singled out as the king who, more than any other, upheld the law (cf. 23:25).

He begins relatively modestly, as though he were another Jehoash, a king concerned for the fabric of the temple (22:3–7: cf. 2 Kgs 12). Indeed, it takes him until his eighteenth year to get this far. But then the 'book of the law' is discovered in the temple. The way this phrase is used in the Pentateuch and Joshua suggests we are to identify this document with Deuteronomy. The law of Moses has been mentioned in connection with various earlier kings: Jehu of Israel (10:31); Amaziah (14:6); Hezekiah (18:6). It seems to have

fallen into disuse during the wicked Manasseh's reign; not surprisingly, given the character of his reign. (On these points, see Provan 1995, p. 271.)

When the book of the law is read to him, Josiah immediately realizes the implications: his people have been violating it for a long time, to an extent that must have provoked YHWH's anger. The first thing to do, then, is to seek YHWH (v. 13).

YHWH responds (22:15–20): his anger has indeed been provoked and cannot be quenched (cf. 21:10–15); the covenant curses will fall (v. 16; cf. Deut. 28—29). But because Josiah was penitent he will be spared from seeing the disaster that is coming.

Josiah does not abandon hope in the face of this prophecy. On the contrary, he does everything in his power to bring his people back to YHWH. First, he summons all the people of Judah to a covenant renewal ceremony, in which king and people bind themselves to observe the terms of the law book (23:1–3; cf. Deut. 31:10–13).

Second (23:4–14), he carries out a comprehensive purge of idolatrous sites and objects of worship in and around Jerusalem. The description of these is the most extensive in Kings, with references to practices which can be traced back to Solomon. It gives a clear sense of Josiah's determination to rid the land of idolatry, but also suggests how deeply idolatry (in many different forms) has become rooted throughout Judah.

Third (23:15–20), Josiah destroys and defiles idolatrous worship sites in the former territory of the North, and kills the priests still offering worship at these sites.

In defiling the site at Bethel he fulfils the ancient prophecy from the time of Jeroboam I (1 Kgs 13:1–3). This passage seems to imply that Josiah attacked the worship practised by the peoples brought into the land by the Assyrians (2 Kgs 17:24–41: note especially that the Israelite priest who established this worship is described at 17:28 as having come to Bethel to do so).

Fourth, and climactically, Josiah holds a Passover the like of which has never been seen before, not since the time of the judges, and not during the reigns of any king up to this point – an astonishingly sweeping statement (23:21–23). Josiah removes all corrupt religious practices from the land, completely upholding the law and showing an unexampled wholeness of heart (23:24–25; cf. Deut. 6:5). Almost everything recorded of him (in considerable detail) relates to his religious faithfulness. He has carried out the programme of Deuteronomy 12:1–7 with unprecedented thoroughness, removing idolatry and establishing the worship of YHWH. He is the greatest of Judah's reforming kings.

And yet Manasseh's sins are still an insuperable obstacle (23:26–27): YHWH will not turn from his anger, and Judah will go into exile like Israel. Jerusalem and the temple will be rejected (a restatement of the prophecy of 21:10–15). Josiah's own end is a sign of what is to come (23:28–30): he dies in battle, having tried to prevent Pharaoh Neco from coming to the aid of Assyria. He does not see the final disaster which comes upon Judah, but only in this sense does he die 'in peace' as Huldah prophesied (cf. 22:20).

The last kings of Judah (2 Kgs 23:31—25:30)
In the aftermath of Josiah's death, Judah briefly becomes a client state of Egypt.

Jehoahaz, appointed as Josiah's heir, is almost immediately deposed by Pharaoh, and a tribute imposed upon the land (23:31–35). Jehoiakim, the king whom Pharaoh installs in his place, makes sure this tribute is paid. (This is the first thing reported about him, even before his opening regnal formula, emphasizing the fact that he comes to the throne as an Egyptian puppet.)

The two kings after Josiah, both of them Josiah's sons, 'did what was evil in YHWH's sight' (23:32, 37). The long description of the idolatrous practices purged by Josiah suggested how deeply rooted they had become, and the speed with which his sons revert to evil-doing may suggest that Josiah's reform, however well intentioned, produced only a superficial change in some hearts.

The incident described in 23:28–30 was the last gasp of the Assyrian empire. Now the Babylonians, the agents of destruction prophesied by Isaiah (20:16–18), arrive in the region, drive Egypt back behind its borders, and take possession of the entire territory once ruled by Solomon (24:1–7; cf. 1 Kgs 4:21, 24). Judah thus exchanges Egyptian control for Babylonian. Jehoiakim rebels against Babylon, but dies just before the rebellion is punished. Raiding bands attack Judah, this being the first outworking of the judgment on Manasseh's sins, which YHWH was 'not willing to pardon' (24:4). The first exile to Babylon ends Jehoiachin's brief reign, and he goes into exile (24:8–17). Much of the remaining finery of Solomon's temple is removed at this time, along with many of the leaders and trained craftsmen of Judah.

Zedekiah, installed on the throne to replace Jehoiachin, does evil like his predecessors, and in his days the long-threatened exile finally takes place (24:18—25:7). He rebels (why?), and Nebuchadnezzar comes to subjugate Judah. The final stages in the history of the kingdom of Judah are precisely marked, the narrator giving day, month and year for the arrival of Nebuchadnezzar outside Jerusalem (25:1), the day when the food ran out (25:3) and the date of the destruction of Jerusalem (25:8). We read of Zedekiah's final, humiliating end: fugitive, abandoned by his men, captured, blinded after he has seen his sons executed, then taken away to Babylon. This seems like the end of David's line.

Jerusalem is similarly humiliated (25:8–12): all its great houses, including Solomon's temple and palace, are burned. Only some of the poorest people are left to maintain the surrounding lands. All the remaining gold, silver and bronze in the temple is removed, treated as so much scrap metal (25:13–17; cf. 1 Kgs 9:6–9). The long history of YHWH's house, which spans Kings, comes to an end. Finally, representatives of the Jerusalem leadership and the population of Judah are executed (25:18–21). This further act of humiliation marks the death of the kingdom of Judah as an independent entity. At that point the narrator concludes (v. 21): 'So Judah went into exile out of its land.'

There are two tailpieces. In the first of them (25:22–26) we read of how Gedaliah, appointed governor of the land, advised leaders of the people still in the land to accept Babylonian rule. One of these men, Ishmael, a man of royal descent, rejects this advice and kills Gedaliah and others with him at Mizpah. Does he still believe, contrary to everything that has happened, that YHWH will somehow establish him as king 'for David's sake'? Those days are long past, and many of those left in the land realize

that the only course left open to them after this foolish act is flight to Egypt.

Finally, in 25:27–30, twenty-six or so years later, Jehoiachin of the line of David, still alive in exile, is shown kindness by the king of Babylon. Although by itself this episode seems noncommittal, against the background of the threat of 2 Kings 21:10–15 (reiterated at other points within chs 22—24) it seems unexpectedly positive: a descendant of David is still alive and enjoying some kind of security, whereas the prophecy seemed to imply an end to David's line as complete as that of Ahab's. Provan seems justified in concluding (1995, p. 281): 'These verses look back beyond Kings . . . to Samuel, and they hang on tenaciously to the words of 2 Samuel 7:15–16: "my love will never be taken away from him . . . your throne will be established forever."'

On the other hand, these last verses show us Jehoiachin as an exile, not a reigning monarch (the contrast with the recent splendours of Josiah's reign is striking). He is dependent on the favour of a foreign king. The post-exilic Histories will suggest that this is at best a mixed blessing.

KEY THEMES

YHWH's uniqueness and sovereignty

Kings presents YHWH as the great king, 'enthroned above the cherubim' in the temple (2 Kgs 19:15), whose glory, from a different perspective, not even the heavens can contain, (1 Kgs 8:27). Allegiance is due to him alone. Even a non-Israelite can come to see this point (2 Kgs 5): all the more is it expected that YHWH's own people will do so. Israel and Israel's king must follow YHWH's commandments (1 Kgs 6:12–13; 8:56–61; 9:3–9), and it is not acceptable to worship other gods alongside YHWH (1 Kgs 18:21).

One like Naaman, when he comes to acknowledge YHWH's power, may be permitted to go through the motions of worshipping another god in whom he no longer believes (2 Kgs 5:15–19); but such concessions do not apply to Israel.

The narrator sees religious unfaithfulness as the greatest failing of both kings and people, and constantly returns to this theme, most obviously in the regnal formulae, where it is the main, almost the only, criterion for a good king.

The theme of YHWH's uniqueness comes across from a different perspective in 1 Kings 20 and especially in 2 Kings 18—19, narratives in which a foreign ruler treats YHWH as merely one of the gods of the nations, limited in power. Both Beh-Hadad and Sennacherib suffer for their presumption.

In line with this Kings explains the exiles of both kingdoms as due to YHWH alone: the exiles happened because YHWH chose to punish sin in this way, and certainly not because Assyria's or Babylon's gods were stronger. If we date the final form of Kings to the sixth century, as is plausible, then this was arguably the main point Kings aimed to convey to its exilic audience. This uncompromising message could, of course, also be a source of hope for the exiles: if YHWH had banished them, then YHWH could deliver them from exile (cf. 1 Kgs 8:46–53).

Failure of the monarchy

Kings refers to, and may well be partly based on, royal annals. But it is not a royal history. Unlike many Assyrian and Egyptian historical accounts, which were written at the command of individual kings to commemorate their deeds (e.g. the conquest accounts referred to in Ch. 3), Kings does not glorify the kings of Israel and Judah. No kings of Israel, and only a few kings of Judah, are unequivocally praised.

Some kings, it is true, clearly illustrate the blessings of Israel's monarchy: in the account of Solomon's reign we see Israel acting as witness to the nations; Hezekiah is a picture of faithfulness under trial; and Josiah's reign embodies the ideal of a people reformed according to the law of Moses (cf. Provan 1995, pp. 99–102, 282–4). But Kings also shows the harm that monarchs can do when they turn from YHWH. The clearest indication of this is, of course, the exiles of Israel and Judah, which are both unambiguously attributed to the sins of their kings, to a persistence in evil-doing which finally drew down YHWH's judgment. (Not that the people are exempt from blame for these disasters.)

The monarchy in both kingdoms led to periods of systemic, state-sponsored evil such as was not really possible, for example, during the period of the judges. The clearest example of this is the account of Ahab, the most prominent Omride king, whom the narrator seems to view with a fascinated horror. Ahab is presented at greater length than any other king apart from Solomon: his reign functions as an anatomy of an apostate kingdom, and plays an important part in the theology of Kings. The accounts of kings such as Ahaz and Manasseh of Judah build upon that of Ahab.

The narrator explains the fall of Israel and Judah along similar lines. For both kingdoms it is persistent wrongdoing that draws down judgment (Dietrich, p. 249). For Israel the narrator highlights the sins of Jeroboam I as a continual stumbling-block.

Jehu's reign, when Baal worship was eradicated, may have marked an 'upturn', but Israel's demise followed swiftly upon the end of Jehu's dynasty. In this context it hardly mattered that Israel's last king Hoshea was less sinful than his predecessors (2 Kgs 17:2): the weight of accumulated sin was then too great to make any difference to the kingdom's fate.

For Judah an additional factor was at work, YHWH's promise to David (see 2 Sam. 7). This promise is first cited as the reason why Rehoboam retained a reduced kingdom in spite of Solomon's sins (1 Kgs 11:12–13); then as the reason why Judah survived even during the reigns of wicked kings (1 Kgs 15:1–5; 2 Kgs 8:18–19); and finally, as the reason why Hezekiah, an exceptionally righteous king, survived siege and near-fatal illness (2 Kgs 19:34; 20:6). One might have expected that for Hezekiah deliverance would be a matter of course: the fact that the narrator explains it instead as due to YHWH's faithfulness suggests that judgment is drawing near. It fits with this that the grievous sins of the next king, Manasseh, finally exhaust YHWH's patience. After Manasseh judgment may be postponed but it is inescapable. Even a great reforming king like Josiah cannot alter this. Verse 6 of 2 Kings 20 is the last time that the narrator refers to the Davidic promise (Provan 1995, pp. 260, 266).

Even righteous kings, then, are not a guarantee against disaster. This theme is prepared for in the accounts of Joash, Amaziah and Azariah of Judah (see 'Outline'), and comes centre-stage in the accounts of Hezekiah and Josiah. Conversely, unrighteous kings are sometimes not punished. Kings takes a long-term view of the issues of judgment and righteousness, and may be contrasted with Chronicles at this point.

The prophetic word

If kings are significant individuals, so are YHWH's prophets. Many incidents suggest the power of the prophetic word to heal and to destroy, and accounts such as 2 Kings 6:15–23 and 2 Kings 19 imply that, notwithstanding the many large human armies which feature in Kings, the 'big battalions' are truly on the side of YHWH's prophets.

The theme of the king as subject to YHWH's word through his prophets, introduced in Samuel, is greatly developed in Kings. Hezekiah receives a prophecy of salvation and, responding in faith, sees it fulfilled (2 Kgs 18—19). Negatively, the dynasties of Jeroboam I, Baasha, Ahab and even Jehu are each destroyed according to prophecy (1 Kgs 14:7–14; 16:1–4; 21:20–24; 2 Kgs 10:30). Behind these texts lies the archetypal prophecy of rejection, Samuel's oracle against Saul (1 Sam. 15).

The narrator regularly draws attention to the fulfilment of prophecy. Sometimes fulfilment follows quickly upon prophecy (compare 1 Kgs 22:23 and 37; 2 Kgs 1:6 and 17); sometimes generations intervene (1 Kgs 21:21–23 and 2 Kgs 9—10), and in one case over 200 years (compare 1 Kgs 13:2 and 2 Kgs 23:15–20). 'In this way we are shown how decisive the word of God is in events in history' (McConville, p. 625).

Von Rad comments on this prophecy-fulfilment schema that 'if one were to try to make a diagram of this structure, the strangest criss-crossings would result' (Vol. 1, p. 340). This may be so, but it does not mean that the schema is contrived or mechanical.

Indeed, the fact that fulfilment is sometimes long delayed suggests a sophisticated perspective, in which the human response to prophecy is as significant as the prophecy itself.

Repentance is one such response: whenever a king repents or seeks YHWH judgment is reversed or postponed (1 Kgs 13:6; 21:27–29; 2 Kgs 13:4–5; 22:19–20). In other passages it is implied that if there had been repentance a threatened judgment would have been averted (1 Kgs 13:33; 2 Kgs 17:13–14). The classic text for this prophetic 'exclusion clause' is Jeremiah 18:1–10.

More generally, the narrator, as well as highlighting the fulfilment of prophecy, draws attention to human choices that led to events assuming the shape they did. (See the comments on Rehoboam's folly in 1 Kings 12, and on the accounts of Ahab and Joram in 1 Kings 17—2 Kings 9.) Last, in at least one case the narrator suggests that a prophecy has *not* been fulfilled: see the comments above on 2 Kings 25:27–30.

Sometimes kings try to manipulate or undermine YHWH's prophets, in the hope of receiving a more favourable prophecy: Jeroboam sends his wife to Ahijah in disguise (1 Kgs 14:1–3); Ahab arrests Micaiah for prophesying defeat (1 Kgs 22:26–27); Ahaziah sends soldiers to make Elijah retract a prophecy (2 Kgs 1); Joram, enraged at YHWH's failure to bring deliverance, orders Elisha's execution (2 Kgs 6:30–31). Manasseh's bloodshed may have included the spilt blood of prophets (2 Kgs 21:16; 24:4).

These kings act as if silencing a prophet automatically neutralizes his message, or as if deceiving him or making him change his message alters YHWH's intention as well. These episodes show the folly of such attempts, for in each case things happen exactly as prophesied.

True and false prophecy

Not all in Kings who claim to prophesy in YHWH's name truly do so. The theme of true versus false prophecy is touched on at various points (e.g. 1 Kgs 13:11–32), but it comes centre-stage in 1 Kings 22. Ahab assembles 400 prophets, who unanimously declare in YHWH's name that the attack on Ramoth Gilead will be a success. They are opposed by the lone prophet Micaiah, who predicts, also in YHWH's name, that Ahab will die in the battle. It turns out that Micaiah was right.

Chapter 22 is not simplistic in its presentation. As the messenger fetches Micaiah the narrator describes the scene (vv. 10–12): the two kings seated on their thrones; Zedekiah the prophet parading the iron horns he has made to symbolize victory, and the other prophets all repeating the same message. Micaiah has prophesied defeat, but he is only one voice against many. And is victory so unlikely? YHWH gave Israel victory over Aram just three years before, and the 400 prophets of chapter 22 are only saying what YHWH's prophets said in chapter 20.

The reader, who knows the history of YHWH's dealings with Ahab, can sense where the truth lies. Ahab seems to have reached the stage where he will not hear negative prophecies (vv. 8, 18). If he believes the 400 prophets, why does he disguise himself before the battle (v. 30)? It seems he is resisting YHWH's word, as in earlier chapters, but unable to silence nagging fears. But someone who does not know this past history (the perspective represented in this narrative by Jehoshaphat of Judah) cannot tell true from false prophecy. Only hindsight makes matters clear. The parallel with Jeremiah 26—29 is close.

David

Kings begins by describing David's last years and Solomon's succession. Throughout Kings the survival of David's line is an important theme, and the very last verses concern a descendant of David (2 Kgs 25:27–30). After David's death Kings continues to speak of YHWH's commitment to his line. David's sons and Judah are spared punishment, or have punishment reduced, for David's sake (e.g. 1 Kgs 11:34; 15:4; 2 Kgs 8:19).

Texts such as these seem to imply an unconditional commitment to David's line which operates irrespective of his descendants' deserts. The same is often said of 2 Samuel 7:11–16, the text from which these passages derive. Here YHWH commits himself to David, promising him a throne which will be 'established for ever' (v. 16), with no conditions stated. If they stray, David's descendants may be punished with 'blows inflicted by human beings', but YHWH's love will never leave them (vv. 14–15). Scholars often contrast these passages with three other passages which are clearly intended as restatements of 2 Samuel 7:11–16, but which apparently make fulfilment of the promise conditional on the faithfulness of David's descendants: 1 Kings 2:2–4 (spoken by David); 1 Kings 8:25 (spoken by Solomon); 1 Kings 9:4–5 (spoken by YHWH). The two sets of passages are often seen as contradictory, but this may oversimplify matters.

In Ch. 5 we questioned whether 2 Samuel 7:11–16 are literally unconditional (i.e. whether they promise David a descendant upon the throne in perpetuity, *no matter what*). The immediate context in 2 Samuel 6, we argued, suggested perhaps not. Having now surveyed Kings we can add two further arguments in support of this position.

First, on a point of linguistic detail, the Hebrew translated 'for ever' (*'ad 'olam*) in 2 Samuel 7:16 need not mean 'for all time' (which clearly *would* imply an unconditional commitment). The use of the same phrase at 1 Kings 9:3 indicates that states of affairs described as lasting *'ad 'olam* may come to an end (see 'Outline').

Second, viewing 2 Samuel 7:14–15 in the light of the history of David's descendants described in Kings, we may conclude (with hindsight) that though the verses could be read as an absolute commitment to the continuation of the Davidic dynasty, other interpretations were possible. Perhaps the verses meant to say that though David's descendants might be chastised, they could still repent. Perhaps the phrase 'I will not take my steadfast love from him' (v. 15) meant that YHWH would repeatedly forgive David's descendants *when they repented* (as was not true of Saul). But what if opportunities to repent were ignored? Certainly Kings describes the gradual running out of YHWH's patience with Judah: perhaps this possibility was not excluded in 2 Samuel 7:14–15.

Turning to the three other texts, 'conditional' may in one sense be a misleading term for them. Clearly they set conditions which must be met if YHWH is to establish David's dynasty; but, when they are read in context they cannot be understood as saying that violation of the stated conditions will terminate the promise to David. Verses 2–4 of 1 Kings 2 come in a setting where David and Solomon seem to do anything but walk in YHWH's ways (v. 3), and yet the dynasty survives; and both 1 Kings 8:25 and 9:3–9 have to be read in the light of 8:46–53, which, building upon Deuteronomy 30, speaks of the possibility of restoration even after invasion and exile.

Moving on from these texts, what actually happens to David's line in Kings? Solomon's son Rehoboam sees ten tribes defect, and so in one sense David's kingdom soon passes out of his descendants' hands. But Rehoboam's descendants continue to rule over a reduced kingdom that outlasts the kingdom of the ten tribes by nearly 140 years. By the end of Kings even that kingdom has been dismantled, and the last descendant of David mentioned in Kings is no longer on any 'throne'. It may seem that the 'conditional' versions of the promise have won out, and that the 'blows inflicted by human beings' of which 2 Samuel 7:14 spoke have assumed such harsh forms (invasion, destruction, exile) as to amount to an overturning of the words which follow in v. 15 ('but I will not take my steadfast love from him'). And yet 2 Kings 25:27–30, when read in context, seems to hold out an unexpected hope that this love is not yet exhausted: perhaps (we can say no more than this) there is still a future, maybe even a future kingdom, for David's line.

Israel and the promise to Abraham

'Israel' is used in two senses in Kings, to denote the 12 tribes of Solomon's united kingdom (1 Kgs 3:28; 8:1) and also the ten tribes of the northern kingdom (1 Kgs 14:14, 19). Kings thus implicitly raises the question: what is Israel? (McConville, p. 631). After the split into two kingdoms, kings in both North and South in different ways lay claim to the term (1 Kgs 12:28; 2 Kgs 19:15), but which kingdom has better claim? The term 'Israel' is most frequently used of the North, but on the other hand the narrative quickly establishes that both monarch and worship in the North are corrupt, and that the kingdom will have no lasting stability (1 Kgs 13—14). The South, by contrast, has an enduring dynasty and the Jerusalem temple, but only two tribes, and is always called simply '(the kingdom of) Judah'. The claims of both kingdoms thus seem to be flawed.

It appears that Kings has a view of Israel as ideally a single, 12-tribe entity. This comes across in the narrative of Elijah on Mt Carmel: he builds an altar using 'twelve stones, according to the number of the tribes of the sons of Jacob' (1 Kgs 18:31). The narrative of Naboth, analogously, upholds an ideal in which each Israelite family of the 12 tribes has a God-given 'inheritance' in the land (1 Kgs 21:3–4). Both these narratives, of course, are set in the North.

If Kings closes with a hint that there may be a future for David's line, and maybe even a restored kingdom of Judah, is a similar possibility held open for the ten tribes of the North? Certainly there is nothing corresponding to the promise to David which acts as a focus of hope for the ten tribes. On the contrary, the North has been ruled by several royal dynasties, the last of which has vanished in Assyrian captivity (2 Kgs 17:4). It appears that Kings envisages no future for the descendants of the ten tribes as a separate kingdom.

And yet, if the kingdom of Israel is never blessed for the sake of any of its kings, there remain the promises to the Patriarchs (ancestors of all 12 tribes), which are invoked at significant moments in the history of the North (1 Kgs 18:36; 2 Kgs 13:23). The reference in 2 Kings 13:23 to YHWH's being unwilling to banish Israel 'until now' probably does not reflect the perspective of the final author or editor of Kings (2 Kings 17 describes precisely such a 'banishing'); but there is no reason to think that even this person believed that YHWH had renounced his commitment to the Patriarchs. Certainly the reference to the Patriarchs just when the threat of exile for the North is becoming a reality is significant (Provan 1995, pp. 229–30). And Solomon's prayer, in which the possibility of repentance and return from exile was first raised, was made on behalf of all 12 tribes. We will return to this issue in the chapters on Ezra–Nehemiah and, above all, Chronicles.

CRITICAL ISSUES

LITERARY-CRITICAL ISSUES

Aspects of Kings as narrative

The bulk of Kings consists of narrative. It is clearly a selective narrative. The references in the concluding regnal formulae to the 'Book of the Annals of the Kings of Israel/Judah' repeatedly imply that there was more the writer could have said. As with Joshua–Samuel, a strongly theological viewpoint informs the narrative, sometimes overtly, sometimes indirectly.

Kings makes use of narrative analogy. At points the reader is expected to compare and contrast what happens in the two separate kingdoms at the same period (1 Kgs 15—16; 2 Kgs 9—12). This applies across generations as well, the accounts of particular kings being narrated so as to suggest parallels with earlier kings: thus both Jeroboam II of Israel and Hezekiah of Judah are in different ways presented as 'lesser

Solomons'; Josiah at the beginning of his reign seems no more radical a reformer than Joash before him, but displays a new zeal when the law is discovered.

There is much formulaic language in Kings. As well as the regnal formulae we find what appear to be stock expressions used for topics like religious faithfulness, questionable religious practices ('on every high hill and under every green tree') and warfare ('from watch-tower to fortified city'). How far such language was a feature of Kings' sources we can only speculate. What is clear is that Kings uses even formulaic language creatively. In the accounts of many kings there seems to be a play between the formulaic phrases and other parts of the account: kings who are introduced as good or largely good behave in ways that call that description in question, or suffer unexpected setbacks; kings introduced as bad are spared judgment.

Formulaic language is used to different effect in 1 Kings 15:27—16:23, where the narrative contrasts the swift succession of northern kings and the long reign of a single king, Asa, in Judah: the names of the northern kings change, but Asa's is repeated (15:33; 16:8, 15, 23), and the mad disorder in the North is offset against the regular formulae relating to the South. The same points apply to 2 Kings 15, the account of the last chaotic decades of the North.

Sources, dating, authorship, editing

No author is named for Kings, and no date is given for the composition of either the final (present) form or possible earlier forms. Clearly the final form cannot predate roughly 560 BC (see 2 Kgs 25:27–30), and it might seem that the failure to mention any returns from exile (a topic which would surely have been of interest; cf. 1 Kgs 8:46–53) suggests it cannot have been written after 538. This may not be an unanswerable argument: there might be other reasons why a writer active in the fifth or fourth centuries chose to end his narrative at an earlier date, as Linville argues (pp. 69–73). Linville spends the bulk of his study, however, exploring what he sees as ambiguities in the presentation of key themes in Kings, and he is reluctant to address the question of possible historical contexts for Kings in any but a tentative and speculative manner (as he himself says on p. 301). This may suggest the difficulties inherent in any attempt to move beyond the fixed point of 560 BC.

As in Joshua–Samuel the phrase 'to this day' is used of certain states of affairs which it seems cannot have been true by the mid-sixth century (1 Kgs 8:8; 9:21; 12:19; 2 Kgs 8:22). Again it is possible that these are 'frozen references', intended to indicate that at these points the writer was drawing on earlier sources. The same probably applies to the phrase 'until now' in 2 Kings 13:23 (see p. 181, 'Key themes'). Other instances of 'to this day' do not clearly imply a particular date of composition (e.g. 2 Kgs 10:27; 14:7), this being a particular problem in the interpretation of 2 Kings 17:41.

Kings names three of its sources: the 'Book of the Acts of Solomon' (1 Kgs 11:41); the 'Book of the Annals of the Kings of Israel' (1 Kgs 14:19, etc.); and the 'Book of the Annals of the Kings of Judah' (1 Kgs 14:29, etc.). Kings seems to refer to these books as available not only to the writers of Kings but also to its readers; though that is not the only way of interpreting these references (see the panel 'Who could consult the three "Books"?').

WHO COULD CONSULT THE THREE 'BOOKS'?

Were the three 'Books' freely accessible in the sixth century or at earlier stages in the composition of Kings? A recent article by Haran argues not. Haran points out that the term 'book' (*sefer*) properly denotes a single, original copy of a document: were such documents accessible to all?

In Haran's view, the editor of Kings did not himself consult the 'Books': rather, he drew on sources written by people who had done so. In other words, the apparent citations of these books in Kings are another type of 'frozen reference': the phrase 'are they not written in the Book of the Annals of . . . ?' is not a 'suggestion for further reading', but a claim that data on which Kings is based can be traced back to such records.

This seems plausible, though it is in the end hard to prove or disprove, simply because the three 'Books' have not survived, and we have little information about the maintenance of official records in Israel or Judah.

Other possible sources may be suggested (cf. Jones, pp. 47–77). The account of Solomon's succession, 1 Kings 1—2, has clear thematic and stylistic links with the second part of 2 Samuel, and may represent a distinct source. So, too, the traditions relating to Elijah and Elisha, and the narrative involving Isaiah in 2 Kings 18—20 (closely paralleled by Isaiah 36—39). A further possibility is that Kings is at points dependent upon royal inscriptions; though there is at present no convincing evidence for this suggestion (Parker).

These suggestions do not exhaust the possibilities. It is entirely likely that many separate traditions and sources have found their way into Kings, even though attempts to identify them soon lead into the realms of speculation. Kings, after all, covers a period of 400 years.

Regarding the question of composition (the combining of these sources to form the present books of Kings), it is possible that Kings grew by stages, somewhat in the manner of royal annals, with periodic updating; or that a work periodically updated in this way formed the basis for Kings. The 'frozen references' noted above may support this.

These suggestions are all rather vague. They are also compatible with the view that Kings is a literary unity with a coherent structure and consistent outlook (which is how the Outline above has interpreted Kings). But historical-critical scholarship on Kings has sought to give more precise answers to the questions of authorship and dating, using the methods of source, form, and redaction criticism. Much of this scholarship finds Kings to be incoherent and inconsistent at points. Here are some examples:

- We noted above that some scholars see within 1 Kings 20 and 22 indications that these chapters did not originally belong in the account of Ahab. These literary observations are combined with a historical argument that the battles with Aram are more likely to date from the period of the Jehu dynasty (see p. 190, 'Historical issues').
- The passage 2 Kings 2—8 has been seen as based on diverse traditions and lacking in thematic unity. As with 1 Kings 20 and 22, it has been suggested that the victories over Aram described in 2 Kings 6 belong in the reign of a later king.
- Chapter 17 of 2 Kings is not a straightforward text: it seems to begin as a denunciation of Israel and yet contains critique of Judah; there is irony; there is the question of when to date the last verses.

For some scholars vv. 29–34a and v. 34b simply represent conflicting viewpoints, and the entire chapter shows signs of having been updated by more than one hand (Jones, pp. 542–5; Hobbs, pp. 224–7, summarizes such approaches, somewhat critically.)

- The account of Hezekiah in 2 Kings 18—19 is incoherent: why should Sennacherib attack (18:17—19:37) after Hezekiah has met his terms (18:13–16)? The latter narrative seems to have arisen as a theologically motivated attempt to 'write up' the events of 18:13–16 as a defeat for Sennacherib – possibly as two such attempts, in fact, as it seems to go over the same ground twice (Jones, pp. 566–9; Hobbs, pp. 246–9, 268–74, again somewhat critically).
- Nelson (1981, pp. 29–42) finds the verdicts in the regnal formulae for the last four kings of Judah unusually inflexible: they all follow the pattern 'he did what was evil in YHWH's sight, just as his fathers had done' (e.g. Jehoahaz, 2 Kings 23:32). Nelson contrasts these 'dry and colourless words' with the greater flexibility of the regnal formulae for Judah up to Josiah. In his view these formulae have been patterned upon earlier examples in which a king is compared to his father or ancestor (2 Kgs 14:3; 15:34; 18:3; 21:20), but rather woodenly, with the result that the entire history of David's line is summed up under a generalizing, negative reference to these kings' 'fathers'. He attributes these last four formulae (and the accounts of Judah's last four kings) to a second, post-Josianic level of Deuteronomistic editing.
- More generally, many scholars see signs of theological incoherence in Kings. Kings seems to hold contradictory views regarding YHWH's commitment to David,

Jerusalem and the temple. Some scholars find Kings' treatment of Manasseh deeply unconvincing: why should his sins have doomed Judah? Why could not even Josiah turn things around, and why did he die so disappointingly? Campbell and O'Brien see this as one of the deepest fault-lines in Kings' theology (p. 327): '[Josiah's death] disavows Deuteronomy. The promise of "life to you and length of days" (Deut. 30:20) is not fulfilled by the gift of an early death. Josiah's unexpected death challenged dtr [Deuteronomistic] theology at its core.' The contrast between 2 Kings 22—23, with their glowing report of Josiah's vigorous reforms, and 2 Kings 24—25, which describe Judah's demise in the decades immediately following Josiah, is one of the main reasons why scholars believe Joshua–Kings underwent two separate Deuteronomistic redactions: one during Josiah's reign, reflecting the hopes entertained for Judah's future at that time; one after the fall of Judah, much more pessimistic in character (see Ch. 7). The passages in 2 Kings 21—24 which make Manasseh's sins responsible for the exile belong (it is argued) to this second redaction.

We have addressed some of these issues directly or implicitly in the Outline, and in some cases suggested alternative readings of the data (on the promise to David, see 'Key themes', p. 179). But it must be admitted that arguments of this sort (there are many others) form a substantial body of raw material for theories regarding editing. This has led to proposals regarding the growth of Kings such as those of Campbell and O'Brien.

The watershed in the formation of Kings as Campbell and O'Brien understand it was a Deuteronomistic edition of Kings carried out during the reign of Josiah. Their analysis of Kings, accordingly, follows a threefold division. They distinguish: (1) materials taken up into the Josianic edition; (2) text added by the Josianic Deuteronomistic editor as he shaped these materials; (3) text added to Kings after the Josianic edition. In more detail:

1 Pre-Josianic materials:

- a Prophetic Record focusing on the role of prophets in relation to the monarchy, covering the period from David to Jehu (see Ch. 5); from 2 Kings 10:35 until 2 Kings 17:23 this is extended by a series of texts focusing on the sins of the kings of Israel after Jehu (Prophetic Record Extension);
- 'other material', including extensive blocks of material relating to Solomon, Elijah, Elisha and Hezekiah;
- a 'Hezekian King List', in which a particular evaluation formula was used for the kings of Judah (this was taken up into the regnal formulae for the South);
- 'Isaiah material': passages in 2 Kings 18—19 which can be paralleled in Isaiah.

2 Deuteronomistic redactional material: numerous, mainly short, pieces of text inserted into the account at frequent intervals. Much of this material is identified on the basis of its affinity with the language and theology of Deuteronomy.

3 Materials added after the Josianic edition:

- 'after the Dtr': further traditions relating to Solomon, and narratives of the last kings of Judah;
- 'revision (royal focus)': Deuteronomistic redactional material focusing on the

responsibility of the kings of Israel and Judah for the national fortunes;

- 'revision (national focus)': Deuteronomistic redactional material focusing on the people's responsibility to uphold the law, and failure to do so;
- 'other material': an extensive and mixed collection of material, some of it early and some of it late, some of it Deuteronomistic in character, some of it not. Whatever its provenance, this material only entered Kings in the later stages.

For more details, see the panel, 'The Make-up of Kings', pp. 186–7.

Campbell and O'Brien's proposal is only one of a number of literary analyses of Kings (or significant portions of Kings) which have been offered in the last two or three decades. For a summary of other proposals see McKenzie; and also Ch. 7 (for Kings has played a leading role in theories of Deuteronomistic historiography.) There is no space to offer a complete response to this entire approach. Often the Outline constitutes an implicit response, which you can compare with the approaches of the scholars whose work we have referred to in this section. Below we simply pick out five points of disagreement.

1 Chapter 5 has already discussed the suggestion that one of the sources of Samuel and Kings was a 'Prophetic Record'. The arguments made there apply here: a number of passages in Samuel and Kings relating to the interactions of prophets and kings have similar wording, and the theme is significant. But none of this need imply that a Prophetic Record ever existed as a separate source.

2 Is a distinction between revisions reflecting respectively a royal and a national focus plausible in Kings, which often seems to link the behaviour of king and people? Consider 1 Kings 11:1–13 and 2 Kings 21:2–15: does it seem necessary or even plausible to divide parts of these two texts along these lines?

3 Can Deuteronomistic editorial insertions be so clearly identified as in (particularly) the second stage of Campbell and O'Brien's analysis? Can they be so neatly detached from their contexts? Chapter 7 will address this question in more detail. Here it is enough to note that, though the influence of Deuteronomy in Kings is most clearly identifiable in those verses which have theological and linguistic affinities to Deuteronomy, the influence of Deuteronomy in Kings (and in Joshua–Samuel) may be much *more* pervasive than this view implies. Is this literary-critical approach the equivalent of trying to remove all the chillies from a curry in the hope of removing all the 'chilli heat'?

4 Nelson's judgment that the regnal formulae for the last kings of Judah are wooden and colourless seems correct, but the conclusion he draws from it may not be. The fact that three of these kings are described as 'doing what was evil . . . just as his fathers had done' (Zedekiah is said to have followed Jehoiakim, 2 Kgs 24:19) is actually highly appropriate. By now the sins of past generations have made exile inevitable: even the misdeeds of unspectacular sinners like the last kings of Judah are enough to start the avalanche. Thus it is fitting to describe these kings with a generalizing formula which suggests that, in spite of kings like Josiah and Hezekiah, the history of Judah's kings has been predominantly one of wickedness. That is, these formulae should be seen, not

THE MAKE-UP OF KINGS

(according to Campbell and O'Brien, pp. 323–470)

Below is a slightly simplified presentation of the details of the literary history of Kings, according to Campbell and O'Brien. It sets out the different categories of material in Kings, and indicates where in their view this material is to be found. Any references of seven to eight or more verses in length have been shaded in grey. Looking up some of these 'shaded' references will give a rough idea of the type(s) of material each category characteristically consists of.

We do not expect that you will work through all the references below. (If you want to follow up Campbell and O'Brien's approach, it is easier to consult their own presentation, in which the text of Kings is set out with different fonts for each different category of material.) We have set out the details of their analysis simply to give an idea of its intricacy (which can be matched in the work of other scholars). This is what literary-critical approaches often look like in practice, with some chapters divided between many different hands (e.g. 1 Kgs 8; 11). We could have provided similarly detailed analyses of Joshua–Samuel, but once is enough!

1 Previously existing materials taken up into the Josianic edition of Kings

Prophetic Record:

- **1 Kings 2**:10, 12; **3**:1; **9**:15–19*, 24; **11**:1a, 3, 7a, 26–31, 37, 38b, 40; **11**:43—**12**:1; **12**:3–24*, **12**:25, 28a, 29–30; **13**:33b—**14**:13*, **14**:17–18a, 20b; **15**:27–29a*; **16**:6, 9–11*, 15b–18, 21–22, 24, 28, 31b–32; **17**:1; **18**:2–46*; **21**:1–24; **22**:40
- **2 Kings 1**:2–8, 17a; **9**:1—**10**:35*; [Prophetic Record Extension] **13**:2, 7, 9, 11; **14**:16, 24, 29; **15**:9–30a*; **17**:2–6, 21–23*

Other material incorporated into the Josianic kings:

- **1 Kings 1**:1—**2**:46*; **3**:4–5, **3**:15—**4**:28; **5**:1–2, 8–12; **6**:2—**8**:1a*, **8**:1c–2, 6a, 12–13, 62–64; **9**:1–2, 25; **12**:2; **14**:25–28; **17**:2—**18**:4*, **18**:12b–14, 19b, **18**:41—**19**:3*, **19**:19–21; **21**:27–29
- **2 Kings 1**:9–16; **2**:1–25; **4**:1—**8**:22*; **11**:1—**12**:16*; **13**:14–24*; **14**:7, 17; **19**:9b–20a*, 32–33, 35; **20**:1–11*; **21**:23–24

Hezekian king list:

- **1 Kings 14**:21–23a*, 31; **15**:3a, 8–14a*, 24; **22**:43, 50
- **2 Kings 8**:18, 24, 27; **12**:2–3, 20–21; **14**:3–5, 19–21; **15**:3–7*, 34–38*; **16**:2b–9*, **16**:20; **18**:3–8*

Isaiah material:

- **2 Kings 18**:17—**19**:2; **19**:5–9a, 36–37

as the handiwork of an uninventive second editor, but as the final proof of the point made above about the regnal formulae being patterned so as to suit their contexts (see the panel 'Regnal formulae in Kings'). This is creative inflexibility!

5 Last, why are Manasseh's sins such a point of difficulty for the theology of Kings? The pattern for Judah is simply the same as for Israel: sin mounts up and after a certain point it makes no difference whether a good or less bad king comes to the throne; there is too much accumulated sin to make exile other than inevitable. In particular, Campbell and O'Brien are mistaken in seeing what happens to Judah after Josiah's reforms as a unique problem for the theology 'this do and live' (cf. Deut.

2 Deuteronomistic additions made as part of the Josianic edition

- **1 Kings 2**:27b; **3**:3a, **3**:6–15a†; **5**:3–7; **6**:1b; **8**:14–29a†, **8**:54–56; **9**:3–5; **11**:4, 6, **11**:34–42†; **12**:15bc, 19, 26–28b*; **14**:8b–9a, 18b–21b*, 29–30; **15**:1–15†, **15**:23–26*; **15**:28—**16**:5†, **16**:8, 12, 14–15a, 20, **16**:23–31a†; **21**:22b–23; **22**:39–45†, 51–53
- **2 Kings 1**:1, 18; **3**:1–3; **8**:16–29†; **9**:7b–10a*, 29, 36–37; **10**:10, 29b, 34, 36; **11**:21—**12**:1; **12**:19; **13**:1, 8, 10; **14**:1–2, 15, 18, 23, 28; **15**:1–2, 6, 8, 11, 13, 15, 17, 21–27†, **15**:30a—**16**:2a, **16**:19; **17**:1, 23a*; **18**:1–2, 9–13*; **20**:20—**21**:7†, **21**:17—**22**:15†; **22**:18b, 20b*; **23**:1–9†, 21–23, 25

3 Material added after the Josianic edition

'After the Dtr':

- **1 Kings 3**:6b; **4**:29–34; **5**:13–18; **9**:16–17a, 23; **9**:26—**10**:29; **11**:33ab; **16**:34;
- **2 Kings 23**:28—**25**:21*

Revision (royal focus):

- **1 Kings 11**:7b–13; **12**:31–33; **13**:2b–3a, 5b, 32b–33a; **14**:14; **15**:12b, **15**:16–22, **15**:30; **16**:2b*, 7, 13, 19, 33*; **21**:20, 25–26
- **2 Kings 12**:17–18; **14**:8–14; **16**:3b–4; **18**:14–16; **20**:12–19; **21**:2b–6*, 10–14, 21–22; **22**:19–20*; **23**:5, **23**:10–20*, **23**:26–27

Revision (national focus):

- **1 Kings 2**:2–4; **3**:3c, 14; **8**:23–26a*, 57–58, 61; **11**:1b–2, 5a, 33ab; **14**:9b, 15–16, 22b; **15**:5
- **2 Kings 17**:7–20; **18**:6, 12; **21**:8–9, 15; **22**:13b, 16–18a

Other:

- **1 Kings 2**:11; **3**:2, 3b; **6**:1a, 11–14; **8**:1b–11*, **8**:27, **8**:29b–53 **8**:59–60, 65–66; **9**:6–14, **9**:20–22; **11**:5b, **11**:14–25, **11**:32, 33c, 39; **12**:17, 21–24; **13**:1–2a, **13**:3b–32a; **14**:23b–24; **15**:6; **18**:18b; **19**:4–18; **20**:1–43; **21**:19b; **22**:1–38, **22**:46–49
- **2 Kings 1**:17b; **3**:4–27; **10**:30–31; **13**:3–6, 12–13, 23; **14**:6, 22, 25–27; **15**:12; **16**:10–18; **17**:24–41; **18**:5b; **19**:3–4, **19**:16–31*, **19**:34; **20**:6b; **21**:16; **23**:8b, 13–14, 24; **24**:2–4, 13–14, 20; **25**:22–30

* = a considerable proportion of the material within these verses is assigned to this source or redactional layer, but not all of it.
† = a fair amount of the material in these verses is assigned to this redactional layer, but the material usually consists of a number of separate pieces of text. (This sign is used only in connection with the editorial additions made during the Josianic redaction of Kings.)

30:15–20), which they regard as the centre plank of Deuteronomistic theology. On the contrary, Joshua, Judges, Samuel and earlier chapters of Kings have provided many examples where this theology, understood in a strict sense, does not fully explain what has happened: righteous people have suffered unexpected fates and (yet more so) sinners have been spared.

Since the beginning of Israel's history in the land, grace has been operative as well as law. But unless divine patience is to become indistinguishable from divine indifference, there must come a point when the penalties of the law have to be imposed. The fact that Kings says this point was reached with the sins of Jeroboam (for the North) and with the sins of Manasseh (for the South) may seem from one point of view arbitrary (why these kings in particular?); but it is hardly surprising. Divine grace, because it is undeserved, can never be explained exactly, and thus can give an appearance of arbitrariness.

As will by now be familiar, then, we find Kings to be a much more finished and consistent literary product than do many who have studied it. While it is likely that it is based on many different sources stemming from different circles and dating from different periods, these sources have been fashioned into a carefully constructed and theologically subtle text whose past history is now more or less untraceable. Where many have confidently spoken of separate sources, divergent viewpoints and sections that are blatantly secondary and redactional, we question the arguments used to arrive at such conclusions and to lay bare the literary history of Kings.

For further comments on the dating of Kings, particularly the question of how significant a role Deuteronomistic redaction of the seventh or sixth centuries played in the formation of the book, see Chapter 7. While it is hard to prove that the final form of Kings should be dated shortly after the date of the events related in 2 Kings 25:27–30, the contrast between the presentation of events in Kings and that in Chronicles seems to argue for a dating in the mid-sixth century. Chronicles has clearly been shaped with the realities of the post-exilic era in view. Kings, by contrast, is more readily understood as 'preaching to the exiles': a presentation of Israel's previous history with the specific purpose of explaining why those in exile had come to be where they were.

HISTORICAL ISSUES

The period covered in Kings extends from 970 to 560 BC. This is a long period to which it is impossible to do full justice here.

To a greater extent than in earlier chapters we will simply refer to accessible discussions of the issues. The major developments in the ancient Near East, as we learn of them from extra-biblical sources, were the resurgence of Assyrian power, which led to two waves of invasion into Syria, Palestine and even Egypt (c. 883–824 and c. 744–660), followed by the rapid rise of Babylonian power and the destruction of the Assyrian empire. Egypt only rarely ventured beyond its borders in this period. These events are reflected in Kings: Assyria is first mentioned at 2 Kings 15:19 and dominates the next five chapters; but the last major power in Kings is Babylon, introduced at 2 Kings 24:1.

The archaeology of Palestine in general confirms the picture from the extra-biblical sources (see the brief but helpful survey in Kitchen, pp. 51–61). As archaeology is less controversial in this period than in those covered in Chapters 3–5 (with the exception of the Solomonic period, for which see below), we simply refer to the treatments by Mazar, Barkay and Stern.

Kings and extra-biblical texts

Kitchen discusses in detail the correlation of biblical and extra-biblical texts for this period (pp. 7–64). He lists all the foreign kings mentioned in Kings, Chronicles and some prophetic texts and, conversely, all the references to kings of Israel and Judah in extra-biblical texts (Egyptian, Aramaic, Moabite, Assyrian and Babylonian), also taking into account 'local records' (inscriptions, ostraca and clay seals from Palestine). He then compares the various sets of texts, with the following results (pp. 62–4):

(1) of 20 foreign rulers mentioned in biblical texts (primarily in Kings) 17 or 18 are also mentioned in extra-biblical texts; (2) from 853 on, when extra-biblical texts (particularly from Assyria and Babylonia) start to refer to kings of Israel and Judah, nine out of 14 kings of Israel and eight out of 15 kings of Judah are named in these texts; (3) the sequence of foreign rulers and Israelite–Judean rulers in Kings matches that of the extra-biblical texts exactly.

Sometimes there appears to be a close fit between events in Kings and events attested in extra-biblical sources. Israel's unexpected survival and (even) flourishing in the period beginning with Jehu and ending with Jeroboam (841–749) took place in the 'false calm' between the two waves of Assyrian expansion. The meeting between Hezekiah and Babylonian envoys described in 2 Kings 20 may be linked to revolts against Assyria in both Babylon and Syria–Palestine in the last decade of the eighth century. Josiah's incursions into the former territory of Israel (2 Kings 23:15–20) took place in the vacuum caused by weakening Assyrian power in the region. Last, Jehoiakim may have been incited to revolt against Babylon (2 Kgs 24:1) by the fact that the Babylonian army in the region was temporarily weakened by a costly battle with Egyptian forces in 601 (Kitchen, p. 44).

If these particular suggestions are correct, however, Kings does not explicitly say so. Kings usually offers 'religious' explanations for events, and has much less to say about 'political' considerations; or so it seems to modern readers, who tend to distinguish politics and religion much more sharply than was the case in the ancient Near East. For instance, Hezekiah's and Josiah's reforms are presented simply as a purging of corrupt religious practices. The possibility that Hezekiah was trying to centralize political power by removing the 'high places', or Josiah trying to expand Judah's borders as he ventured north, is not even mentioned.

In general, while Kings tells us much about Israel's and Judah's relations with their near neighbours (Aram, Moab, Edom) and with Assyria, Babylon and Egypt, it tells us less than we might like to know. There are also gaps in the extra-biblical sources. This said, however, it is possible to cross-reference Kings (and other biblical sources) with extra-biblical accounts at many points. Some clear examples (discussed in Kitchen, pp. 32–45) are:

- Pharaoh Shoshenq's invasion of Israel (1 Kgs 14:25–26; stela fragment at Megiddo and triumphal inscription at Karnak);
- conflict between Mesha and Israel during the Omride period (see the panel 'The Moabite Stone');
- the deaths of Joram of Israel and Ahaziah of Judah (2 Kgs 9; Tel Dan Stela, *COS* II, pp. 161–2);
- Tiglath-Pilcser III's dealings with Israel and Judah (2 Kgs 15:19—16:20; inscriptions of Tiglath-Pileser, *COS* II, pp. 284–92);
- Shalmaneser V's and Sargon II's dealings with Israel and Judah (2 Kgs 17; Babylonian Chronicle, *COS* I, p. 467; inscriptions of Sargon, *COS* II, pp. 293–300);
- Sennacherib and Jerusalem (see panel on p. 171);
- Josiah and Pharaoh Necho (2 Kgs 23:29–30; Babylonian Chronicle, *COS* I, pp. 467–8);
- siege of Jerusalem in 598–597, capture of Jehoiachin, appointment of Zedekiah in his place (2 Kgs 24:10–17; Babylonian Chronicle, *COS* I, p. 468).

The relationship between biblical and extra-biblical texts in these examples is not always straightforward. Sometimes extra-biblical texts tell us things we do not read about in Kings: e.g. Omri's capture of part of Moab (Moabite Stone); Ahab's participation in a coalition which fought against Shalmaneser III in 853 (*COS* II, pp. 263–4); Jehu's payment of tribute to Shalmaneser III in 841 (*COS* II, p. 270).

(For further discussion of these issues from a variety of perspectives, see the essays by Na'aman, Grabbe and Long; also Provan, Long and Longman, pp. 259–85.)

The dating of events in I Kings 20—2 Kings 8

The question of whether some incidents in the central section of Kings have been narrated out of historical sequence is partly a question of how to correlate biblical and extra-biblical evidence. Miller and Hayes see a discrepancy in the account of Ahab and his sons (pp. 259–62): parts of the account seem to portray them as powerful (for instance, the Elijah narratives, where Ahab is 'autocratic' and 'in full control' of his kingdom, and 2 Kings 9:14, which suggests that Joram controlled Ramoth Gilead). This picture is supported by Shalmaneser's inscription (*COS* II, pp. 263–4), which portrays Ahab as one of the most powerful kings in the coalition against him in 853, with a contingent of 2,000 chariots and 10,000 foot soldiers; and also by the Moabite Stone, which implies that Ahab dominated Moab. Over against this, other parts of Kings seem to portray Ahab and his sons as weak and constantly under threat from Aram: the accounts of the three battles in 1 Kings 20 and 22 (note especially 20:27); the accounts of Elisha and the Arameans in 2 Kings 5—8.

There are other apparent inconsistencies in these chapters: the varying relations of Israel and Aram (now allies, as in 1 Kings 20:33–34, 22:1 and Shalmaneser's inscription, now at war, as in other parts of the account); the varying relations of kings and prophets (sometimes confrontational, sometimes friendly). Miller and Hayes conclude that those parts of the account which portray Israel and Israel's kings as weak originally described events from the period of the Jehu dynasty (cf. their treatment of this period, pp. 297–302).

Miller and Hayes seem to build partly on the work of literary-critical scholars who point to the lack of evident continuity between the separate incidents of 1 Kings 20—2 Kings 8: if this section is seen as a loose collection of diverse traditions, then it may seem reasonable to rearrange them so as to produce a more straightforward sequence of events. But is the presentation of events in these chapters so difficult? It is true that connections between events are not always spelled out, but there seem to be many implicit thematic links, and, arguably, a coherent sequence of events overall (see 'Outline').

Regarding Shalamanezer's inscription, it has been suggested that the figure given for Ahab's chariots (2,000) is, for whatever reason, too high (see *COS* II, p. 263, n. 25); but even if we take the figures in this inscription as accurate, then Aram (Damascus) still emerges as more powerful than Ahab overall (20,000 foot soldiers, 1,200 chariots, 1,200 cavalry), which brings us closer to the picture in 1 Kings 20 and 22 than Miller and Hayes imply. And it is easy to envisage Aram and Israel joining forces against the Assyrian threat, but reverting to hostile relations once the threat had receded.

Certainly the picture of the period which emerges if we follow the order of the biblical account (Israel now allied to Aram, now at war; now victorious, now defeated) is more complex, and has more ebb and flow than in Miller and Hayes' simple contrast between the period of Ahab (Israel powerful, on good terms with Aram) and the period of Jehu's dynasty (Israel weak, at war with Aram). But it is hardly an impossible picture: sometimes events *are* complex.

(See Provan, Long and Longman, pp. 263–5 for an account of the Omrides based upon the order of events in Kings.)

Solomon

One figure in Kings who is not mentioned in any extra-biblical text discovered up to this point is Solomon. The panel 'Solomon's glory: fact or fiction?' invited you to consider the implications of this fact. Further to the authors cited there, you can consult the following treatments: Knoppers' survey of recent scholarship on the United Monarchy; Dever 1997, which builds up a picture of tenth-century Palestine solely on the basis of archaeological data (setting the biblical account on one side, that is) and is still able to conclude that the evidence for the existence of a centralized state is such that 'if we have never heard of a "Solomon" in the biblical texts, we should have to invent a tenth century BCE Israelite king by another name' (p. 251); Niemann's essay in the same volume as Dever's, which is much less optimistic about the amount of archaeological data that can securely be dated to the tenth century.

Chronology of the kings of Israel and Judah

The regnal formulae for the kings of Israel and Judah regularly give three types of chronological data: (1) the king's age at accession; (2) the number of years he ruled; (3) (during the period of the divided monarchy) a synchronism linking each king's year of accession with a particular year in the reign of his counterpart in the other kingdom (see the panel 'Early kings of Israel and Judah'). In principle these data should be enough to provide us with both a *relative* chronology for the two kingdoms and (via synchronisms with Assyrian and Egyptian chronology) an *absolute* chronology. In practice the figures in the regnal formulae are one of the knottiest problems in Kings. (See the summary of the issues in Provan, Long and Longman, pp. 242–6.)

Some difficulties are immediately apparent to the attentive reader:

- 2 Kings 1:17 states that Jehoram of Israel became king 'in the second year of King Jehoram son of Jehoshaphat of Judah', whereas 2 Kings 3:1 puts his accession in Jehoshaphat's eighteenth year.
- 2 Kings 16:2 states that Ahaz was 20 years old when he began to reign, and that he reigned for 16 years; 2 Kings 18:2 states that Hezekiah, Ahaz' son, was 25 years old when he came to the throne. Taken together, these figures seem to imply that Ahaz was 11 years old when he fathered Hezekiah.
- 2 Kings 18:9 implies that Hezekiah became king around 727, but 18:13 places Sennacherib's invasion (701) in Hezekiah's fourteenth year, which implies he became king around 714.

Once one examines these and other examples, it becomes apparent that the chronological data in Kings 'cannot be understood just by totting up figures as if this were some modern, "Western" composition' (Kitchen, p. 26). The figures must, rather, be understood on the basis of ancient Near Eastern usage. In practice this involves considering several possibilities (Kitchen, pp. 26–32):

- that the lengths of some reigns are calculated according to 'accession-year dating' as practised in Mesopotamia (Year 1 of a king's reign is the first full year which falls within his reign, and no portion of the previous year is credited to him, even though he may have reigned for many months of that year);
- that the lengths of other reigns are calculated according to 'non-accession-year dating' as practised in Egypt (the first full year of a king's reign is counted as his Year 2, and any period between his accession and the beginning of that year is counted as his Year 1, even if this period was only a few days);
- that both 'accession-year dating' and 'non-accession-year dating' may have been used at different times in Israel and Judah;
- that two different calendars were in use in Israel and Judah, one running from spring to spring, and another from autumn to autumn;
- that the figures given for the reigns of particular kings involve 'co-regencies', according to which a king was reckoned to begin his reign during that of his predecessor. Co-regencies 'usually have political significance, e.g. to affirm the succession under threats (real or potential) from within or without' (Kitchen, p. 29). A king who began as co-regent might choose, when his predecessor died, to make a fresh start, reckoning the beginning of his period as sole ruler as the

beginning of his reign. Such factors may explain the discrepancy between 2 Kings 18:9 and 18:13 noted above.

On this basis Kitchen is able to claim that Kings provides 'a very remarkably preserved royal chronology, mainly very accurate in fine detail, that agrees very closely with the dates given by Mesopotamian and other sources' (p. 29). This would constitute an argument for the accuracy of Kings' sources as regards chronology and perhaps also therefore in other aspects. Kitchen does not argue his case in detail, however, leaving this for a future volume.

The picture of Israelite religion

Kings presents a mixed picture of Israelite religion during the monarchy. On the one hand, it contains strong statements of YHWH's uniqueness and his superiority to the gods of the nations (e.g. 1 Kgs 8, 2 Kgs 19). Some of these come early in Kings. On the other hand, many texts state that king and people frequently failed to acknowledge YHWH as they should have, engaging in questionable forms of worship (e.g. the references to the 'high places' in 1 Kgs 3), and even turning to the worship of other gods and goddesses (e.g. 1 Kgs 11).

The same mixed picture can be found in Samuel and (particularly) Judges: a strongly expressed commitment to the uniqueness and power of YHWH, coupled with an acknowledgement that the people's worship was at times corrupt, even idolatrous (in Samuel, this theme only surfaces in 1 Sam. 1–7). Joshua does not describe the Israelites of the conquest generation as worshipping other gods (unless Josh. 24:14 implies this), but is clear regarding both YHWH's uniqueness and the danger posed by other gods (see particularly chs 23—24).

The same picture emerges from the other Histories, except that neither Ruth nor Esther explicitly address the question of the worship of other gods. (As this is the only place in Chapters 3—11 where we deal with the issue of Israelite religion, we shall widen the discussion here to take in the other Histories as well.)

Joshua–Kings do not claim that the Israelites consistently recognized YHWH as the only true god, but that there were periods when this was so, from the time of Joshua down to the reigns of the reforming kings of Judah (Asa, Hezekiah, Josiah). Interspersed with these periods were periods in which the people worshipped other gods, or tried to combine the worship of YHWH and other gods. It may even be said that Joshua–Kings present idolatry as the 'default state' to which the people revert unless restrained. But the worship of other gods is always presented as a lapse which the people and their leaders should have known better than to allow: from their earliest days the Israelites knew that their obligation was to YHWH alone, no matter how imperfectly they fulfilled that obligation.

Many archaeological finds at sites within Palestine, particularly from the period of the divided monarchy, support what Joshua–Kings say about the people's tendency to engage in forms of worship that they themselves condemn. There is evidence from various periods for household shrines and for local shrines, for instance at Hazor and Dan (cf. Kings' reference to 'high places'). Figurines have been recovered which were seemingly intended for use in worship, including female figures which may plausibly be linked to the goddess Asherah (cf. 1 Kgs 15:13; 18:19). Wall-paintings and paintings on jars reinforce this picture. An eighth-

century inscription from Khirbet el-Qom (probably biblical Makkedah) contains the words: 'blessed is Uriyahu by Yahweh; from his enemies he has been saved by his a/Asherah'; a wall inscription in a shrine in the ninth- or eighth-century fort at Kuntillet 'Ajrud (eastern Sinai Desert) dedicates the shrine 'to [Y]ahweh (of Teiman) [= Yemen] and to his Asherah'. (For all this, see Dever 2005; Keel and Uehlinger.)

But what about the other side? Are Joshua–Kings also correct in their claim that YHWH's uniqueness was recognized from the earliest days of Israel's presence in Canaan? Some scholars argue that this belief was a late development within Israel: for much of their history Israelites were polytheists, like the Canaanites, and the goddess Asherah was widely venerated as YHWH's consort (Dever 2005). Only towards the end of the monarchic period, or perhaps even only in the post-exilic period, did the view that YHWH was alone worthy to be worshipped come to be at all widely held. (For this view, see Gnuse and Smith; Gnuse, pp. 321–45, draws an explicit parallel between the development of monotheism in Israel and biological evolution.)

This implies, of course, that Joshua–Kings are seriously misleading at this point. It is regularly argued that their presentation is a retrojection of later beliefs on to an earlier period. Monotheism was a minority view (if that) for much of Israel's history, but the minority view later became the dominant view, which has deeply influenced the perspective of Joshua–Kings. Joshua–Kings, on this view, are an example of the general claim that 'history is written by the winners'. Similar arguments have been applied to Chronicles (which closely follows Samuel and Kings in its general view of Israel's religion during the monarchy). Ruth and Esther have not featured much in this discussion, and Ezra–Nehemiah's presentation of post-exilic religious life in Judah, because it is generally held to have been composed 100–150 years after the events it describes, is not so vulnerable to the charge of 'misleading retrojection'.

The view that Joshua–Kings and Chronicles give a distorted picture of Israel's religion in the pre-exilic period raises methodological issues discussed in earlier chapters: the relationship of biblical and archaeological data; the issue of historical reliability. Literary-critical discussions are as important here as they are elsewhere: much of the impetus for seeing monotheism as a late development in Israelite thinking comes, in the Histories at least, from a widespread belief that the 'Deuteronomistic' editing of Joshua–Kings is a late stage in their formation (see Ch. 7).

We must content ourselves here with restating positions for which we have already argued: the Histories are a more reliable guide to Israel's early history than is often accepted; and we are less confident than many about the ability of modern scholars to unravel the literary history of Old Testament books (hence, in this instance, about the plausibility of regarding the strongest statements of monotheism in the Histories as expressions of a distinctively late viewpoint).

The weaknesses of the 'evolutionary' approach to Israelite religion are elegantly summed up by Bauckham (pp. 198–9):

> The conclusion that exclusive Yahwism did not exist until the late monarchical period results mainly from treating the biblical

texts not just with historical scepticism but with historical scepticism based on very considerable ideological suspicion of the texts, along with the use of religio-historical models for interpreting the non-biblical evidence and making a plausible story out of it. Such models are inescapable in any history of religions and the smaller the amount of evidence and the more ambiguous it is the more it is the models that control the conclusions drawn from the evidence. Once the biblical texts have been discounted as reliable evidence, not only because of very late datings given them but also because they are so ideologically shaped, the remaining evidence is, it must surely be admitted, rather easily malleable according to the models and analogies employed. While the historical reconstruction may fully respect the integrity of this evidence, it is not so easy to tell whether an alternative historical reconstruction might not do so just as well. Ironically, there is a clear danger of historiography that is no less ideologically shaped than it considers that of the Deuteronomists to have been. In particular, most such reconstructions seem controlled by a developmental model, however nuanced, that envisages a series of steps that advance by stages towards full monotheism and cannot reckon with serious departure from monotheism once this has been attained.

(Further on the question of contemporary ideologies as a factor shaping some modern accounts of Israelite religion, see Provan 1997, pp. 68–82.)

Bauckham in general regards the Old Testament as displaying a consistent 'monotheising' tendency (pp. 206–17):

coming from a context in which polytheism was the rule, the Old Testament writers repeatedly contend for YHWH's 'transcendent uniqueness' (YHWH is not merely greater than other gods; he is in a class of his own). It is not that the question of YHWH's uniqueness was only raised at a late stage (and then answered affirmatively); rather, the Old Testament bears witness to a continual struggle with polytheism, the issue not being decisively resolved until (at the earliest) after the Babylonian exile. In our view, the grounds for reading Kings and the other Histories in this way are as strong, if not stronger, than those for the 'evolutionary' treatments cited earlier.

KINGS IN THE CANON

Kings continues the account of Israel in Joshua–Samuel. In particular, it continues the history of Israel's monarchy begun in Samuel, and develops many themes introduced there. There are also frequent allusions to Genesis, Exodus and (particularly) Deuteronomy. By the end of Kings the narrative of Genesis–Kings has come full circle: Abraham came from Mesopotamia, and his descendants have now returned there.

Most of the Old Testament prophetic books have their origins in the events described in 2 Kings. The prefaces to many of these books date the prophet's activity to the reigns of one or more kings of Israel and–or Judah (e.g. Hos. 1:1; Isa. 1:1; Jer. 1:1–3). Chapters 18–20 of 2 Kings overlap to a considerable extent with Isaiah 36–39, and 2 Kings 25 with Jeremiah 52. It is therefore not surprising to find in Kings both general references to prophetic activity (e.g. 2 Kgs 17:13; 24:2), and particular references to individual prophets (Jonah, 2 Kgs 14:25;

Isaiah, 2 Kgs 18–20). Indeed, it may seem surprising that more prophets are not mentioned by name, Jeremiah being perhaps the most striking absentee in this regard. A possible explanation of this is that the final stages in the composition of Kings took place at a time when many of the prophetic books had reached their final form. The present form of Kings was perhaps always meant to be read alongside the prophetic books.

Certainly points of interest emerge when we do this. The prophetic books, first, give us more details on particular points than Kings. Amos builds on the portrayal of the Jehu dynasty in 2 Kings 13—15, portraying the reign of Jeroboam II as one of false confidence. Isaiah 7—9 and 2 Kings 16 are mutually illuminating regarding the Syro-Ephraimite war (though it is not clear why Isaiah is not mentioned in 2 Kings 16). Jeremiah 25—29 and 34—44 give a far fuller and much more colourful picture of the period after Josiah than does Kings. The oracles against the nations in (especially) Isaiah, Jeremiah and Ezekiel reinforce the picture in Kings of the eighth–sixth centuries as a time of international tumult, though these oracles, being themselves often obscure, do not usually make our picture of the period any clearer.

Kings and the prophetic books also have a number of themes in common: the interplay of prophecy and human response; the issue of true and false prophecy; the promise to David (for these, see 'Key themes', p. 177–9). Jeremiah is well known for his insistence, during the chaotic years of the early sixth century, that the immediate future of God's people lay in Babylon, not in Palestine or Egypt (e.g. Jer. 29; 44). The last two incidents in Kings (25:22–26, 27–30) perhaps make the same point implicitly, contrasting a failed revolt in Palestine (whose instigators had to flee to Egypt) with Jehoiachin's kind treatment many years later at the Babylonian royal table.

Along the lines of comments at the end of Chapter 5, we may speak of a 'proto-messianism' in Kings: just as Samuel seemed to draw a contrast between David at his best and David's failings, so figures such as Solomon, Hezekiah and Josiah show what David's line was (intermittently) capable of and thus, when set against the dismal performance of David's line as a whole, partly anticipate prophetic texts regarding a future descendant of David who will restore the fortunes of the line and Israel as a whole.

Solomon also forms a link with the Old Testament wisdom books, being cited either as author or on other grounds in Proverbs, Ecclesiastes and the Song of Songs. Interestingly, while Proverbs, making him the author of much of the book, reinforces the picture of him in Kings as a wise king (cf. 1 Kgs 4:29–34), Ecclesiastes and Song of Songs seem to echo those parts of Kings which portray Solomon's folly, Ecclesiastes making him express the view that the pursuit of wealth, luxury and even architectural glory is ultimately futile (Eccl. 2:1–16), and Song of Songs portraying him as trying to buy love and being rejected (Song 8:10–12).

Finally, in the New Testament, many of the figures in Kings are seen as prefiguring Jesus: not only Solomon and the leading kings of Judah, but also Elijah and Elisha. Jesus, indeed, has a prophetic ministry like those of Elijah and Elisha and accompanied by similar miracles, in which Israel is offered life but warned of judgment if it refuses the offer.

FURTHER READING

COMMENTARIES

M. Cogan and H. Tadmor, *2 Kings*. New York: Anchor, 1988.

S.J. De Vries, *1 Kings*. Waco: Word, 1985.

W. Dietrich, '1 and 2 Kings', OBC, pp. 232–66.

T.R. Hobbs, *2 Kings*. Waco: Word, 1985.

G.H. Jones, *1 and 2 Kings*. Grand Rapids/London: Eerdmans/Marshall, Morgan and Scott, 1984.

B.O. Long, *1 Kings*. Grand Rapids: Eerdmans, 1991.

B.O. Long, *2 Kings*. Grand Rapids: Eerdmans, 1991.

I.W. Provan, *1 and 2 Kings*. Peabody: Hendrickson, 1995.

OTHER BOOKS AND ARTICLES

A.G. Auld, *Kings without Privilege. David and Moses in the Story of the Bible's Kings*. Edinburgh: T. and T. Clark, 1994.

G. Barkay, 'The Iron Age II–III' in A. Ben-Tor (ed.), *The Archaeology of Ancient Israel*. New Haven: Yale University Press, 1992, pp. 302–73.

R.J. Bauckham, 'Biblical Theology and the Problems of Monotheism' in C.R. Bartholomew *et al.* (eds), *Out of Egypt: Biblical Theology and Biblical Interpretation*. Grand Rapids/Milton Keynes: Zondervan/Paternoster, 2004.

H.C. Brichto, *Towards a Grammar of Biblical Poetics. Tales of the Prophets*. New York: Oxford University Press, 1992.

A.F. Campbell and M.A. O'Brien, *Unfolding the Deuteronomistic History. Origins, Upgrades, Present Text*. Minneapolis: Fortress Augsburg, 2000.

P.R. Davies, *In Search of 'Ancient Israel'*. Sheffield: Sheffield Academic Press, 1992.

W.G. Dever, 'Archaeology and the "Age of Solomon": A Case-Study in Archaeology and Historiography', in L.K. Handy (ed.), *The Age of Solomon. Scholarship at the Turn of the Millennium*. Leiden: Brill, 1997, pp. 217–51.

W.G. Dever, *Did God Have a Wife? Archaeology and Folk Religion in Ancient Israel*. Grand Rapids: Eerdmans, 2005.

R.K. Gnuse, *No Other Gods. Emergent Monotheism in Israel*. Sheffield: Sheffield Academic Press, 1997.

L.L. Grabbe, 'Are Historians of Ancient Palestine Fellow Creatures – or Different Animals?' in L.L. Grabbe (ed.), *Can a 'History of Israel' be Written?* Sheffield Academic Press: 1997, pp. 19–36.

L.K. Handy (ed.), *The Age of Solomon. Scholarship at the Turn of the Millennium*. Leiden: Brill, 1997.

M. Haran, 'The Books of the Chronicles "of the Kings of Judah" and "of the Kings of Israel": What Sort of Books Were They? *VT* 49 (1999), pp. 156–64.

R.S. Hess, 'Hezekiah and Sennacherib in 2 Kings 18–20' in R.S. Hess and G.J. Wenham (eds), *Zion, City of Our God*. Grand Rapids: Eerdmans, 1999.

V. Hurowitz, *I Have Built You an Exalted House. Temple Building in the Bible in Light of Mesopotamian and Northwest Semitic Writings*. Sheffield: Sheffield Academic Press, 1992.

O. Keel and C. Uehlinger, *Gods, Goddesses, and Images of God in Ancient Israel*. Minneapolis: Augsburg Fortress, 1998.

K.A. Kitchen, *On the Reliability of the Old Testament*. Grand Rapids: Eerdmans, 2003.

G.N. Knoppers, 'The Vanishing Solomon: The Disappearance of the United Monarchy from Recent Histories of Ancient Israel', *JBL* 116 (1997), pp. 19–44.

J.R. Linville, *Israel in the Book of Kings. The Past as a Project of Social Identity*. Sheffield: Sheffield Academic Press, 1998.

V.P. Long, 'How Reliable are Biblical Reports? Repeating Lester Grabbe's Comparative Experiment', *VT* 52 (2002), pp. 367–84.

J.G. McConville, 'Kings, Books of', *DOTHB*, pp. 623–34.

S.L. McKenzie, 'The Books of Kings in the Deuteronomistic History' in S.L. McKenzie and M.P. Graham (eds), *The History of Israel's Traditions. The Heritage of Martin Noth*. Sheffield: Sheffield Academic Press, 1994, pp. 381–05.

A. Mazar, *Archaeology of the Land of the Bible, 10,000–586 B.C.E.* New York: Doubleday, 1990.

C. Meyers, 'Temple, Jerusalem', *ABD VI*, pp. 350–69.

A.R. Millard, 'King Solomon in His Ancient Context' (with response by J.M. Miller) in L.K. Handy (ed.), *The Age of Solomon. Scholarship at the Turn of the Millennium*. Leiden: Brill, 1997, pp. 30–56.

J.M. Miller, 'Separating the Solomon of History from the Solomon of Legend' (with response by A.R. Millard) in L.K. Handy (ed.), *The Age of Solomon. Scholarship at the Turn of the Millennium*. Leiden: Brill, pp. 1–29.

J.M. Miller and J.H. Hayes, *A History of Ancient Judah and Israel*. Philadelphia: Westminster Press, 1986.

N. Na'aman, 'The Contribution of Royal Inscriptions for a Re-Evaluation of the Book of Kings as a Historical Source', *JSOT* 82 (1999), pp. 3–17.

R.D. Nelson, *The Double Redaction of the Deuteronomistic History*. Sheffield: JSOT Press, 1981.

H.M. Niemann, 'The Socio-Political Shadow Cast by the Biblical Solomon', in L.K. Handy (ed.), *The Age of Solomon. Scholarship at the Turn of the Millennium*. Leiden: Brill, 1997, pp. 252–99.

S.B. Parker, 'Did the Authors of Kings Make Use of Royal Inscriptions?' *VT* 50 (2000), pp. 357–78.

D. Penchansky, *What Rough Beast? Images of God in the Hebrew Bible*. Louisville: Westminster John Knox Press, 1999.

I.W. Provan, *1 and 2 Kings*. Sheffield: Sheffield Academic Press, 1997.

I.W. Provan, V.P. Long, T. Longman, *A Biblical History of Israel*. Louisville: Westminster John Knox Press, 2003, pp. 259–85.

G. von Rad, *Old Testament Theology*, 2 vols. Edinburgh: Oliver and Boyd, 1962.

P.E. Satterthwaite, 'The Elisha Narratives and the Coherence of 2 Kings 2–8', *TB* 49 (1998), pp. 1–28.

M.S. Smith, *The Early History of God. Yahweh and the Other Deities in Ancient Israel*, 2nd edition. Grand Rapids: Eerdmans, 2002.

E. Stern, *Archaeology of the Land of the Bible, Volume II. The Assyrian, Babylonian and Persian Periods (732–332 B.C.E.)*. New York: Doubleday, 2001.

N. Wyatt, 'Of Calves and Kings: The Canaanite Dimension in the Religion of Israel', *SJOT* 6 (1992), pp. 68–91.

Chapter 7

JOSHUA–KINGS AND THEORIES OF DEUTERONOMISTIC HISTORIOGRAPHY

INTRODUCTION

The 'Critical issues' sections of Chapters 3–6 have referred to an entity known as 'the [or 'a'] Deuteronomistic History', and have discussed the possibility that these books contain one or more layers of 'Deuteronomistic' editing. Chapters 3–6 have expressed reservations about such views, and it is now time to address this topic in more detail. This chapter is necessarily somewhat technical and detailed, but it builds upon much of what Chapters 3–6 have said regarding the literary shaping and theology of Joshua–Kings.

THE DEUTERONOMISTIC HISTORY: A SURVEY OF SCHOLARSHIP

'The Deuteronomic or, more properly, Deuteronomistic History is a modern theoretical construct which holds that the books of Deuteronomy, Joshua, Judges, Samuel and Kings constitute a single work, unified by a basic homogeneity of language, style and content' (Knoppers, 'Introduction', p. 1).

This quotation brings out two key points: 'Deuteronomistic History' is a modern term, and there is no ancient document which

---

DEFINITIONS: 'DEUTERONOMIC' AND 'DEUTERONOMISTIC'

The literature on the Deuteronomistic History often uses the two terms 'Deuteronomic' and 'Deuteronomistic'. Ideally it ought to be possible to distinguish these two adjectives along the following lines:

Deuteronomic = pertaining to Deuteronomy, found in the book of Deuteronomy
Deuteronomistic = expressing ideas somewhat similar to those found in Deuteronomy, but derivative or secondary in character

That is, it would be easiest if the two terms drew a clear distinction between Deuteronomy itself

and other parts of the Old Testament possibly influenced by Deuteronomy. In practice things are not so simple, but we shall try to use 'Deuteronomic' and 'Deuteronomistic' in their 'ideal' senses wherever possible.

Following a common convention, we use the abbreviations DH (for 'Deuteronomistic History') and Dtr (for 'Deuteronomistic Historian' or 'Deuteronomist'). Further refinements can be introduced later.

corresponds precisely to the DH as modern scholars understand it. (All texts and ancient versions of the Old Testament separate Deuteronomy from Joshua–Kings, grouping it with Genesis–Numbers.) But on the other hand, there are clear thematic and verbal links between the books Deuteronomy–Kings which modern theories of Deuteronomistic historiography attempt to explain.

NOTH'S THEORY

The German scholar Martin Noth was the first to set out a coherent theory of a Deuteronomistic History, in a volume originally published in 1943. In Noth's view, a decisive stage in the literary history of Joshua, Judges, Samuel and Kings was the creation, around 550 BC, possibly in Palestine, of a Deuteronomistic History (DH). This DH was the work of a single man ('the Deuteronomist', Dtr), and encompassed most of Deuteronomy–Kings in their present form. It was a history of Israel from the conquest to the Babylonian exile, with Deuteronomy, Moses' farewell speech to Israel, acting as preface. Noth believed that parts of our present Joshua–Kings were later additions to the DH, most notably: Joshua 13—22 and 24; most of Judges 1:1–3:6 (Noth attributed only 2:6–16, 18–19 to Dtr); Judges 13—16 and 17—21; 2 Samuel 21—24.

In Deuteronomy, Noth argued that Dtr had taken an earlier form of the book (essentially Deut. 4:44—30:20, that is, the central law code of chs 12—26 with preface and conclusion) and added to it most of the narratives in chapters 1—3, along with verses (now part of chs 31 and 34) which described Moses' death and prepared for Joshua's leadership. The fact that Deuteronomy in something close to its present form became the first section of the DH was highly significant for the shape of the entire work: Dtr made the theology of Deuteronomy, particularly its teaching that obedience brings blessing and disobedience judgment, the interpretative grid for his account of Israel from conquest to exile.

This theology is restated in speeches placed at key points in the later sections of the work: YHWH's words to Joshua in Joshua 1 (Noth viewed vv. 7–9, which focus on law-keeping, as a later addition); Joshua's farewell (Josh. 23); Samuel's farewell (1 Sam. 12); Solomon's prayer at the dedication of the temple (1 Kgs 8). Noth saw these as Dtr's own compositions. Comments by Dtr in his own voice at other key points had similar functions: the overview of the judges period at Judges 2:11–19; the survey of later developments at Judges 10:6–16; the lengthy explanation for the fall of the northern kingdom at 2 Kings 17:7ff. These insertions all reinforced the theological perspective of the first section. The speeches also marked major structural divisions in the DH.

In making the theology of Deuteronomy so determinative for the shape of Joshua–Kings, it could be said that Noth took seriously the designation of Joshua–Kings in the Hebrew biblical canon as 'Former Prophets'. That designation seems to draw a link between the theological viewpoint of Joshua–Kings and that of the Old Testament prophetic books (the 'Latter Prophets' in the Hebrew canon). The link between the prophetic books and Deuteronomy has long been recognized. (Noth also followed the lead of the Hebrew canon in finding no place for the book of Ruth in his DH.)

Noth argued that Dtr 'was not merely an editor but the author of a history which brought together material from highly varied traditions and arranged it according to a carefully conceived plan' (p. 26). Noth did not mean that Dtr thoroughly reworked all the traditions available to him, putting them all 'in his own words'; he believed that Dtr respected these traditions, using them selectively but reproducing them faithfully. Thus in Joshua he argued that Dtr based his account on a pre-existing collection of stories relating to the conquest of Canaan, this earlier collection now forming the basis for Joshua 2—11. All Dtr did was to supply this collection with an introduction (most of ch. 1), a summary (ch. 12) and a theological conclusion (ch. 23). The point of describing Dtr as an 'author' was, rather, that it was Dtr who combined the separate traditions underlying Deuteronomy–Kings into a single work.

The traditions themselves varied in form and extent, and Dtr handled them in correspondingly different ways. In the sections dealing with the conquest and with Saul, David and Solomon, the traditions were already quite extensive and required little editing. The traditions relating to the period of the judges were shorter and relatively unformed, and so Dtr's editorial hand is more obvious in Judges: he supplied frameworks for the separate narratives, and brought together two originally separate sets of traditions, one relating to military heroes (Judg. 3—8) and the other relating to local lawgivers (Judg. 10:1–5; 12:7–15), to produce a single account of 'the judges of Israel'.

Dtr wanted to explain the destruction of the northern and southern kingdoms. His account emphasized Israel's persistent unfaithfulness, which drew down increasingly severe judgments until both kingdoms were destroyed. YHWH displayed great patience during Israel's history, raising up saviours in the judges period in spite of Israel's disobedience, allowing Israel to have kings though not really approving of the idea, and giving the monarchy a fair chance to bring blessing to the people. But Israel and their leaders broke the covenant (Dtr particularly focuses on violations of the laws relating to worship), and so Israel's history came to an end.

This in Noth's view was Dtr's main burden, to explain why Israel's history, the last stages of which he would himself have witnessed, was now over. Dtr says nothing about any possible future for Israel. Specifically, though key passages view deportation as the appropriate final punishment for apostasy (Deut. 4:25–28; Josh. 23:15–16; 1 Sam. 12:25) and these warnings are fulfilled, there are no corresponding passages in the DH which explicitly speak of the possibility of return from exile. (Noth argued that 1 Kings 8:44–53 was not such a passage.) The note about Jehoiachin in 2 Kings 25:27–30 simply recorded the last fact about the line of David available to Dtr. In ending his account with this note Dtr did not intend (as some before Noth had argued) to hold open the hope of restoration, but to mark a full stop.

Noth found the DH's silence about Israel's possible restoration striking, particularly compared with prophetic texts from the same period (Isa. 40—55; Ezek. 36—37). The DH was thus somewhat distinct from other strands of contemporary Israelite thought represented in the Old Testament. Noth argued that it was best seen as the work of a single man who had been moved to investigate Israel's history after having witnessed the Babylonian exile. It did not represent any official or necessarily widely held viewpoint.

NOTH'S CASE IN OUTLINE

- A single, mid-sixth-century DH encompassed most our of present Deuteronomy–Kings.
- This DH was the work of one man, Dtr.
- Dtr brought together a variety of traditions into a single account, treating these traditions on the whole with respect.
- The key idea of the DH: Israel's decline was the result of their continuing disobedience to YHWH.
- Dtr expressed no hopes concerning Israel's future.

For a clear statement of Noth's views regarding pre-existing traditions available to Dtr, Dtr's editorial work and later additions to the DH, see Campbell 1994, pp. 58–62.

SCHOLARSHIP AFTER NOTH

These last points were quickly picked up by other scholars. Was Noth's view of Dtr's aims plausible? Would one write a comprehensive history of Israel simply to reach the conclusion that this history was now over? Wolff argued persuasively that the different stages of Israel's history as described by Joshua–Kings followed a common pattern: the Israelites sinned and fell under judgment, but were restored when they repented and cried out to YHWH. Repentance and returning to YHWH are key ideas in Deuteronomy–Kings (Judg. 2:16–18; 1 Sam. 7; 12:19; 2 Kgs 17:13; 23:35). Viewed in this light, the DH is best seen as a call to repentance: the southern kingdom may have gone into exile, but the appropriate response is to plead with YHWH to restore Israel's fortunes. Dtr has no such act of restoration to report, and so his history ends somewhat ambiguously with the note about Jehoiachin; but, in the light of Israel's previous history, the ending of the DH leaves open the possibility of restoration in future.

Arguments along these lines suggested a theological interpretation of Deuteronomy–Kings different from Noth's, and also tended to narrow the gap Noth had perceived between these books and other parts of the Old Testament. However, they left most parts of Noth's case untouched. Thus Wolff, for all that he interpreted the DH differently from Noth, accepted that it was the work of a single, sixth-century Dtr. Later scholarship, however, subjected Noth's theory to a more radical critique, partly confirming but also partly modifying his original proposal. In his discussion of this later scholarship Campbell uses a helpful analogy: Noth built a 'house' – set out his theory of a single, exilic DH – and later scholars, depending on their responses to this theory, may be divided into 'restorers', 'rebuilders' and 'redecorators' of 'the house that Noth built'. The following summary of these scholars' work is largely based on Campbell's presentation.

Restorers

'Restorers' scrape away layers of wallpaper and plaster in order to reveal original stonework and beams, or dig into the foundations to discover the remains of earlier buildings. In a similar way, the response of some scholars to Noth's theory was to recover earlier stages in the DH, pre-existing literary units used by Dtr. Noth himself had accepted the existence of such units. The work of the 'restorers' was merely to identify them more accurately than they believed Noth had done. Thus, where Noth had briefly mentioned the possibility that some of the deliverer stories in Judges 3—8 had been collected together before Dtr came to use them, Richter (1964, 1966) provided detailed support for a very similar view, arguing that traditions relating to Ehud,

Deborah/Barak, Gideon and Abimelech had been formed into a single collection during the period of the northern kingdom, two centuries or more before Dtr (see Ch. 4, 'Literary-critical issues'). And where Noth had not paid much attention to the narratives relating to prophets in 1 and 2 Samuel, McCarter (1980, 1984) argued that this material had earlier belonged to a history of the beginnings of the monarchy written from a prophetic perspective; and Campbell himself linked the prophetic material in Samuel with that in 1 and 2 Kings, arguing that a pre-Deuteronomistic 'Prophetic Record' formed the basis of much of 1 Samuel 1—2 Kings 10 (see Ch. 5, 'Literary-critical issues').

Such investigations were perfectly compatible with Noth's view of a single, post-exilic Dtr. They were not trying to address the question whether there was more than one Dtr. This question, however, was a major focus of the next two groups of scholars.

Rebuilders

'Rebuilders' denotes those scholars who held that Noth's theory needed extensive restructuring to be tenable. Chief among them was the American scholar Cross. In an essay published in 1973 he argued (following Wolff and others) that Noth had not convincingly accounted for the purpose of the DH. But he also questioned Wolff's view that the work could be explained as an appeal to sixth-century exiles to return to YHWH. Cross suggested that Joshua–Kings had undergone two stages of Deuteronomistic editing, the first and much more extensive stage dating to the reign of Josiah (late seventh century), the second dating to the exilic period. He called these two editions Dtr1 and Dtr2.

Cross focused on two themes in Kings which, when taken together, provided the key to identifying the scope and intent of Dtr1: the sin of Jeroboam, responsible for the downfall of the northern kingdom (1 Kgs 13:34; 2 Kgs 17:20–23); and the preservation of the southern kingdom because of YHWH's promise to David (1 Kgs 11:36; 15:4; 2 Kgs 8:19; 19:34; 20:6). This second set of texts, of course, is linked to 2 Samuel 7, a chapter which Cross believed was a Deuteronomistic editorial composition on a par with passages such as Joshua 23 and 1 Samuel 12. Dtr1 presented Jeroboam and David as opposites, the one an apostate whose sin doomed the North, the other a servant of YHWH whose faithfulness secured the survival of the South. These two themes came to their head in the account of Josiah, David's faithful descendant, who restored the Jerusalem temple, recommitted his people to keep the law, and recaptured many of the territories of the former northern kingdom, raising hopes of a revived Davidic kingdom.

Cross argued that the aim of the first edition (Dtr1) was to glorify Josiah: the account of Josiah's reign was designed as the resounding finale to the entire Dtr1. Dtr1 did indeed summon its readers to return to YHWH, but it was a call to seventh-century Judeans to commit themselves to Josiah's reforms, not a call to sixth-century exiles to seek YHWH.

Cross thus saw the events of Josiah's reign as a key to understanding Deuteronomy–Kings. The present form of Deuteronomy–Kings is basically that of the Josianic edition of these books (Dtr1). The contributions made by the second, exilic editor were relatively slight: a final section continuing Judah's history down to the Babylonian exile

(2 Kgs 23:26—25:30); and additions explaining why not even Josiah had been able to prevent the exile (2 Kgs 21:2–15; 23:26–27). Some other passages outside Kings were also assigned to Dtr2: texts in Deuteronomy which promised restoration after exile (Deut. 4:27–31; 30:1–10); and a series of minor additions which either speak of the destruction of the nation and its exile (Deut. 28:26–37, 63–68; 29:27; Josh. 23:11–13, 15–16; 1 Sam. 12:25; 1 Kgs 8:46–53; 9:7–9; 2 Kgs 17:19; 20:17–18) or seem to make the promise to David conditional upon the obedience of David's descendants (1 Kgs 2:4; 6:11–13; 8:25b; 9:4–6). Cross advanced no detailed arguments regarding these additions, but he seems to have felt that they more naturally belonged to the exilic Dtr2 than to the 'upbeat', pre-exilic Dtr1.

Dtr2's additions were intended to turn the DH into an exilic call to repentance: that is, Cross' second editor had aims similar to those which Wolff (modifying Noth at this point) had attributed to his single, exilic Dtr. Cross' approach explained why it was so hard to identify the DH's theme and purpose: the DH actually reflected the conflicting aims of two separate editors, the second superimposed on the first. This was why the ending of the work seemed so ambiguous, and why other contradictory perspectives could be perceived within Joshua–Kings, for instance regarding whether the promise to David was conditional or unconditional.

Cross did not provide much detailed literary analysis in support of his views, but this was supplied by later scholars who accepted his position: for example, Nelson (1981), who identified a number of passages which, on the basis of literary and linguistic arguments, seemed to belong to a secondary

Deuteronomistic layer (Josh. 24:1–28; Judg. 1; 2:1–5; 6:7–10; 1 Kgs 8:44–51; 9:6–9; 2 Kgs 17:7–20, 23b–40; 21:1–18; 22:15–20; 23:31–25:30). These passages stand out because of their pessimism about the people's ability to obey YHWH; some of them also seem to presuppose the fact of exile, or speak of it as inevitable. In support of the view that 2 Kings 23:31—25:30 was the work of a second, exilic editor Nelson cited the uniformity of the regnal formulae in the accounts of Judah's last four kings (those who came after Josiah) compared to the relative flexibility in the formulae before Josiah (see Ch. 6, 'Literary-critical issues').

THE 'CROSS SCHOOL'

- There were two editions of the DH, Dtr1 (Josianic) and Dtr2 (exilic), to be distinguished by their different perspectives on key theological issues.
- Dtr1 was essentially optimistic in tone, focusing on YHWH's continuing faithfulness to the southern kingdom, and on Josiah as the restorer of the fortunes of David's line.
- Dtr2 was written to update Dtr1, to explain why Josiah had not effected a permanent change, and to call the exiles to repentance.
- Relatively few passages belong to Dtr2: the shape of Deuteronomy–Kings is essentially that of the first edition, Dtr1.

Nelson also developed the distinction between Dtr1 and Dtr2 in relation to a number of key themes: the promise to David; the ark; the land; heroes and villains; the northern kingdom. Dtr1 treats all these themes in a distinctive way; Dtr2 is either silent about them or takes a different viewpoint from Dtr1. Thus whereas Dtr1's account contains a number of heroes all of whom, especially Joshua, are depicted in a way which makes them prefigure the achievements of Josiah, there are no heroes in Dtr2's work. Cross' thesis as developed by scholars such as Nelson has come to be known as the 'Cross school'.

Redecorators

Campbell describes the third category of post-Noth scholars as 'redecorators'. Unlike Cross and those who followed him, this group accepted most aspects of Noth's thesis but aimed to give it a 'new look', restating Noth's position to address weaknesses which had since become apparent. They agreed with Noth that the DH was exilic in date, but argued that more than one level of Deuteronomistic editing could be detected in it.

The German scholar Smend, in an article published in 1971, produced a detailed literary-critical study of a series of passages in Joshua and Judges which Noth had treated as secondary additions to his DH (Josh. 1:7–9; 13:1b–6; 24; Judg. 2:17, 20–21, 23). Smend accepted that these passages were secondary to their present contexts, but he pointed to linguistic and theological links between them which suggested that they were the work of a second Deuteronomistic editor. He also attributed Joshua 23 to this second editor, seeing Joshua 24 as the first editor's conclusion to the book. The first editor (whom Smend termed DtrH) had presented the period covered in Joshua as a time of obedience which resulted in the complete conquest of Canaan, and the period covered in Judges as a time of disobedience which brought down YHWH's judgment in the form of enemy invasion. In contrast, the second Deuteronomistic editor presented the conquest of Canaan as incomplete when Joshua died, and contingent upon the people's continued faithfulness, specifically upon their keeping the law of Moses (Josh.

1:7–9; 23:6–8). In this editor's view it was the people's law-breaking after Joshua's death that led to YHWH's decision not to drive out the remaining Canaanites within Israel (Judg. 2:20–21).

Smend gave this second editor the siglum DtrN (N for 'nomistic' = 'concerned with legal observance') because of his focus on law-keeping. DtrN in his view was also responsible for the inclusion of the material in Judges 1:1—2:9, much of it a previously existing text which he found congenial because it described the conquest of Canaan as only partially successful. Judges 1:1—2:5 was another passage which Noth had treated as a secondary addition.

Smend believed that DtrN had also made additions in Deuteronomy, Samuel and Kings, and ended by noting the need for further study which might confirm this suggestion. This was provided by Dietrich's work on the theme of prophecy in Kings (1972) and by Veijola's studies of kingship in Samuel (1975, 1977). These scholars argued that three editorial hands could be detected in Judges–Kings: DtrG, responsible for the first edition of the DH, corresponding to Smend's DtrH (G for 'Grundschrift' = 'base text'); DtrP, an editor who introduced a focus on prophets and the fulfilment of the prophetic word (P for 'prophetic'); and DtrN, who, as Smend had suggested, focused on the theme of law-keeping. DtrG was to be dated after 586, DtrP between 580 and 560, DtrN around 560.

This position has come to be known as the 'Smend school'. An example of how these scholars identified different editorial hands is Veijola's work on Judges and Samuel. Veijola argued that the three editors each took a different view of the Israelite monarchy: DtrG was favourable towards it; DtrP was qualified in his evaluation, applying the criterion of obedience towards the prophetic word; DtrN was openly critical, basing his assessment on the failure of most kings to observe the laws regarding worship. Veijola's work was also notable for the fact that he detected Deuteronomistic editing in Judges 17—21, which Noth had excluded from his DH. The panel 'The Smend school' gives further details of which texts this approach assigned to DtrP and DtrN.

THE 'SMEND SCHOOL'

- The DH was exilic with three layers of editing, identified as DtrG/H (to be dated after 586), DtrP (580–560), DtrN (c. 560).
- DtrP's additions focused on prophecy. They included: 1 Samuel 3:11–14 (Samuel's prophecy against Eli's house); 15:1—16:13 (Samuel's rejection of Saul and anointing of David, a somewhat tentative attribution); parts of 2 Samuel 12:7–14 (Nathan's prophecy); 1 Kings 11:29–31 (prophecy by Ahijah); 12:15 (its fulfilment); 14:7–11 (further prophecy by Ahijah); 15:29 (its fulfilment); and other similar texts in 1 Samuel—2 Kings.
- DtrP also incorporated pre-existing prophetic traditions into the DH (e.g. 1 Kgs 20; 22; 2 Kgs 18:17—20:19).
- DtrN's additions focused on law-keeping. They included 1 Samuel 8:6–22a and 12:1–25 (Samuel's warnings regarding kings); 1 Samuel 13:13–14 (Samuel rebukes Saul); 2 Samuel 7:1b, 6, 11a, 22–24 (texts whose theme is the king's role in the fulfilment of YHWH's purposes); 1 Kings 9:1–9 (YHWH's warning to Solomon); 1 Kings 11:32, 34b, 36, 38; 2 Kings 8:19; 13:4–6, 23; 14:26–27; 15:12 (texts which explain the limitation or postponement of judgment in spite of law-breaking); 2 Kings 17:12–19; 21:7b–9; 23:26–27; 24:3–4 (texts describing judgment on Israel because of law-breaking).

(For more details, see Campbell 1994, pp. 48–50.)

The panel 'Editorial layers in 1 Kings 11:29–38' illustrates how this approach works out when applied to a single text.

Digging deeper:
EDITORIAL LAYERS IN 1 KINGS 11:29–38

Dietrich's analysis of 1 Kings 11:29–38 attributes all these verses to either DtrP or DtrN, with the exception of the last words of v. 38 ('and I will give Israel to you'), as follows:

DtrP: vv. 29–31, 33a (up to 'Ammonites'), 34a (up to 'from him'), 35a (up to 'to you'), 37b (from 'and you shall reign')

DtrN: vv. 32, 33b (from 'and has not walked'), 34b (from 'but will make him'), 35b ('that is, the ten tribes'), 36, 37a ('I will take you'), 38 (apart from the very end)

Write out the text according to this division, in a way that makes the distinction between DtrP and DtrN clear. (This is easiest if you have access to an electronic biblical text on a computer.) What is to be said for and against Dietrich's approach? You can compare the analysis of these verses in Campbell and O'Brien, pp. 369–70.

LATER DEVELOPMENTS

So far we have described Noth's thesis and three major approaches, dating mainly from the 1960s and 1970s, which sought to modify Noth's thesis. Scholarship has not stood still since then (see, for example, the extensive survey in Römer and de Pury). The following paragraphs offer merely the briefest summary of some more recent developments.

Combinations of viewpoints

Campbell and O'Brien (pp. 11–23) combine elements of Cross' and Smend's approach. Campbell 1994 (p. 50) argues that the

Smend school tends to place the 'pessimistic' or 'warning' elements in later redactional layers, and that this makes it more likely that the first Deuteronomistic edition was Josianic and not (as Smend and those who followed him argued) early-exilic in date. It is true that at some points the Cross school's Dtr1 and Dtr2 correspond (respectively) to the Smend school's DtrG and DtrP/DtrN.

A DH or separate books influenced by Deuteronomy?

Continental scholarship has recently asked whether it is right to speak of Joshua–Kings as parts of a single DH, given the different narrative structures and styles of these books (explicit comment by the narrator at regular intervals in Judges and Kings, but a rather different method in Joshua and Samuel). Are they not better viewed as books displaying different degrees of Deuteronomic influence, each edited separately before being placed next to each other? The point about the different styles of Joshua–Kings is obvious enough, but the question then arises how to account for the careful transitions between the four books (and between Joshua and Deuteronomy), as well as other links and allusions within Deuteronomy–Kings (see p. 208).

Newer literary perspectives on the DH

Other studies, while still in some sense working with the concept of a DH, introduce unusual perspectives into the discussion. Polzin's three studies of Deuteronomy–Samuel argue for greater literary subtlety and theological paradox within these books than is generally recognized by DH scholarship (whose approach is generally 'literary-critical' in the sense defined in Ch. 1, 'The Histories as literary texts'). The result is an unresolved tension in Polzin's work: is he really talking about a DH like that conceived of by Noth and most of his successors?

Somewhat similar to Polzin is Eslinger. Eslinger argues texts such as Joshua 1 and 23, Judges 2, 1 Samuel 12, 2 Kings 17, which played so important a part in Noth's understanding of the DH, are set in contexts which ironically undercut their authority. In Eslinger's view Dtr's theology is much less conventional than is usually thought, and Dtr's own voice is to be distinguished from the strident tones of Noth's 'key passages'. Eslinger's study subjects many of the established procedures of DH scholarship to a radical critique.

'Pan-Deuteronomism'

'Pan-Deuteronomism' denotes a tendency in scholarship to suggest that Deuteronomic influence may be detected not merely in Joshua–Kings and in other books (such as Jeremiah) where it had long been recognized, but within collections such as the Pentateuch or the Twelve Prophets or Proverbs where few of the usually accepted indicators of Deuteronomistic editing are present. But this has been countered by calls for methodological caution. Why is it that there are no agreed answers to such basic questions as who 'the Deuteronomists' might have been, and when and where they might have worked? And are not some of the criteria which scholars use to trace Deuteronomic influence within the Old Testament excessively vague? These issues are explored in the volume edited by Schearing and McKenzie. It can be argued that the term 'Pan-Deuteronomism' is itself misleading, as few of the scholars whose work is criticized in that volume actually argue for Deuteronomic influence in *all* parts of the Old Testament. But the question of criteria for such influence remains.

What is Deuteronomistic? What is the direction of influence?

Noth's thesis gave pride of place to Deuteronomy: Deuteronomy (in something close to its present form) stood at the head of the DH, and later texts within the DH, composed by Dtr, were intended to remind the reader of key elements of Deuteronomy's theology. The direction of influence was clear: Deuteronomy had influenced the presentation and interpretation of Israel's history in Joshua–Kings. Joshua–Kings were thus 'Deuteronomistic' – influenced by Deuteronomy.

Auld (1999) argues that the direction of influence was probably the opposite of what Noth supposed. The nucleus of the DH was not Deuteronomy but the text shared by Chronicles and Samuel–Kings which Auld terms the 'Book of the Two Houses'. Earlier parts of the DH (and perhaps parts of the Pentateuch) appear to have been composed under the influence of this 'Book'. In Auld's view, verbal parallels between Samuel–Kings and Deuteronomy suggest that many of the themes of Deuteronomy 1, 4 and 9–11 were drawn from the 'Book'; while (further) Deuteronomy 16—18 and 27—30 echo sections of Samuel–Kings which were added at a later stage, as Samuel–Kings started to develop around the nucleus of the 'Book'. So now it is Deuteronomy which is secondarily influenced by different stages in the growth of Samuel–Kings! Indeed, Auld suggests elsewhere, it is 'attractive to think of the royal story underlying Samuel–Kings [the material common to Chronicles and Samuel–Kings] as the root-work that supports the whole tree of Genesis–Kings' (Auld 1998, p. 67).

Auld's approach partly follows the lead of other scholars who have argued that the literary history of Deuteronomy is more complex than Noth allowed, with sections of chapters 5—30 to be assigned to secondary layers, thus in effect 'Deuteronomistic' in character (see the brief summary in Römer and de Pury, pp. 109–11). The tendency of these arguments is to undermine Deuteronomy's status as the touchstone for what is Deuteronomistic. If Auld is right, then Deuteronomy–Kings can no longer be described as a Deuteronomistic History, unless we revise the definition of the term to mean something like 'a history with Deuteronomy as its first volume', so that 'Deuteronomistic' simply reflects the shape of the finished DH and not the processes of its growth.

EVALUATION

Are you still awake? The above sections, believe it or not, simplify previous and contemporary scholarship on the DH. It is now time to draw the discussion to a close, not commenting on all the different scholars reviewed above, but drawing out some points relevant to the approach adopted in this book.

POINTS OF AGREEMENT

The interpretation of Joshua–Kings offered in Chapters 3–6 agrees with some of the observations made by the scholars surveyed above.

Deuteronomy–Kings as a literary unit

Chapter 3 noted the careful transition in Joshua 1 between the end of Deuteronomy and the beginning of Joshua. Chapters 3–6 also noted significant thematic links between Deuteronomy and Joshua–Kings, links which are often reinforced by verbal echoes (e.g. compare Josh. 1 and Deut. 31 and 34;

Judg. 20 and Deut. 13; 1 Sam. 8 and Deut. 17; 2 Sam. 7 and Deut. 12; 1 Kgs 8 and Deut. 28—29). Chapters 3–6 also identified other passages where Deuteronomic themes seem to lie behind the text: the account of Solomon's growing folly in 1 Kings 9—10; other narratives which describe violations of the law (idolatry and acts of injustice); narratives of judgment and narratives of YHWH's unexpected grace and forgiveness (this, too, is a theme of Deuteronomy: see chs 4, 9—10, 30).

Chapters 3–6 noted many similar links *within* Joshua–Kings. They drew attention to the carefully structured transitions between the beginnings and ends of each book, and to other themes which unite the books (leadership and administrative structures; the importance of hearing YHWH's word through the prophets; the role of prophets in appointing and bringing down kings; the Canaanites as a threat to Israel's faithfulness; wisdom and knowledge in the accounts of David and Solomon). They also noted allusions and narrative analogies which link different parts of Joshua–Kings: the account of the third attack on Gibeah (Judg. 20:29–48) echoes the account of the second attack on Ai (Josh. 8); many parts of 1 Samuel 1—15 seem to refer back to Judges; 1 Kings 2:27 picks up the prophecy against Eli's line in 1 Samuel 2:27–36; prophecies against royal dynasties in Kings echo the account of Saul's rejection in 1 Samuel 15; the condemnation of Israel in 2 Kings 17:1–20 echoes but goes beyond that in Judges 2:11—3:6. Our view of passages like Joshua 23, 1 Samuel 12, 1 Kings 8 and 2 Kings 17 is close to Noth's: these passages, as he argued, act as narrative signposts, reviewing previous events and pointing forward to future developments.

The implication of these observations is that Joshua–Kings together form a history of Israel from conquest to exile, in which many different types of narrative, reflecting a diversity of underlying traditions, have been combined into a single literary entity; and that the theological perspective of Deuteronomy is frequently and significantly reflected in this history.

Sixth-century perspective

A further implication of what we have been saying is that the perspective of Joshua–Kings is ultimately that of the sixth century BC, simply on the basis that 2 Kings ends its account in that century. This implies that Noth and others were right to focus on the question of the 'message' of Joshua–Kings for sixth-century Israelites.

POINTS OF DISAGREEMENT

It might seem, then, that Chapters 3—6 have been arguing for something rather like a DH as envisaged by Noth and others. However, we also differ at many points from most of the scholars whose work we have been surveying.

Dating

Joshua–Kings have been formed into a recognizable literary entity, and the latest stages of this formation process cannot predate the sixth century. But what more can be said? Did these latest stages involve extensive revision of the entire work, so that large parts of Joshua–Kings are basically the product of the sixth century, or (following Cross) the product of the seventh century with a sixth-century overlay? Or had Joshua–Samuel (at least) assumed something very close to their present form centuries previously, say by the time of Solomon?

A common approach to such questions is that biblical texts may be dated on the basis of the perspectives and concerns they seem to reflect. Scholars often argue, for example, that narratives of judgment and texts which dwell on the possibility of exile are most likely to have been composed or at least edited into their present form during the Babylonian exile. Nelson's argument that the heroes of the DH all prefigure the achievements of Josiah is basically similar in form, except that in his view the DH mainly reflects the concerns of the seventh, not the sixth, century.

Historical accounts do, of course, usually reflect the concerns of a period later than that which they are describing (cf. the definition of history writing as 'an ongoing conversation between the past and the present' in Ch. 1). However, the suggestion that narratives of apostasy, judgment and exile in Joshua–Samuel reflect Israelite thinking of the seventh or sixth centuries is much less convincing. The underlying ideas, after all, are attested in the ancient Near East throughout the second and first millennia BC. It was widely believed that a nation's gods might cause the nation to suffer military defeat, famine and plague if king or people did not honour them appropriately. And invasion, dispossession and exile were realities of life in the region long before the seventh century. This makes it rather unlikely that Israelites should not have thought about these matters until the seventh and sixth centuries. We could envisage Israelites of, say, the tenth century reflecting on events in Israel's history up to that point and producing theological accounts of these events (many ancient Near Eastern historical accounts are theological in character), perhaps with the specific aim of encouraging later generations of Israelites to reflect upon YHWH's dealings with them.

In such a scenario, Joshua–Samuel (or something close to them) might have come into existence much earlier than is often argued. Indeed, if pressed to say which parts of Joshua–Samuel positively demand to be dated to the seventh or sixth centuries, we would answer, entirely contrary to the conclusions of most scholars on this point: none; though there is no reason in principle why revisions should not have taken place then.

Joshua–Kings are often dated in relation to Deuteronomy. According to a standard view Deuteronomy in its present form is a largely seventh-century work, linked to Josiah's reforms, and Joshua–Kings, in which the thinking of Deuteronomy is a major influence, must have received their decisive shaping in the wake of (or perhaps as part of) the processes which produced Deuteronomy. This, of course, runs contrary to the testimony of Joshua–Kings, according to which something like Deuteronomy ('the Book of the Law') was current long before the seventh century (see, e.g., Josh. 1:8; 1 Kgs 2:3; 2 Kgs 18:6), and there are, and always have been, scholars who dissent from the standard view, arguing that neither the literary form nor the concerns of Deuteronomy obviously mark it out as a seventh-century work. But in any case, Auld's point about possible directions of influence between the books of the DH should be borne in mind: Deuteronomy may stand before Joshua–Kings, but that does not necessarily mean that it reached its present form (or close to it) earlier than Joshua–Kings.

We can imagine a sequence of events in which, for example, the account of Solomon in 1 Kings 9—11 reached its present form before Deuteronomy 17:14–20 (the law of the king): perhaps an earlier form of Deuteronomy 17 stated simply that the king should not acquire much wealth, and the references to 'many horses' and 'many wives' (vv. 16–17) were added by an editor who wished to 'set up' a clear contrast between Solomon's behaviour and the requirements of the law. When we read Deuteronomy and Kings in their present order, of course, we naturally read 1 Kings 9—11 as echoing Deuteronomy 17, and that is how we are meant to read it. But chronological sequence is not necessarily the same as order of composition or editing.

But what if the conventional model, in which Deuteronomy influences Joshua–Kings rather than the other way round, seems in most cases to offer a better explanation of the thematic links between particular texts? Even then, the issue is not resolved, for the arguments for seventh- or sixth-century dating are not equally strong for all parts of Deuteronomy. One could accept that some parts of Deuteronomy are most likely to have originated in these centuries (an example might be the sanctuary law of Deuteronomy 12, which is frequently linked with Josiah's religious reforms described in 2 Kings 23), without going on to conclude that all of Deuteronomy or all those parts of Joshua–Kings felt to be influenced by Deuteronomy must be dated then (or later). It is always possible to invoke putative earlier editions of Deuteronomy, or earlier collections of laws which eventually found their way into Deuteronomy and which at an earlier stage played a part in the shaping of Joshua–Kings. The testimony of Joshua–Kings, as noted above, is that an entity described as 'the law of Moses' had existed since the days of Joshua. And the theological framework of Deuteronomy

(linking faithfulness with blessing, unfaithfulness with judgment), which is what scholars often have in view when they argue that a text in Joshua–Kings reflects Deuteronomic influence, is not properly Deuteronomic at all, but a theological commonplace of the ancient Near East. Deuteronomy does not provide a fixed point for dating Joshua–Kings.

Leaving Deuteronomy on one side, if Joshua–Samuel had reached largely their present form at an earlier period, then the picture which emerges of the formation of Joshua–Kings is rather different from that usually accepted. No longer are the events of the seventh and sixth centuries decisive for the shape and tone of Joshua–Samuel. Rather (one can argue) the already formed theology of apostasy and judgment in Joshua–Samuel supplied seventh- and sixth-century Israelites with a framework for understanding the events they lived through. Similarly, when Kings attributes national decline to religious unfaithfulness and other violations of the law, it does so partly because it is following the lead of Joshua–Samuel. The earlier stages influence the later, and not the other way around: the accounts of Hezekiah and Josiah remind us of Joshua son of Nun because the writer of Kings wishes us to see similarities between these two righteous kings and a great leader from an earlier period, not because the figure of Joshua is a cipher for Hezekiah or Josiah.

Finally, we should not assume that even Kings received its decisive shaping in the seventh and sixth centuries, though parts of Kings clearly cannot be dated earlier than that. Quite possibly Kings grew by stages, with successive revisions in which the earlier parts influenced the shape and tone of the later parts. Royal annals tend to be written in this way, and Kings claims to be partly based on, or at least familiar with, royal annals.

(For further details on some of the points in this section, see Kitchen, pp. 299–307; McConville 1984 and in *DOTP*; Wenham, *EOT I*; Provan 1997, pp. 72–81.)

Detecting of Deuteronomistic redaction; Deuteronomistic theology

Most scholars who have worked on the DH hold that it is relatively easy to distinguish between underlying traditions and Deuteronomistic redactional layers in Joshua–Kings: basically, Deuteronomistic redaction is to be found in those parts of Joshua–Kings whose style, vocabulary and concepts resemble those of Deuteronomy (as set out, for example, in the Appendix in Weinfeld 1972, pp. 320–65). Thus, Judges 2:6—3:6 and also the frames of the accounts of the 'major judges', seem (in contrast to other parts of Judges 2:6—16:31) to echo the many passages in Deuteronomy which warn Israelites against unfaithfulness. On these grounds they are usually seen as Deuteronomistic redactional material. Reversing the argument, Noth (p. 23) argues against the possibility of Judges 1 ever having formed part of the DH on the basis that the language and contents of this chapter nowhere echo Deuteronomy. Arguments of this sort have been standard fare in DH scholarship.

But is this approach defensible? Why assume that Deuteronomy's influence is restricted to those parts of Joshua–Kings whose language clearly echoes Deuteronomy's? Many of the items of vocabulary usually identified as Deuteronomic are terms of explicit evaluation, the kind of language a writer uses when he 'lays his cards on the table'.

Thus it is noticeable that Kings echoes Deuteronomy most clearly at climaxes in the narrative where the writer wishes to be unambiguous in his evaluations, whether positive or negative: for example, the description of Solomon's sins (1 Kgs 11), the description of Manasseh's sins (2 Kgs 21:1–9), and the account of Josiah's covenant renewal ceremony (2 Kgs 23:1–3). Deuteronomic language has a clear rhetorical and structural function within Kings.

But do Old Testament writers always want to express themselves unambiguously? We can imagine a scenario in which a writer influenced by Deuteronomy deliberately adopted a 'neutral' style in a particular section of his work, withholding explicit evaluation until it would have greater impact. Such a writer might avoid obviously 'Deuteronomic' vocabulary in that section, in spite of the fact that Deuteronomy was in general an influence on his work.

This is precisely what we believe has happened in Judges 1 (Ch. 4, 'Outline'). But this, if correct, undermines Noth's justification for splitting off Judges 1 from 2:1—3:6, for the implication then is that Judges 1 is not necessarily any less 'Deuteronomic' than the rest of 1:1—3:6. The writer's aim throughout 1:1—3:6 (entirely in keeping with the spirit of Deuteronomy) is to characterize the judges period as one of growing apostasy. The fact that he sometimes avoids and sometimes uses Deuteronomic language is more a matter of literary strategy than of underlying viewpoint. Noth's focus on Deuteronomic language as a criterion of Deuteronomistic editing in Judges 1:1—3:6 may have led him to fragment a literary unity unnecessarily.

Another example is 1 Kings 2:1–9, which Alter, not a scholar normally given to such judgments, sees as a blatant example of Dtr editing. Commenting on verses 2–4 of this passage, he states that every word 'shows the fingerprints of the Deuteronomist . . . these long-winded sentences loaded with didactically insistent synonyms are nothing like the sentences spoken by characters in the David story' (p. xiii). These verses were inserted, Alter argues, because Dtr was unhappy with the tone of David's last words in vv. 5–9, and wished to put into David's mouth some more conventionally pious 'last words'.

But this proposal involves a rather crass piece of editing on Dtr's part. Could Dtr not have omitted or at least toned down vv. 5–9? Was it not clear to him that inserting vv. 2–4 while leaving vv. 5–9 unchanged exacerbated the problem rather than solving it? The proposal also ignores the possibility that the clash between the first and second parts of David's words is deliberate. What if the writer (influenced by Deuteronomy) wished to bring out the grating contrast between David's brutal instructions and the standards of the law of Moses, and did so by having David on his deathbed give Solomon what are basically two contradictory pieces of advice? Then again the distinction between base text (2:1, 5–9) and Deuteronomistic redaction (2:2–4) collapses, and 2:1–9 becomes a single text with a unified perspective.

Other cases where we disagree with the kind of redactional analysis regularly practised in DH scholarship are the frames in Judges 3:7—16:31 and the regnal formulae in Kings. In each of these cases we suggest that the formulaic material is better integrated with its context (and actually less formulaic) than usually held, again calling in question the conventional distinction between base text and redactional insertion. In general we find the kinds of literary analysis regularly practised in DH scholarship problematic.

To argue in this way is, of course, to attack a main pillar of the entire approach. Weinfeld, for example, stated that 'style is the only objective criterion for determining whether a biblical passage is Deuteronomic or not' (1972, p. vii): the fact that he included the lengthy Appendix (pp. 320–65) shows how important he considered this issue. More recently Person has argued that 'the methods of source and redaction criticism necessarily depend upon linguistic criteria. Therefore, unless we are willing to abandon source criticism and redaction criticism altogether, we must have some basic understanding of what Deuteronomic language is' (p. 21).

But surely such an approach at best isolates the minimum body of text in Joshua–Kings which reflects the influence of Deuteronomy? It does not necessarily reveal the full extent of that influence. It may be that many studies of redaction in the DH, because they have focused too exclusively on the explicitly evaluative sections of Joshua–Kings (which do indeed often have affinities with the language and thought of Deuteronomy), have not considered the possibility that Deuteronomic influence in these books may be much more pervasive than usually accepted, and that this has led to a faulty literary analysis of many passages within these books. That Joshua–Kings are in some sense 'Deuteronomic' seems clear enough: but it is less clear that those parts of Joshua–Kings which are usually identified as Deuteronomistic redactional material can be as easily detached from their contexts as is often argued or assumed.

This means that our view of Deuteronomic/ Deuteronomistic theology may also need to be revised. Eslinger sums up the message of the theologically explicit sections of Joshua–Kings (where most scholars believe Deuteronomistic editing is primarily to be found) as follows (p. 228): 'Israel has sinned. See, here is the evidence. Sin upon sin upon sin. And so, God has punished Israel. Rightly so and good riddance to the wicked. Sinners, repent!' This message he rightly describes as trite. But if our picture of Deuteronomistic theology must include not merely the explicitly evaluative parts of Joshua–Kings, but also the sections dominated by implicit commentary, if the theology of Joshua–Kings, indeed, emerges in the *interplay* between these two types of material, then the picture becomes more complex.

It is true that the many passages which contain clear echoes of Deuteronomy in Joshua–Kings tend to reinforce in our minds a rather simplistic-seeming schema (faithfulness brings blessing, unfaithfulness judgment). But the narratives, particularly in Judges–Kings, do not always conform to that schema; on the contrary, there are many unforeseen twists in Israel's history, and they almost all relate to unexpected displays of divine grace. The Israelites in the period of the judges repeatedly turn away from YHWH (as the narrative frames emphasize), but YHWH does not cast them off, in spite of what Joshua 23 stated. The kings of the northern kingdom all persist in the false worship instituted by Jeroboam I (as their regnal formulae uniformly state), and yet the northern kingdom continues to survive beyond all reasonable expectation. In these cases the use of explicit, 'Deuteronomic' formulae to enclose sections of narrative draws attention to the fact that the expected judgment often does not fall: the schema is invoked only to be thwarted, and it becomes clear that YHWH's dealings with Israel cannot be entirely captured by the formula: faithfulness → blessing, unfaithfulness → judgment. For further comments on this topic with particular reference to Kings, see Provan 1997, pp. 93–7.

Separation of different Deuteronomistic redactional layers

The previous section has questioned the criteria by which Deuteronomistic redactional material in Joshua–Kings is usually identified. We are equally uneasy about the criteria regularly used to distinguish different redactional layers (as in the approaches which have argued that there was more than one Dtr). It is not necessary to go into detail here, as Chs 3–6 have already addressed most of the relevant topics: the debate as to whether two views of the Israelite conquest are found in Joshua and Judges; the frequent characterization of different texts in 1 Samuel as 'pro-' or 'anti-monarchic'; the claim that the promise to David is variously presented as conditional or unconditional; the viewpoint of the last chapters of 2 Kings compared to what has gone before.

In general, arguments for multiple redaction centre around the question of the 'polarity' of particular texts: assigning a passage to a redactional layer depends on showing that it is 'positive' or 'negative' in relation to key theological criteria (as in Cross' and Nelson's distinction between optimistic- and pessimistic-seeming layers in Joshua–Kings, or as in the arguments of the 'Smend school' that DtrG, DtrP and DtrN each viewed the Israelite monarchy differently). But making such judgments is not necessarily straightforward. 'Pseudo-objective' narrative such as we have argued is present in Judges 1 and 1 Kings 9—10 is one case in point, a narrative style whose purpose is deliberately to *avoid* taking an overtly positive or negative stance. And even in the case of passages whose 'polarity' seems unambiguous, consideration of the wider context may complicate the issue: 2 Samuel 7, often said to present YHWH's promise to David as entirely unconditional, comes after a narrative (2 Sam. 6) which emphasizes the need for David to be humble and obedient, and which thereby strongly hints at conditionality; the allegedly 'conditional' version of the promise given in 1 Kings 2:1–4 is, by contrast, set in a context which emphasizes YHWH's grace, and David's and Solomon's failure to conduct themselves righteously, which implies that conditionality will not have the last word.

To this we must add McConville's point, made in connection with Kings, that the allocation of apparently contradictory viewpoints to different editorial layers is in danger of ignoring the ironies within the narrative (McConville 1993, pp. 85–90). The narrator's portrayal of kings like Hezekiah and Josiah is more ambivalent and subtle than is sometimes supposed, and the way to handle this fact is not to dissolve the ironies by dividing the text up. This point can be extended to other parts of Joshua–Kings, for example the narratives of David and Solomon, which are yet more complex and ambiguous than those of the later kings.

Other considerations come into play. Dietrich (pp. 171–5) has questioned the tendency of the 'Cross school' to link optimistic passages with the period of Josiah and pessimistic passages with the period after 586 (he has in mind particularly passages such as 2 Kings 8:19; 19:34; 20:6):

even after 586 some in Israel may have continued to entertain the hope that YHWH would continue to show mercy to his people. But equally, the view of the Smend school that Joshua–Kings were shaped by one Deuteronomistic editor (DtrG) and then passed through two Deuteronomistic revisions (DtrP, DtrN), all within the space of no more than 30 years, seems intrinsically unlikely (so McConville, 1993, pp. 83–5). McConville notes that the Smend school does not offer a convincing analysis of the account of Josiah: can it be right to attribute to the (exilic) DtrG a form of the Josiah narrative wholly unclouded by notes of warning and coming judgment? That is what is implied by the allocation of 22:16–20 and 23:26–27 to DtrP and DtrN. But 'any exilic portrayal of Josiah that did not try to account for the events that followed his death would be nonsensical' (McConville 1993, p. 85).

Campbell states clearly what is at stake in this discussion (1994, p. 52, fn. 1):

> The issue is why these finely nuanced differences of expression are distributed across the text with a remarkable and determined regularity. They are not random variations. There is a patterned regularity, and it is this that needs explanation – whether it is from one author or several.

That is, verbal links can be observed between different parts of Deuteronomy–Kings, and different texts seemed to be linked by different sets of key words. The three passages in Judges in which YHWH confronts Israel (2:1–5; 6:7–10; 10:6–16) are linked by form, content, tone and vocabulary in a way which distinguishes them from (say) the narrator's survey of the period at 2:6—3:6. This is clearly not accidental: the same applies to other such cases in Deuteronomy–Kings.

The question then becomes how to explain this 'patterned regularity'. Our tendency is to prefer explanations involving a single author: Joshua 1:7–9 and 13:1b–6 are to be linked to each other (as Smend argued), and do play a part in the structure of Joshua, but they are not secondary to their present contexts; the three confrontation passages in Judges are a distinct element within the book, but they have an intelligible function within Judges' narrative economy and do not have to be seen as a distinct redactional layer. Further comments along these lines may be found in the 'Critical issues' sections of Chapters 3–6.

Why only Deuteronomy?

Deuteronomy, in some shape or form, was a major influence in the formation of Joshua–Kings. This is hardly surprising: of all the books of the Pentateuch, Deuteronomy is the one that most explicitly anticipates Israel's life in the land. In both the MT and the LXX canon Deuteronomy functions as a hinge between the Pentateuch and Joshua–Kings, and it is plausible that Deuteronomy's present position and function reflect the role that the book (or an earlier form of it) had already come to assume at earlier stages in the formation of Genesis–Kings. Under these circumstances it was natural that Deuteronomy should cast a long shadow over Joshua–Kings' account of Israel's life in the land.

But is Deuteronomy the only influence? We have noted significant echoes of Genesis–Numbers (particularly Genesis and Exodus) in Joshua–Kings (see, for example the comments in the 'Outline' sections on Joshua 2, 5 and 7, Judges 6, 1 Samuel 4—6, 2 Samuel 7, 1 Kings 8 and 1 Kings 12). Focusing on Deuteronomy may have led some scholars to neglect links with the rest of the Pentateuch. It may also have led to a neglect of themes which do not feature prominently in Deuteronomy but which are significant within parts of Joshua–Kings. Examples are the 'proto-messianism' of Samuel–Kings and the theme of true versus false wisdom in the accounts of David and Solomon in 2 Samuel and 1 Kings (see Provan 1999). Wherever the roots of these themes are to be found, it is probably not Deuteronomy. Part of the problem may be that scholars tend not to pay attention to thematic links within Joshua–Kings if the themes in question have not first been identified as Deuteronomic.

FINAL COMMENTS

This chapter has questioned some of the leading tenets of a broad and well-established consensus in the study of Joshua–Kings: the dating of Deuteronomy and the DH; the criteria for discerning Deuteronomistic editing (whether a single layer or multiple redactional layers); the tendency to focus on Deuteronomic influence in Joshua–Kings to the exclusion of other possible influences. It has also sketched an alternative approach to the question of Deuteronomic editing, partly taking up comments made in Chapters 1 and 3–6. Because of space this chapter cannot be a full-dress presentation of our approach, though it should be clear from this and earlier chapters how we might attempt to argue our case in a longer presentation.

This chapter has illustrated the point made in Chapter 1 about the tendency of 'historical-critical' and 'narrative-critical' approaches to interpret the same data in very different ways. DH scholarship has been and remains almost without exception historical-critical in orientation. Given the general tendency of narrative-critical approaches to see complex unity and a single author where historical-critical approaches see conflicting perspectives, literary awkwardness and more than one author, it is perhaps not surprising that we have ended up questioning the viability of the whole DH enterprise.

The points in favour of our position are not necessarily stronger than those underlying the consensus position: all that we claim is that they are no weaker. But these are not matters on which certainty is possible. As regards the dating of Joshua–Kings in particular, almost all the arguments are indirect (once one gets beyond obvious points such as that accounts cannot be dated earlier than the events they describe), and most of them not terribly compelling.

What, then, can be said about the formation of Joshua–Kings, and about Deuteronomy's influence upon them? Perhaps little more than the following: 'I am persuaded . . . that the books of the OT generally grew gradually into their present form in dialogue with each other, each shaping the developing tradition and being shaped by it' (Provan 1995, p. 4): note the absence in this quotation of hard dates or even definite statements as to directions of influence between particular Old Testament books!

So, extending Campbell's metaphor in a direction he might not welcome, we are perhaps best described as demolition men, or as surveyors questioning whether the foundations of 'Noth's house' were ever sound in the first place. This does not, of course, mean that we think that all the scholarship that has gone into restoring, restructuring and redecorating that house

can be discounted. On the contrary, the works we have surveyed contain much useful reflection on the literary structure and theological implications of Deuteronomy–Kings, and we encourage you to read some of them for yourself. In particular, you may find Campbell and O'Brien's lucid, widely researched and passionate presentation of their version of 'DH Orthodoxy' a good counter-balance to the more sceptical approach offered in this chapter.

FURTHER READING

Surveys of scholarship on the DH are provided by McKenzie's *ABD* article, and by Campbell's 1994 essay. The survey of Römer and de Pury (2000) is also helpful, but longer and more technical.

Attention should also be drawn to four useful collections of essays: Knoppers and McConville (2000); McKenzie and Graham (1994); Schearing and McKenzie (1999); de Pury, Römer and Macchi (2000).

R. Alter, *The David Story*. New York: Norton, 1999.

A.G. Auld, 'The Former Prophets' in S.L. McKenzie and M.P. Graham (eds), *The Hebrew Bible Today. An Introduction to Critical Issues*. Louisville: Westminster John Knox, 1998.

A.G. Auld, 'The Deuteronomists and the Former Prophets or What Makes the Former Prophets Deuteronomistic?' in L.S. Schearing and S.L. McKenzie (eds), *Those Elusive Deuteronomists. The Phenomenon of Pan-Deuteronomism*. Sheffield: Sheffield Academic Press, 1999, pp. 116–26.

A.F. Campbell, *Of Prophets and Kings: A Late Ninth-Century Document (1 Samuel 1–2 Kings 10)*. Washington: Catholic Biblical Association of America, 1986.

A.F. Campbell, 'Martin Noth and the Deuteronomistic History', in S.L. McKenzie and M.P. Graham (eds) *The History of Israel's Traditions. The Heritage of Martin Noth*. Sheffield: Sheffield Academic Press, 1994, pp. 31–62.

A.F. Campbell and M.A. O'Brien, *Unfolding the Deuteronomistic History. Origins, Upgrades, Present Text*. Minneapolis: Fortress Augsburg, 2000.

R.E. Clements, *Deuteronomy*. Sheffield: Sheffield Academic Press, 1989.

F.M. Cross, 'The Themes of the Book of Kings and the Structure of the Deuteronomistic History' in *Canaanite Myth and Hebrew Epic: Essays in the History of the Religion of Israel*. Cambridge: Harvard University Press, 1973, pp. 274–89 (reprinted in G.N. Knoppers and J.G. McConville, *Reconsidering Israel and Judah. Recent Studies on the Deuteronomistic History*. Winona Lake: Eisenbrauns, 2000, pp. 79–94).

W. Dietrich, *Prophetie und Geschichte. Eine redaktionsgeschichtliche Untersuchung zum deuteronomistischen Geschichtswerk*. Göttingen: Vandenhoeck and Ruprecht, 1972.

W. Dietrich, 'Martin Noth and the Future of the Deuteronomistic History', in S.L. McKenzie and M.P. Graham (eds), *The History of Israel's Traditions. The Heritage of Martin Noth*, Sheffield: Sheffield Academic Press, 1994, pp. 153–75.

L. Eslinger, *Into the Hands of the Living God*. Sheffield: Almond Press, 1989.

K.A. Kitchen, *On the Reliability of the Old Testament*. Grand Rapids: Eerdmans, 2003.

G.N. Knoppers, 'Introduction', in G.N. Knoppers and J.G. McConville (eds), *Reconsidering Israel and Judah. Recent Studies on the Deuteronomistic History*. Winona Lake: Eisenbrauns, 2000, pp. 1–18.

G.N. Knoppers and J.G. McConville (eds) *Reconsidering Israel and Judah. Recent Studies on the Deuteronomistic History*. Winona Lake: Eisenbrauns, 2000.

P.K. McCarter, *1 Samuel*. Garden City: Doubleday, 1980.

P.K. McCarter, *2 Samuel*. Garden City: Doubleday, 1984.

J.G. McConville, *Law and Theology in Deuteronomy*. Sheffield: JSOT Press, 1984.

J.G. McConville, *Grace in the End. A Study in Deuteronomic Theology*. Carlisle: Paternoster, 1993.

J.G. McConville 'Deuteronomy, Book of', *DOTP*, pp. 182–93.

S.L. McKenzie, 'Deuteronomistic History', *ABD* II, pp. 160–8.

S.L. McKenzie and M.P. Graham (eds), *The History of Israel's Traditions. The Heritage of Martin Noth*. Sheffield: Sheffield Academic Press, 1994.

R.D. Nelson, *The Double Redaction of the Deuteronomistic History*. Sheffield: JSOT Press, 1981.

M. Noth, *The Deuteronomistic History*, 2nd edition. Sheffield: JSOT Press, 1991 (English translation of German original dated 1943).

R.F. Person, *The Deuteronomic School. History, Social Setting, and Literature*. Atlanta: Society of Biblical Literature, 2002.

R. Polzin, *Moses and the Deuteronomist: A Literary Study of the Deuteronomic History, Part 1: Deuteronomy, Joshua, Judges*. New York: Seabury, 1980.

R. Polzin, *Samuel and the Deuteronomist: A Literary Study of the Deuteronomic History, Part 2: 1 Samuel*. Bloomington: Indiana University Press, 1989.

R. Polzin, *David and the Deuteronomist: A Literary Study of the Deuteronomic History, Part 3: 2 Samuel*. Bloomington: Indiana University Press, 1993.

I.W. Provan, *1 and 2 Kings*. Peabody/Carlisle: Hendrickson/Paternoster, 1995.

I.W. Provan, *1 and 2 Kings*. Sheffield: Sheffield Academic Press, 1997.

I.W. Provan, 'On "Seeing" the Trees while Missing the Forest: The Wisdom of

Characters and Readers in 2 Samuel and 1 Kings' in E. Ball (ed.), *In Search of True Wisdom. Essays in Old Testament Interpretation in Honour of Ronald E. Clements*. Sheffield: Sheffield Academic Press, 1999, pp. 153–73.

A. de Pury, T. Römer and J.-D. Macchi (eds), *Israel Constructs Its History. Deuteronomistic Historiography in Recent Research*. Sheffield: Sheffield Academic Press, 2000.

W. Richter, *Die Bearbeitungen des 'Retterbuches' in der deuteronomischen Epoche*. Bonn: Peter Hanstein, 1964.

W. Richter, *Traditionsgeschichtliche Untersuchungen sum Richterbuch*. Bonn: Peter Hanstein, 1966.

T. Römer and A. de Pury, 'Deuteronomistic Historiography (DH): History of Research and Debated Issues' in A. de Pury, T. Römer and J.-D. Macchi (eds), *Israel Constructs Its History. Deuteronomistic Historiography in Recent Research*. Sheffield: Sheffield Academic Press, 2000, pp. 24–141.

L.S. Schearing and S.L. McKenzie (eds), *Those Elusive Deuteronomists. The Phenomenon of Pan-Deuteronomism*. Sheffield: Sheffield Academic Press, 1999.

R. Smend, 'The Law and the Nations. A Contribution to Deuteronomistic Tradition History' in G.N. Knoppers and J.G. McConville (eds.), *Reconsidering Israel and Judah. Recent Studies on the Deuteronomistic History*. Winona Lake: Eisenbrauns, 2000, pp. 95–110 (English translation of German original dated 1971).

T. Veijola, *Die ewige Dynastie: David und die Entstehung seiner Dynastie nach der deuteronomistischen Darstellung*. Helsinki: Suomalainen Tiedeakatemia, 1975.

T. Veijola, *Das Königtum in der Beurteilung der deuteronomistischen Historiographie: Eine redaktionsgeschichtliche Untersuchung*. Helsinki: Suomalainen Tiedeakatemia, 1977.

M. Weinfeld, *Deuteronomy and the Deuteronomic School*. Oxford: Oxford University Press, 1972.

M. Weinfeld, 'Deuteronomy', *ABD* II, pp. 168–83.

H.W. Wolff, 'The Kerygma of the Deuteronomistic Historical Work' in G.N. Knoppers and J. G. McConville, *Reconsidering Israel and Judah. Recent Studies on the Deuteronomistic History*. Winona Lake: Eisenbrauns, 2000, pp. 62–78 (English translation of German original dated 1961).

Chapter 8

RUTH

INTRODUCTION

The book of Ruth is a short narrative gem. It tells of the family of Elimelech, driven from their home in Bethlehem by famine to make their lives in the land of Moab. The sons of Elimelech and Naomi, Mahlon and Chilion, take Moabite wives, Ruth and Orpah. The action develops when in due course all the men die, leaving Naomi and her Moabite daughters-in-law facing the question of how to survive.

The four chapters of Ruth give a simple structure to the book. Chapter 1 tells how Elimelech's family moves to Moab and later returns to Israel. Chapter 2 relates events in the fields, where Ruth gleans with the servants of Boaz. Chapter 3 concerns Ruth's meeting with Boaz at his threshing-floor. And the action of the final chapter takes place in the city-gate of Bethlehem, where the legal issues surrounding Ruth's future are settled.

The structure can be described in more detail. Chapters 2 and 3 portray the development of the relationship between Ruth and Boaz. These middle chapters have similar threefold structures: Ruth and Naomi make a plan, Boaz shows favour to Ruth,

and Ruth and Naomi discuss what has happened (Nielsen, pp. 1–2). The outer chapters correspond because they tell of leaving home and of death and bereavement (ch. 1), and of returning home and of birth and new life (ch. 4). The shape of the whole story, therefore, is chiastic (an ABB'A' structure). This shape can be described simply in terms of the four chapters, as we have just done (where 1 and 4 correspond, and 2 and 3 also correspond). But it can also be described in a more complex way, involving a threefold division of each chapter, in which chapters 2, 3 and 4 are all chiastic in themselves (Gow). The book of Ruth has been skilfully composed.

STRUCTURE OF RUTH	
1:1–22	Famine and bereavement
2:1–23	Ruth meets Boaz
3:1–18	Naomi seeks a 'resting-place' for Ruth
4:1–22	A redeemer

OUTLINE

1:1–22: FAMINE AND BEREAVEMENT

The scene is quickly set in the days 'when the judges ruled' (1:1), when Israel lived in its tribes and clans. Bethlehem is neither more nor less important than anywhere else. With minimum comment, we are told that Elimelech and his family leave their home in Bethlehem because of famine (ironically, 'Bethlehem' means 'house of bread'). They go to the more fertile Moab. We are left to imagine most of the circumstances: why did they go and not others? Why did they go to Moab in particular? The interest is not in the famine, or the history, but in the family. By the end of v. 5, we know everything we need to know for the story to begin to unfold. In Moab, Elimelech dies, leaving Naomi a widow. Moreover, both Mahlon and Chilion die, also leaving widows, who were Moabite. The men of the family are no more. Only the three women are left, all widows, and two of them not even Israelite. What does the future hold for them?

Naomi decides to return to her homeland. Nothing is said about her life in Moab, nor is it implied that it was harsh there. We learn only that she hears that there is food again in Bethlehem. But can there be a home in Israel for her Moabite daughters-in-law? Naomi thinks it would be better for them to stay among their kin. This shows how much the means of life is bound up with family in the societies Naomi knew. It tells us she is fearful for her foreign daughters-in-law back in her homeland. So she appeals three times to Ruth to stay (1:8, 11–13, 15). The emotional quality of this exchange is intensified by the comparison between Ruth and Orpah. Orpah is grieved to leave Naomi, yet does the safer, wiser thing. But Naomi's appeals only succeed in calling forth Ruth's moving declaration of loyalty to her (1:16–18). And not only to Naomi: Ruth's decision involves a painful leaving, which brings with it a deep-seated change in who she is and where she belongs. There would be no expatriate Moabite community in Bethlehem.

In the last stage of chapter 1, Naomi and Ruth arrive in Bethlehem. It is no triumphant entry. Naomi calls her life bitter, says she is 'empty' (possessing nothing), and laments that YHWH has done this to her.

Background note:
WIDOWS IN ANCIENT ISRAEL

The book of Ruth assumes that widows in Israel were in a weak position socially. But in what sense? In a recurring formula in the laws of Deuteronomy, they are grouped with orphans and resident aliens (Deut. 14:28–29; 24:19). However, these groups were not necessarily poor. Widows could inherit and own property, as Naomi herself apparently did (4:3). Their weakness as groups probably lies in not having the same legal standing as adult male Israelites. In that case, the laws in Deuteronomy are meant to give them some legal access to the produce of the land, in case of need.

Widows are also in a dependent position within their former husband's family. This comes to the fore in the 'levirate' customs, which we shall meet in chapter 4. They could remain within that family, and have a certain social status because of it. This was not dependent on the levirate custom, since that custom only applied in certain specific circumstances. Even so, the widow may have been in an uncomfortable position in the family, without the immediate protection of a husband. Ruth may have been particularly vulnerable in a future without Naomi. This would explain the importance Naomi attaches to finding a suitable husband for Ruth.

For more on widows in Israel see the essay by Frick.

The narrator has raised the question of YHWH's hand in events with increasing insistence during this chapter. In v. 6 he notes that 'YHWH had had consideration for his people and given them food' (v. 6), the first reference to YHWH in the book, and one that raises questions about events in the previous five verses: if the giving of food is a sign of YHWH's consideration, then was the famine (v. 1) an act of judgment like others in the period of the judges?

In verses 8–9, her first appeal to Ruth (and Orpah), Naomi speaks of YHWH in conventionally pious terms: 'May YHWH deal kindly with you . . . YHWH grant that you may find security . . .' In v. 13 a much rawer note emerges, apparently revealing her true feelings: 'It has been far more bitter for me than for you, because the hand of YHWH has turned against me.' And in her final attempt to dissuade Ruth from coming with her to Bethlehem, she urges her to follow Orpah in returning 'to her people and to her gods' (v. 15): no longer 'may YHWH deal kindly with you', but almost 'wouldn't you be better off with the gods of Moab?'

The lament in verses 20–21 is the most forceful protest of all: 'the Almighty has dealt bitterly with me . . . YHWH has brought me back empty . . . YHWH has dealt harshly with me and the Almighty has brought calamity upon me.' There is an irony here, of course: Naomi has not come back entirely empty, for Ruth is with her, and has committed herself to Naomi and to Israel's god (v. 16). Naomi has apparently forgotten about her: she does not mention her, nor do the citizens of Bethlehem. But the narrator reminds us that 'Naomi returned together with Ruth the Moabite', and adds the comment that 'they came to Bethlehem at the beginning of the barley harvest' (v. 22). Is this a hint that YHWH's compassion will now extend towards them (cf. v. 6)?

2:1–23: RUTH MEETS BOAZ

Boaz is introduced in v. 1 by the narrator as a relative of Naomi, but Naomi herself has apparently formed no plan for Ruth to meet him. Instead, Ruth simply says that she will go and glean in the harvest fields, 'behind someone in whose sight I may find favour' (2:2). It is presented as accidental that Ruth stumbles on Boaz's field (2:3), though the narrator indicates that there is more than happenstance in the unfolding of these events.

When Boaz arrives to greet his workers Ruth is already gleaning, and he asks his foreman about her (2:5–7). This scene is a good example of how biblical narrative presents events and people from different viewpoints. Here we see Ruth as she appears from the foreman's perspective: a Moabite woman, who has expressed her commitment to Naomi by returning from Moab with her; a modest woman, who has not simply started gleaning but has asked permission; and a hardworking woman, who has taken only a short break. She has clearly made a favourable impression.

When Boaz speaks to Ruth (2:8–9) we realize that she has done something risky, for he warns her to keep with his servant-girls and tells her he has instructed the young men to leave her alone. We sense the vulnerable position of a lonely foreign woman. We also learn that Boaz admires Ruth's loyalty to Naomi (2:11). From what he says, he knew about her already. Strikingly, he describes what she has done in terms which remind us of Abraham's call: 'you left your father and mother and your native land and came to a people that you did not know before' (cf. Gen. 12:1).

As yet, the relationship between Boaz and Ruth is one of master to servant. But Boaz accepts Ruth's decision to identify with Israel's people and Israel's god (2:12), and extends her the protection that his wealth and authority afford. It is a first recognition of her as a member of the Israelite community in Bethlehem. His prayer for her ('May you have a full reward from YHWH, the God of Israel, under whose wings you have come for refuge!') introduces an image that will feature significantly in chapter 3, one that depicts YHWH as willing to care for and protect those who come to him. His words are particularly powerful because he himself has shown such an attitude towards Ruth.

When Ruth reports back to Naomi (2:17–23), we begin to see Naomi's sense of purpose. The narrator does not suggest that Naomi has actually plotted that things should go as they have done, for she is not in a position to control events. Certain things are in the hands of YHWH. But events are indeed going in the way she hoped. Her blessing in v. 20 is ambiguous: does the phrase 'whose kindness has not forsaken the living or the dead' refer to YHWH or to Boaz? (NRSV does not quite bring this point out). But either way, hope seems to be reviving in her, for she sees more clearly than Ruth the shape that events may take. It is now that she reveals that Boaz is a relative, a 'kinsman-redeemer' (2:20, NIV; NRSV translates the Hebrew term, *go'el*, as 'nearest kin' or 'next-of-kin').

The point of this seems to be lost on Ruth. Going on with her story, she curiously misreports Boaz: Boaz had told her to stay close to his young women (2:8), but Ruth now says that he told her to stay close to his young men (2:21). What kind of slip was that? Clearly Ruth is not yet thinking of Boaz

as a future husband. Her sights are not set so high. But Naomi knows what Boaz intended – even if she wasn't there when Boaz said it (2:22)!

Ruth does as Naomi says (v. 23): 'she stayed close to the young women of Boaz, gleaning until the end of the barley and the wheat harvests; and she lived with her mother-in-law.' This verse picks up the reference to 'the beginning of the barley harvest' in 1:22. But it also reminds us of the matters that have yet to be resolved: the position of Naomi and Ruth in Bethlehem, and the possible role of Boaz. Boaz has shown Ruth and Naomi great generosity, but has taken no further action during the seven weeks of harvest (cf. Deut. 16:9–12).

3:1–18: NAOMI SEEKS A 'RESTING-PLACE' FOR RUTH

Naomi now takes active steps to ensure Ruth's place in the family and society. What she seeks for Ruth (3:1) is literally a 'resting-place' (NRSV, 'some security').

Her plan seems astonishingly bold. Ruth is to lie down with Boaz when he falls asleep after his day's work (3:1–5). This will clearly symbolize an offer of herself in marriage to him. The plan is a bold one, with presumably a serious risk of rejection. The reader might well think Ruth's action at least manipulative, and perhaps find an analogy with Tamar's ploy to make Judah sleep with her (Gen. 38; see Nielsen, p. 70). Note, however, how Ruth makes clear what she wants in her first words to Boaz after he wakes up (3:9): 'I am Ruth, your handmaid [not "servant" as in NRSV; a different Hebrew term is used compared to 2:13, implying a more elevated status and also her availability for marriage]; spread the corner of your garment over your handmaid, for you are next-of-kin.' She is not inviting Boaz to sexual pleasure, but to assume responsibility for her needs. ('Corner' is literally 'wing', echoing Boaz's reference at 2:12 to 'the God of Israel, under whose wings you have come for refuge'. Ruth asks him to extend that same protection to her.)

Characteristically, Boaz responds with a blessing (3:10; cf. 2:4). He welcomes Ruth's act as an act of 'loyalty' (*hesed*). This is the kind of faithfulness that belongs in covenantal relationships, and is used of both YHWH (sometimes called his 'steadfast love') and humans. Boaz now says that all Ruth's behaviour to Naomi has been of this kind, and that this new action of hers towards him is the same (3:10). He is willing to act as 'kinsman-redeemer', but reveals that another relative has a prior claim (3:12). He reinforces his words with symbolic actions, telling Ruth to 'lie down until the morning' (3:13), showing her the protection he will extend to her if he can, and giving her barley to take back (3:15).

When Ruth returns, Naomi asks her how things have gone. Most of Ruth's answer is not quoted, the narrator simply saying, 'she told her all that the man had done for her' (3:16). When the narrator does quote Ruth's words, it is to reveal a new detail: 'He gave me these six measures of barley, for he said, "Do not go back to your mother-in-law empty-handed"' (3:17). Boaz's thoughtful words are quoted where they have the greatest impact. We can imagine Naomi's response to this unexpected consideration on Boaz's part. We are also reminded of Naomi's complaint that 'YHWH has brought me back empty' (1:21, using the same Hebrew word). It seems that YHWH has responded. Naomi knows now that things will be settled quickly (3:18).

4:1–22: A REDEEMER

The last chapter gives one of the clearest insights in the Old Testament into how legal agreements were made in ancient Israel. In it we read how Boaz 'redeems' Ruth, along with a piece of property belonging to Naomi, which we now hear of for the first time. (For the legal background, see 'Ruth and biblical law', p. 227). The other next-of-kin is interested in the piece of land, but not in taking Ruth as his wife. His refusal puts Boaz's willingness in a good light, for it implies that there is some cost in accepting the duty of redeemer.

The story ends with the joyful marriage of Ruth and Boaz, completing her 'homecoming' in Israel. The prayer of the people at the gate signifies her acceptance in the most positive of terms, linking her with Rachel and Leah, Israel's ancestresses, and with Tamar, ancestress of the tribe of Judah (4:11–12). Ruth, in fact, not only becomes accepted herself in Israel, but even becomes an ancestress of Israel's greatest king, David (4:18–22). The shock-value of the story thus continues to the very end. For according to one law, Moabites should not enter the 'assembly' of Israel (Deut. 23:3–6), that is, they should not become full members of the worshipping people of YHWH. Ruth has not only done that, but has entered what would become the royal line.

Note, too, how the words of the women of Bethlehem at the birth of Ruth's and Boaz's son provide the book's final answer to Naomi's complaint in chapter 1:

Blessed be YHWH, who has not left you this day without next-of-kin . . . He shall be to you a restorer of life and a nourisher of your old age; for your daughter-in-law, who is more to you than seven sons, has borne him.
(v. 15)

And, more simply, 'A son has been born to Naomi' (v. 17). This time Naomi does not reject their words.

KEY THEMES
Ethos of Israelite life

The book of Ruth does not spell out its main theological concerns. We have to try to recognize them by our interpretation of the story. The book breathes a certain atmosphere. When the issues in the characters' lives are finally settled, it rejoices in the life of ancient Israel. The society in Bethlehem, in which Naomi and Boaz play their part, is able to produce a condition of prosperity and joyfulness. In drawing the vulnerable outsider Ruth into their very heart and life, the citizens of Bethlehem have shown their faithfulness to YHWH and his laws. The echoes of biblical law in the story seem to serve this purpose, to show how YHWH blesses his people when they organize their lives in faithfulness to him.

Think about
WOMEN'S ROLES IN THE BOOK OF RUTH

Two of the leading characters in the book of Ruth are women, both of them positively portrayed. But, it might be said, the book is no less patriarchal in perspective than other Old Testament books where the leading characters are all men. Who make most of the significant decisions in this book? Men, surely: it was Elimelech who took his family to Moab in the first place; and it is Boaz and the elders at the gate who decide Naomi's and Ruth's futures at the end. Female happiness, indeed, seems to be defined on the basis of male concerns: being married to a wealthy male; giving birth to a son who will continue a dead man's family line; being the great-grandmother of a king.

Or is the book more subversive than that? Bauckham notes that in chapters 1—3 women take the initiative and the narrative focuses upon them. True, in chapter 4 men dominate events, and the book ends with a male genealogy; but even there the scene of Obed's birth (4:13–17) is dominated by women. So Ruth is a book in which the male perspective is contrasted with a more unusual female perspective, this point becoming clear in chapter 4. The book may end with a male genealogy, but this genealogy is set in a context which makes clear that it does not express the book's primary concerns (p. 17):

The genealogy [4:18–22] says in effect: 'This is how the usual men's perspective views the history of this period of David's ancestors. This is the way you readers are accustomed to thinking of this period. Everything the narrative you have just read has taught you to see as important is here left out.'

Bauckham concludes (p. 17):

In effect this gives Ruth an important canonical function, that is a function in relation to the rest of the contents of the canon of Scripture, or, in this case, in relation to the other narratives in Scripture. By revealing the Israelite women's world which is elsewhere invisible in biblical narrative it makes readers aware of the lack of this women's perspective elsewhere, expanding the hints and filling in the gaps which they can now see to be left by the narratives written purely or largely from a male perspective.

What do you think of this? Do you agree with the claim that the Old Testament generally reflects a male perspective to which a book like Ruth can act as a corrective?

Loyalty and law

The main characters also show the best qualities in human relationships. We have seen that Ruth and Boaz correspond to each other in this respect, for each shows the quality of *hesed*, 'loyalty'. The point is brought out more fully by the comparison of Ruth with Orpah, and Boaz with the other next-of-kin. Ruth 3:10 is thus a key text for the message of the book. Ruth's faithfulness is seen when she commits herself to Naomi and the god of Israel in words that are surely meant to remind us of YHWH's own covenant faithfulness (Ruth 1:16–17; see also Lev. 26:12; Jer. 30:22). And in showing *hesed*, YHWH's covenant partners are imitating him, for he is the one who shows it above all (Deut. 7:9).

This centrality of *hesed* puts the book's interest in law in a certain light. There is no doubt that the law and its practice are regarded favourably in Ruth. Yet it seems that it is the *spirit* of the law that is really in view, as several writers have suggested. This may even be why it is hard to match the actions in Ruth with known laws. When Boaz acts as *go'el*, he may be under no obligation at all to fulfil the duties of the brother-in-law, but he chooses to interpret his role broadly and generously (see Block, p. 715 and note 35).

CRITICAL ISSUES

LITERARY-CRITICAL ISSUES

'Almost all who have worked on the book of Ruth agree that it is a unity, with the possible exception of the genealogy in 4:[18–]22,' comments Bush (p. 10). He goes on to argue convincingly that the genealogy forms a 'fitting and appropriate conclusion' to the book (p. 16). Source-criticism has featured hardly at all in scholarship on this book, whose literary skill has generally been greatly admired.

Date

There is no clear evidence about the date of the book. It is set in the period of the judges, yet it looks back on that period (1:1), so it must have been written during the monarchy at the earliest. But it is difficult to say how long after the judges the book was written. A number of kinds of evidence have been advanced.

1 *Linguistic.* The Hebrew of Ruth is unusual in some respects. Some verb-forms have a final 'n' ('paragogic nun') which is not standard. There are also some apparently masculine verb-forms used where feminine forms would be expected. These may be evidence of an earlier form of Hebrew, in which, for example, a dual verb-form similar to the masculine might have been used for either masculine or feminine. However, it is not clear that these forms are in fact archaic; and even if they were, the author of Ruth could have deliberately adopted them for literary reasons. Other peculiarities are not conclusive either.

2 *Law.* A number of biblical laws are alluded to in Ruth (see 'Ruth and biblical law'). This has been taken to mean that Ruth must be later than the law-codes in which these laws appear. On most views, this would require a post-exilic dating, since the latest law-codes are usually dated to that time. However, this is questionable for a number of reasons. The dates of the law-codes are themselves uncertain. In any case, the date of a law-code may not tell us much about the age of a particular law or custom found in it. Finally, a custom may be attested first in a narrative, and only afterwards in a law.

3 *Relations with Moab.* One might look for a period in history when relations between Israelites and Moabites were good enough for a man from Bethlehem to settle

in Moab, and for his family to form marriage relations with Moabites. The problem is that quite different dates might meet this criterion, either as early as David (1 Sam. 22:3–4) or well after the exile, perhaps in a time when there was reaction against the strict reforms of Ezra and Nehemiah.

4 *Canonical links*. Ruth shows particular similarities and differences to other parts of the Old Testament. For example, it has some connection with the story of Tamar in Genesis 38. And, as just noted, it has been contrasted with Ezra. Does this mean that canonical relationships are a guide to dating? Again, there is no sure way here. This is because we cannot be sure whether Ruth *intends* to be a reaction to some other biblical work, or whether it just happens to have a similar or contrasting theme.

Opinions are about evenly divided between pre-exilic and post-exilic settings for the book. It may be a tribute to its masterly art that it conceals its origins so well. Ruth is unique in the Old Testament, a short tale that touches on major topics in Israelite religion and Old Testament theology. It should not be reduced to a polemical response to some other biblical book, or limited by linking it to a single situation.

RUTH AND BIBLICAL LAW

The action in chapter 4 involves several laws and customs. These are related to known biblical laws, although the connections are not exact. There are other allusions to biblical law, such as when Boaz instructs his harvesters to leave some of the grain for Ruth (cf. Deut. 24:19–22). However, the two main laws that underlie the story are the law of levirate marriage (Deut. 25:5–10) and the law of 'redemption' (Lev. 25:23–28, 47–55).

These seem to be somehow combined in Ruth.

The concept that is most to the fore in the story is 'redemption', since Boaz is several times called a *go'el*, that is, a 'redeemer' or 'kinsman-redeemer'. The last act in the book turns on who will take on this role. In Leviticus 25, redemption can apply to both land and persons. Land may be sold in hard times to pay debts, and later 'redeemed' by a near relative or the original seller (vv. 25–28). Persons can be redeemed when they have been forced through poverty to sell themselves into the service of 'resident aliens' (vv. 47–54). If they are not redeemed they must in any case be released in the year of the jubilee (the fiftieth year in a 50-year cycle). Only Israelites who are enslaved in this way to foreign residents may be redeemed. Israelites who become enslaved to other Israelites must serve till the jubilee (vv. 39–43). Only foreigners who become slaves can become slaves permanently (vv. 44–46).

None of this quite applies to the redemption of Ruth. According to Leviticus, as a foreigner she would not be entitled to redemption. Nor has she arrived in Bethlehem as a slave in the first place. So the 'redemption' of Ruth goes well beyond these laws, both because Ruth is a foreigner and because she obtains more than her freedom, since with it will come marriage to Boaz.

It is the levirate law (Deut. 25:5–10) that relates specifically to marriage. The point of the levirate law is that, when a man dies childless, his brother should have a child by the widow, in order to provide an heir for the dead man. This is also the concern in Ruth 4:5, 10, where Boaz's marriage to Ruth will have the effect of providing an heir for Ruth's former husband Mahlon. Again, the custom assumed here is not quite like the one that the law addresses. (When Ruth has a son, the women of Bethlehem call him a son 'born to Naomi'; 4:17. This is probably not intended legally, but as a recognition that the child belongs properly within her family.)

In Ruth, the 'levirate' intention of Boaz's marriage to Ruth is bound up with the 'redemption' of a field belonging to Naomi (4:3). This means that the legal procedure in Ruth 4 is not based exactly on either of the laws that are close to it in theme. The levirate custom may have had a secondary concern with land, since the widow may have had title to property from her marriage, which she would have taken out of the family if she married outside it. However, this does not quite explain the procedure in Ruth 4.

It is not wholly surprising that biblical narratives give a picture that is slightly different from what biblical laws lead us to expect. The full legal situation may have been more complex than appears from any of the laws we happen to have. For example, a *go'el* may have been obliged to marry a widow in certain circumstances (Hubbard, pp. 48–63). Or the explanation may simply be that there was no unified law-code that applied to all Israel at all times. The law-codes themselves differ from each other on certain topics (see, for example, Exod. 21:1–6 and Deut. 15:12–18). In that case Ruth would simply let us see one kind of practice, while the laws we have noticed point to others.

Finally, we have to ask whether the narrator intends merely to base the narrative on laws or in some ways to oppose them. The most obvious example is in relation to Deuteronomy 23:3–6 (see following section). For further discussion of the legal issues, see Bush, pp. 211–15.

RUTH IN THE CANON

In the Hebrew Bible, Ruth is placed among the Writings. It is part of a group of five texts called the Megilloth (Scrolls); the other four are Song of Songs, Esther, Ecclesiastes and Lamentations. These were each associated with one of the annual Jewish feasts, in Ruth's case the Feast of Weeks. This may have been because the story of Ruth takes place between Passover and the Feast of Weeks, or between the times of the barley and wheat harvests (1:22; 2:23). But the Feast of Weeks was also associated with the giving of the law at Sinai, and in Jewish writings Ruth was considered a model convert (or 'proselyte'), that is, one who subjected herself to the Jewish law, or Torah (Nielsen, pp. 17–21).

In English Bibles, which follow the order of LXX, Ruth is placed between Judges and Samuel. This is because both the setting and the narrative itself fit comfortably there. The first line of Ruth shows that the events take place in the time of the judges. The last chapters of Judges tell of a socially chaotic time, and sum it up by saying: 'In those days there was no king in Israel; all the people did what was right in their own eyes' (Judg. 21:25). At the beginning of Ruth, a man and his family have to flee Israel because of famine. And the book goes on to tell of the origins of King David. The books of Samuel then relate how David became king in Israel. So in English Bibles Ruth provides an important link in the larger story of the transition from judges to kings in Israel.

To understand the theology of Ruth, we have to think of how it functions in relation to other parts of the Old Testament. How important is it that Ruth was a Moabite? The earliest Jewish interpretation of the story, the Targum of Ruth (an Aramaic translation and interpretation) shows that this was felt to be a problem. Chilion and Mahlon, in marrying foreign women, had broken YHWH's law, and were punishable by death (cf. Deut. 7:1–5; 23:3–6; see Nielsen, pp. 17–18). The same text, however, regards Ruth herself as a model of those who are converted to become followers of YHWH (proselytes). A later Jewish commentary, the Midrash on Ruth, shows how nonsensical the idea of a pure genealogy can be, since David, and before him Tamar, were of mixed descent (Nielsen, pp. 18–19).

The incorporation of Ruth into Israel is the single most startling aspect of the story. The acceptance of Ruth is a key feature, even in the language used. For example, Naomi describes Boaz as 'a relative of *ours*', implying that Ruth belongs in her family just as much as she does herself (2:20). And Boaz, at first meeting, calls her 'my daughter' (2:8).

The boldness of the book on this reminds us of the equally surprising story of Jonah, in which the Assyrian Ninevites repent and are saved from judgment, much to the prophet Jonah's dismay! Ruth firmly insists that true belonging to the people of YHWH cannot be by physical descent only.

The openness of Ruth prepares for a similar point, in a very different book, when the apostle Paul shows that the promises of God are received by faith (Rom. 4). More generally, it counsels an open, welcoming attitude to all weak and vulnerable people – foreigners, asylum-seekers, economic migrants – however different they may be from ourselves.

FURTHER READING

COMMENTARIES

D.I. Block, *Judges, Ruth*. Nashville: Broadman and Holman, 1999.

F.W. Bush, *Ruth, Esther*. Dallas: Word, 1996.

E. Campbell, *Ruth*. New York; Doubleday, 1975.

R.L. Hubbard, *The Book of Ruth*. Grand Rapids: Eerdmans, 1988.

P. Joüon, *Ruth: Commentaire philologique et exégétique*. Rome: Biblical Institute Press, 1986.

M.S. Moore, 'Ruth' in J. Harris, C. Brown and M.S. Moore, *Joshua, Judges, Ruth*. Peabody/Carlisle: Hendrickson/Paternoster, 2000, pp. 293–374.

K. Nielsen, *Ruth*. London: SCM Press, 1997.

OTHER BOOKS AND ARTICLES

R.J. Bauckham, *Is the Bible Male? The Book of Ruth and Biblical Narrative*. Cambridge: Grove Books, 1996.

A. Brenner (ed.), *A Feminist Companion to Ruth*. Sheffield: Sheffield Academic Press, 1993.

A. Brenner (ed.), *Ruth and Esther. A Feminist Companion to the Bible (Second Series)*. Sheffield: Sheffield Academic Press, 1999.

E.W. Davies, 'Ruth IV 5 and the Duties of the Go'el', *VT* 33 (1983), pp. 231–4.

H. Fisch, 'Ruth and the Structure of Covenant History', *VT* 32 (1982), pp. 425–37.

F.S. Frick, 'Widows in the Hebrew Bible' in A. Brenner (ed.), *A Feminist Companion to Exodus to Deuteronomy*. Sheffield: Sheffield Academic Press, 1994, pp. 139–51.

M.D. Gow, *The Book of Ruth: Its Structure, Theme and Purpose*. Leicester: IVP, 1992.

K.J.A. Larkin, *Esther and Ruth*. Sheffield: Sheffield Academic Press, 1996.

B.G. Webb, *Five Festal Garments: Christian Reflections on the Song of Songs, Ruth,* *Lamentations, Ecclesiastes and Esther*. Leicester; Apollos, 2000.

E. van Wolde, *Ruth and Naomi*. London: SCM Press, 1997.

Chapter 9

ESTHER

The book of Esther tells the story of a Jewish community living in exile in the Persian empire. (See Map 6.) While Ezra and Nehemiah focus on the return to Jerusalem following Cyrus' decree, Esther has no such interest. In Esther, Jewish life goes on at the heart of empire itself, with no apparent sense that Jews ought to return there.

The issue in Esther is how Jews can survive as a community under a foreign king and empire. The heroes of the story are Esther herself, who becomes queen of Persia, and her uncle, Mordecai, who also rises to a position of great power. They do so, however, as a result of desperate opposition to the Jews as a people.

Esther is one of the Bible's great 'diaspora' stories: that is, it is about the life of Jewish people 'scattered' among non-Jewish nations. It has remained tremendously important for Jewish people throughout the centuries, since most of them have lived in 'diaspora', under all kinds of non-Jewish rule.

In the Christian Bible, Esther follows Ezra and Nehemiah, and is therefore classed as one of the Histories. In the Hebrew Bible, it comes in the third section, the Writings. Like Ruth, it is also counted as one of the five short books called the 'Megilloth' (scrolls). This may suggest that Jewish reading is more concerned with the issues raised than with the history in itself. One remarkable feature of the book is that it nowhere mentions God. This will be an important issue to consider below.

Esther is a carefully constructed narrative. Its plot falls into closely connected scenes, according to the following structure:

STRUCTURE OF ESTHER

1:1–22   A queen deposed
2:1–23   Esther is queen, Mordecai a hero
3:1–15   Haman's plot, Mordecai's dilemma
4:1–17   Esther's dilemma
5:1–14   Esther's dinner party for the king – and Haman!
6:1–14   Mordecai is rewarded
7:1–10   Haman is condemned
8:1–17   The decree overturned
9:1–32   Purim
10:1–3   Mordecai honoured

Note: in the Structure and Outline given here we follow the most familiar form of the book, as found in most English Bibles. But see 'Text' (p. 237) for another form of the book, which is regarded as authoritative in some churches.

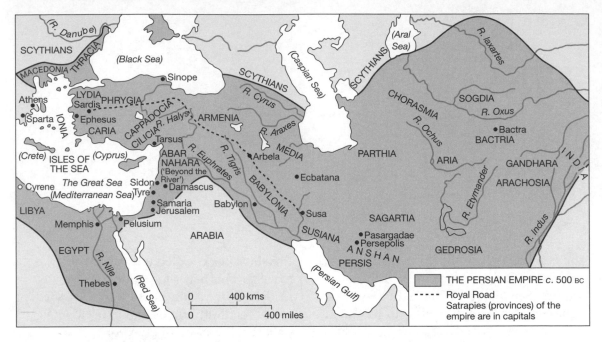

Map 6   The Persian empire

OUTLINE

1:1–22: A QUEEN DEPOSED

King Ahasuerus is better known as Xerxes, one of the great Persian kings (486–465 BC). His empire stretched 'from India to Ethiopia' (1:1), though he failed to extend it into Europe, losing a war against Greece. Susa was one of three capitals of the Persian empire (with Babylon and Ecbatana). The great banquets (1:3–9) are intended to display the extent of the empire and the machinery of power. Their lavishness is in line with what is known of the Persian court of the period.

The action of the story begins when the king summons his queen, Vashti, to appear before his officials and show her beauty. Vashti does the unthinkable and defies the king. The king, powerful in the world, cannot rule in his own home. Humiliated and angry, he takes counsel, deposes Vashti from her throne, and delivers a decree throughout the empire that women should honour their husbands.

2:1–23: ESTHER IS QUEEN, MORDECAI A HERO

Now that we have seen the power and pride of the king, we meet the two main characters of the story. Esther's selection as queen puts the next building-block of the story in place. The key is that she is Jewish, a fact which Mordecai tells her to conceal. In doing so, he shows keen insight into the dangers to Jews under foreign rule.

At the same time, and by coincidence, Mordecai shows his loyalty to the king by uncovering a plot against him. This also becomes a building-block in the story, though as yet it seems unrelated to the main line. Behind the apparent randomness of events, a plot is being skilfully constructed. Mordecai's action has no immediate consequences – but it will be remembered (2:23).

Think about
ESTHER AND MORDECAI: COMPROMISERS OR LOYAL JEWS?

In chapter 2 Esther, encouraged by Mordecai, engages in what might be seen, from the perspective of other Old Testament books, as a series of compromises: she becomes the queen of a foreign king after spending the night with him (vv. 13–18; contrast Ezra–Nehemiah's position on intermarriage); she eats the food she is given, and raises no objections based on Jewish food laws (vv. 9–10; contrast Daniel in Dan. 1).

How are we to view Mordecai's and Esther's behaviour in this chapter? (Remember that it is only because of what Esther does in ch. 2 that she is later in a position to deliver her people. Note also Mordecai's *un*compromising stand at the beginning of ch. 3.) Is it appropriate to apply the standards of Ezra–Nehemiah to Jews living outside Palestine? Consider the narrator's final description of Mordecai in 10:3: does that amount to a commendation of everything he has done in the book?

Along somewhat similar lines, chapters 1 and 2 invite a comparison between Esther and Vashti. Who behaves with greater dignity, Vashti, the queen who refuses to be displayed as an adornment of royal power (1:11), or Esther, the woman who beautifies herself in order to be accepted as queen (2:8–12)?

3:1–15: HAMAN'S PLOT, MORDECAI'S DILEMMA

The plot thickens with the introduction of Haman. Haman's promotion to 'prime minister' seems another random event. It is unexpected because Haman is introduced suddenly, and because we might instead have expected an honour for Mordecai. But in fact Haman is an 'Agagite', a term which suggests a connection with the ancient Amalekites, enemies of Israel (1 Sam. 15:1–9). Haman's anger when Mordecai refuses to bow to him turns against the Jews. The issue which lay hidden in chapter 2 – whether the Jews could survive under foreign rule – is now brought to a head by a powerful figure who stands symbolically for historic enmity to the Jews.

Before approaching the king, Haman casts lots (Hebrew *purim*), probably to decide the day on which the Jews should be destroyed. His murderous intention is later remembered by the Jews, when they celebrate 'Purim' on the day that Haman chose (9:24–28).

For now, the king is easily fooled by Haman, who accuses the Jews of disloyalty because of their other loyalty, namely to their laws and customs. This is a reference to the Mosaic Law, though it is not put in those terms. The accusation is false, as we know, because Mordecai has already shown his loyalty. But the proud and foolish king is easily worried into believing it, and he gives his signet ring to Haman 'the enemy of the Jews' (3:10). He does not know that in allowing the decree he is condemning his own queen. The narrative brings out the danger posed for the Jews by this irresponsible and gullible ruler: the description of Ahasuerus sitting down to drink with Haman while Susa is in turmoil because of the decree (3:15) neatly sums up the character of his rule.

4:1–17: ESTHER'S DILEMMA

Esther's position as queen and her Jewishness, concealed up to this point, now come into play. But in taking the initiative to go to the king she must risk her own life in order to save her people. Mordecai persuades her that she has a duty to take the risk. This leads to the theological centre of the story. Mordecai believes that the events which have led to the present situation have a pattern in them: Esther has been brought to her unique position in order to protect her people. But even if she does not accept the role, 'relief and deliverance will rise for the Jews from another quarter' (4:14) – an indirect statement of faith in Israel's god.

5:1–14: ESTHER'S DINNER PARTY FOR THE KING – AND HAMAN!

Esther now takes the leading role; she will do things her way. Her banquet for the king and Haman sums up the tensions and ironies in the story. Haman is delighted to be honoured by the queen (v. 12) – yet unknown to him, she is one whom he has planned to destroy. Esther's power is now emphasized, as the king offers her anything she desires. This puts two contrary forces in action: the decree against the Jews, which cannot be taken back, and the king's gift to Esther, which puts enormous power into her hands. Surprisingly, she asks only for a second banquet with the king and Haman, increasing the dramatic tension. Meanwhile, Haman's anger with Mordecai comes to a head, and he prepares to destroy his rival by setting up gallows.

This chapter displays the power relations in the story. While the Jewish characters may feel that their position is desperate, the readers see in the deployment of power here that it is really Haman whose cause is hopeless. The last episode (5:9–14)

suggests his insecurity and irrationality. Even when he seems to be doing so well, one thing is enough to put him in a bad mood (v. 9); so much so that, in order to compensate himself for a perceived slight, he has to summon his family and friends to hear him boast about his successes (vv. 10–12). His wife soothes his feelings by suggesting that he erect the gallows (vv. 13–14), pandering to his anger with ridiculous-seeming advice (cf. Ahasuerus' courtiers in ch. 1).

6:1–14: MORDECAI IS REWARDED

When things seem worst for the Jews, events take a hand yet again. During a sleepless night the king has the chronicles of the kingdom read to him, and is reminded of Mordecai's loyal action. So he resolves to honour Mordecai, just when Haman thought he was going to execute him! In a scene rich in irony the king asks Haman what should be done for the man whom the king favours. Haman has always been obsessed with a desire that people should honour him, and now, thinking the king means him, he devises the most extravagant honours possible without usurping royal prerogatives – only to discover that the king meant Mordecai! But even as Haman mourns his humiliation, his friends hint that worse could be in store. For if Mordecai is Jewish (and we know he is, even if Haman does not), he cannot prevail against him (6:13).

7:1–10: HAMAN IS CONDEMNED

With his family's gloomy words in his ears, Haman is rushed off to Esther's second feast. Haman's position has changed drastically since the day before. But he has another surprise to come – when Esther reveals that she is Jewish! Esther's request to the king, which the king has granted before she asks, is the life of her people. Esther then explains how Haman has plotted against the Jews, and the trap closes on Haman. (Note 7:6, 'Haman was terrified before the king and the queen', which suggests with brilliant economy how Esther has turned the tables on him: she and Ahasuerus are now 'the king and the queen', standing over against him, and Haman is cut off from his source of power.) The climax touches farce when Haman, in begging for his life from Esther, appears to be assaulting her (7:8). After this, he is hanged on the gallows he had made for Mordecai.

8:1–17: THE DECREE OVERTURNED

Mordecai's triumph over Haman is complete (8:1–2). But the matter is not yet closed, because the decree against the Jews remains in force and must still be countered. The threat remains because the Jews have enemies everywhere, and they are planning to attack the Jews on the day assigned, the 13th of Adar (3:7, 13). Esther has to prevail on the king again, and he authorizes a counter-decree, allowing Jews throughout the empire to defend themselves against any who would attack them. Mordecai leaves the royal court clothed in royal finery, and this becomes the signal for general rejoicing among the Jews, the four terms 'light and gladness, joy and honour' (8:16) reversing the 'mourning . . . fasting and weeping and lamenting' which greeted Haman's original decree (4:3).

9:1–32: PURIM

The Jews' self-defence is now told. The action described does not look very like defence, however, but rather revenge on those who had sought the Jews' downfall, and who had 'hated' them (9:2, 5). This impression is strengthened when Esther requests a second day to finish the job in Susa, and in particular to complete the action against Haman by hanging his ten sons (9:13). In the provinces one day was enough to seal the fate of 75,000 enemies (9:16). The whole action reminds us strongly of the ancient 'holy war' against the Canaanites (Deut. 20:16–18). Echoes of earlier accounts are particularly clear at 8:17, where we are told that the dread of the Jews fell on the peoples in the empire (cf. Josh. 2:9), and also in the repeated phrase, 'they did not touch the plunder' (9:10, 15–16; cf. Josh. 6:18–19).

These events give rise to the annual celebration of Purim, which the king himself ordered should be held on the 14th and 15th of Adar. The feast was called 'Purim', because Haman had cast the lot in his bid to wipe out the Jews (9:24–26). The feast receives royal authorization, by the hand of Queen Esther herself, together with Mordecai (9:29).

Digging deeper:
PURIM

Purim is the only Jewish feast that has origins in the Bible but is not commanded in the biblical laws. In this it is quite different from the three major feasts of Israel, Passover/Unleavened Bread, Weeks and Tabernacles (Lev. 23). Its name ('Lots') might seem to be out of keeping with the biblical belief in God's providence. This is one among a number of features of Esther which seem to be at odds with the theology of other parts of the Old Testament.

Scholars have often thought that Purim was originally not a Jewish festival at all, but had Babylonian or Persian roots. To follow this up, see Moore, pp. xlvi–xlix.

10:1–3: MORDECAI HONOURED

The last verses focus on Mordecai rather than Esther, and recall his great honours, honours that Haman had desired for himself, but which events denied him. But Mordecai is remembered finally not for his power in the kingdom, but for his devotion to his people's welfare, for whom he 'interceded' (10:3). All Mordecai's achievements are recorded 'in the annals of the kings of Media and Persia' (10:2). This phrase, similar to the 'regnal formulae' of Kings (e.g. 1 Kgs 14:19, 29), suggests a comparison with earlier periods of Israel's history, and reminds us that the fundamental earthly reality in this period has been Persian imperial power.

KEY THEMES

The following theological points relate to the Masoretic Text of Esther. On the variant textual traditions of Esther, see p. 237.

God and events

An obvious fact about Esther is that the book nowhere mentions God. This can hardly be accidental, because the issues at stake inevitably raise the question of God's power and will to help the Jewish people – just as the terrible persecution of the Jews in Nazi Germany did. Does the silence about God in the narrative mean that the author has written him out of history? The structure of the book brings out strongly the close connection between events, as cause and effect. The series of random coincidences might imply unpredictability, the events of life governed by nothing more than chance, or the throw of a die (hence 'Purim'). Is the writer saying that the only cause of events is events themselves? Other Old Testament narratives also portray the connection between events, but they still see God clearly behind them (e.g. 2 Sam. 11—20, note 12:15b; Gen. 37—50, note

45:5–8). Perhaps Esther has taken a step towards agnosticism?

It seems, in fact, that Esther takes a more positive view of God's working in history. The coincidences can be seen as evidence, not of randomness, but of God's providential ordering of things. The key text is 4:14, where Mordecai's words to Esther would be meaningless unless he believed that events were ordered by God. Perhaps the huge improbability of Esther's becoming queen just at the time of her people's greatest danger is due to a higher purpose. And if Esther refuses to do her duty, relief will arise from 'another quarter' (literally 'place'): God will find another way of saving his people. If we understand Mordecai's words in this way, then the theology of Esther is very like that of the Joseph story. For there too God is said to have achieved his own purposes by a quite unpredictable chain of events, even overruling the brothers' evil plans (Gen. 45:5–8; 50:19–20). (For an extended treatment of this topic, see Rodriguez.)

It now appears that Esther, by not naming God at all, goes beyond the Joseph story: even when God appears to be absent from events, he is still actually present in them, carrying out his own saving purposes.

Providence, prayer and responsibility

Mordecai's words to Esther (in 4:14) have another important message. If Esther has been brought to her position by God's purpose, she has a responsibility to act in accordance with it. Mordecai's warning to her is chilling: 'you and your father's family will perish'. There will be a serious loss if she deliberately does not do what she is uniquely able to do, knowing that she should.

The book of Esther, therefore, reflects on the relationship between God's overruling in history and the responsibility of human beings. Proverbs poses the relationship in this way:

> The human mind plans the way
> But YHWH directs the steps.
> (Prov. 16:9)

Esther adds to this that the human action may frustrate or forestall the divine plan: God will overrule in the end, but people have real choices, for good or ill.

Esther agrees to do her part (4:16b). But at the same time she knows that she does not control events. Therefore she fasts (v. 16a). The narrative is consistent here: as it does not mention God, so it does not speak of prayer. Yet we may take fasting to imply prayer. Esther knows that she cannot take matters entirely into her own hands; she is dependent on a higher power.

Finally, she is willing to accept the risks of her action. In her words 'if I perish, I perish' (4:16) we may read, not resigned fatalism, but faith that is ready to face consequences. God may not be manipulated. Her attitude may be compared with that of Shadrach, Meshach and Abednego. When they are threatened with King Nebuchadnezzar's 'furnace of blazing fire', they declare that God will save them, but they add the telling words: '*But if not . . .*', and go on to say that even so they will be faithful to God (Dan. 3:17–18).

Retribution

The other theological issue in Esther concerns the retribution exacted by the Jews on their enemies. As we saw in the Outline, their actions seem to go beyond self-defence: they mete out to others the terrible treatment that was devised against them. If we are right in reading the book in this way, it is hard find anything positive in this. How should we understand the narrative at this point?

First, in the case of Haman, we have an example of evil plans being turned on their head against the person who made them. There is huge irony in Haman being hanged on the very gallows he had had constructed for someone else. This can be read as a cautionary illustration of the point we have already noted, that the plans of human beings are limited because they do not have full knowledge of what causes events. Esther humbly recognized her limitations in this respect, but Haman did not.

Second, we must bear in mind the nature of the story. The events are told in comic vein, in order to ridicule the false pretensions of the powerful. Human beings, even when powerful, are ludicrous in their pretensions, so much so that their plans may actually have the opposite effect of that intended, and when they are evil, fall back on themselves. (See also the panel 'Esther 9 and 10: later additions?')

CRITICAL ISSUES

TEXT

So far, we have considered the book of Esther in the form in which it is printed in most English Bibles. That form is based on the Hebrew of the MT. There are several ancient forms of Esther, however, which have complicated relationships with each other. In particular, a longer form of the book existed in early times, which is now found in the LXX of Esther. NRSV gives this form in its entirety in the Apocrypha section.

(Most editions of the Apocrypha translate only those parts of LXX which were additional to the MT, and these are called 'Additions to Esther'. To see them in context, however, it is necessary to read the whole text, as given in NRSV.)

Esther LXX is a translation of an older Hebrew text, different from MT. It is not just a matter of additions. There are differences in the parts of the book that the two versions have in common. To the story-line of MT the following is added:

A/11:2—12:6 (before ch. 1): Mordecai sees in a dream that God will save the Jews.
B/13:1-7 (after 3:13): A copy of the king's decree to destroy the Jews.
C/13:8—14:19 (after 4:17): Prayers of petition by Mordecai and Esther.
D/15:1–16 (immediately after C): God turns the king's heart to favour Esther; Esther twice faints, showing her great inner turmoil.
E/16:1–24 (after 8:12): A copy of the king's letter through Mordecai, allowing the Jews to defend themselves.
F/10:4—11:1 (after 10:3): Mordecai interprets the events of the story, according to his dream at the beginning.

The two forms also differ theologically. The main differences are as follows:

- Esther LXX makes explicit the hand of God in events (A/11:10).
- LXX conforms Esther to central Old Testament theology. The main characters are models of piety: they pray and their motives are clearly noble (e.g. Esther shows her hatred of being married to a Gentile, and holding the position of queen, which she only occupies for the sake of her people; C/14:15–16). Parts of LXX are close to Daniel, with its dreams and visions, and symbolic language (A/11:6–7, 10–11, interpreted in F/10:6–9).
- LXX fills gaps in the story. For example, the king's letter (E) stresses that many in authority throughout the empire have spilt innocent blood, and sought to harm the king's subjects. Haman is shown to have been treacherous towards the king. This gives greater justification to the Jewish acts of retribution.
- The king is portrayed as pious, honouring the god of Israel (E/16:18, 21). The LXX thus carefully maintains a respectful attitude to the empire.

> **Think about**
> **GREEK ESTHER**
>
> Some of the new emphases in LXX Esther may show what the book's earliest Jewish interpreters found puzzling or even offensive about the book. In what ways do they try to 'rescue' the two heroes' reputations? Do they place Esther closer to other post-exilic literature, for example Ezra and Nehemiah, by means of these 'orthodox' changes?

One further form of the text should be mentioned, the so-called Alpha text (A-text). This is a Greek text which apparently had separate origins in Hebrew from both MT and LXX, but which is based, finally, on this independent textual tradition together with additions from LXX. This text is not preserved in any canonical tradition, and the first edition of it appeared only in the seventeenth century. However, modern study regards it as a witness to how the story of Esther developed in ancient times. (For more on the A-text, see Levenson, pp. 32–4. Clines 1984b, pp. 215–17, gives the text in its entirety in both Greek and English, and analyses it on pp. 71–92.)

LITERARY-CRITICAL ISSUES

Esther as narrative

The skilful literary construction of Esther has often been praised, and is apparent in many aspects of the narrative: the subtle interweaving of the different strands of the plot and the artful construction of individual episodes (Clines 1984b, pp. 9–24, 31–8); the balancing of different episodes of this tale of reversals around the turning-point in chapter 6 (Levenson, pp. 5–10); the use of clothing and luxury goods as symbols in the narrative (1:1–9; 4:1–4; 6:8–11; 8:15); the role played by banquets in the book (there are ten, and it is usually significant who is present at them). The narrator satirizes the Persian royal court, particularly in chapter 1, and at a number of points he parodies the 'officialese' of the Persian empire (e.g. in chs 1, 3 and 9; in the last chapter, amusingly, Esther and Mordecai show themselves able to write fluently in this 'dialect').

Genre and historicity

A distinctive feature of the narrative is the contrast between its comedic aspects and the grim things which threaten the Jews and finally fall on their enemies. The central critical issue of Esther concerns what kind of writing it is. Is it meant as history? In kind (or genre) Esther could be similar to the Apocryphal/Deuterocanonical books of Judith and Tobit. Judith and Tobit also tell

---

Think about
ESTHER 9 AND 10: LATER ADDITIONS?

Clines 1984b (pp. 26–30, 39–63) argues that whereas chapters 1—8 are an artful literary unity, chapters 9—10 are clumsy, illogical and best explained as having arisen through a series of later additions. These additions have taken up many terms from chapters 1—8, but together form an 'ending' which is not a logical conclusion to those chapters.

His arguments include the following:

- Chapter 8 describes the writing of a second decree permitting the Jews to defend themselves against any who attack them. This decree aims to neutralize the earlier decree of Haman without explicitly revoking it, which would be impossible (1:19; 8:8). The intended result is a stalemate: no non-Jew will attack a Jew, and no Jew will need to engage in self-defence. Both decrees seem to be ignored in ch. 9 where there is no mention of any attacks on Jews (in spite of Haman's decree), and the Jews do not simply defend themselves (as the second decree permitted), but take the initiative against 'their enemies' (9:1, 5, 16).

- The references in chapter 9 to the Jews' 'enemies' are strange: previously there has been only one enemy of the Jews, Haman (3:10); the inhabitants of Susa, by contrast, are distressed by Haman's decree (3:15) and rejoice when Mordecai is exalted (8:15). Where have the 75,000 enemies of 9:16 come from?

- Much of 9:20—10:3 seems repetitious, confused or vague, very different in style and technique from chapters 1—8.

Work through Clines' arguments: do you find them convincing, or is there more to be said for chapters 9—10 as the proper conclusion of the book? Bear in mind that the book clearly has been subject to some additions, as the LXX evidence shows. You can compare the comments of Levenson (pp. 118–34), who is sympathetic to Clines, but not entirely persuaded.

stories about Jews living under the rule of an empire (Assyria), but it is clear from internal evidence that these books are not telling accurate history. (For example, in Judith Nebuchadnezzar is portrayed as king of Assyria, whereas he was king of Babylon.) Esther is canonical, while Judith and Tobit are not, but that fact by itself does not tell us that Esther is more historical.

Some general features favour historicity. The historical Ahasuerus did reign over a huge empire stretching from India to Ethiopia. In addition, the description of the empire's administration and its customs fits in many details with what is known: for example, the postal system, the recording of deeds deserving reward, impaling as a form of punishment (Clines 1984a, pp. 261, 293; Moore, p. xli). There are also a number of Persian names and other words. (On the accuracy of many of these names, see Millard.)

The events of the book could fit with what is known of the chronology of Ahasuerus' reign from other sources (mainly the Greek historian Herodotus, who wrote soon after the reign of that king). They must allow for Ahasuerus' four-year absence fighting the war with Greece (483–479). According to Clines (1984a, pp. 260–2), the banquet and deposal of Vashti in Ahasuerus' third year (1:3) could have happened before the war, and Esther's installation in the seventh year (2:16) could have happened after it. Fox (p. 133) disputes this, thinking that Ahasuerus would still have been away in the seventh year. However, as Fox (p. 14) takes the beginning of Ahasuerus' reign as 485, the seventh year would be 479, and thus Esther's accession could indeed have taken place soon after Ahasuerus' return.

None of this proves that the book is historical, as most of these details are circumstantial. A fictional work might get the local colour right just as easily as a historical work.

An important consideration is the central events narrated: a plot to kill all the Jews in the empire, foiled by the actions of a queen and a high official, and an actual slaughter of 75,000 Persians by Jews. Of these there is no independent evidence. Some have judged that such a thing probably did happen, and that 'there is nothing intrinsically impossible or improbable in the central incident' (Gordis, p. 388). However, what is 'probable' is always disputable. It may be thought *im*probable that a king, who is bound to be interested in stability, would sanction wholesale slaughter throughout his empire.

So how do we judge if the book is historical? To answer this we come back to the question of genre. As we saw in the Outline, Esther is a carefully crafted tale. It is a story based on a series of unlikely coincidences (such as Esther becoming queen at just the right time; and the king happening to be reminded of Mordecai's noble deed just when Haman was about to have him executed; 5:14—6:3). It even has comic features (as when Haman mistakenly thinks the king means to honour him, when in fact he is talking about Mordecai; 6:6–9). Indeed, the opening scene of the book, which sets up all the action, borders on farce: the all-powerful king is humiliated by his wife, and the empire's magnificent communications system is set in motion to declare something ordinary and obvious (for then), that men should rule in their own houses – though the king himself evidently could not! The portrait of the king as pompous, weak and easily manipulated seems closer to caricature than historical actuality. The idea that Esther is a *comedy* is not always recognized in scholarly literature. It is a major emphasis of the recent commentary of Berlin.

Think about
COMEDY IN THE BIBLE

Readers may be wary of the idea that a biblical book may be comic in character. Comedy, however, can be very serious, indeed close to tragedy.

Berlin says of Esther: '. . . even commentators who recognize the comic nature of Esther do not take it into account sufficiently when they interpret the book' (p. xviii). She sees aspects of farce, or *burlesque* in the book (p. xix), and she thinks that 'all the characters are types' (p. xx). She goes on: 'The largest interpretive problems melt away if the story is taken as a comedy associated with a carnival-like festival' (p. xxii).

Do you agree that reading Esther as comedy diminishes some of the ethical problems readers have found in the book? What kind of modern literature or performance do you think is closest to Esther? It may help to read Berlin, pp. xvi–xxii.

Along similar lines, Levenson argues:

the book of Esther is best seen as a historical novella set within the Persian empire. This is not to say that the book is false, only that its truth, like the truth of any piece of literature, is relative to its genre, and the genre of Esther is not that of the historical annal (though it sometimes imitates the style of a historical annal. (p. 25)

The book is not aiming to enlighten us historically, but to illustrate the situation of Jews living in the diaspora. As for date, it probably comes from late in the Persian period, some time after Ahasuerus' reign (since 'Ahasuerus' has to be identified for the reader in 1:1), and perhaps from Susa, where the action is set (p. 26).

So perhaps Esther is best interpreted as a 'What if . . . ?' story: what would happen if sudden destruction, even destruction decreed by an imperial power, were to threaten the Jews? Would they survive, and how? Alternatively (one might speculate) Esther is a tale told to challenge the pride of Palestinian Jews. If Jews in Palestine were tempted to question the loyalty of those Jews who did not return with them, then perhaps Esther was written to ask them: how do you know that there are not some of your people far away who show as much courage and commitment as you do? Can you be certain that you do not owe your continued existence to such people, whom you dismiss as compromisers?

Against all this it may be argued that, while some of the actions and behaviour described in Esther seem for various reasons implausible, strange things very often do happen, not least in the courts and empires of powerful, megalomaniac kings. We should also bear in mind the possibility, noted above, that chapters 9—10, in which a number of the most implausible-seeming events in the book are described, are a secondary addition. Removing them from the discussion would certainly ease the historical difficulties. But at the very least, those who wish to maintain the essential historicity of the book must take account of its style (part comic, part serious), and of the unquestionable elements of parody in parts of the narrative.

ESTHER IN THE CANON

There is no clear allusion to Esther in the New Testament. At most, we find a similar kind of accusation brought against the Jews under Roman rule (Acts 16:21) as brought against the Jews by Haman (Esther 3:8). The place of Esther in the canon must be judged, first, by reference to other Old Testament books.

In its context, we have observed that Esther is unusual. The extra material in LXX removes some of the oddities, and was seemingly intended to make Esther conform more fully to Old Testament norms. Esther even differs from its closest canonical neighbours (Ezra and Nehemiah), because it sets no store by the call to Jews to return to Jerusalem.

In certain of its emphases, however, it resembles other Old Testament books. It is like the stories in Daniel (Dan. 1—6) and the Joseph narrative (Gen 37—50) in that it deals with the place of Jews under foreign rule, far from the homeland (the term 'Diaspora Novella' has been applied to these). All of these show that it is possible for Jews to live, even succeed, under such rule. Daniel and Esther also show that dangers can arise because of Jewish identity. This point is more strongly made in Daniel, where the main characters openly practise their Jewish faith in defiance of decrees. In Esther the danger lies in Jewish identity itself. This question of how to live under foreign rule was plainly an issue for Jews after the exile, and has remained so.

We have also noted how Esther deals with the matter of human responsibility and divine sovereignty. In comparison with other narratives that handle this question, it goes further by posing the hiddenness of God as a fact of experience. It is here that the comedy of Esther lies close to some of the Bible's deepest soul-searching: in those psalms, for example, which express perplexity because God does not answer. Comedy lies close to tragedy because of the haunting question: what if in fact the unexpected happy ending had not materialized? We also noted similarities to themes in Proverbs. Like Proverbs 16, Esther stays on the side of confidence in the face of God's apparent absence.

How might this most Jewish of Old Testament books be read from a Christian point of view? One way is to attempt a typological reading of the book, in which Esther becomes a type of Christ, as in Beckett's recent study: Esther is in some respects like Moses before Pharaoh (p. 42), but more profoundly she is like Christ. She is an 'agent of deliverance . . . [a] mediator', who puts herself under the threat of death for others (pp. 43–4).

A little differently, we can see an analogy between the Jews in exile or diaspora and Christians in 'metaphorical' exile, 'strangers and exiles' (as in Hebrews 11:13). Christian life in the world may bring both privilege and danger because of the Christian's ultimate loyalty to God.

Some of the theology of Esther, however, is common to Jew and Christian: a belief that God is at work in the world in unseen ways, and often when there is no immediate and apparent sign of his working.

Think about
TWO PERSPECTIVES ON ESTHER

Esther, particularly the ending of the book, can be read from two perspectives: a diaspora perspective and a Jerusalem perspective.

From a diaspora perspective the book seems to conclude on an entirely positive note: Mordecai has a position of great influence, which he uses on behalf of his people (10:3) – indeed, his achievements can be compared to those of Israel's kings (10:2); the decisions in favour of the Jews have been entered in the Persian records, so that they will not be forgotten when Mordecai dies (9:20: 10:2); there are references to future generations of Jews who will observe Purim (9:27–32). We can reflect that by the end of the book the Jews, through a series of 'coincidences', have survived, which perhaps implies that they will continue to do so.

So perhaps Esther aims to commend an alternative mode of existence for God's people? That is, it may be right for some to return to Jerusalem to engage in the rebuilding (so Ezra–Nehemiah); but equally it may be right for others to remain behind, even close to the centre of imperial power, and do what they can for their people there.

A Jerusalem perspective, by contrast, raises questions: what has happened to the prophetic promises concerning the rebuilding of Zion, the nations coming to Zion to acknowledge the god of Israel? The Jews may have survived as a result of Mordecai's and Esther's initiatives, but what steps have been taken towards these larger goals? Mordecai may have accomplished much, but he is a servant of Persian power, hence his deeds are recorded in Persian, not Israelite, annals (10:2). Is the Persian empire, with its arbitrary and comical (but also dangerous) leadership really a permanent resting-place for God's people?

Which of these readings do you find more plausible? Are they incompatible?

FURTHER READING

COMMENTARIES
A. Berlin, *Esther*. Philadelphia: Jewish Publication Society, 2001.

D.J.A. Clines, *Ezra, Nehemiah, Esther*. London: Marshall, Morgan and Scott, 1984a.

J.D. Levenson, *Esther*. London: SCM Press, 1997.

C.A. Moore, *Esther*. New York: Doubleday, 1971.

OTHER
M. Beckett, *Gospel in Esther*. Carlisle: Paternoster, 2002.

D.J.A. Clines, *The Esther Scroll: The Story of the Story*. Sheffield: JSOT Press, 1984b.

M.V. Fox, *Character and Ideology in the Book of Esther*, 2nd edition. Grand Rapids: Eerdmans, 2001.

R. Gordis, 'Religion, Wisdom and History in the Book of Esther: A New Solution to an Ancient Crux', *JBL* 100 (1981), pp. 359–88.

K.J.A. Larkin, *Ruth and Esther*. Sheffield: Sheffield Academic Press, 1996.

A.R. Millard, 'The Persian Names in Esther and the Reliability of the Hebrew Text', *JBL* 96 (1977), pp. 481–8.

A.M. Rodriguez, *Esther: A Theological Approach*. Berrien Springs: Andrews University Press, 1995.

E. Yamauchi, *Persia and the Bible*, 2nd edition; Grand Rapids: Baker, 1996.

Chapter 10

EZRA AND NEHEMIAH

INTRODUCTION

The book of Ezra falls into two main sections. Ezra 1—6 tells the story of those who returned from exile in Babylon following the decree of Cyrus in 538 BC. The historical period is the first two decades after that event, until 516, when the new temple was completed. The key figures in this period were Zerubbabel, Joshua, Haggai and Zechariah. The second section is Ezra 7—10, in which Ezra himself is the main figure. This relates to a later period. Ezra probably came to Jerusalem in 458, assuming the king in the narrative is Artaxerxes I (464–424; see 'Dates and dating', p. 257).

PERSIAN KINGS, 550–358 BC

Cyrus	550–530
Cambyses	530–522
Darius I	522–486
Xerxes	486–465
Artaxerxes I	465–424
Darius II	423–404
Artaxerxes II	404–358

The story in Ezra 1—6 is mainly of local opposition to the temple project, from a population that had not experienced the Babylonian exile. The success of Zerubbabel's project depends on his managing to get continuing support from the Persian authorities. Letters are exchanged between the two opposed groups in Judah and the imperial officials, and the final result is that Darius I upholds Cyrus' original decree (Ezra 6).

Ezra 7—10 falls into two parts: the account of his commission to supply the worship of the temple and to teach the laws of the LORD in Judah (Ezra 7—8); and the account of how he faced the problem of intermarriage between Jews who had returned from Babylon and non-Jewish people who lived in Judah (Ezra 9—10).

While Ezra tells of the return to Jerusalem by waves of exiles, who built and maintained the temple, the book of Nehemiah mainly describes the rebuilding of the city walls. The central figure in this book is Nehemiah himself, whose mission is distinct from Ezra's. Nehemiah arrives in the twentieth year of Artaxerxes (Neh. 2:1), that is, 446–445, or 12 to 13 years after Ezra. However, the two projects overlap, as is clear from

Nehemiah 8—9, in which Ezra reappears and takes a leading role in a ceremony of covenant-renewal.

The first and longest section of Nehemiah (chs 1—7) reports Nehemiah's successful mission to rebuild the walls of Jerusalem. The second (chs 8—10) has the covenant-renewal at its centre. The final section (chs 11—13) tells of the dedication of the walls, and of Nehemiah's attempts to maintain order in the community. Nehemiah himself tells a large part of the story, especially in chapters 1—7 and in parts of chapters 12—13 (in the so-called 'Nehemiah memoir'; Williamson 1985, p. xxiv). In places, however, another voice tells the story, referring to Nehemiah in the third person (e.g. 8:9).

STRUCTURE OF EZRA AND NEHEMIAH

Ezra 1:1—6:22	Return from exile and rebuilding the temple
Ezra 7:1—10:44	Ezra's mission: Torah, and the problem of mixed marriages
Neh. 1:1—7:73	Rebuilding the wall of Jerusalem
Neh. 8:1—10:39	Covenant renewal
Neh. 11:1—13:31	Dedication of walls, and further reforms

The book of Ezra belongs closely with Nehemiah; indeed, the two were originally thought of as one. (We know this from the earliest Jewish references to them. For the evidence, see Williamson 1985, p. xxi.) Ezra himself reappears in Nehemiah 8, and the missions of the two men, Ezra and Nehemiah, are presented in the combined work as integrally related.

OUTLINE

EZRA 1:1—6:22: RETURN FROM EXILE AND REBUILDING THE TEMPLE

Cyrus' decree (1:1–11)

The story of the book of Ezra is the continuation of the story of Chronicles. This is immediately clear because the opening passage (1:1–4) repeats and slightly expands the closing words of Chronicles (2 Chron. 36:22–23). The logic of this continuation is clearly seen in English Bibles, where Ezra is placed after Chronicles.

In 539 Cyrus king of Persia overthrew the Babylonian Nabonidus, and this marked the end of the Babylonian domination of the biblical world, and the beginning of the Persian empire, the greatest empire known to the world until that time. Persia's policy on subject peoples was different from Babylon's. Whereas Nebuchadnezzar of Babylon had taken the conquered Jewish people into exile in 597 and 586, Cyrus now pursued a policy of allowing subject peoples to remain in their homeland and maintain their own traditions. His decree regarding the people of Judah is in line with this policy. Independent evidence for the policy comes from the so-called 'Cyrus Cylinder' (*COS* II, pp. 314–16), a clay cylinder which tells how he resettled other populations besides the Jews. (We suggest you look this text up: while offering confirmation of what is said in Ezra 1:2–4 and 6:2–5, it presents Cyrus' policy from an interestingly different perspective.) The narrator adds at this point that Cyrus also personally supervised the return of temple treasures plundered by Nebuchadnezzar 50 years before (1:5–11; cf. 2 Kgs 25:8, 13–17). He had also made a decree that the temple should be rebuilt, though this is not reported until 6:3–5.

The meaning of the decree, from the point of view of the author of Ezra, is explained as a fulfilment of prophecy (1:1). Jeremiah had foretold that Babylon, after a period of supremacy over other nations, would in turn fall to another power (Jer. 50:9), named in another text as the 'king of the Medes' (Jer. 51:11). Texts in Isaiah also pointed to the triumph of Cyrus as part of YHWH's salvation of Judah (Isa. 44:28; 45:1, 13). The rebuilding and maintaining of the temple is an essential part of the programme pursued first by Zerubbabel and later by Ezra.

The exiles who returned (2:1–70)

There follows a list of those who came to resettle in the towns of Judah. (The list closely resembles Neh. 7:6–73.) Zerubbabel and Jeshua are at their head. Zerubbabel was a descendant of David (1 Chron. 3:17–19), and a grandson of Jehoiachin, who was taken captive in 597. (In 1 Chronicles 3:19 Zerubbabel is the son of Pedaiah, while here, and in Haggai 1:1, he is the son of Shealtiel. Williamson 1985 (p. 32) suggests the difference may be accounted for by a levirate marriage). Jeshua was the grandson of Jozadak (Ezra 3:2), the last high priest before the exile (1 Chron. 6:14). The leaders therefore represent the political and religious authorities of Judah from before the exile.

The largest part of the list consists of the ordinary people of Judah (2:3–35), followed by the priests (vv. 36–39), the Levites (v. 40) and other officials of the temple (vv. 41–58). The concern in this list is to establish the legitimacy of those who returned, that is, that they had roots in known Jewish families, and in some cases links with places (e.g. vv. 22–23, 25–28). This concern appears in verses 59–63. Finally a connection is made between the resettlement in the land and the project to rebuild the temple (vv. 68–69).

Foundations (3:1–13)

The narrative now portrays the returned community as zealous to re-establish the worship of YHWH in Jerusalem. Sacrificial worship is instituted at the Feast of Booths (or Tabernacles) in the first year (3:3–6), while in the second year a start is made on the foundations of the temple. Everything is done properly, with the priests and Levites fully involved (v. 8; cf. 1 Chron. 23:4). There is an echo here of Solomon's building of the first temple, and also in the reference to trade with Tyre and Sidon for building materials (v. 7; cf. 1 Chron. 22:2–4). David's detailed preparations for that temple, a major topic in Chronicles, are also recalled (v. 10), and there are further hints of Chronicles in the praise (vv. 10–11, cf. 1 Chron. 16:4–7, 34; 2 Chron. 5:11–13). By comparison with the first temple the new one is poor; even so, it is clearly important that a temple has been re-established on its old site.

Opposition finally overcome (4:1—6:22)

The new arrivals from Babylon did not find themselves alone. Rather, there was a population in and around Judah which evidently did not welcome the incomers. These are called 'the people of the land' in 4:4, and distinguished from 'the people of Judah'. By calling the returning exiles 'the people of Judah' the author is declaring them the rightful occupants of the land, while 'the people of the land' (v. 4) are introduced as 'the adversaries of Judah and Benjamin' (v. 1), and excluded from the project (cf. also 3:3). This is why the local people's approach to Zerubbabel is rejected (vv. 2–3). Zerubbabel plainly regards their claim to worship YHWH as suspect.

The local opposition to the temple project persisted until it was built, as 4:5 shows, since Darius was the king who finally authorized the building (ch. 6). Following 4:5, the author includes an account of such opposition which goes well beyond the time-frame of the temple project under Zerubbabel. In 4:6 we read of an accusation against Judah in the reign of Ahasuerus (= Xerxes, 486–465). And 4:7–23 records a correspondence between officials of the Persian province 'Beyond-the-River' and Artaxerxes I (465–24), in which they protest about the building of Jerusalem's walls, a project which was undertaken long after Zerubbabel in the time of Nehemiah. The resettlement of Judah by the returning exiles involved a long struggle with the neighbouring peoples.

It is at this point (4:8) that the language changes from Hebrew to Aramaic. The change is occasioned by the verbatim report of the letters that are exchanged in chapter 4, which were actually in Aramaic. The narrative itself is also in Aramaic up to 6:18. An effect of this is to illustrate the importance of the imperial power in the affairs of the region: the success of the projects to rebuild both temple and city depends on demonstrating the legality of the projects according to royal decree.

After the digression about events in the time of Artaxerxes, 4:24 brings us suddenly back to the time described in 4:4–5, when the issue of the temple had not yet been resolved. The temple project is revived by the preaching of the prophets Haggai and Zechariah (5:1), the prophets whose prophecies are recorded in the books that bear their names (see *EOT IV*, pp. 229–57). Haggai urges the people to remember their true priorities, while Zechariah encourages them with visions of a more glorious future. So the temple project resumes (5:2).

This brings the local authorities into play once again. Tattenai and his associates do not seem to be opposed to the project as such, but they act as careful officials, setting down names and relevant facts. Tattenai's report to Darius puts the case of the people of Judah as they might have set it out themselves, pointing out especially that Cyrus had permitted them to build the temple (5:6–17). Tattenai therefore asks for an investigation to settle once for all the issue of the Judeans' right to build. The result of the search in the imperial capitals is that a copy of Cyrus' decree is discovered (6:1–5), and Darius instructs Tattenai to permit the building to go ahead (6:6–12).

So the temple is completed a little over 20 years after the first return from Babylon (6:15).The account closes with another celebration by the people of Judah, and a Passover. Passover was particularly symbolic of escape from oppression in a foreign land and occupation of the land of promise (see also Josh. 5:10–12).

Digging deeper:
UNDERSTANDING CHRONOLOGY IN EZRA 4—6

Our author has a way of putting things together that actually happened at different times. We have already noticed his long insertion in 4:6–23 which interrupts the account of the immediate events to give a picture covering a long period. There are two more instances in ch. 6. First, the mention of Artaxerxes in 6:14 is unexpected: he cannot have helped with the temple project, since he came to the throne only later. Second, the reference to the 'king of Assyria' (6:22) is not historically accurate, since Darius was Persian, and the Assyrian empire had been overthrown two centuries earlier.

Is the author just mixed up about history? Or do these features of the narrative have a purpose? An answer may lie in his wish to bring out the character of events. Note that Artaxerxes did send more silver and gold for the temple (7:15–16).

Compare the different ways of understanding this problem in Williamson 1985, pp. 56–60, and Grabbe, pp. 133–4.

EZRA 7:1—10:44: EZRA'S MISSION: TORAH, TEMPLE AND THE PROBLEM OF MIXED MARRIAGES

We move on to the time of Artaxerxes, some 60 years later (7:1). As we have noticed, our author is quite happy to juxtapose events from different periods for his own purposes.

Ezra himself is introduced with a priestly pedigree going back to Aaron, via Zadok, chief priest in David's time (7:1–5). He comes as part of another wave of settlers from Babylon. This shows that the return did not happen all at once, but that the Persian authorities kept up their policy towards the people of Judah. As before, there were priests and Levites among the returnees, as well as lay people (7:7).

Ezra's purpose was to study and practise the 'law of the LORD', and teach it to the people of Judah (7:10). He too came armed with a decree from a Persian king (7:11–26). The main theme of the decree is once again provision for the work and personnel of the temple. This makes a strong link between the two parts of the book (chs 1—6, 7—10). But Artaxerxes also clearly authorizes Ezra's mission to teach YHWH's law to the people (7:25–26). Keeping the law and providing for the temple are closely linked. The king's concern may have been that the Persian contributions to the temple service were being properly used.

From 7:27, Ezra begins to speak in his own voice, first giving thanks that YHWH has once again put it into the heart of a king to act for the benefit of his people in Jerusalem. Ezra's 'memoir' continues to 9:15.

Ezra now tells of those who gathered to go with him to Jerusalem (8:1–14). He is concerned that there are no priests or Levites among the party, so arranges for some to join them, along with other temple servants (8:15–20). After fasting, Ezra solemnly makes over the gold and other Persian offerings for the temple to the priests and Levites (8:24–30). The journey is a great procession out of Babylon to the temple itself, which is at the heart of the enterprise. The real arrival in Jerusalem is the giving of the gifts for worship, and the worship celebrations which follow (8:31–36).

The remainder of the book (chs 9—10) is taken up with the problem of mixed marriages. Ezra sees marriage of Jews to non-Jews as a breach of the covenant. He uses the strong word 'faithlessness' (*ma'al*) to describe it (9:4), the word which is frequently used in Chronicles for deep-rooted rebellion against YHWH (1 Chron. 10:13).

Intermarriage had evidently taken root in the community, as the lists in 10:18–44 show. The mass divorce is undertaken with great solemnity and care. In spite of Ezra's belief that it was a terrible sin, he believed that by repentance and the grace of YHWH there could still be hope for the future of the people (10:2).

NEHEMIAH 1:1—7:73a: REBUILDING THE WALLS OF JERUSALEM
The project established (1:1—4:23)
Nehemiah held the important position of 'cupbearer to the king' (1:11), like other Jews who became eminent in exile (Daniel, Mordecai). He is distressed at news that the walls of Jerusalem are in poor repair (Neh. 1:1–3). The news probably refers to the event described in Ezra 4:7–23 (Artaxerxes' decree to put a stop to repairs on the walls).

Think about
MIXED MARRIAGES

Why is mixed marriage so grave a sin in Ezra's eyes? To answer this, recall that for Ezra the return to the promised land is like the first exodus from Egypt and the first possession of the land. This means that the book of Ezra is a little like Deuteronomy, Moses' sermons to Israel before they entered the land for the first time. See Deuteronomy 7:1–5 (Ezra seems to have this passage in mind in 9:10–12). Why do you think such warnings about purity come at new entrances to the land? Notice the importance of 'covenant' here, as also in ancient Israel (10:3, 8).

Nehemiah's prayer reflects a theme of Chronicles: that misfortune for Judah and Jerusalem is the result of sin, but that repentance can bring restoration (1:6–9; cf. 2 Chron. 7:14; Ezra 10:2–3). Nehemiah now brings a request to the same Artaxerxes that he might continue that work of repair (2:1–8). And once again a Persian king supports the project of re-establishing the Jewish community in Judah.

Nehemiah inspects the walls and announces the plan to rebuild (2:11–17). The project immediately provokes the anger of certain leading people among the local population (2:9–10, 19–20). The building of the walls will lead to the same kind of trouble as the building of the temple.

Chapter 3 gives a detailed account of those who built and the sections for which they were responsible. It shows that the entire people of Judah was involved, including the priests. The account of the building begins with the Sheep Gate in the north-eastern corner of the city and goes anti-clockwise to the Dung Gate at the southern tip, then up the eastern slope; in this last section it apparently takes a new line.

The hostility of Sanballat, Tobiah and others goes from angry mockery (4:1) to outright threat of attack (4:7–9). So the labourers have to contend with preparing to defend themselves, on top of the great difficulties of the building itself. Nehemiah's trust in YHWH for help goes hand in hand with great watchfulness (4:15–23).

Trouble within and without: but success! (5:1—7:73a)

Progress is matched by setbacks. The first setback comes from within the people. In contrast to the picture of unity in chapter 4 it now appears that some of the people of Judah are being impoverished by the actions of others (5:1–5). The crisis has apparently been brought about by famine, but perhaps also by the fact that the men are occupied with wall-building. People are complaining about shortage of food, having to give property to creditors in 'pledge', or having to borrow to pay tax (the contribution to royal tribute). In this crisis, some are even having to allow sons and daughters to become slaves.

The things reported remind us of the serious abuses in the community that the prophets preached against. For example, Isaiah had condemned taking houses in pledge (Isa. 5:8). The post-exilic community has clearly fallen back into some of its old sinful ways.

In his criticism of them, Nehemiah lays stress on the fact that the people are 'brothers' (vv. 1, 7–9, NRSV 'people', 'kindred', 'kin'), an important theme of Deuteronomy (as in Deut. 15:1–18), to argue that such activities

---

ENSLAVEMENT IN ISRAEL

How could Israelites have become slaves to fellow-Israelites? Old Testament laws provided means for those who became poor to get back on their feet economically. They could allow creditors to use their goods or land temporarily, or they could even become slaves, also temporarily, in order to repay debt. The purpose of all this was to restore the poor to a position where they could again provide for their own needs. The Old Testament maintains a clear distinction between debt-slaves (of the type just mentioned) and so-called 'chattel-slaves', a type known in the ancient world, who became the actual property of their masters (see Lev. 25:39–46).

The classic texts for this Old Testament institution are in Deuteronomy. See Deuteronomy 15:1–18; 23:19; 24:6, 10–13.

---

are wrong. He also admits that he and his own family are implicated in lending at interest (v. 10). The assembly of the people agree to return land and houses held in pledge and to return money taken as interest.

Nehemiah now claims that he did not take from the public purse payment to which he was entitled as 'governor' (5:14–19). He presumably did this in order to avoid adding to the tax burden on the people, and he now records it in order to set an example of the sort of generosity that is needed in order to make the restoration project succeed. This note was apparently added at a later time in Nehemiah's term as governor.

The 'memoir' returns to the theme of opposition from outside. The first strategy of Sanballat, Tobiah and Geshem is to persuade Nehemiah that they want to come to an agreement with them (6:2). But they soon threaten to turn the authorities against the Jews with false reports of plans to rebel (the same strategy used on an earlier occasion, Ezra 4:12–13), and they use other trickery to discredit Nehemiah. However, the threats come to nothing, and the walls are completed in an astonishingly short time (6:15). Even so, the influence of Tobiah remains a problem because, as we now discover, he is related by marriage to some in the Jewish community (6:18). It seems the intermarriage problem, which Ezra tried to deal with, has not entirely gone away!

With the city now properly protected, Nehemiah organizes a plan to guard it. With this in mind, and because the numbers in the city are low (7:4), he decides to ensure that it is sufficiently well populated to be secure. So he turns to the genealogy of the first arrivals (v. 5) which we have already seen in Ezra 2, presumably in order to establish who should be living in Jerusalem (7:6–73).

NEHEMIAH 7:73b—10:39: COVENANT RENEWAL

The next three chapters have the form of a covenant renewal ceremony. The 'book of the law of Moses', which is read as the first part of the ceremony, is the basis of the covenant (ch. 8); the reading is followed by confession of sin (ch. 9), and finally the people commit themselves to renewed loyalty (ch. 10).

Ezra's sudden reappearance at this point is surprising. Nothing is said about Ezra between his arrival in Jerusalem 12 or 13 years before Nehemiah, and the events we have just been reading about. For this reason, scholars often argue that Nehemiah 8 originally belonged after Ezra 8, where it would fit well. In that case it would have

been brought to its present position afterwards by the final editor of the two books, perhaps in order to give the ceremony a more climactic position in the whole story, and in order to present the missions of Ezra and Nehemiah as united. It has also been suggested that Nehemiah 9 originally came after Ezra 10 because of its tone of sorrowful repentance, so different from the joy of Nehemiah 8. See Williamson 1987, pp. 20–5, for a treatment of some of these issues. In their present context, however, Nehemiah 8 and 9 together mark distinct elements in a covenant renewal ceremony.

The 'book of the law of Moses' probably refers to the Pentateuch. (On most accounts the whole Pentateuch would have been in existence by this time.) The importance of the law (*torah*) in this part of the book cannot be overemphasized, and its prominence here is clearly meant to show its great significance in the life of the post-exilic community.

The form of the reading ceremony seems to mark the beginning of the tradition of *interpretation* of the law, or Scripture, which became so important in Judaism. Ezra reads from a sort of pulpit, and the physical layout of the event and the people's responses resemble a form of liturgy (8:5–6). As Ezra reads, the Levites move among the people making sure they understand (vv. 7–8).

The people at first weep (v. 9), as the reading of the law reminds them how serious it is to ignore YHWH's word, but the keynote of the event is joy (8:12). This theme continues as Ezra, the priests and the Levites proclaim a celebration of the autumn festival, the Feast of Booths (or Tabernacles), which was a joyful memorial of YHWH's deliverance from Egypt

251

long before (8:13–17; cf. Lev. 23:39–43; Deut. 16:13–15). The reason for joy is the same in this event: the release from captivity, which has made possible this new possession of the promised land (v. 17).

The heart of Nehemiah 9 is a great confessional prayer (9:6–37). It is prepared for by a solemn separation of the people from all non-Israelites (9:2). The sudden change from joy in chapter 8 to sorrow in chapter 9, the absence of Ezra, and the reference to separation from foreigners (v. 2) at this late stage, have (as noted) suggested to scholars that chapters 8 and 9 did not originally belong together. (According to NRSV, the prayer is introduced by the words 'And Ezra said'. However, NRSV is following LXX at this point; the words are not in the Hebrew, which is followed by NIV and others.)

The liturgy of penitence, however, makes sense in the general picture of covenant renewal. The form of the chapter resembles some of the great psalms of penitence which also celebrate the grace of YHWH in his past dealings with Israel (e.g. Pss 78; 106). There are also prayers of confession in Ezra 9:6–15; 10:2–4. In each case the confessions express the hope of mercy. The present confession is also a hymn of praise and thanks (9:6–15).

The final part of the prayer (9:32–37) is interesting for the attitude it expresses towards Persian rule. Hitherto in Ezra–Nehemiah, Persia has been cast in the role of benefactor, providing everything needed for the people of Judah to re-establish themselves in their homeland. Now the prayer sees the people as 'slaves in the land that you gave to our ancestors', and laments that the land's wealth must go in tribute to an overlord (9:36–37). Nehemiah 9 expresses an eschatological hope, that is, a hope for a future far better than the present conditions, even though there is cause to celebrate even these.

The final phase in the covenant renewal (ch. 10) is the solemn undertaking to keep the covenant. This is in written form (9:38), on a document bearing the names of Nehemiah, priests, Levites and senior representatives of the people (10:1–27). The solemnity of it is expressed in the words 'enter into a curse and an oath to walk in God's law' (10:29), meaning that the people accept the terms of the covenant, which involved 'blessings and curses' (see, for example, Deut. 28). The 'commandments, ordinances and statutes' (10:29) are the individual commands in the various law-codes contained in the Pentateuch. The language is very like Deuteronomy's (e.g. Deut. 5:31). These commands form the content of the covenant. A strong theme in the undertaking is that they will keep separate from the other peoples of the land (10:30–31). Finally, they resolve to maintain the regular worship of the temple by making all the due offerings (10:32–39), especially the offerings for the priests and Levites (cf. Num. 18:21–25; Deut. 14:28–29; see also Neh. 12:44).

The temple thus remains in the centre of the call to faithfulness. But the leading idea is the need to obey YHWH's commandments in their totality.

NEHEMIAH 11:1—13:31: DEDICATION OF WALLS, AND FURTHER REFORMS
Residents of Jerusalem and Judah (11:1—12:26)
The final section of Nehemiah brings to a conclusion the twin themes of the two books: the establishment of temple worship and the

rebuilding of the walls of Jerusalem. Before the account of the dedication of the walls, we are given further lists of the inhabitants of Judah, following on from chapter 7. To a large extent, the lists contain information already met. The first list (11:1–20), comprising groups of ordinary inhabitants of Judah and Benjamin, then priests, Levites and gatekeepers, resembles the list in 1 Chronicles 9:2–17. The time perspective has shifted back to the period of the first return, a century before Nehemiah. The point of returning to this theme is to show that the events described in Nehemiah continue and complete the story of resettlement. It also shows that specific measures were taken to ensure that Jerusalem in particular was repopulated (11:1).

Further lists occupy 11:21—12:26. These are mostly records of priests and Levites; 11:25–36 is an exception, showing the settlement of towns in Judah and Benjamin. There is some repetition of the names in 12:1–7 and 12:12–21, as also with 10:2–8. Blenkinsopp (1989, p. 337) helpfully tabulates the correspondences.

Two points may be made about these lists. First, they are not systematic genealogical records. This is clear from the element of repetition that we have noticed. Presumably the author of this part of the book has gathered similar records which formerly existed separately. Furthermore, the names recorded actually come from two different periods: the time of the first return under Zerubbabel and Jeshua, and the time of Nehemiah.

The second point follows from the first, namely that the lists are used to promote a theme: the resettling of Judah and Benjamin in fulfilment of YHWH's promise, and

according to his command – hence the strong emphasis on the proper ordering of temple worship by the stationing of priests and Levites in Jerusalem.

Rededication (12:27—13:3)

The dedication of the walls of Jerusalem echoes the account of their building, with two groups of leaders of the people making a procession round the walls. The procession climaxes in a ceremony of worship in the temple (12:40). As at the completion of the temple itself, the keynote is rejoicing (12:43; cf. Ezra 6:22).

The unity of the temple and wall projects is clear from the return to the temple theme in 12:44—13:3. Two paragraphs beginning 'on that day' (12:44; 13:1) take their cue from the wall-dedication ceremony, but tell of measures taken to ensure proper worship arrangements. The first focuses on offerings for the maintenance of the clergy (see on 10:37–39), but also reflects other practices from Nehemiah's time. The second (13:1–3) connects with Deuteronomy 23:3–4 (cf. Numbers 22—24). It fits with Ezra–Nehemiah's theme of maintaining the purity of the people.

Final reforms (13:4–31)

The final verses of Nehemiah abandon the note of triumph and turn to consider problems in sustaining the community's faithfulness. These apparently arose during a time when Nehemiah had returned to Persia, and were discovered by him on a second visit to Jerusalem (13:6–7). In 13:4–9 we find the undertakings in 12:44—13:3 overturned, since the space given over to storing the tithes in the temple has been allocated instead to Tobiah, one of those who had opposed the building of the walls, and an Ammonite (cf. 2:19; and see again

6:17–19)! The problem lies not only in the temple but at the grass roots, for the offerings have not even been set aside by the people (13:10–11). Nehemiah also records other abuses that have crept into the community: trading on the Sabbath (13:15–22) and, once more, intermarriage (13:23–24). In each of these cases Nehemiah enforces a reform. His repeated prayer ('remember me, O my God') suggests his personal struggle to carry through his ministry despite opposition from within and without, and his memoir closes the book on this note (13:31).

KEY THEMES

YHWH's favour

The narrator traces YHWH's hand in events: Cyrus issues his decree because the LORD 'moved his heart' (Ezra 1:1); Ezra and Nehemiah both testify to YHWH's hand upon them (Ezra 7:27; Neh. 2:8); YHWH encourages the people to rebuild the temple (Ezra 5:1; 6:14) and similarly blesses the work of rebuilding the walls (Neh. 4:15; 6:16). The people respond to YHWH in worship (Ezra 3:10–13; 6:19–22; Neh. 12:27–43), and by committing themselves to keep his law (Neh. 8—10).

Force of personal example

Ezra and Nehemiah are leading figures in the narrative, men of piety and determination who each accomplish significant things, even in the face of opposition. The first-person 'memoirs' of Ezra and Nehemiah ensure that their personalities and actions stand out among the many other names listed at different points.

Continuity

In various ways Ezra–Nehemiah makes clear that the migrations of Jews to Jerusalem in the period after 538 are a continuation, not a new beginning. The returnees stand in continuity with Israel before the exile. This is reflected in the concern with the ancestry of those who returned (Ezra 2; Neh. 7). It also explains the echoes of earlier parts of the Old Testament such as the accounts of the exodus and of Solomon's temple; a further example is Nehemiah 6:16 (reminiscent of Josh. 2:24; 5:1).

Israel

So the post-exilic community are the legitimate successors of pre-exilic Israel. They return to the territory of the former kingdom of Judah, but apparently see themselves as somehow linked to the Israelites of the former northern kingdom as well: when the temple is built they offer sacrifices for all the twelve tribes (Ezra 6:17; 8:35). Similarly, the extensive review of Israel's history in Nehemiah 9 mostly covers the period when Israel was still one nation (vv. 7–25 at least). Ezra–Nehemiah, like Chronicles, seems to hold that the ideal Israel is a 12-tribe entity (see Ch. 11).

Law of Moses; worship

This point must be balanced by noting the great weight Ezra–Nehemiah lays upon law and upon worship in Jerusalem. The climax of Ezra–Nehemiah, the account of the dedication of Jerusalem's walls in Nehemiah 7—12, brings together law-keeping (chs 8—10) and worship (12:27–43), and in so doing merely highlights what are major themes throughout. Worship in Jerusalem and law-keeping almost define Israel in Ezra–Nehemiah: Israel, or at least the nucleus of a restored Israel, consists of those who are committed to maintaining worship in the rebuilt Jerusalem temple, and to keeping YHWH's law.

This is another point of agreement with Chronicles, which shows the same interest in priests and Levites, and so in the proper arrangements for worship (Ezra 2:36–41; Neh. 11:10–24; 12:1–26), and, like Ezra–Nehemiah, insists on the legitimacy of the Jerusalem temple and the law of Moses as non-negotiable points in the definition of Israel.

Success or failure?

Ezra 3:10–13 states that when the foundations for the new temple were laid, there were those who wept, because they remembered the former temple. That event neatly sums up one aspect of Ezra–Nehemiah: by the end of Nehemiah, in spite of the further rebuilding which has by then occurred, not even the old kingdom of Judah has been restored, let alone the kingdom of Solomon. The territory the returned exiles inhabit includes at most parts of the former allocations of Judah and Benjamin (Neh. 11), and it is not an independent kingdom, but under Persian rule. The permission of Persian kings is required at every stage in the process of return and rebuilding.

Eskenazi (p. 95) summarizes Nehemiah 8—13 under the heading 'Success (Objective Reached)'. But is Ezra–Nehemiah simply a success story? Arguably not: Ezra 7—10, the section describing Ezra's mission, ends on the negative note of banned intermarriage (Ezra 10:18–44); Nehemiah 8—10, in some ways the climax of Ezra–Nehemiah, has at its heart the extended confession and lament of Nehemiah 9; Nehemiah ends with a chapter describing violations of the law (Neh. 13), suggesting the possibility that, in spite of the pledges of Nehemiah 10, there will be further violations in future. There is, it emerges, a negative side to continuity with the past: the post-exilic community repeats the sins of pre-exilic Israel (Ezra 9:1–2; Neh. 13:26–27).

The return as fulfilment of prophecy

Ezra 1:1 describes the return to Jerusalem and Judah after the exile as a fulfilment of Jeremiah's prophecy (Jer. 25:11; 29:10). The term often used in Ezra to describe the returned exiles (*golah*, Ezra 1:11; 2:1; 6:19–20, etc.) is a further link with Jeremiah, where it refers to those who would go into exile in Babylon as against those who stayed behind in the land (Jer. 28:6; 29:1; cf. 24:5). The role of Cyrus in the events of Ezra 1—6 reminds us of Isaiah's vision of a deliverer who would conquer nations in order to bring Israel back to its land (Isa. 41:2, 25; 44:28—45:7).

So does the author think that every prophecy about the restoration of Israel and Judah has been fulfilled in the events recorded in Ezra–Nehemiah? For all the allusions to prophecy that we find, there are other prophecies which seem to be passed over in silence: for instance, prophecies of the union of northern and southern kingdoms (Ezek. 37:15–23), of a new Davidic king (Ezek. 37:24; Jer. 23:5–6), of other nations being subject to Israel (Isa. 60:12) and coming to Zion to learn the Torah (Isa. 2:2–4). Nothing described in Ezra–Nehemiah matches up to these prophecies.

Why is there so little allusion to such prophecies in Ezra–Nehemiah? One answer might be that the author of Ezra–Nehemiah looks so favourably on Persia's role in restoring Judah that he looks for no further fulfilment of prophecy beyond the re-establishing of the temple worship, and ensuring that the people obeyed the law.

This picture is only partly true, however. The protection of Persia certainly demonstrates YHWH's power to keep his promises, but this does not mean that the relationship with the empire is regarded as a permanent good in itself. As noted above, there are signs that the present reality falls short of what might be hoped for. This is clearest in the prayer in Nehemiah 9, especially at 9:32–37. The complaint there that 'we are slaves in the land' (v. 36), because of the heavy tax demands of the imperial authorities, is in line with other passages where it is clear that Persian rule was oppressive in its own way (Ezra 4:13; 7:14; Neh. 5:4; see also Ezra 9:8–9; and Blenkinsopp 1989, pp. 307–8). There are also texts in which Persia seems to be deliberately equated or classed with the arch-oppressor, Assyria (Ezra 6:22; cf. Neh. 9:32).

The situation portrayed in Ezra–Nehemiah, therefore, is like that in the books of Haggai and Zechariah (the prophets named in Ezra 5): that is, while the return is seen as an act of salvation brought about by YHWH, there remains a hope of better things yet to come.

Hope for the future?

The great confessional prayers (Ezra 9:6–15; 10:2–4; Neh. 9:6–37) are like certain of the psalms (e.g. Pss 78; 106). As well as confessing past sins, they express hope of YHWH's mercy. Confession and repentance may be seen as a prelude to salvation. The concern to put right the wrongs in the community, as well as institute proper worship, has the purpose of preparing for the salvation which YHWH might yet bring.

Is this eschatological? If there is eschatological hope in Ezra–Nehemiah (involving the overthrow of all the enemies of YHWH and Israel) it is very muted (see, for example, the comments on Neh. 11:25–36).

David?

In Ezra–Nehemiah David is mainly referred to in connection with temple worship (e.g. Ezra 3:10; Neh. 12:24, 36–37, 45). There is, however, no mention of the promise to David (contrast Chronicles), and no living descendant of David is described as such in Ezra–Nehemiah, apart from Hattush (Ezra 8:2–3). It is striking that the author does not identify Zerubbabel as of Davidic descent (contrast 1 Chron. 3:17–19), particularly as Zerubbabel plays a leading role in rebuilding the temple (Ezra 3:8; 5:2). Temple building was a project dear to David, and yet the author does not bring out the point that a descendant of David was following in his ancestor's footsteps.

Eskenazi (pp. 22–23) argues that this is a deliberate omission: the author saw no significance in the promise to David for his own day, hence Davidic descent was no longer important. This argument is hard to refute, in view of Ezra–Nehemiah's silence on the topic, but perhaps the omission can be taken another way, as reflecting the fact that no descendant of David since the exile had ruled as king over an independent nation. Does the author feel that, until the situation of 'slavery' (Neh. 9) is at an end, the promise has not really been fulfilled, hence that it is inappropriate to refer to someone like Zerubbabel as of Davidic descent?

CRITICAL ISSUES

LITERARY-CRITICAL ISSUES

Aspects of Ezra–Nehemiah as narrative

Is it appropriate to consider Ezra–Nehemiah as narrative? It presents a highly uneven appearance, being made up of diverse

Digging deeper:
SIMILARITIES WITH CHRONICLES?

As we shall see below, the common authorship of Chronicles and Ezra–Nehemiah, which used to be widely accepted, has been challenged. This is partly because Ezra–Nehemiah appears to differ from Chronicles in certain theological themes. We have noted one such theme above, the promise to David. Do you think that this is a real point of difference?

Consider also the question of 'immediate retribution'. Some have argued that Ezra–Nehemiah does not share this concept with Chronicles, since none of the characters experience dramatic reversals of fortune caused by a sudden change in themselves. But again, is there a real difference between the two works on this point? In Ch. 11 we will see that 'immediate retribution' in Chronicles is best not seen as a universal theory of morality. Rather, it aims to persuade readers that repentance can always bring about a change in circumstances. Can this basic idea be found in Ezra–Nehemiah also?

For a discussion of other aspects which some have cited as points of difference between Chronicles and Ezra–Nehemiah (e.g. mixed marriages, the centrality of the exodus) see Blenkinsopp 1989, pp. 51–4 and Williamson 1977, p. 66, n. 1.

Think about
INTENTIONAL UNEVENNESS?

Ezra–Nehemiah's literary diversity has not stopped commentators treating it as a coherent entity with recognizable theological themes, but Eskenazi's study is unusual in that she makes the literary unevenness the starting-point for her approach: in her view it is deliberate, and part of the 'message' of Ezra–Nehemiah. Her arguments include the following:

- Ezra–Nehemiah aims to suggest that many hands played a part in the rebuilding of Jerusalem and the temple. A chapter like Nehemiah 3 could have been related much more briefly, but the compiler wanted the sheer weight of names. So, too, with many other lists in Ezra–Nehemiah (pp. 186–7).
- Similarly, the first-person sections could have been rewritten as third-person narrative; but the use of both narrative styles is another way of suggesting that many people were involved.
- The repetition of Ezra 2 (the list of those who returned in the first wave) at Nehemiah 7, after the walls have been finished, is intentional (pp. 88–95). As one reads through Ezra–Nehemiah, one senses that the earlier and later post-exilic generations are all contributing towards what is really one endeavour, even though they returned at different times, and engaged in different tasks. The repetition of Ezra 2 at Nehemiah 7 links the beginning with the end: when Jerusalem's wall is rebuilt, that accomplishes the aim which even the earliest groups of returnees had in mind. (Compare her similar treatment of the list of priests and Levites at Neh. 12:1–26, pp. 183–4).

Do you find this plausible?

materials: third-person accounts (much of Ezra 1—6; Neh. 8), first-person accounts (parts of Ezra 7—10; Neh. 1:1—7:5; Neh. 12:31—13:31); royal decrees and letters (Ezra 1:2–4; the Aramaic letters in Ezra 4—6 and at 7:12–26); many lists (Ezra 2; 8:1–14; 10:18–44; Neh. 3; 7:6–68 [= Ezra 2, with some variations]; 9:38—10:29; 11:3–24;

12:1–26); prayers, individual (Ezra 9:6–15; Neh. 1:5–11) and corporate (Neh. 9:5–37). These different materials could have been rewritten into a more uniform account, but this has not been done.

Dates and dating

The plain reading of Ezra–Nehemiah is that Ezra came to Jerusalem first, Nehemiah followed some years later, and the work of the two men in Jerusalem overlapped. The dating system in the books puts Ezra's arrival in Jerusalem at 458, that is, in the reign of Artaxerxes I (but see the panel 'Did Ezra and Nehemiah know each other?'). Nehemiah followed in 445, stayed for 12 years (to 433) and made a second visit a few years later. It is not clear exactly when this second visit is to be dated, but presumably it took place before the death of Artaxerxes in 424: Nehemiah 13:6–7 seems to imply that Artaxerxes was the king who gave him permission to return to Jerusalem. We do not know how long he stayed on that occasion. Assuming these to be the raw data for dating, the books cannot have been written before about 430, but they could have been written not long after.

Besides the dates given in the books themselves, other evidence may come from the lists of those who returned. On the basis of the lists of priests and Levites in Nehemiah 12:1–26, Williamson puts the earliest date for the books at about 400. This is based on the view that the compilation in this section goes up to the time of Johanan (12:23: on this view Jaddua, who according to Josephus was high priest later in the fourth century, is an addition in 12:22; Williamson 1985, pp. 359, 361). It should be observed, however, that these lists are not necessarily comprehensive, that we do not know accession dates, and that they cannot

Digging deeper:
DID EZRA AND NEHEMIAH KNOW EACH OTHER?

Most recent commentaries follow the order of events in Ezra–Nehemiah, though with reservations (Williamson, Blenkinsopp, Clines). An alternative view, less popular now than at one time, puts Ezra's work later than Nehemiah's, in the reign of Artaxerxes II. In the most common form of this view, Ezra arrived in Jerusalem in 398, not 458. This theory helped explain why, for the most part, Ezra and Nehemiah appear to work separately. While this solution is now felt to be less attractive, some questions remain. For example, why did Ezra wait for 13 years, till Nehemiah's arrival, to undertake a public reading of the law which he came to establish (Neh. 8—9)? Why are there no other signs that they knew each other? These questions have led to the sort of proposals we noted above about earlier forms of the text in which the narratives about Ezra and Nehemiah were separate from each other. Such proposals imply that their activities were quite unrelated. They would also imply that an author has deliberately shaped the material in order to make an artificial connection between the two men's work, in order to emphasize that the establishment of the law and the defence of the city were thematically inseparable (Clines, pp. 11–12).

The view that Ezra came after Nehemiah arose in part from their apparently separate ministries, but was also based on a range of points of interpretation. Clines lists 13 of these, with responses to each (Clines, pp. 16–24). Consider their strength individually and cumulatively. What kind of arguments are they? Note also Clines' arguments for the priority of Ezra (p. 21).

be compared in detail with independently known records. Blenkinsopp (1989, pp. 336–8) sees 12:1–26 as an incomplete list spanning the period up to Jaddua, around the time of Alexander the Great in the late fourth century.

A final issue concerns Ezra 1—6. This account of the building of the temple under Zerubbabel (completed in 516) refers to a time well before Ezra's arrival in Jerusalem. It may be, therefore, that it was composed by someone other than the author of Ezra 7—10. However, the fact that it deals with events up to 516 does not necessarily mean that it was composed close to that time. Williamson puts it around 300, and thinks it was written as a response to the Samaritans' building their temple on Mt Gerizim about then (1985, p. xxxv). By contrast, Blenkinsopp finds that Ezra 1—6 and 7—10 both derive from the Chronicler (1989, pp. 43–4, 47–54).

The date of Ezra–Nehemiah is subject to some of the uncertainties surrounding the date of Chronicles. The genealogical data seem to point to around 400 (or later if we include Jaddua). An occasion for the book could be the building of the temple on Mt Gerizim around 300. However, as little is known about the period 516–325, apart from Ezra–Nehemiah, there may well have been other occasions for writing at any time after 430, the time of Nehemiah's second visit to Jerusalem.

Sources, authorship, editing

The authorship of Ezra–Nehemiah is closely connected with dating, yet it is strictly separate. The writings may come from soon after the time of Ezra and Nehemiah, but is the author reliable, and are the writings based on actual events? In particular, can we be sure that the author had access to reliable accounts of the earliest events recorded in the books, in Ezra 1—6?

One feature of Ezra–Nehemiah is its use of sources. In the first place, we hear the voices of Ezra and Nehemiah themselves in what are known, respectively, as the Ezra Memoir (EM, Ezra 7—8, Neh. 8, Ezra 9—10) and the Nehemiah Memoir (NM, Neh. 1—7, and parts of Neh. 12—13). The authenticity of NM is generally accepted, partly because of the unusualness of the first-person account, and the authentic-looking personal touches, such as the prayers (Grabbe, pp. 154–5). It may have been written initially as a report intended for the king to give an account of Nehemiah's successfully accomplished mission (which would mean that 'memoir' would not be an appropriate term). However, in that case it must have been expanded later to include events in the second visit, and these additions, including his prayers, may have aimed to answer criticisms within his own community (Williamson 1985, pp. xxvii–xxviii).

The EM has been more controversial. The term 'memoir' is even less appropriate to it, because it is not a first-person account throughout. If Nehemiah 8 was originally in EM (see above), then of course it must have been removed from its setting there at some point. Arguments about the reliability of EM have ranged from regarding it as complete fiction to seeing it as authentic (Williamson 1987, pp. 20–2). There are mediating views (e.g. Noth's belief that the Chronicler wrote up the story of Ezra on the basis of certain sources; see Williamson 1987, p. 21). A more sceptical modern position is that of Grabbe (pp. 125–53).

One's view of the reliability of Ezra 1—6 depends on how one evaluates the sources that it presents: the decree of Cyrus, the list of those who returned (ch. 2), and the letters that passed between the province and the imperial authorities. It is likely that the author wrote the narrative on the basis of these sources. But this leaves room for disagreement about the likely reliability of the picture that emerges. Williamson and Grabbe take different views of this.

HISTORICAL ISSUES
Historical context
Most of the events in Ezra–Nehemiah take place in Jerusalem, the administrative centre of the province of Yehud. ('Yehud' is an Aramaic name used at Ezra 5;1, 8 and 7:14,

---

Digging deeper:
DID THE CHRONICLER WRITE EZRA–NEHEMIAH?

Or indeed, did Ezra write Chronicles? The belief that Chronicles and Ezra–Nehemiah were written by the same author goes back to the nineteenth century. There are, on the surface, two obvious factors that might support this conclusion: the story-line of Ezra follows immediately from that of Chronicles, as we noted above; and both works were written at some time in the Persian period, and arise out of concerns relating to that period.

There are also thematic parallels between the two, especially their interest in the temple and priest-hood. These parallels are strongest in Ezra 1—6, where there are clear echoes of the planning and building of the first temple (Ezra 3; cf. I Chron. 21—22, 28). The place of music in worship is also important in both (Ezra 3:10, cf. I Chron. 16:4–7, 34; 2 Chron. 5:11–13).

In recent times important arguments have been made for the independent origins of the two works, based on their language and themes (Williamson 1977; 1985; Japhet 1969). For example, Ezra–Nehemiah is said to show less interest in David or the former northern kingdom (Williamson 1977, pp. 37–70). An important part of Williamson's case is his argument that Ezra 1—6 is one of the latest sections of Ezra–Nehemiah, and was edited in line with emphases of the Chronicler (Williamson 1985, pp. xxiii–xxiv, xxxiii–xxxv). This enables him to account for the similarities between Chronicles and that part of Ezra.

The thematic and linguistic arguments for separate authorship have been criticized, partly because they rest on a narrow basis (since Ezra–Nehemiah is a small sample, composed to an extent of independent sources), and partly because certain differences are to be expected due to the works' different settings. For criticism of the arguments of Williamson and Japhet, and an argument for the conceptual unity of Chronicles and Ezra–Nehemiah, see Blenkinsopp 1989, pp. 47–54.

Another version of parts of Ezra–Nehemiah is found in the Septuagintal book I Esdras. It begins with 2 Chronicles 35:1 and is largely composed of the same material as the book of Ezra, with the addition of Nehemiah 8:1–12. It could there-fore be evidence that Chronicles and Ezra–Nehemiah originally belonged together. Williamson, however, has argued that I Esdras is not an original witness, but dependent on the MT form of the books (1977, pp. 12–36). Therefore, I Esdras cannot decide whether the Chronicler wrote Ezra–Nehemiah.

and on Persian-period coins and seals.)
The province included much of the former
territory of the kingdom of Judah (hence
the name). It was part of the larger Persian
administrative district (satrapy) named
Beyond-the-River (Ezra 4:10–20;
Neh. 2:7–9), which extended from the
region west of the Euphrates river near
Tiphsah down to Gaza.

(For surveys of the Persian period and the
historical issues raised by Ezra–Nehemiah,
see Miller and Hayes, pp. 437–75; Winn
Leith; Williamson 1999; and Provan, Long
and Longman, pp. 278–303; along with the
essays in the volumes edited by Davies and
by Eskenazi and Richards.)

Among the issues discussed by these scholars
are:

- What is the authenticity of Cyrus' decree
  (Ezra 1:2–4) and of the Aramaic
  documents in Ezra 4—7?
- What was Ezra's mission, precisely,
  and what was his status?
- How did the missions of both Ezra
  and Nehemiah relate to Persian imperial
  policy?
- Who were the 'adversaries of Judah
  and Benjamin' (Ezra 4:1) in the early
  post-exilic period, and why were their
  claims to worship the same god as the
  returned exiles so summarily dismissed?
- What was the reason for local opposition
  to the rebuilding in Jerusalem at that time
  and for many decades following
  (Ezra 4:5–23; Neh. 4:15; 6:1)?

That such issues continue to be debated
is partly due to the fact that Ezra–Nehemiah
is far from offering a complete account of
the period. Ezra–Nehemiah begins in 538
(Cyrus' decree), and the latest event recorded

dates to around 400 or even later, but the
two books cover only a small part of these
140 or so years in any detail. They are also
mainly concerned with theological issues:
right worship, law-keeping and the religious
purity of the community. As regards Persian
rule, the focus is on YHWH moving the heart
of Persian kings to treat the Jews favourably
(Ezra 1:1; 7:27, etc.), and it is not spelled
out how the returns of the Jews from exile
and the missions of Ezra and Nehemiah
fitted into Persian imperial policy. Clearly
it was in Persian interests that provinces
should be efficiently administered by
officials loyal to the Persian ruler; hence the
accusation of sedition was always potent
(cf. Ezra 4:11–22; Neh. 6:5–9). But beyond
that, little is said of Ezra's and Nehemiah's
roles as Persian officials, even though that
is clearly what they both were.

This last issue is explored by Hoglund, who
suggests that in the 460s and 450s Persian
control of the Levant was threatened by Greek
military operations and by the Egyptian
revolt in the 450s. He notes that a number
of new fortifications were built in the Levant
in the mid-fifth century, seemingly with
the aim of defending the main lines
of communication. In his view Artaxerxes
may have had similar aims in sending Ezra
and Nehemiah. The rebuilding of Jerusalem's
walls, the imposition of taxes (Neh. 5), and
even Ezra's and Nehemiah's actions regarding
mixed marriages can all be explained as
intended to strengthen Persian control of the
region, though the biblical account does not
emphasize this point. (Williamson 1999,
pp. 259–61, briefly summarizes and
responds to Hoglund's arguments.)

The history of the exile
The premise of Ezra–Nehemiah is that those
who returned from Babylon after the exile

were the legitimate possessors of the land. But did this pose a problem in relation to people who had not gone into exile in Babylon? A considerable time had passed since Nebuchadnezzar's deportations (nearly 50 years by 538). Those who now returned were not the same people who had gone away. Equally, a couple of generations had grown up in the vicinity of Judah and Jerusalem, for whom those events lay well in the past.

So was the land of Judah an empty land, simply waiting for its rightful possessors to return? Recent scholarship has spoken of 'the myth of the empty land' (Carroll), implying that it was a fiction intended to advance the interests of the group that returned from Babylon in opposition to the local population who had never been exiled. The 'myth' is thought to be strongest in 2 Chronicles 36:20–21, Leviticus 26:34–35 and 2 Kings 25:21. The Chronicles passage states that the land 'lay desolate' in order to 'keep sabbath' and so 'to fulfil seventy years'. The logic of this is spelt out in Leviticus 26:34–35: that for generations the people had not observed the seventh 'sabbatical' year, when the land should not be sown (Lev. 25:1–7), therefore it must now lie fallow for a number of years equal to those that had been lost. This is supported by Jeremiah 24, where those who went into exile are depicted as the ones with whom YHWH will renew a covenant relationship, while those who remained, or went to Egypt, are regarded as apostate.

This picture is contested in modern historical reconstructions. While some hold, on the basis of archaeology, that Judah's towns were indeed comprehensively destroyed by Nebuchadnezzar, others believe that the record shows that there was basic continuity of settlement during the period of the exile (see the debate between Blenkinsopp 2002 and Stern 2001 and 2004). The point of 'the myth of the empty land' would have been that those who now returned had a pedigree going back to ancient times, while all others were usurpers. Blenkinsopp puts the motive thus: 'the avoidance at all costs of having to admit that the land had always been shared with others' (2002, p. 174).

The historical reality is probably that only a proportion of the people of Judah was taken into captivity in 586. The account in Kings acknowledges that the Babylonian commander left 'some of the poorest people of the land' to maintain the agriculture (2 Kgs 25:12). This had already happened in 597, when it was really members of the social elite who were taken (2 Kgs 24:14–16). We should notice too the numbers who are said to have been deported, with the relatively low figure of 4,600 given in Jeremiah 52:28–30 likely to be the realistic one. (The larger figures in 2 Kings 24:14–17 are perhaps intended to emphasize the devastating effect of the Babylonian action on Judah.)

So it seems that we should read between the lines of the Kings accounts and conclude that a substantial part of the population was left – enough to warrant the appointment of a 'governor' after Zedekiah was removed (2 Kgs 25:22). The story of this remaining group is told in more detail in Jeremiah 40—44.

We also read that in this same period people continued to come from the former northern territory to worship in Jerusalem (Jer. 41:4–5). This implies that there was not a rigid boundary between the populations of Judah and the former northern territory, and that there were worshippers of YHWH there who maintained an interest in Jerusalem.

The picture in Ezra–Nehemiah is, in any case, more nuanced. Its picture of resettlement is indeed based on the idea that the people who return from exile are the rightful possessors of the land. But it does not pretend that the land was empty. The 'adversaries of Judah and Benjamin', or 'the people of the land' (Ezra 4:1, 4) are not presented as people who come from outside the borders of Judah (even though the centre of local government in the province Beyond-the-River was Samaria). It is possible that in the conflicts depicted in Ezra–Nehemiah we may see the beginning of the Samaritan–Jewish split of later times. But in fact the adversaries seem to be more concerned with political power, and the implications of the re-emergence of Jerusalem for power structures in the area, than with a religious conflict. From the point of view of Zerubbabel, Ezra and Nehemiah, however, the issue is religious, a matter of loyalty to YHWH. The lines are drawn between faithful Israelites who returned from Babylon and the 'people of the land', who were not faithful. This belief does indeed entail a territorial claim: Ezra–Nehemiah may not present Judah as an empty land awaiting the return of the exiles, but it clearly believes that the returned exiles are the rightful possessors of this land.

THEOLOGY

Like the other Histories, Ezra–Nehemiah portrays YHWH as sovereign over the nations of the world: we have seen, for example, how the author traces YHWH's hand in the favourable attitudes of Persian kings towards the Jews. Ezra–Nehemiah also implies YHWH's consistency in his dealings with

Israel: the prayers of Ezra 9 and Nehemiah 9 are appeals to YHWH to continue to show Israel mercy as in earlier eras, and the prayer in Nehemiah 9 begins with a lengthy review of Israel's previous history. In a similar way the return from Babylon is a fulfilment of Jeremiah's prophecy (though other prophecies of Israel's restoration remain unfulfilled). The portrayal of YHWH fits with Ezra–Nehemiah's emphasis on continuity with the past.

Loyalty to YHWH in Ezra–Nehemiah involves drawing clear boundaries: only those who can prove their priestly lineage can serve as priests (Ezra 2:61–63); groups from outside the community of returned exiles in Jerusalem are told that they have no part in the rebuilding work (Ezra 4:3; Neh. 2:20). Most notably, those who have married women from the neighbouring peoples have to divorce these women and their children by them (Ezra 10). This seems extremely harsh: should a people whose purpose is to bring YHWH's blessing to the nations of the world adopt such an exclusive and seemingly uncompassionate stance? We take this matter up in the following section.

EZRA–NEHEMIAH IN THE CANON

Like Chronicles, Ezra–Nehemiah has different positions in the Christian and Jewish canons. In the former, it is placed with the Historical Books, coming after Chronicles, which in turn follows Kings. The whole section, Chronicles–Nehemiah, is thus treated as an alternative history of Israel, from Adam (1 Chron. 1:1) to Babylon and after. With Nehemiah, the history of Israel comes almost to its close, with only Esther following. As a history, it leaves major questions open about the future of the people. This is because of its story of a partial fulfilment of prophecy, and the feeling that the great hopes kindled by Cyrus's decree, allowing the exiles to return to Judah, have not come to fruition. In the Christian canonical order, the disappointing note at the end of the Histories leaves the way open for prophecy to gain new and different interpretations.

In the Hebrew canonical order, Ezra–Nehemiah precedes Chronicles at the end of the Bible. This is a curious reversal of the natural chronology, since the events narrated in Chronicles are earlier. Moreover, the editorial bridge between the two books (2 Chron. 36:22–23; Ezra 1:1–4) seems designed to highlight the fact that Ezra–Nehemiah is the sequel. So it seems that the order has been deliberately reversed to allow Chronicles to come last. This has the effect of letting the canon close on a high note, the decree of Cyrus affirming the open possibilities for the future of Israel in its historic land. Here too the disappointments of Ezra–Nehemiah have been downplayed so as to allow hope to override the returned exiles' constricting circumstances.

Yet Ezra–Nehemiah has an indispensable role in the story. The books stand as a warning against complacency. Haggai and Zechariah are named in Ezra in connection with the rebuilding of the temple (Ezra 5:1). The book of Zechariah in particular looks back on the salvation that has already occurred in the deliverance from Babylon, but also knows that a greater salvation lies in the future (see *EOT IV*, pp. 251–3; also p. 235). Ezra–Nehemiah provides the necessary back-cloth to such prophecies, and shares this theological perspective with them.

Finally, Ezra–Nehemiah focuses on the Jewish community after the exile, in such a way that they are often regarded as among the most exclusive books in the Old Testament. That is, they are at the opposite end of the spectrum from books like Isaiah (chs 40—55), Jonah and Ruth, all of which, in their own ways, proclaim that YHWH has an interest in non-Jewish people. Ruth, indeed, with its assertion that David had a Moabite ancestress, seems to present a direct challenge to Ezra's severe attitude to mixed marriages. Ruth and Ezra together raise the question: what really counts as truly belonging to the people of YHWH? If Ezra asserts that the qualification is by birth, then the challenge of Ruth is effective, and left its mark on later Jewish interpretation. Ezra, however, harks back to the perspective of Deuteronomy (Ezra 9:11–15; cf. Deut. 7:1–5). Within the canon, this vision also has its function: to call communities to guard what is central to their life, traditions and identity. Parts of the New Testament echo this concern (2 Cor. 6:14–18).

FURTHER READING

COMMENTARIES

J. Blenkinsopp *Ezra–Nehemiah*. London: SCM Press, 1989.

D.J.A. Clines, *Ezra, Nehemiah, Esther*. Basingstoke/Grand Rapids: Marshall, Morgan and Scott/Eerdmans, 1984.

G.F. Davies, *Ezra and Nehemiah*. Collegeville: Liturgical Press, 1999.

L.L. Grabbe *Ezra–Nehemiah*. London/New York: Routledge, 1998.

H.G.M. Williamson *Ezra, Nehemiah*. Waco: Word Books, 1985.

OTHER BOOKS AND ARTICLES

J. Blenkinsopp, 'The Bible, Archaeology and Politics; or The Empty Land Revisited' *JSOT* 27 (2002), pp. 169–87.

R.P. Carroll, 'The Myth of the Empty Land', *Semeia* 59 (1992), pp. 79–93.

P.R. Davies (ed.), *Second Temple Studies 1: Persian Period*. Sheffield: Sheffield Academic Press, 1991.

T.C. Eskenazi, *In an Age of Prose: A Literary Approach to Ezra–Nehemiah*. Atlanta: Scholars Press, 1988.

T.C. Eskenazi and K.H. Richards (eds), *Second Temple Studies 2: Temple and Community in the Persian Period*. Sheffield: Sheffield Academic Press, 1994.

K.G. Hoglund, *Achaemenid Imperial Administration in Syria–Palestine and the Missions of Ezra and Nehemiah*. Atlanta: Scholars Press, 1992.

S. Japhet, 'The Supposed Common Authorship of Chronicles and Ezra–Nehemiah Investigated Anew' *VT* 18 (1969), pp. 330–71.

J.M. Miller and J.H. Hayes, *A History of Ancient Israel and Judah*. Philadelphia: Westminster, 1986.

I.W. Provan, V.P. Long, T. Longman, *A Biblical History of Israel*. Louisville: Westminster John Knox, 2003.

E. Stern, *Archaeology of the Land of the Bible, II: The Assyrian, Babylonian and Persian Periods (732–332 B.C.E.)*. New York: Anchor, 2001.

E. Stern, 'The Babylonian Gap: The Archaeological Reality', *JSOT* 28, 3 (2004), pp. 273–7.

H.G.M. Williamson *Israel in the Books of Chronicles*. Cambridge: Cambridge University Press, 1977.

H.G.M. Williamson, *Ezra and Nehemiah*. Sheffield: JSOT Press, 1987.

H.G.M. Williamson, 'Exile and After: Historical Study' in D.W. Baker and W.T. Arnold (eds), *The Face of Old Testament Studies. A Survey of Contemporary Approaches*. Grand Rapids/Leicester: Baker/Apollos, 1999, pp. 236–65.

M.J. Winn Leith, 'Israel among the Nations. The Persian Period', in M.D. Coogan (ed.), *The Oxford History of the Biblical World*. New York: Oxford University Press, 1998, pp. 276–316.

Chapter 11

1 AND 2 CHRONICLES

INTRODUCTION

The 'books' of Chronicles are really a single book, and the twofold division in our Bibles is not original. The book is usually divided up into a three-part structure as here (or very similar to this), because the long middle part that deals mainly with the reigns of David and Solomon is regarded as a unified section.

STRUCTURE OF CHRONICLES	
1 Chron. 1:1—9:44	From Adam to the restoration from Babylon
1 Chron. 10:1— 2 Chron. 9:31	The reigns of David and Solomon
2 Chron. 10:1—36:23	From Rehoboam to the restoration from Babylon

The first section, with its lists of the tribes of Israel, is often called 'genealogies', but this is just a convenient umbrella term for the mixture that we find in these first nine chapters. In fact it is very much part of the story of Chronicles, as the title given to it above is meant to indicate. It shows how YHWH's purpose for Israel was rooted in creation.

The middle section on David and Solomon shows Israel at its height. David is the successful king who establishes the kingdom in the face of enemies; Solomon presides over a peaceful kingdom and builds the temple.

The last section takes us from the first major crisis in Israel's history under the kings, the split between North and South, to the decision of the Persian King Cyrus to restore the Jewish exiles to their land. The titles given above to the first and third sections of the book are meant to show that there is a kind of parallel between them. Both the 'genealogies' and the story of the book as a whole lead up to a time after the exile in Babylon. The structure of the book is intended to focus on the situation of the community in Judah after the exile.

OUTLINE

1 CHRONICLES 1:1—9:44: FROM ADAM TO THE RESTORATION FROM BABYLON
Genealogies
The main type of material in these chapters is genealogies. In them we find lines of descent from the ancestors of Israel.

The dominant effect is of a series of long, almost unreadable lists! But there is more to these lists than meets the eye.

THE NATURE OF GENEALOGIES

One important study finds nine different functions that genealogies have in the Old Testament (Johnson, pp. 77–82; cf. Braun, p. 3). In general, they can: establish kinship between tribes or peoples; demonstrate the continuity of a people over long periods, supplementing historical narratives; have military purposes; confirm the legitimacy of a person in his office. The main function in Chronicles seems to be to show the continuity of the people of Israel from early times through to the period after the exile. In the case of Levi, they also support the legitimacy of the Levitical priests who served the second Jerusalem temple. They may also serve the theological purpose of asserting YHWH's purposeful control of history.

It follows that biblical genealogies do not work like a visit to the Public Record Office. They have a range of purposes according to the needs of those who use them. They may be changed and developed in accordance with their purpose. They are not necessarily historical sources in the sense that they might at first appear.

The first question that we face is how these lists fit with the rest of the book. From 1 Chronicles 10 the type of literature is narrative, interspersed with speeches, songs and prayers. Some have thought 1 Chronicles 1—9 so different from the body of the book that they do not belong with it (Cross). The question is not only about literary type but also about theme. For example, these chapters show a concern for the 12 tribes of Israel, while the rest of the book focuses mostly on Judah. We shall see if such distinctions hold up as we continue. For now we simply notice that

most recent studies regard these chapters as integral (see Williamson 1977, pp. 71–82, for an important argument along these lines).

So how do they fit? It will help first to look at the beginning and the end of the section. The first chapter gives the impression that it is going somewhere fast. But where?

We learn a lot about Chronicles from its first four verses. Even the opening words 'Adam, Seth, Enosh' show the method. Why Adam– Seth, and not Adam–Cain, or Adam–Abel? The Chronicler is writing for people who know Genesis, and they would see what he is doing. He is retelling the creation story with a very clear purpose: to highlight the line that would lead finally to Israel and Judah. Notice his method as he covers Genesis 1—11 in the space of 24 verses.

So these 'genealogies' are not just a list, but a story. Now look at the end of this story, in chapter 9. In 9:1–2 we have an important clue to the Chronicler's purpose and interests. He points to the exile of the people of Judah to Babylon, and then to the return of the exiles to the historic land, and their resettlement there. In this chapter we see where the Chronicler has been going: he wanted to tell the story of his people from creation down to the time of the community who lived in Judah after the return from exile and the rebuilding of the temple.

The composition of chapter 9 makes this very clear. In verses 3–9, the main emphasis falls on the people of Judah and Benjamin, who made up the main part of the post-exilic community (though other tribes are named, for reasons that we shall see). Then the rest of the chapter, to verse 34, is devoted to the priests, the Levites (a second level of temple officials), gatekeepers and other office-holders in the temple administration. Chapter 9 is a miniature picture of the post-exilic community; right at its centre is the temple and those who administer and serve it. The Chronicler's interests are beginning to stand out clearly.

Now let us fill in some of the story between chapters 1 and 9. Note first how the Chronicler adopts and adapts the lists of the tribes that make up Israel. He does this first in the heading of the genealogies in 2:1–2, and then rather differently in the genealogies themselves in 2:3—8:40. To understand how he is using the traditional material, we need to look briefly at the tribal lists in the Pentateuch.

Twelve-tribe lists in the Pentateuch vary in both order and content. The Genesis lists have Levi and do not divide Joseph into Ephraim and Manasseh (Gen. 29:31—30:24 + 35:16–20; 35:22–26; 46:8–27; 49). The Numbers lists divide Joseph into Ephraim and Manasseh and omit Levi. Some of them begin with Reuben (Num. 1:1–5; 1:20–43; 13:4–15; 26:5–51), others with Judah (Num. 2:3–31; 7:12–83; 10:14–28). The reasons for the variations within the Pentateuch are partly historical and partly theological. (See the panel 'Variations in tribal lists'.)

Verses 1–2 of 1 Chronicles 2 lie closest to the Genesis lists (all beginning Reuben, Simeon, Levi, Judah). The order in chapters 2—8 is individual in a number of ways: (1) it resembles those Numbers texts in which Judah has precedence; (2) it divides Joseph into Ephraim and Manasseh, like all the Numbers texts, but goes further by subdividing Manasseh, in accordance with the division of Manasseh into two

> **Background information:**
> **VARIATIONS IN TRIBAL LISTS**
>
> The replacement of Reuben by Judah is prepared for in Genesis by the story of Reuben's sexual misconduct (Gen. 35:22). The prominence of Judah begins to appear in Jacob's blessing (Gen. 49:8–12), and in his leading role in the Joseph story (Gen. 37:26; 43–44). The large Joseph tribe effectively divided into two parts, named after Joseph's sons, Ephraim and Manasseh (Gen. 48:1–7 explains why Ephraim and Manasseh came to be regarded as Jacob's own sons; see also Josh. 16:1—17:18). The omission of Levi reflects the fact that, as the priestly tribe, it was given no land inheritance in the settlement, but lived among the other tribes and served the place of worship (Deut. 10:9; Josh. 13:14).

groups that occupied territory east and west of Jordan respectively in the settlement of the land (Deut. 3:13–15); (3) it includes Levi (differently from the Numbers lists which divide Ephraim and Manasseh); (4) it omits Zebulun and Dan; (5) it lists Benjamin twice.

The order and composition of the tribal lists in Chronicles tell us something about the Chronicler's interests. The list in 2:1–2 is closely based on the Genesis lists, but the order adopted in the expansion is more telling: it is striking that a traditional list with Reuben in first place is immediately followed by an expansion which gives priority to Judah.

In putting Judah first, the Chronicler is not doing something new, since some of the Numbers texts also did this (Num. 2:3–31; 7:12–83; 10:14–28). In style, however, the genealogies in 1 Chronicles 2—8 most resemble those in Genesis 46 and Numbers 26, though these are 'Reuben' lists. It follows

**ORDER OF THE TRIBES IN GENESIS AND
1 CHRONICLES**

Genesis 29—30	1 Chronicles 2—8	
Reuben	*Judah*	(2:3—4:23)
Simeon	Simeon	(4:24–43)
Levi	Reuben	(5:1–10)
Judah	Gad	(5:11–22)
Dan	1/2 Manasseh	(5:23–26)
Naphtali	*Levi*	(6:1–80)
Gad	Issachar	(7:1–5)
Asher	*Benjamin*	(7:6–12)
Issachar	Naphtali	(7:13)
Zebulun	1/2 Manasseh	(7:14–19)
Joseph	Ephraim	(7:20–29)
Benjamin	Asher	(7:30–40)
	Benjamin	(8:1–40)

Note the positions of Judah, Levi and Benjamin.

that the Chronicler is not simply following one line of the tribal lists tradition. Instead, it seems that he has drawn freely on different traditions in a way that reflects his distinctive theological perspective. The chief points to observe are the priority of Judah, the inclusion of Levi and the heightened profile of Benjamin.

The tribal lists show that the Chronicler wants to tell the story of all Israel. However, he tells it in a way that reflects his own (post-exilic) setting. We have already noticed that the story-line in chapters 1—9 ends in the post-exilic period, and an emphasis on the tribes of Judah, Benjamin and Levi. Indeed, the whole structure of the genealogies also expresses this interest. Williamson points out that it is designed have Judah first, with Benjamin in the final position, Levi in the middle, and a number of tribes either side of Levi: the tribes of Judah, Levi and Benjamin provide the framework for 1 Chronicles 2—8 (Williamson 1982, pp. 46–7). And we shall see that the Chronicler's story will go on to focus heavily on Judah, the tribe of King David, and Levi, which in his day too serves the Jerusalem temple. Yet even with this focus, he does not lose sight of the idea of all Israel: the other tribes are not excluded, but rather enclosed, by this framework (Williamson 1982, p. 47).

The genealogy of *Judah* is not only first but occupies most space (2:3—4:23). The 'sons of Judah' are introduced twice (2:3 and 4:1), and the lines traced have slight differences. A genealogy of David (3:1–24) has also been introduced before the second block of Judah material, hinting at the importance of David in the story to come. These are probably signs that diverse materials have been gathered by an editor (Williamson 1982, pp. 48–9).

Simeon is closely attached to Judah (4:24–43), as also in Joshua, where it is said that 'its inheritance lay within the inheritance of the tribe of Judah' (Josh. 19:1–9; cf. Josh. 21:9). Simeon's independent existence seems to have been short-lived, and this is reflected also in Jacob's blessing of the 12 sons, in which Simeon is paired with Levi as a tribe that will be scattered throughout Israel (Gen. 49:5–7). The traditional close attachment to Judah accounts for its being listed next to it here.

Reuben, Gad and the *half-tribe of Manasseh* (5:1–26) make up the group that flank Levi on one side. They also belong together, as they are the tribes who first possessed land, allotted to them on the east of the Jordan by Moses (Deut. 3:12–17; Josh. 13:15–33). The records contain memories of wars fought to control their territory (5:10, 19—22), as well as a note about their fall in the end to the Assyrian king Pul (Tiglath-Pileser III; 5:26).

The genealogy of *Levi* shows the priority of Aaron, as also in the Pentateuchal ('priestly') tradition, in which the descendants of Aaron were priests, and the rest of the tribe of Levi took lesser roles in attending the sanctuary (Num. 3:5–10). The lineage of Aaron is traced here from Moses to the exile (6:1–15). As for the other Levites, the focus is on their service in the temple of Solomon. According to Chronicles, this was organized by King David, even though the temple was built only later by his son (6:31; cf. ch. 23). The final part of the chapter (6:49–81) shows how the Levitical tribe was distributed in the land. Aaron's sons did the priestly work at the temple. But they and the rest of the tribe lived in settlements allocated to them in the territories of the other tribes throughout the land. This is the pattern also in Joshua 21.

Issachar, *Benjamin*, *Naphtali*, *Manasseh* (west of the Jordan), *Ephraim* and *Asher* form the second group that flanks the Levi genealogy (7:1–40). There is no obvious pattern to the order in which they come. But between them they account for all the territory north of Judah and west of the Jordan. Benjamin's first appearance at this point reminds us that it could count as a northern tribe, as it did in the days of the civil war between David of Judah and followers of the Benjaminite Saul (2 Sam. 2—4; note 2 Sam. 2:8–9). There are strong military features in this group (note the recurrence of 'mighty warriors' in vv. 1–12, and v. 40). The reference to 'the days of David' (v. 2) is a further pointer to the Chronicler's interest in that king.

Finally, it is striking that *Zebulun* and *Dan* are missing from the list (and it is in this group that we might have expected to find them). It is possible that their omission is due to some corruption of the text, which could also account for the very brief mention of Naphtali (Williamson 1982, pp. 47–8).

The roll-call of the tribes returns in the end to Benjamin (8:1–40). This passage is different from the former section on Benjamin, and may be based on territorial groupings. It records that some of the tribe of Benjamin lived in or near Jerusalem, which was on its border (vv. 28, 32). It is likely that Benjaminites migrated there especially after the fall of the northern kingdom.

In chapter 9, the 'genealogies' section is rounded off with an account of the return of exiles from Babylon to their former territories (9:2). This shows clearly that 1 Chronicles 1—9 corresponds to the story of Chronicles as a whole, and shares a similar concern with the situation of the post-exilic community. In fact, 1 Chronicles 9 is very like Nehemiah 11, on which it is generally held to be based (Braun, p. 132; Nehemiah, of course, deals directly with the post-exilic period).

The genealogies finish, therefore, by highlighting that Israel is in principle still united (even though Ephraim and Manasseh do not reoccupy their historic land). And they signal the importance of the temple and its ministry in the life of the post-exilic community.

1 CHRONICLES 10:1—2 CHRONICLES 9:31: THE REIGNS OF DAVID AND SOLOMON

The long middle section of the book is dominated by the reigns of David and Solomon, with a single chapter given to Israel's first king, Saul (1 Chron. 10). We are struck by things that are left out. There is no account of the exodus from Egypt, nor of the

270

Sinai covenant. The narrative that runs from 1 Chronicles 10 to the end of the book is like the genealogies in this respect. Moses, the central figure in the Pentateuchal story, and the leader of Israel in Egypt and the Sinai wilderness, is barely mentioned in Chronicles (only in the genealogies of Levi; 1 Chron. 6:3; 23:14–15). If a single figure stands out in Chronicles, it is David.

Saul (1 Chron. 10)

The account of Saul deals only with the end of his life, his defeat and death at the hands of the Philistines. The chapter is largely based on 1 Samuel 31, and the reader is presumably expected to know the fuller story of Saul in 1 Samuel. The Chronicler adds his own assessment of Saul in verses 13–14. The key idea is his 'unfaithfulness' (Hebrew *ma'al*). This term recurs frequently in Chronicles (always in passages where the Chronicler is not following an earlier biblical text). It is often specifically related to offences against the temple (e.g. 2 Chron. 26:16, 18). The consequence of 'unfaithfulness' is loss of land, including the exile to Babylon (1 Chron. 5:25–26; 2 Chron. 36:14, 17–21).

The account of Saul is important in Chronicles, because it is set in opposition to the portrayals of David and Solomon. Saul represents the danger of losing the gift of the land by unfaithfulness, while David and Solomon together represent the possibility of holding and enjoying it (so Mosis 1973; Williamson 1982, pp. 92–3). Another way of reading this account of Saul is proposed by Johnstone, who thinks Saul's 'unfaithfulness' represents the guilt of Israel which must be atoned by the service of the temple and its altar (Johnstone 1998, pp. 95–106). Japhet (1993, pp. 229–30) thinks that the Chronicler's idea of

'unfaithfulness' has only general significance. This is a key issue in interpreting the book (see p. 279, 'The Chronicler's interpretation of history').

David becomes king (1 Chron. 11—12)

As with Saul, the story of David is remarkable for what it does not say. There is no mention of Saul's attempts to kill David (1 Sam. 18—27), apart from brief references at 12:1 and 12:19. The account also passes over the subsequent war between northern Israel, loyal to Saul, and David's Judah (2 Sam. 2—4). Instead chapter 11 begins with 'all Israel' declaring its loyalty to David at Hebron (vv. 1–3). The narrator carefully notes that Benjaminites (Saul's tribe) supported David (12:2, 16–18).

There is also no mention of David's adultery with Bathsheba and murder of Uriah, and the consequent civil war between his sons, narrated at length in 2 Samuel 11—20 (see 1 Chron. 20:1 and compare 2 Sam. 11:1, then notice how each passage continues). While in Samuel the birth of Solomon is the consequence of David's sinful liaison, and Solomon has to fend off a strong claim to the throne from his older brother Adonijah (2 Sam. 3:2–5; 1 Kgs 1), in Chronicles there is no hint of the dubious circumstances of Solomon's birth, nor of a rival for the succession to David (1 Chron. 28—29).

Instead, the account of David builds up a picture quite distinct from that in Samuel. Several of the important building-blocks are still there. David becomes king in Hebron (1 Chron. 11:1–3); he then establishes his kingdom in Jerusalem by overcoming the Jebusites (11:4–9); he brings the ark of the covenant to Jerusalem (chs 13—16); he receives a promise from YHWH of an everlasting kingdom (ch. 17); he wins victories against enemies (chs 18—20); he takes a census of the people, and discovers the site on which the temple would be built (21:1—22:1).

However, not only are there important omissions compared to Samuel, but the material in common with Samuel has been rearranged, and fresh material added. Thus 1 Chronicles 11:1–9 is drawn from 2 Samuel 5:1–3, 6–10, while verses 10–41a are drawn from 2 Samuel 23:8–39. This rearrangement draws together lists of David's warriors, bringing out the idea that he had all Israel behind him. (Verses 41b–47 have no parallel in Samuel.)

Besides this rearranged material in chapter 11, the Chronicler has added two further long lists in chapter 12 (vv. 1–22, 23–40). The first consists of those who came to David while he was in the southern wilderness fleeing from Saul; the second group came while he was at Hebron.

The point of this section is to stress the unity of Israel in making David king. Key passages in building up the picture are 11:10 and 12:23 (Williamson 1982, pp. 96–7). It is no accident that all the tribes of Israel are represented here (numbering 13, with Joseph subdivided). A further important theme is that of help, not only the help of supporters (12:22), but above all of YHWH (12:18).

David brings the ark to Jerusalem (1 Chron. 13—16)

The account of the bringing of the ark to Jerusalem also differs significantly from that in Samuel (2 Sam. 6). The theme is begun in chapter 13, where verses 1–5 (not in Samuel) admit guilt for having neglected the ark in the days of Saul, and call for Israelites far and wide to join the project. The story is greatly elaborated in chapters 15—16. Chronicles stresses that David, after the tragedy of Uzzah (13:9–14), dealt properly with the ark, allowing only Levites to carry it (15:2). The narrative becomes an occasion to show how David organized the proper attendance of the ark (15:4–15; 16:1–7). He also organizes Israel's worship more generally, by the appointment of singers and musicians (15:16–28).

Developing the theme of Israel's worship, 16:8–36 includes a number of examples of it, in the form of excerpts from the book of Psalms (vv. 8–22 = Ps. 105:1–15; vv. 23–33 = Ps. 96:1–13; v. 34 = Ps. 106:1; vv. 35–36 = Ps. 106:47–48). The choice of these psalms is hardly accidental. They are united by a theme of YHWH's salvation of Israel, even though Israel is weak and small, an important message for the post-exilic community.

The covenant with David (1 Chron. 17)

Chapter 17 of 1 Chronicles is of central importance, because it contains YHWH's promise to David that his son will sit on the throne of Israel. It corresponds to the equally crucial 2 Samuel 7. Here too the Chronicler has made a significant change. The promise itself now focuses on Solomon more expressly than it did in 2 Samuel 7. Most importantly, and in contrast to 2 Samuel 7:16, YHWH here says that he will confirm Solomon, not David, in the kingship, and the kingdom is described as YHWH's, not David's (17:14). This change goes with a tendency to make the promise conditional (1 Chron. 28:2–10; 2 Chron. 6:15–17; 7:17–18; Williamson 1982, p. 133; cf. Braun, p. 199). The note of conditionality implies a warning that the continuance of the covenant depends on

Israel always remaining faithful. (See also Ch. 6, 'Key themes'.)

David prepares for the building of the temple (1 Chron. 18—29)

The accounts of David's wars (chs 18—20), drawn from Samuel, illustrate the point that David was a 'man of wars', and explain his disqualification from building the temple (22:8; 28:3; cf. 1 Kgs 5:3). This does not mean that David is blamed for fighting the wars, as is clear from the repeated comment that YHWH was with him (18:6b, 13b). David's role was to defeat Israel's enemies, so that Solomon would enjoy peace, and so be able to build the temple (22:18–19). In Chronicles the time of peace, or 'rest', from enemies, which was the final piece in the jigsaw of the conquest of Canaan, arrived only with Solomon, and not with David.

> **Digging deeper:**
> **THE 'MAN OF PEACE'**
>
> Compile all the evidence in 1 Chronicles 17—29 for the focus on Solomon as the man of peace. Begin by noting the difference between 2 Samuel 7:1 and 1 Chronicles 17:1. Then consider the significance of this in relation to Deuteronomy 12:10–11. See also comments on 2 Samuel 7:1.
>
> In addition to differences noted above in the Samuel and Chronicles accounts of the promise to David, consider the altered wording in 2 Samuel 7:12 and 1 Chronicles 17:11: is there any significance in it? (See Williamson 1982, p. 135; Braun, p. 199.)

The story of David's census (21:1—22:1) differs in two important respects from that in 1 Samuel 24. First it attributes the incitement of David to sin to Satan (v. 1), rather than YHWH (2 Sam. 24:1), in a theological development in the thinking about evil. But second, and in close connection with the main theme, the site is expressly identified as the place where the temple should stand (21:28—22:1).

The remainder of 1 Chronicles (chs 22—29) has no parallel in Samuel, and is devoted to one theme: David's preparations for the building of the temple, and his charge to Solomon and the people to carry the project through and be faithful. Solomon is said to be 'young and inexperienced' (22:5), an echo of Solomon's words about himself in 1 Kings 3:7. Here it gives grounds for David undertaking the detailed planning, including acquiring materials from Hiram of Tyre (22:4), which in 1 Kings 5 Solomon himself undertakes. There is an echo of the making of the tabernacle (22:15–16; cf. Exod. 31:1–4). David's preparations go hand in hand with his exhortation to Solomon to remain faithful to YHWH (22:13), his prayer that YHWH will help Solomon as he helped David (22:11–12), and his command to Israel's leaders that they too should help Solomon (22:17–19).

A lengthy section (chs 23—27) portrays David as organizing the Levites (ch. 23; 24:20–31), the priests (ch. 24:1–19), the musicians (ch. 25), gatekeepers and other officials (ch. 26), and military and tribal officials (ch. 27).

The picture given in these chapters (23—27) is usually held to represent the organization of the priesthood in the second temple (post-exilic) period, as there is no other evidence of it having arisen in the time of David or Solomon. The system is still visible in Luke 1:5, where Zechariah, father of John the Baptist, is of the division of Abijah (1 Chron. 24:10).

The account of David now returns to the theme of his provision for the building of the temple. Chapter 28 strongly resembles chapter 22, repeating the prohibition of David's building the temple, the choice of Solomon to do so, and David's plans and provision for it (see Braun, p. 267). There are again echoes of the tabernacle (28:11–19, cf. Exod. 25—30). Chapters 22 and 28 thus frame the section on the organization of the temple worship. The scene has changed slightly from chapter 22, for now an official assembly of all Israel is called (28:1, 8). The term 'assembly' (*qahal*) denotes Israel as constituted for legal and religious purposes; it was the *qahal* that stood before YHWH at Sinai (Deut. 9:10). 'All Israel' is sometimes used to refer to the same thing (Deut. 29:2; Josh. 24:1). David again urges the assembly to keep YHWH's commandments, in order to continue to possess the land (28:8). The charge to the assembly has YHWH's choice of Solomon as temple builder at its centre (28:5–6).

There follows the well-known charge to Solomon (vv. 9–10), which is significant for the Chronicler's theology. Solomon must 'seek' YHWH, so that YHWH will 'be found' by him. But the stakes are high. If he does not do so, he will be cast off 'for ever' – in a negative echo of the eternal promise! In this solemn command to the king lies a similar call to the people of post-exilic Judah.

The temple itself is the real centre of attention here. It is now called 'a house of rest for the ark of the covenant of YHWH' (28:2). The phraseology here is very like Psalm 132:8, 14. The 'rest', or peace, that would only fully come with Solomon (cf. 22:9) is now seen to be attached to the temple.

David's charge here goes beyond chapter 22 in another sense, for he now gives his son detailed plans for constructing the temple, as revealed to him by YHWH (28:11–19). David declares to the assembly what he has provided for building the temple, and the leaders respond with their 'freewill-offerings' (29:1–9). Then, in a foreshadowing of Solomon's prayer at the dedication of the temple, David prays for the people's and Solomon's future faithfulness (29:10–19; cf. 1 Kgs 8; 2 Chron. 6), and huge sacrifices are offered.

Finally, in much shorter order than in 1 Kings 1—2, Solomon is anointed king, and the death of David is recorded (29:22b–30).

The major difference from the Samuel–Kings account of the transition from David to Solomon is its strong focus on the temple. Everything else is subordinated to this. We hear nothing of the tussle between David's sons over the succession, nor of the moral weakness of David, nor of Solomon's own brutal suppression of his enemies (1 Kgs 2). The transition is clean and the issues are clear.

Solomon (2 Chron. 1:1—9:31)

The story of Solomon is governed by the themes we have already noticed. The Chronicler focuses on his building of the temple, by which he fulfils the role prescribed for him in the promise to David (1 Chron. 17; 22; 28). Most of 2 Chronicles 1—9 is devoted to this topic, and what we read here is largely familiar from Kings. But here again the Chronicler has re-presented the material to support his main themes.

We have already seen that there is no mention of Solomon's suppression of his

Think about
SOLOMON'S SUCCESSION: TWO CONTRADICTORY ACCOUNTS?

Compare the accounts of Solomon's succession in I Kings I—2 and I Chronicles 22, 28–9. The two accounts clearly have very different focuses: indeed, for most of the time they each relate events that the other account either does not mention at all or refers to only briefly. But where the accounts do overlap, can they be reconciled? In I Kings I—2 the aged David is portrayed as indecisive, out of touch and vindictive; he advises Solomon on how to get rid of potential trouble-makers; and the succession is confused and messy. In I Chronicles 22, 28—29 David is firmly in control of events and a model of piety; he encourages Solomon to build the temple and follow YHWH faithfully; and there is not a hint of opposition to Solomon's succession.

How would you harmonize these two accounts so as to produce a single sequence of events in chronological order? Alternatively, if you wished to argue that the accounts cannot be harmonized, which parts of them would you focus on? How do you explain the differences between them?

enemies (1 Kings 2). Nor do we read here of Solomon's marriages with many foreign women, or his turning to false gods at the end of his life, which, in the Kings account, led to the division of the kingdom (1 Kings 11). Omitted too is any reference to the time and effort which he gave to building his own palace (1 Kgs 7:1; though note 2 Chron. 2:1; 7:11; 8:1).

Instead, Solomon is introduced with an account of his wealth and wisdom (2 Chron. 1); his story also ends on this theme, with the account of the Queen of Sheba (ch. 9); and everything between these 'bookends' is devoted to the temple-building (chs 2—8).

Solomon's visit to the 'high place' at Gibeon (2 Chron. 1:3) is free here from any implication that it was an illegitimate worship centre (contrast 1 Kgs 3:2–3). Indeed, we read here that the tent of meeting was there. (1 Kgs 3 says nothing of this.) This fact also serves to connect the vision at Gibeon with the temple project (note 1:5 and cf. 2:7). The substance of the vision is still his prayer for wisdom, and the gift of wealth as well. But the illustration of his wisdom in 1 Kings 3:16–28 is omitted. Instead, the positioning of the story of the vision suggests that both the wealth and the wisdom are for the purpose of the temple-building (1:14–17 in its present setting also has an effect very different from that of the parallel passage in 1 Kings 10:26–29, which leads directly into the account of Solomon's sin in ch. 11).

The point of Solomon's portrayal in Chronicles is to show that he has fulfilled the conditions for the establishment of the dynasty according to YHWH's promise (1 Chron. 17). His centrality in the Chronicler's scheme is best illustrated by the key text 2 Chronicles 7:14. This text is part of YHWH's response to Solomon's prayer at the temple dedication (cf. 1 Kgs 9:1–9). There YHWH promises that he will always respond to Israel's repentance after he has punished them for sin (v. 13 refers to 'covenant curses' that would come upon Israel for sin, and v. 14 shows that sin has been the cause of YHWH's action in judgment). This passage becomes a key to interpret all the history of Israel and Judah that follows Solomon's time (see p. 282, 'Fresh opportunity').

The other main differences from the account in 1 Kings 1—11 are as follows.

- Solomon takes all the initiatives in the relationship with Huram of Tyre (Hiram in Kings); e.g. 2 Chronicles 2:3, 10; cf. 1 Kings 5:1, 6. Huram's acknowledgment of Israel's god is also developed. The effect of these changes is that Huram's role in the relationship is more clearly subordinate than in Kings (Williamson 1982, p. 200).
- Chronicles makes it clear that Solomon did not conscript Israelites as forced labour (2:17–18, cf. 1 Kings 5:13–18, though note that this is qualified at 1 Kings 9:20–22).
- Chronicles links the temple site with Mount Moriah (3:1), where Abraham was commanded to sacrifice his son Isaac (Gen. 22).
- The plan for the temple largely follows Kings. But Chronicles also depends on the plan in Ezekiel 40—48, e.g. at 2 Chronicles 4:9. The link between the temple and tabernacle is also brought out more fully than in Kings (5:5; 7:1–3, cf. Lev. 9:23–24; Williamson 1982, p. 222).
- The importance of the exodus is played down. For example, Solomon's prayer in Chronicles leaves out 1 Kings 8:50–51; see 2 Chronicles 6:39. (But see also 1 Chron. 17:21–22, and p. 279, 'The Chronicler's interpretation of history').

Solomon in Chronicles is a much less colourful figure than in Kings. His weaknesses are virtually passed over. He is portrayed as a king who presides over a peaceful kingdom, and puts in place the arrangements for worship prescribed by his father David. His portrayal is crucial to the Chronicler's moral vision; everything depends on Solomon's obedience. But this becomes a paradigm for the evaluation of all the kings and people.

We have now seen three kings of Israel: Saul, David and Solomon. These have been described as 'types' (representing, respectively, apostasy, war and peace). The kings who follow are judged according to whether they conform to one or other of these types. (See p. 281, 'The kings as "types"?'.)

2 CHRONICLES 10:1—36:23: FROM REHOBOAM TO THE RESTORATION FROM BABYLON

The remainder of 2 Chronicles tells of the period of the monarchy after Solomon, down to the Babylonian exile and the restoration. The major and obvious difference from Kings is that Chronicles has no separate account of the northern kingdom. In 1 Kings 11, Solomon is told by YHWH that his kingdom is to be divided because of his sin in following other gods (1 Kgs 11:11). Kings then proceeds by interleaving the stories of two kingdoms ('Israel' and 'Judah'). In Chronicles, as we have seen, Solomon's sin and the judgment upon him are played down.

The division of the kingdom is still reported, however (2 Chron. 10). The Chronicler clearly expects his readers to know the story as told in Kings, because he refers to the prophecy of Ahijah to Jeroboam as a familiar fact (10:15). The facts of the division are told essentially as in Kings, with Rehoboam alienating the northerners. However, no direct blame attaches to Solomon here, and it is simply stated that this was 'from YHWH' (11:4).

The story of Rehoboam continues in chapters 11—12, and in it we see some important features of the Chronicler's method in this last section of the book. Rehoboam's reign, after the withdrawal of the northern tribes, falls into two distinct parts. First, Rehoboam is obedient to YHWH (ch. 11), then he is disobedient (ch. 12), though he finally 'humbles himself' (12:12). This is a much more varied picture of Rehoboam's religious life than we find in Kings, where (1 Kgs 14:21–29) we find a summary of Rehoboam's reign, characterized as a time of rebellion against YHWH (vv. 22–24). The relationship between Rehoboam himself and the fortunes of the kingdom is not emphasized (in fact it is 'Judah' that is accused of doing evil there, v. 22).

Chronicles, however, makes clear links between Rehoboam's obedience or disobedience and the events of his reign. When he listens to the prophet Shemaiah, and so does not go to war with Jeroboam, we read how he fortified the cities of Judah (11:5–12), how priests and Levites and other faithful Israelites joined him from the territory of the northern tribes (vv. 13–17), and how he ruled wisely and had many sons who also participated in his good administration (vv. 18–21). These are all signs of blessing and security, and they are deliberately connected with Rehoboam's obedience. None of this material is found in the Kings account.

Similarly, when Rehoboam 'abandons the law [torah] of YHWH' (12:1) this also has its consequences. For his disobedience is the direct cause of the invasion of Judah by the Egyptian pharaoh Shishak (12:2–12). The connection is made clear in 12:5, where YHWH says: 'You abandoned me, so I have abandoned you.'

Finally, Rehoboam 'humbles himself' (12:12). This is one of the terms used in the key passage in 2 Chronicles 7:14, in which repentance leads to YHWH turning back to the people to 'heal their land'. When Rehoboam 'humbles himself', the worst effects of Shishak's invasion are allayed.

These differences from Kings are part of a general pattern in Chronicles. Another striking example is Manasseh. In 2 Kings 21 Manasseh is depicted as the worst king of Judah. In sharp contrast to his reforming father Hezekiah, he made the idolatrous worship of foreign gods official in Judah (2 Kgs 21:3–9), and was also guilty of great oppression (21:16). Because of Manasseh, the good effects of the reforms of King Josiah, his successor but one, were made null and void (2 Kgs 23:26). In 2 Chronicles 33, this apostasy of Manasseh is also recorded (33:1–9), and is seen as the cause of his defeat and capture by the Assyrians, a thing not recorded at all in Kings (33:10–13).

However, like Rehoboam, Manasseh, while in captivity, 'humbled himself' and prayed, and so YHWH turned back to him (33:12–13). The pattern is again that of 2 Chronicles 7:14. And as a result, Manasseh was restored to his kingdom, where he was able to re-fortify its cities and re-establish the worship of YHWH in the temple (33:14–17).

Rehoboam and Manasseh, near the beginning and end, respectively, of the kingdom of Judah, illustrate the Chronicler's method in writing his history. It is as if the kings are used as illustrations of his theology. That theology wants to demonstrate a close correspondence between the faithfulness or otherwise of king and people and the consequences for them.

Digging deeper:
THE CHRONICLER ON THE KINGS OF JUDAH

Trace the pattern described above in relation to Rehoboam and Manasseh through the accounts of the other kings of Judah. Consider whether it is regular and holds up. Asa (2 Chron. 14—16; cf. 1 Kgs 15:9–24), and Uzziah (= Azariah; 2 Chron. 26; cf. 2 Kgs 15) are further examples of kings whose reigns have distinct phases. Notice how Chronicles diverges from the Kings accounts in these cases.

King Jehoshaphat offers a different angle on the Chronicler's method (2 Chron. 17—20; cf. 1 Kgs 22:1–50; 2 Kgs 3:9–12). Jehoshaphat, like Asa, was one of the few faithful kings according to Kings. Chronicles largely builds on this picture. Notice in this case how Jehoshaphat's good qualities are highlighted. Notice the prayer of Jehoshaphat, and the exhortation by the Levite Jahaziel, in 2 Chronicles 20:5–12, 13–17. 'Levitical sermons' such as these have been thought to be important vehicles of the book's theology.

(For help, see von Rad, Dillard, pp. 77–80, and the other commentaries.)

Hezekiah (2 Chron. 29—32) and Josiah (2 Chron. 34—35)

As in Kings (2 Kgs 18—23), Hezekiah and Josiah stand out for their reforming zeal and piety. The Chronicles accounts are quite distinctive, however. Hezekiah's reform is told at greater length than Josiah's, the reverse of Kings in this respect. It focuses much more directly on the temple than the Kings account of Hezekiah, and is steeped in the language and ideas that we have seen in connection with David and Solomon. While Kings says almost nothing about the corruption of the temple worship, focusing rather on high-place worship, Chronicles highlights the defilement of the temple itself, in the past in general and by Ahaz in particular (2 Chron. 29:3–11; and note vv. 6, 19). This leads into an account of his reform of its organization and worship. In this reform, the role of the priests and Levites is emphasized (not an issue in Kings), and they carry out a reform which harks back clearly to David's preparations for both sacrifice and music (2 Chron. 29:12–30).

The cleansing of the temple is followed by a restoration of its worship, beginning with the Passover (ch. 30), and going on to a destruction of false places of worship, and the re-institution of sacrifices and offerings, according to Pentateuchal laws (ch. 31). The account of the Passover, notably, shows that Hezekiah aimed to unite people from all parts of Israel (30:1, 5, 10–11, 18–19).

The account of the deliverance from Assyria, also in Kings (2 Kgs 18—19), is told in the Chronicler's manner, much simplified, and focusing on YHWH's answer to Hezekiah's prayer (32:20–21). Finally, there are elements even in the story of Hezekiah of the Chronicler's typical explanations of misfortune, coupled with his theology of repentance (32:24–26).

The story of Josiah has the main elements of the Kings account (discovery of the book of the law, covenant-renewal, Passover, Josiah's death at Megiddo). However, it is remarkable for the following features:

- It tells that Josiah began his reform while still a boy (34:3), and some years before the discovery of the book of the law in the temple (34:8–18), in contrast to 2 Kings 22:1–10. The effect of this is to make that discovery rather more incidental to the reform than in Kings: in Chronicles the reform was already proceeding according to the Chronicler's usual criteria of faithful religion even before the discovery (e.g. 34:12–13).

- While Josiah meets his death at the hands of Pharaoh Neco in battle as in Kings, Chronicles attributes this to his refusal to hear the words of YHWH from the mouth of the pharaoh (35:21–22), thus explaining what had been left in Kings as a surprising culmination of Josiah's faithful reign (2 Kgs 23:28–30).

Exile and restoration (2 Chron. 36)
The end of Chronicles differs from Kings in one obvious way, that the last event narrated is not the exile of the people of Judah to Babylon, but the decree of Cyrus allowing the people of Judah to return to their homeland (36:22–23). The exile itself is explained as the fulfilment of Jeremiah's prophecy that the exile would last 70 years (36:21, cf. Jer. 25:11–12; 29:10). In the Chronicler's scheme the exile is just one in a long series of judgments, all of them in principle reversible by repentance. Even so, there is a point of contact with the perspective of Kings here, for Chronicles allows that the exile happened because the people of Judah had persistently failed to hear YHWH's prophets (36:15–16).

The end of Chronicles overlaps with the beginning of Ezra (Ezra 1:1–4), which relates the next phase in the life of Judah.

KEY THEMES
The Chronicler's interpretation of history
It is obvious from the Outline that the Chronicler attaches tremendous importance to David and Solomon, and to the Jerusalem temple. But why? To answer this we have to ask: what is his view of Israel's history as a whole? This means accounting for the path he traces from creation to the post-exilic period. The Chronicler's omissions are as important as what he records. For example, he omits not just the story of the northern kingdom but even the exodus from Egypt, the Sinai covenant, and the conquest and settlement under Joshua. Since this story is so prominent in Exodus–Joshua it is striking that it is omitted here. Does the Chronicler simply take all this for granted, or does his omission of it give a clue to his real concerns?

Japhet's important analysis of the Chronicler's theology (1989) lays much emphasis on what Chronicles has omitted. In her view, the Chronicler deliberately played down the traditions about Israel's covenant with YHWH, leaving out Exodus–Sinai because he did not want to attach the covenant to particular events (p. 105). According to the Chronicler, the tribes in the land were descended directly from Jacob, and possessed it without the need for exodus from Egypt, conquest or settlement. That is, Chronicles deliberately paints a picture of a relationship between YHWH and Israel that has been in place from the beginning, and which nothing, not even the Babylonian exile, has seriously disturbed (pp. 117–18; 378–86, 393). Covenant, then, becomes closely connected with keeping the commandments, which is a duty laid upon all members of the community (p. 116).

Within this reconstruction, the covenant with David has no special significance (p. 459). YHWH's ways unfold within time, without major changes or surprises: 'Time provides illustrations of unchanging principles'

(p. 501). The temple worship and organization is important because it represents the continuous presence of YHWH with Israel. The institutions of Israel are themselves timeless, just like YHWH's relationship with Israel (pp. 218–31).

A quite different view of the significance of historical events in Chronicles is taken by Johnstone (1998), who believes that the purpose of the temple arrangements is to allow atonement to be made for Israel's past unfaithfulness (*ma'al*), which he understands to mean 'guilt'. Chronicles is in fact a 'midrash' on Leviticus 5:15—6:7, that is, an extended theological interpretation of this section of Leviticus (pp. 95–106: on 'midrash', see Porton, *ABD* IV). The reason that David and Solomon have reigns free from *ma'al* (guilt), in contrast to Saul, was that David, though he became guilty in taking a census (1 Chron. 21), put in place the arrangements for sacrificial worship in the temple, by which the guilt might be atoned for (pp. 117–18).

Johnstone's approach is more open than Japhet's to the possibility of real change in history. He points out that Chronicles draws on Leviticus for another idea, that of jubilee (Lev. 25:8–55), calculating that in Chronicles the exilic generation is the fiftieth from Adam. This is suggestive for an eschatological interpretation of Chronicles (pp. 125–6).

While Johnstone and Japhet agree that temple worship is a central concern of Chronicles, they place it within very different reconstructions of the Chronicler's view of history. In doing so they illustrate the chief problem of interpreting Chronicles' theologically: how to read what it does and does not say. (See also p. 287, 'Chronicles in the canon'.)

Eschatology/Messiah

Does Chronicles have an eschatological hope? This question follows from our discussion of the Chronicler's view of history. It has been answered both negatively and affirmatively with equal emphasis. In addition to the points made by Japhet, those who find no eschatology in Chronicles point to its apparently favourable view of Cyrus and the Persian empire. It was Cyrus who decreed that the exiles held in Babylon might return home and rebuild their temple. He even declared that YHWH himself had commissioned him to build the temple. This interpretation of Chronicles also owes much to the long-held (but now widely disputed) opinion that the Chronicler was also the author of Ezra and Nehemiah. Those books are widely thought to reflect a contentment with subject status and a readiness to co-operate with empire (see Ch. 10, 'Key themes').

Another reason given for the non-eschatological interpretation is that Chronicles' preoccupation with the organization of temple worship suggests that it regards the promises as having already been fulfilled in the Jerusalem temple and its ministry. The importance of David, on this view, lies in his role in establishing that worship. The Chronicler aimed to show his post-exilic audience that the rebuilt temple took its legitimacy from the fact that David had authorized its personnel and forms of worship. For example, Riley (1993, p. 191) thinks that the assembly of Israel at worship effectively fulfils the promise to David. (Other important advocates of a non-eschatological view are Plöger and Hanson. See also Mason, pp. 31–2; and for a critical treatment of non-eschatological views of Chronicles, Kelly, pp. 137–47.)

Chronicles is certainly not eschatological in any overt sense: it is not like prophetic texts which promise a full repossession of land, with a Davidic king bringing peace and prosperity (e.g. Isa. 11:1–9; Ezek. 34:11–31). However, there are some grounds for thinking that it entertains the possibility of a future that fulfils Israel's hopes more fully than had happened by the Chronicler's own day.

An eschatological interpretation depends largely on how we read the portrayal of the kings, especially David and Solomon. Although some (like Japhet) argue that the kings are merely used to illustrate moral and religious points, it is possible that Chronicles attaches weight to the Davidic promise itself, which is so prominent in the portrayal. As we have seen, a great proportion of the book is taken up with David and Solomon. Moreover, there are key texts which make the transition from the father to the son crucially important (1 Chron. 17; 28). And as Solomon is made the pattern of obedience, so king, temple and land belong to the picture of the future that is promised in return for obedience. This is perhaps clearest in 2 Chronicles 7:19–22, in the context of YHWH's second appearance to Solomon, in which the key 'repentance' text also occurs (7:14). In the pattern proposed by Mosis, the time of peace represented by Solomon, which was not realized again by any historical king, remains a vision which might yet come to reality.

If so, is the Chronicler's vision not only eschatological, but also messianic? Messianic hope attaches importance to an individual who will be YHWH's instrument in bringing about salvation. (In Isa. 11:1–9, for example, the 'messianic' figure is a descendant of David who will establish a kingdom based on justice and righteousness.) The prominence of Solomon in the promises, a son of David

who will faithfully keep YHWH's commandments and bring peace, wisdom and security to Israel, conforms in large measure to the overtly messianic images of kings in passages like Isaiah 11. It may be, therefore, that the Chronicler's presentation of the dynastic promise, with its strong emphasis on Solomon, does not just indicate future hope in a general way, but ties that hope expressly to a king, a 'son of David'. The final note in Solomon's prayer at the dedication of the temple hits a thoroughly 'messianic' note:

O LORD God, do not reject your anointed one [*mashiakh*, 'messiah', 'anointed one']. Remember your steadfast love for your servant David.

(2 Chron. 6:42)

The term *mashiakh* does not have to be used for a 'messianic' hope to be present. However, it does seem that this passage asserts a strong hope for the fulfilment of the Davidic promise. As Williamson points out, the verse contains an echo of Isaiah 55:3. In that text the Davidic promise appears to have been reinterpreted so as to allow it to be fulfilled not in the king himself, but in the people as a whole. Here, perhaps in deliberate contrast, a specifically royal interpretation of the promise to David is once again expressed (Williamson 1982, pp. 220–1).

The kings as 'types'?

Mosis has argued that the Chronicler sees Saul, David and Solomon as 'types' of the attitudes that other kings are seen to have elsewhere in the narrative. Briefly, Saul represents unfaithfulness, David represents times of war and re-establishment, and Solomon represents times when the full blessing of peace is known. Thus, Joash resembles David when he makes provision for the restoration of the temple (2 Chron. 24:4–14). But in later life he turned away from proper care for the temple of YHWH and worshipped other gods. And so, as a result of this 'Saul' period, Judah was invaded and suffered much destruction at the hands of Aram. Joash's death in a palace coup is also presented as a consequence of his unfaithfulness (2 Chron. 24:23–27; Mosis, pp. 180–2).

In Mosis' analysis Ahaz and Hezekiah are close parallels to Saul and David (Mosis, p. 192). But no part of 2 Chronicles fully corresponds to Solomon's time of peace (Mosis, p. 203). In this way the pattern leaves open the possibility of a future time which will be as peaceful and successful as that of Solomon.

Fresh opportunity

As noted, Chronicles presents a number of kings of Israel and Judah quite differently from Samuel and Kings. This is regularly the case with kings of Judah in 2 Chronicles 10—36. The reigns of kings frequently fall into separate phases, with periods of success and failure which are closely related to the king's faithfulness or unfaithfulness to YHWH. Manasseh is a prime example, with a repentance about which Kings is entirely silent.

The Chronicler is rather systematic in tracing the correspondence between faithfulness and blessing, unfaithfulness and judgment. It is established already with King Saul, who becomes the paradigm of unfaithfulness (1 Chron. 10:13–14). But the pattern dominates the book. As Dillard points out, about half of 2 Chronicles 10—36 is unique to the Chronicler, and 'the vast majority of this non-synoptic material is directly in the service of retribution theology' (Dillard, p. 78).

Why does Chronicles re-present Israel's history in this way, so as to bring out what Dillard terms a 'retribution theology'? Many scholars have viewed the Chronicler's portrayal of history in just this way. Some have spoken of 'immediate retribution'. That is, Chronicles is said to have a doctrine of morality and justice which demands that actions are rewarded or punished by YHWH immediately, and in ways that are clear to all.

**Digging deeper:
'IMMEDIATE RETRIBUTION'?**

Does Chronicles' pattern of close correspondence between act and consequence really aim to teach a universal truth about divine justice? For a long time critical scholarship believed that it did. Recently, however, Kelly (pp. 29–45) has questioned this view. He cites, for example, Weiser (p. 324): 'The dominating viewpoint of the Chronicler's presentation of history is the idea of retribution carried through mechanically and, as regards the individual, down to the smallest details; when history does not fit with it, it is usually distorted.'

Notice Weiser's emphasis here on 'individual' and 'mechanical'. In another, older work, it is claimed that the Chronicler 'made a *universal* [my italics] connection between piety and prosperity and wickedness and adversity' (Curtis and Madsen, p. 9). These extracts show that the Chronicler was believed to have adhered to a universal theory of ethics and judgment. Moreover, that theory was invariably judged negatively ('mechanical'), and was probably a factor in the low esteem in which Chronicles was widely held.

Follow up this older critical view as documented by Kelly, then consider his analysis and criticism of it in the chapter cited.

But is this the right way to think of the theology of Chronicles? In fact, if the Chronicler were trying to argue that events could always be traced to certain moral actions he would have had to make things more cut and dried than he has (cf. Williamson 1982, pp. 31–3). For example, he has deliberately not attributed the division of the kingdom to any sin on Solomon's part, though that explanation was available to him in 1 Kings 11. Instead, Chronicles is rather quiet about the causes of the division, saying only that it was a 'turn of affairs brought about by God' in fulfilment of prophecy (2 Chron. 10:15).

It is better to think of the pattern of reward and punishment in Chronicles as offering fresh hope in a bleak situation. A key text in this regard is, as we saw above, 2 Chronicles 7:14: 'if my people who are called by my name humble themselves, pray, seek my face, and turn from their wicked ways, then I will hear from heaven, and will forgive their sin and heal their land.'

The verse is based on an important passage in Kings, 1 Kings 9:4–9, where Solomon is warned that Israel's future possession of land and temple depends on their obedience to YHWH's commandments. In the Chronicler's version, while the significance is similar to Kings, its function as a model for future generations is brought out by the form of vv. 13–14, which envisages any future case of unfaithfulness. A pattern is set here according to which YHWH will always act. The horizon, however, is set by the life of Judah in its land (hence 'I will heal their land'). The language of healing and forgiveness has some echoes of Jeremiah (cf. Jer. 8:22; 14:19; 31:34).

The Chronicler's so-called retribution theology, therefore, is best understood as an essential part of his belief that YHWH will act in grace towards his people, even though they may at any time be at a low ebb. The point is similar to that of Ezekiel 18. That is, the fate of the present generation (*any* present generation) is not determined by anything that past generations have done. There is always time for repentance. This theology, therefore, is not a legalistic doctrine of mechanical rewards and punishments. It is not a theory of ethics at all, but an offer of hope to a community that may be discouraged.

At the same time, there is a call to remain faithful, so that YHWH's blessing may continue (1 Chron. 28:8; 29:18–19). This call is centred on proper care for the temple, but also on commandment-keeping.

Chronicles' theology of repentance can be linked with eschatology. As the point of the retribution theology was to demonstrate YHWH's grace and bring to repentance, so it also opened up the possibility of a better future. The strong link between 'retribution' and eschatology is argued at length by Kelly.

Prophecy

The preaching of the prophets in Chronicles also serves the theme of YHWH's grace, because it shows that he gives a chance to think again and avert judgment. For example, in 2 Chronicles 12:5–7 a prophetic word leads directly to Israel 'humbling themselves', and YHWH decides not to punish. Prophecies were not always heeded, however (e.g. 2 Chron. 16:7–10; Williamson 1982, p. 32; Japhet 1989, pp. 154–66). At the end of the book YHWH acts graciously because of the prophetic word that he has spoken (2 Chron. 36:22–23).

All Israel

We have seen that Chronicles in some sense holds out hopes of a better future for the post-exilic community in Judah and Jerusalem. But what kind of 'Israel' did the Chronicler have in mind when he thought about the future? For a long time, scholars began from the fact that the Chronicler writes mainly about the kingdom of Judah and leaves aside the entire history of the northern kingdom. In 2 Chronicles 11:3 we find the phrase 'all Israel in Judah and Benjamin'. This seemed to confirm the view that the Chronicler saw the future of 'Israel' as lying only with the descendants of the tribes that made up the former kingdom of Judah (for examples, see Williamson 1977, p. 97 and note). Recent scholarship, however, has argued that Chronicles works with an ideal of a united, 12-tribe Israel. The question of his view of Israel depends in part on deciding what actually belongs to the Chronicler's own work. Now that the genealogies (1 Chron. 1—9) are agreed to be substantially authentic to Chronicles, it follows that he was interested in the whole people. The picture is confirmed in other places, especially in Hezekiah's Passover, in which the king sent throughout Israel to invite people from all the tribes (2 Chron. 30). While the invitation was only partially taken up, Hezekiah's intention can be taken to represent the Chronicler's view that all the historic tribes remained in principle part of Israel. Another important text is 1 Chronicles 12:23–40, in which all the tribes gather to David to make him king. (The case for an ideal 12-tribe Israel is argued in detail by Williamson 1977, pp. 87–140; and by Japhet 1989, ch. 3.)

CRITICAL ISSUES

LITERARY-CRITICAL ISSUES

Chronicles as narrative

Much of Chronicles is based on earlier biblical texts, selected and reshaped to reflect the Chronicler's theological perspective. The Chronicler apparently expects his readers to be aware of these earlier texts. We have noted passages where the Chronicler briefly mentions something described in more detail in Samuel or Kings, passages which are not really intelligible except to a reader familiar with Samuel or Kings: David's flight from Saul (1 Chron. 12:19); Ahijah's prophecy against Solomon (2 Chron. 10:15); Hezekiah's illness (2 Chron. 32:24). But more generally, many sections of Chronicles make their point most clearly to the reader who is aware of what has been omitted, or of how the Chronicler has reshaped the traditions available to him: only a reader familiar with the tribal genealogies in Genesis–Numbers will note the distinctive features of the arrangement in 1 Chronicles 2—8; only the reader familiar with the narratives of David and Solomon in Samuel and Kings will be aware how consistently the Chronicler emphasizes the positive and downplays the negative in his account of these two kings.

Chronicles, therefore, is not an entirely free-standing narrative. But this does not usually mean that it is incoherent unless the reader mentally fills its gaps with materials from the earlier biblical texts. The Chronicler has shaped his material carefully. We have noted the tendency to bring out the pattern of reward and punishment in the accounts of Israel's kings, and also the use of Saul, David and Solomon as 'types'.

Date, authorship, sources, editing

Chronicles must be dated some time after the return of the Babylonian exiles to Judah. The story-line itself makes this clear, as it ends with the decree of Cyrus (538), which permitted the Jews to return, and even commissioned them to rebuild their temple. The words attributed to Cyrus in 2 Chronicles 36:23 are in line with what is known of Persian imperial policy: while the Assyrians and Babylonians dispersed and exiled populations, the Persians sought the loyalty of subject peoples by returning them to their homelands and enabling them to cultivate the worship of their own gods. The so-called 'Cyrus Cylinder' contains a record of Cyrus' policy in respect of Babylon (see Ch. 10).

Not only the main story-line but also the genealogies (1 Chron. 1—9) indicate a post-exilic date. As we have seen above, 1 Chronicles 9 gives a miniature picture of the post-exilic community, with its people, priests, Levites and other temple officials.

Can we date the book more precisely? The genealogies help us again, because in one place they go at least two generations beyond Zerubbabel, a key figure in the building of the second temple, completed in 515 (1 Chron. 3:17–24; cf. Ezra 5:1–21). This suggests that Chronicles cannot be dated earlier than about 450.

Chronicles, therefore, was written well after the return to the land, and the rebuilding of the temple, the formative events of the post-exilic community. For Zerubbabel, and the prophets Haggai and Zechariah, those events were of critical importance. But for the readers of Chronicles, they are already history, and the rebuilt temple is an established fixture in their life. As we saw,

> **Digging deeper:**
> **THE SONS OF ZERUBBABEL**
>
> Verses 17–24 of 1 Chronicles 3 take us at least two generations after Zerubbabel. This is clear from verses 19–21. But do they take us further? Compare the translations of verse 21 in NRSV and NIV, and see also the marginal note in NRSV.
>
> For further explanation of the possible readings, see Williamson 1982, p. 58.

the descriptions of the arrangements for the temple worship (as in 1 Chron. 23—27) may reflect conditions from that time.

However, it is impossible to be precise about the dating. Indeed, if we allow for the possibility of growth in the book, the dating becomes even more open. For example, commentators often ascribe parts, or all, of the genealogies to later hands than the Chronicler. And 1 Chronicles 23—27 is also often thought to be later than the bulk of the book. This means that an argument based on the latest data in the genealogies or on Chronicles' description of the temple worship need not prove the date of the bulk of the book. The Chronicler could then have worked closer to the time of the building of the temple than the final form of the book implies (see Cross).

Recent work, however, tends to date Chronicles closer to the end of the Persian period (332 BC) than its beginning (Mason, pp. 132–3; Japhet 1989, p. 5). Japhet, for example, finds the organization of the temple worship in 1 Chronicles 23—27 more advanced than anything in Ezra–Nehemiah. She argues that these chapters are not a later addition (Japhet 1993, pp. 26–7). This last judgment depends upon a decision as to what is central to the book's theology. The entire discussion illustrates the problems of a precise dating of Chronicles.

Finally, it was once widely held that the author of Chronicles also wrote Ezra and Nehemiah. In that case the dating of Chronicles would depend on how one dates those books too, which could take Chronicles into the fourth century (see Ch. 10, 'Critical issues'). However, now that many scholars have argued against this common authorship (especially Williamson and Japhet), the dating of Chronicles can float free of arguments about those books. This need not mean, however, that Chronicles must be dated earlier than Ezra–Nehemiah. Johnstone, for example, argues that Chronicles is later, on the grounds that 1 Chronicles 9:2–17 seems to be dependent on its parallel in Nehemiah 11:3–19 (Johnstone 1998, p. 93).

HISTORICAL ISSUES
Historical context
The historical context of most of the events described in Chronicles has been set out in the chapters on Samuel and Kings. The historical context of the post-exilic period was briefly described in Chapter 10.

Historicity
Chronicles has usually been regarded as less valuable historically than Samuel and Kings. This is because of its method of presenting events and people according to a schematic pattern. Scholars suspected that the Chronicler invented episodes in order to make history conform to his theological message. Thus, since Kings portrayed Manasseh as a thoroughly evil king, the Chronicles account of his repentance was judged to carry less weight. Chronicles has been called 'midrashic', because of its interpretation of existing texts and its perceived tendency to make theological or didactic points out of them.

On individual points it is often impossible to reach a definite conclusion. For example, in the case of Manasseh the Chronicler may have known something that the author of Kings did not know, or that he knew but deliberately omitted. But there is no way of resolving the differences between the two accounts because we have no independent evidence to corroborate either of them.

Judgments about historicity, however, do not depend entirely on individual cases, but on one's view of the nature of the writing. And here it is the regularity of the Chronicler's portrayals of kings and events, and the fact that they uniformly support his theology of repentance, that seems, in the opinion of many scholars, to tell against historicity.

Does the Chronicler use historical sources? We know, of course, that he draws on Genesis–Kings, because we have seen that his work often corresponds closely to parts of those books. But what of the parts that contain no such parallels? The Chronicler names certain sources that he draws on, both historical records (e.g. 'the Book of the Kings of Israel and Judah', 2 Chron. 27:7), and works attributed to prophets (e.g. 1 Chron. 29:29; 2 Chron. 9:29). We do not have independent evidence for such works: the historical books referred to are not the same as the canonical books of Kings. But these references show at least that the Chronicler presents his own work as drawing on the authority of other sources, and may also imply that these sources were known to his readers, perhaps even available to them.

It is now thought that the Chronicler may indeed have used other sources as well as the biblical ones. To begin with, it seems dogmatic to rule out the possibility in advance, since we know that written annals were widely used in the ancient Near East. In addition, there are a number of passages where it seems that the Chronicler may have been drawing on state records, for instance 2 Chronicles 11:5–12, describing cities fortified by Rehoboam, and 1 Chronicles 12:23–40, giving figures for the tribal contingents who made up David's army at Hebron. For more on the Chronicler's sources see Jones, pp. 68–71.

To say that the Chronicler used sources does not mean that he is, after all, a historian as we understand the term. He has used sources creatively and freely according to his purpose, and it is likely that where he based his account on earlier biblical texts, he expected his readers to note the fact. His method may not fit modern canons of history writing, but perhaps these are not entirely appropriate categories to apply in this case.

(The essays in the volume edited by Graham, Hoglund and McKenzie offer detailed treatments, from various perspectives, of the issues raised in this section.)

CHRONICLES IN THE CANON

In English Bibles Chronicles comes immediately after Kings. This canonical order goes back to LXX, and is based on the fact that Chronicles covers much ground that is also covered in the 'primary history' (Genesis–Kings), especially Samuel and Kings. The close relationship between the Genesis–Kings and Chronicles is also reflected in the name of the book in LXX, *ta paraleipomena*, or 'things left out':

Chronicles was seen as a book that filled in gaps left by the former history. From early times, therefore, interpretation of Chronicles was undertaken by means of close comparison with other canonical books.

Such comparative interpretation is unavoidable. In our outline of the book, we have seen how a reading of Chronicles constantly has to cross-refer to Samuel and Kings. But what does it show us? Critical investigation of Chronicles since the early nineteenth century has given priority to historical aspects of the comparison between Chronicles and Samuel–Kings, and until recently this tended to be unfavourable to Chronicles. However, careful comparison can also be done for the theological purpose of showing the place of Chronicles in the biblical canon. As we drew out theological themes of the book, we saw that the differences between Chronicles and Samuel–Kings could be explained by its distinctive theological message. It was a time of opportunity: repentance could lead to renewal; people need not feel crushed under the weight of a huge disaster; the possibilities for a peaceful, fulfilled life in covenant with YHWH were unlimited.

This message makes a contrast with Kings, which was written much closer to the time of the Babylonian exile, and which was attempting to offer an explanation of that disaster. It is not that there are fundamental theological differences between Chronicles and Kings – they share a belief in YHWH as lord of history, in his justice and forgiveness. However, Chronicles puts more emphasis on grace and forgiveness, and on the possibility of change if the people will turn to YHWH in wholehearted obedience. The comparison between Kings and Chronicles leads to reflections on how the word of YHWH comes differently in different situations. After judgment there is still the possibility of renewal. No single event marks the end of history – except (from a Christian perspective) the one event which reveals the 'end' of history, in the sense of its ultimate meaning and goal, the resurrection of Jesus Christ.

What is true of the comparison with Kings is true of comparisons with other canonical texts which reflect on the meaning of the exile. With respect to Lamentations' repeated cry 'there is no one to comfort' (Lam. 1:7, 16, 21), Chronicles looks back to the 'comfort' which came in the form of Cyrus of Persia and affirms that the cry of desolation that sees no future is only a partial vision. YHWH did act to relieve that anguish. In respect of other comparisons, however, Chronicles adopts a note of warning. While Jeremiah could go beyond the vision of Kings by holding out the hope of a glorious return to the land (Jer. 30—33), Chronicles knows that the return to the land after the exile could no more be the last act in history than was the exile. The Chronicler wrote for a people who were in some measure disappointed, and who still awaited a better future. It remained for the people to look to themselves, in order to see how YHWH's promises might yet be fulfilled in them.

Chronicles' assessment of the people's hopes after the exile leads on to the other unavoidable canonical comparison, namely with Ezra and Nehemiah. Whether in the English or Hebrew canonical order of the biblical books, Chronicles is placed in close connection with Ezra and Nehemiah. The effect of this is different in the two forms of the canon, however.

English Bibles (following the LXX order) place Ezra–Nehemiah after Chronicles, following the natural order of the story: Ezra–Nehemiah takes up from where Chronicles left off, with the report of Cyrus' decree allowing the exiles to return. This is what might be expected in a canonical form which puts all three books in a section that tells the history of Israel. The 'historical' section is then rounded off with the book of Esther. This grouping of stories about the fortunes of the Jews after the exile adds up to a mixed picture: a struggling community in Jerusalem, and a 'diaspora' (scattered people) in Persia subject to the whims of kings. This unpromising end to the 'history' of Israel leaves an open question in English Bibles to which the prophetic section of the Old Testament gives an answer, with its predominant structure of judgment followed by salvation.

Hebrew Bibles, however, place Chronicles after Ezra–Nehemiah. This suggests that the Hebrew canonizers wished to allow Chronicles' report of deliverance from exile (2 Chron. 36:22–23) to be the final word in the story of the post-exilic community, rather than the downbeat note of Nehemiah's struggle to contain that community's waywardness (Neh. 13). This effect is the greater because Chronicles thus closes the entire Hebrew canon.

The placing of Chronicles at the end of the canon marks a major divergence from the English canonical order. It arises because Chronicles, together with Ezra and Nehemiah, is placed in the third division of the Hebrew canon, the Writings. The historical reasons for this arrangement are lost to us. But it suggests an emphasis less on Chronicles as a historical account than as a theological reflection on history. These distinctions are not hard and fast, of course, since all biblical history writing is also theological. Nevertheless, it is Chronicles that gives us the word 'midrash' (2 Chron. 13:22; 24:27), with its emphasis on new applications of known texts (or in the words of Neusner, 'creative philology and creative historiography'; cited in Johnstone 1998, p. 95, n. 8).

Finally, Chronicles may be linked with the New Testament. In English Bibles the New Testament comes after the prophets and particularly the book of Malachi with its expectation of a coming 'day of YHWH' (Mal. 4:5; cf. 3:1–2). This seems to suggest a weak connection between Chronicles and the New Testament. However, a comparison between the genealogies of Chronicles and the genealogy of Jesus Christ in Luke 3:23–38 is instructive. Luke's genealogy is in reverse order, beginning with Jesus and tracing a line backwards through the royal Davidic line to Adam and the creation. Luke's genealogy is itself an interpretation of the history of Israel, just as the Chronicler's is. That is, it follows the line of promise. In fact in doing so it follows Chronicles, not only in its compact style, but in that its names from Adam to Abraham can all be found in 1 Chronicles 1:1–27, and those from Judah to David mostly in 1 Chronicles 2. (For David's son Nathan (Luke 3:31), see 1 Chronicles 3:5.) The important canonical point, of course, is that Luke makes the story of promise to Israel culminate in the birth of Jesus, and thus in his narrative of Jesus' life, death and resurrection. Luke's genealogy is given not for purposes of historical information, but as a deliberate reinterpretation of the story of Israel.

FURTHER READING

COMMENTARIES

R.L. Braun, *1 Chronicles*. Waco: Word Books, 1986.

E.L. Curtis and A.A. Madsen, *The Books of Chronicles*. Edinburgh: T. and T. Clark, 1910.

R.B. Dillard, *2 Chronicles*. Waco: Word Books, 1987.

P.K. Hooker, *First and Second Chronicles*. Louisville: Westminster John Knox, 2001.

S. Japhet, *I and II Chronicles*. London: SCM Press, 1993.

W. Johnstone, *1 and 2 Chronicles*, 2 vols. Sheffield: Sheffield Academic Press, 1997.

J.G. McConville, *Chronicles*. Edinburgh/Philadelphia: St Andrew Press/Westminster, 1984.

J.M. Myers, *I Chronicles, II Chronicles*. New York: Doubleday, 1965.

M.J. Selman, *1 Chronicles, 2 Chronicles*. Leicester: IVP, 1994.

J.A. Thompson, *1, 2 Chronicles*. Nashville: Broadman and Holman, 1994.

H.G.M. Williamson, *1 and 2 Chronicles*. Grand Rapids/London: Eerdmans/Marshall, Morgan and Scott, 1982.

OTHER

F.M. Cross, 'A Reconstruction of the Judean Restoration', *JBL* 94 (1975), pp. 4–18.

M.P. Graham, K.G. Hoglund, S.L. McKenzie (eds), *The Chronicler as Historian*. Sheffield: Sheffield Academic Press, 1997.

P.D. Hanson, *The Dawn of Apocalyptic*. Philadelphia: Fortress, 1975.

S. Japhet, *The Ideology of the Book of Chronicles and its Place in Biblical Thought*. Frankfurt/New York: Peter Lang, 1989.

M.D. Johnson, *The Purpose of the Biblical Genealogies*. Cambridge: Cambridge University Press, 1969.

W. Johnstone, *Chronicles and Exodus: An Analogy and its Application*. Sheffield: Sheffield Academic Press, 1998.

G.H. Jones, *1 and 2 Chronicles*. Sheffield: JSOT Press, 1993.

B.E. Kelly, *Retribution and Eschatology in Chronicles*. Sheffield: Sheffield Academic Press, 1996.

J.W. Kleinig, 'Recent Research in Chronicles', *Currents in Research: Biblical Studies* 2 (1994), pp. 43–76.

R.A. Mason, *Preaching the Tradition: Homily and Hermeneutics after the Exile*. Cambridge: Cambridge University Press, 1990.

R. Mosis, *Untersuchungen zur Theologie des Chronistischen Geschichtswerkes*. Freiburg: Herder, 1973.

O. Plöger, *Theocracy and Eschatology*. Oxford: Blackwell, 1968.

G.G. Porton, 'Midrash', *ABD* IV, pp. 818–22.

G. von Rad, 'The Levitical Sermon in I and II Chronicles' in *The Problem of the Hexateuch and Other Essays*. London and Edinburgh: Oliver and Boyd, 1966, pp. 267–80.

W. Riley, *King and Cultus in Chronicles: Worship and the Reinterpretation of History*. Sheffield: Sheffield Academic Press, 1993.

W.M. Schniedewind, *The Word of God in Transition; From Prophet to Exegete in the Second Temple Period*. Sheffield: Sheffield Academic Press, 1995.

M.A. Throntveit, *When Kings Speak: Royal Speech and Royal Prayer in Chronicles*. Atlanta: Scholars Press, 1987.

A. Weiser, *Introduction to the Old Testament*. London: Darton, Longman and Todd, 1961 (English translation of German original dated 1948).

H.G.M. Williamson, *Israel in the Books of Chronicles*. Cambridge: Cambridge University Press, 1977.

INDEX